foundations

POLICING

in canada

PAUL F. MCKENNA

Ontario Ministry of the Solicitor General and Correctional Services

Prentice Hall Canada Career & Technology
Scarborough, Ontario

Canadian Cataloguing in Publication Data

McKenna, Paul F. (Paul Francis), 1952-
       Foundations of policing in Canada

Includes bibliographical references and index
ISBN 0-13-899436-6

1. Police - Canada. I. Title.

HV8157.M34 1998   363.2'0971   C97-931404-6

© 1998 Prentice-Hall Canada Inc., Scarborough, Ontario
A Division of Simon & Schuster/A Viacom Company

Prentice-Hall, Inc., Upper Saddle River, New Jersey
Prentice-Hall International (UK) Limited, London
Prentice-Hall of Australia, Pty. Limited, Sydney
Prentice-Hall Hispanoamericana, S.A., Mexico City
Prentice-Hall of India Private Limited, New Delhi
Prentice-Hall of Japan, Inc., Tokyo
Simon & Schuster Asia Private Limited, Singapore
Editora Prentice-Hall do Brasil, Ltda., Rio de Janeiro

ISBN 0-13-899436-6

Vice-President, Editorial Director: Laura Pearson
Acquisitions Editor: David Stover
Editorial Assistant: Ivetka Vasil
Copy Editor: Ann Keys
Production Editor: Mary Ann McCutcheon
Signing Representative: Samantha Scully
Production Coordinator: Leora Conway
Photo Research: Susan Wallace-Cox
Art Direction: Mary Opper
Interior and Cover Design: Julia Hall
Cover Photograph: Kalunzy-Thatch/Tony Stone Images
Page Layout: Heidi Palfrey

1 2 3 4 5   RRD   02 01 00 99 98

Printed and bound in United States

Every reasonable effort has been made to obtain permissions for all articles and data used in this edition. If errors or omissions have occurred, they will be corrected in future editions provided written notification has been received by the publisher.

Visit the Prentice Hall Canada Web site! Send us your comments, browse our catalogues, and more. **www.phcanada.com** Or reach us through e-mail at **phabinfo_pubcanada@prenhall.com**

To my wife, Lee, who gently leads me in understanding that beautiful things are difficult.

And, to my daughter Kathleen, who always inspires me with hope for a better future.

CONTENTS

CHAPTER THREE

POLICE JURISDICTIONS IN CANADA   46

CHAPTER FOUR
BECOMING A POLICE OFFICER IN CANADA   73

CHAPTER SEVEN
ASSIGNMENT TO DUTY   127

CHAPTER EIGHT
ORGANIZATIONAL STRATEGIES: MAKING THE BEST USE OF RESOURCES   158

CHAPTER NINE
COMMUNICATION AND INFORMATION TECHNOLOGY   191

CHAPTER TEN

LEADING INNOVATION IN CANADIAN POLICING   209

CHAPTER ELEVEN

LOOKING FORWARD TO THE NEXT MILLENNIUM OF CANADIAN POLICE SERVICE   244

FOREWORD

Over the last few decades, policing in Canada has undergone substantial and significant change. This change has resulted from challenges arising out of a growing need for effective and efficient public services, unprecedented technological development, and profound organizational demands that directly impact the delivery of police services. The Canadian Association of Chiefs of Police (and its predecessor, the Chief Constables' Association of Canada, formed in 1905) has been deeply engaged in the process of change and is dedicated to responding to these challenges.

In light of the need for leadership and creativity in the face of such change, it is increasingly important that individuals seeking careers in law enforcement be fully prepared to understand the complexity of Canadian policing. The history of policing in Canada is rich and reveals a continuous commitment to both innovation and service. This textbook provides a current and practical introduction to the subject of Canadian policing. It is designed to facilitate learning about the nature of this profession and builds on a wealth of research and analysis originating from a variety of sources, including many police services across Canada.

While this publication is geared to students at a community college level, it offers worthwhile reading for anyone seeking a comprehensive understanding of the growth and development of policing within a distinctively Canadian context. Such a perspective is extremely important as we near the end of the 20th century, and anticipate the beginning of the new millennium.

John D. Moodie
Assistant Commissioner, "D" Division (Manitoba), Royal Canadian Mounted Police
President, Canadian Association of Chiefs of Police

This book is designed as an introductory textbook on policing in Canada. It is intended for new students planning a career in law enforcement and for continuing students who happen to be currently engaged in the police profession. While it is primarily aimed at those who are at the beginning of their police learning, it is anticipated that there will be broad interest in both the academic and the police community for a Canadian treatment of the fundamentals of law enforcement. Even though there are several valuable and detailed textbooks on the basics of police administration, none of them provides this kind of in-depth coverage of current Canadian policing experience, which has its own history, growth, and complexity. In order to help address the increasing challenges that face the future of Canadian policing, in order to provide learners, at all levels, with a reliable source of information and insight on this country's policing experience, and, finally, in order to offer a cohesive vision of how leadership can contribute to the enhancement of policing in general, this book has been assembled.

Chapter 1 begins with a brief look at the origins of policing in Canada, particularly the British experience, which gave shape to so many of our institutions and traditions. However, an ongoing openness to other influences has made the Canadian approach to law enforcement distinct. As the nation grew throughout the 19th century, so did its policing requirements. As the country matured through the sobering experience of the First and Second World Wars, so did those organizations responsible for providing police services to the Canadian public. With strong historical ties to Great Britain and France, with geographic proximity to the United States, and with a uniquely Canadian approach to multiculturalism, we saw the development of an approach to policing that revealed a special blend of influences.

In Chapter 2 we attempt to learn something about the context in which the enterprise of policing takes place. Canada's social, political, legal, and technological settings are explored to better understand why we have the kinds of policing we experience today. The question of what police organizations do is treated in general terms, including the fundamental goals and objectives of police organizations.

A great deal of attention is given in Chapter 3 to the various police jurisdictions in Canada. The richness and diversity of the policing experience is portrayed in order to give the reader a firm grasp of where we are in the evolution of our police services. Moving from federal law enforcement agencies, through the various provincial, territorial, regional and municipal police organizations, we also explore some of the important and growing special categories of police services, including private security.

Chapter 4 provides a careful evaluation of what it takes to become a police officer, which is critical to the purpose of any introductory textbook on policing. Clearly there is nothing constant but change in this regard; however, it is possible to highlight the current qualities and capabilities that are most in demand for the person who would become a police officer. Aspects of particular importance include the growing role of women in policing, reflecting the ethnic and racial diversity of the community, and the impact of civilianization. This leads inevitably to a review of the fundamental duties and core functions of a police officer. Again, this is open to wide variation depending upon jurisdiction, specific assignment, and career pathing; however, this textbook provides details on the widest range of operational, administrative, and other functions that can be found in a variety of police organizations.

At the core of this book is Chapter 5, which offers an analysis of leadership. We would suggest that leadership, properly understood, has the potential to make its appearance at all levels of an innovative police organization and that the successful future of Canadian policing is assured if senior managers understand the importance of fostering and freeing up the capacity for leadership within their organizations. It is more than a public relations ploy to propose that the organizational chart could be turned on its head in order to display the front-line service personnel as the "leading edge" of the police service. A clear framework for understanding leadership is presented with a discussion of specific skills and abilities that should be fostered.

Chapter 6 then moves to consider the basics of police administration. Without oversimplifying this topic, there is an effort to offer a straightforward understanding of Canadian organizations as systems. In this context of systems analysis, some fundamental elements of police agencies are explored.

Chapter 7 looks at the topic of assignment to duty and reviews the various areas where police personnel may apply their skills and talents on behalf of their organizations.

Chapter 8 considers police organizations as integrated units, examines the ways in which they meet their specific mandates, and answers the question: how do Canadian police services make the best use of their human, financial, and technological resources? The investments made in the provision of these important public services are staggering, and it is essential that the reader have an understanding of the decision-making processes that relate to the use of these various resources.

Chapter 9 deals with the topic of communication and information technology, which is increasingly important to the effectiveness and efficiency of any police organization.

Chapter 10 recognizes that at this time many organizations, including police organizations, are facing massive levels of change and upheaval. It is valuable to examine how Canadian police agencies have dealt with change and have, in many instances, risen to the challenge of change with some innovative and compelling approaches which demonstrate a promising capacity for leadership. Since police services cannot, and should not, operate in a vacuum, we take this opportunity to look at some areas of organizational learning, renewal, and change in the larger corporate context. Of particular application in the police realm is the notion of community policing. This philosophy is given special consideration in combination with particular case studies from across Canada.

Finally, in Chapter 11, we spend some time speculating on the future and what it may hold for Canadian policing. As the 21st century, a new millennium, rapidly approaches, it is worthwhile to reflect on how change might affect police organizations in Canada, the profession of policing, and the individuals who are now, or wish to become, part of the policing experience in Canada.

Because this textbook is intended for use by learners who are committed to the serious study of policing in Canada, it was felt that a number of appendices would be useful for pursuing independent and deeper lines of inquiry. Therefore, this book contains an extensive Selected Bibliography that lists a sampling of important Canadian and other sources for the reader to consider for further study. Next, a collection of Canadian Police Case Studies is provided for use in illustrating a number of the chapters throughout the textbook. This is followed by a Selected Listing of Associations, Organizations, and Web Sites for Canadian Policing, which should be valuable for all readers and particularly for computer literate readers who may wish to explore and, by exploring, expand their understanding. This textbook is also accompanied by an Instructor's Manual that offers additional background on the topics addressed.

Policing in Canada has always held a strong attraction for many people as a career or a vocation. Unfortunately, police work has often been subjected to wildly exaggerated portrayals in the media and the overzealous efforts of Hollywood. On the other hand, it has also borne the weight of academic study that often operates at a high theoretical level without the benefit of practical grounding in actual police operations. The Canadian public usually has little or no direct contact with the women and men who are sworn to protect their safety and security, except in circumstances of either profound distress or mundane routine. The special characteristics and profound challenges of policing in Canada today have never been fully explored in a basic textbook that is designed as a practical guide for a wide audience of learners. This book represents a sincere effort at beginning such an exploration, and you are invited to join in this voyage of discovery.

ACKNOWLEDGEMENTS

This book is the result of research and reflection on issues relevant to learning policing. In order to gain a clear focus on the current practice, and future prospects, of policing in Canada, I have relied on the input and insight of police practitioners who have provided me with the benefit of their knowledge or have facilitated access to materials that have been invaluable in the preparation of this textbook.

While it is impossible to be exhaustive in such a listing, I wish to formally acknowlege the following persons who made important contributions to my better understanding of the enterprise of Canadian policing. I am grateful for their generous assistance and will emphasize that they are blameless for any deficiencies in presentation, which rest exclusively with the author.

I have arranged these persons in accordance with their organizational affiliation, and not by order of importance.

Belleville Police Service: Chief Dave Klenavic

Brantford Police Service: Chief Alvin Barber

Brockville Police Service: Chief Barry V. King

Calgary Police Service: Chief Christine Silverberg

Centre of Criminology, University of Toronto: Philip Stenning, Tom Finlay

Cornwall Police Service: Chief Joseph G. St. Denis

Edmonton Police Service: Chief John Linsay; Const. Al Davis

Essex Police Service: Chief Thomas Wilson; D/Chief Chris Southward

Fredericton Police: Chief G.M. Carlisle; D/Chief Chipperfield

Hawkesbury Police Service: Chief Paul L. Roy

KPMG Investigation and Security Inc.: Mr. Norman Inkster

Kingston Police Service: Chief Bill Closs; Sgt. Bob Napier; Const. Brian Begbie

Lethbridge Police Service: Chief John D. LaFlamme

Metropolitan Toronto Police: Chief David Boothby; D/Chief Joseph Hunter; D/Chief Robert Molyneux; D/Chief Mike Boyd; D/Chief Bob Kerr; D/Chief Steven Reesor; A/D/Chief Al Griffiths; Retired S/Superintendent Jack Webster; Supt. Doug Reynolds; S/Insp. John Mellor; A/Insp. Wes Ryan; S/Insp. Ron Relph; S/Insp. "Rocky" Cleveland; S/Insp. Cheryl Ingwersen; A/Insp. Mike Sale; S/Sgt. Mike Farrar; S/Sgt. Steven Grant; S/Sgt. Garry Silliker; Sgt. John Howell; Const. Deb Abbott; Const. Vic Lochhead

National Search & Rescue Secretariat: Carol O'Rourke-Elliott; Jayanti Roy

Niagara Regional Police Service: Chief Grant Waddell; Insp. Robert Ciupa

Ontario Provincial Police: Commissioner Thomas B. O'Grady; Insp. Phil Duffield; Mr. Angelo Sabatini; Mr. Ray Kolly

Ottawa-Carleton Regional Police Service: Chief Brian Ford; Dr. Gail Johnson

Peel Regional Police: Retired Chief Robert Lunney; Mr. John MacNeil

Pembroke Police Service: Deputy Chief Blair McIssac

Police communauté urbaine de Montréal: Director Jacques Duchesneau; Christiane Gauthier

Prescott Police Service: Chief F.A. (Rick) Bowie

Royal Canadian Mounted Police: Asst. Comm. John Moodie ("D" Division); S/Sgt. Tom Trueman ("D" Division); Dr. Frum Himelfarb (HQ, Ottawa); Insp. Brian Roberts ("F" Division); C/Supt. D.L. Bishop ("H" Division); Sgt. Bill Price ("H" Division)

Royal Newfoundland Constabulary: Chief Leonard Powers; Lieut. E.C. Snow; Supt. Gary Browne; Sgt. John C. House

Sault Ste. Marie Police Service: Chief Robert D. Davies

Vancouver Police Department: Sgt. Valerie Harrison

Victoria (Australia) Police Service: Supt. Trevor Parks

Wallaceburg Police Service: Chief Del Lunn

Windsor Police Service: Chief John Kousik; D/Chief Glenn Stannard

Winnipeg Police Service: Chief Dave Cassels

Fred Peters and Mike Mitchell, Policing Services Division, Ministry of the Solicitor General and Correctional Services are to be thanked for permitting me to take a leave of absence in order to pursue this project. I would also like to thank the following individuals who reviewed the manuscript: John Grime, Mohawk College; Uldis Kopstals, Seneca College; Ken Smith, Confederation College; Al Rudolph, Lethbridge Community College; Sandie McBrien, Mount Royal College; and Rob Gerden, Niagara College.

Sincere thanks to Yolanda de Rooy, John Fleming, David Stover, Marta Tomins, Ivetka Vasil, and Mary Ann McCutcheon at Prentice Hall Allyn and Bacon Canada for carefully guiding me throughout this adventure, and also to my insightful copy editor, Ann Keys. Special thanks to Peter Bregg and Christina Strong at *Maclean's* for assisting me with some excellent photographs, and also to Mike Pinder for his photographic contribution. Particular thanks to Doreen Simpson for her tea service and secretarial skills. Appreciation to Dennis Roughley, Georgian College and Gina Antonacci, Centre for Justice Studies, Humber College for offering me the opportunity to teach while writing this book, and, finally, to my students in the Advanced Private Policing course, who questioned my thinking and made me better understand the purpose of learning: the mutual campaign to examine things anew and to challenge our understanding of the things we think we know.

CHAPTER ONE

ORIGINS AND BEGINNINGS

LEARNING OBJECTIVES

1. Identify the basic origins of policing in Canada
2. Identify reasons for the development of provincial policing in Canada
3. Understand the forces shaping the development of Canadian policing
4. Identify Sir Robert Peel's nine principles of policing
5. List key reasons for the development of auxiliary police officers
6. Identify examples of the three main levels of policing in Canada
7. Cite five specific periods in the development of policing in Canada

INTRODUCTION

Canada has a reputation for policing that is extremely high. Canada is also one of few countries with a police service that is world-renowned as an important national symbol. Like the Canadian Rockies, Niagara Falls, the Hudson's Bay Company, Donovan Bailey, and other icons of Canadian identity, the Royal Canadian Mounted Police (the RCMP) represents Canada around the world. The mere presence of the distinctive red serge uniform is enough to convey an image of the Canadian heritage in policing.

However, policing in Canada is much more than simply the history of the RCMP. In many ways, the development of police service in Canada mirrors the larger development of the country as a whole. Settlement began early on the continent that is now Canada. More than 100 centuries ago, early Native peoples arrived on the North American continent from Asia. These earliest settlers migrated across enormous stretches of land. In many instances, nations joined together in order to provide mutual support and protection. For example, the Mohawk, Oneida, Onondaga, Cayuga, and Seneca nations formed a confederacy long before the arrival of European explorers. The waves of Norse and European explorers came in search of timber and fur. They found that and a great deal more when they arrived in the New World.

In 1867, when Canada was created by the Fathers of Confederation through the passage of the *British North America Act* (*BNA Act*), there were specific powers and responsibilities assigned to the newly formed federal government. There were other specific powers and responsibilities given to the various provinces that were to become the Dominion of Canada. There were, of course, people who were responsible for maintaining the peace before Confederation in 1867; however, the *BNA Act* made distinctive arrangements for policing. This legislation also highlighted some of the fundamental principles which make policing in Canada so much different from policing in the United States. It is important to have a good understanding of these differences.

As in many things Canadian, our policing heritage is an example of compromise, blending, and survival within the context of the harsh landscape which we have chosen to inhabit. The growth of police service in that landscape tells us a great deal about our traditions, our roots, and our aspirations. This chapter will be general and highly selective. It will, by no means, do justice to the richness of our policing history. There is room for more work to be done on writing the history of policing in Canada. While some excellent work has already been accomplished, the scope for further research and writing is virtually unlimited (Higley, 1984; Kelly and Kelly, 1976; Marquis, 1993; Talbot, Jayewardene, and Juliani, 1985).

ENGLISH ANCESTORS

After 1763 Canada, as a colony of Britain, was guided by the traditions and practices which were in place on the European continent. As a territory that was also settled and structured by people from France, the country also followed the styles of administration found in French society. The English and French influences on the development of policing in Canada are important; however, they should be placed in the context of early 19th century Canada and the particular issues that would affect the growth of policing. For instance, our close proximity to the United States was both a threat and an inspiration. On one hand, there existed the danger that Americans opposed to Britain would attack (as was the case with the Fenian raids in the mid-19th century); on the other hand, there were lessons to be learned from this new American republic in the making. There was also a diversity of First Nations territories throughout the country, and the relationships between them and the newest settlers were important for future development.

CONSTABLES

The presence of police constables in Canada is a direct inheritance from British practice. The roots of the office of constable have been traced to medieval England (Guth,

1994). These earliest constables were agents of the Crown, but were also direct representatives of the communities over which they presided. From the beginning, the constable was responsible for finding evidence, recording facts, and executing lawful orders. They were not judges, but servants of the Crown responsible to the local magistrate (Cooper, 1981). The following list of a constable's duties from the 1600s reveals the wide range of varied responsibilities held by these officers (Guth, 1994):

- performing court-related activities;
- arrest and seizure;
- peacekeeping;
- regulating prices in the marketplace and taverns;
- prosecuting players of illegal games (e.g., bowling);
- responding to the College of Physicians for the control of "quacks";
- supervising the collection of monies for the feeding of prisoners in local gaols;
- pursuing persons in default of the poor tax;
- enforcing statutes of labourers against the unemployed;
- accounting for fines and forfeitures applied to the maintenance of highways;
- ensuring weights and measures conform to royal standards; and
- prosecuting owners and users of bawdy houses or gaming clubs.

By 1852, there were over 2800 police constables operating in Upper Canada (i.e., Ontario). In addition to constables, there was a further British feature that was applied in Canada:

Inspection of Toronto Police Officers (circa 1912)

Metropolitan Toronto Police Museum and Discovery Centre

the night watch. In Britain, these persons, either paid or volunteer, were organized to be on guard for danger or disruption. Other elements that were directly applied from British experience included the police magistrate, the recorder (who were both judicial officials), and the chief constable, who was, and is, similar to the chief of police (Stenning, 1981).

SIR ROBERT PEEL

The name of Sir Robert Peel is at the centre of discussions about modern policing. His observation that the police are the public and the public are the police has become a benchmark in presentations on community policing and forms the basis of its underlying principles. In his earlier career, Peel was also responsible for the creation of a territorial police service for the 35 counties in Ireland, known as the Peace Preservation Force (PPF). The PPF was intended as an experiment to provide emergency response to real and anticipated disruption in the rural areas of this farming-based society. Part of Peel's aim in this project was to reduce the existing reliance on the militia. However, unlike Peel's model for an urban police force, the PPF was closer in form to a paramilitary unit with uniformed officers who were armed and housed in barracks with strict discipline and rigid command.

In 1829, Robert Peel went on to develop the London Metropolitan Police in Britain. This innovation became the model for urban policing and further enhanced Peel's reputation for advancing the cause of public policing. The structure of the police model created by Peel evolved substantially under his guidance. The Home Office (headed by the Home Secretary) had centralized control of the London City Police. Eventually, police forces were established in various boroughs lead by chief constables who reported to elected watch committees. Finally, county forces developed under chief constables responsible to magistrates. What accelerated this evolution in Peel's model was the incorporation of cities. With municipalities gaining more authority and a formally recognized structure, they were able to pass bylaws that permitted them to have greater control over their own affairs, including the direction of a municipal police force. In order to better understand the enduring impact of Sir Robert Peel's thinking, it is worthwhile to refer to his principles for policing.

THE POLICING PRINCIPLES OF SIR ROBERT PEEL

1. To prevent crime and disorder as an alternative to their repression by military force and by severity of legal punishment.
2. To recognize always that the power of the police to fulfill their functions and duties is dependent on public approval of their existence, actions, and behaviour, and on their ability to secure and maintain public respect.
3 To recognize always that to secure and maintain the respect and approval of the public means also the securing of the willing cooperation of the public in the task of securing observance of laws.
4. To recognize always that the extent to which the cooperation of the public can be secured diminishes, proportionately, the necessity of the use of physical force and compulsion for achieving police objectives.

5. To seek and to preserve public favour, not by pandering to public opinion, but by constantly demonstrating absolutely impartial service to law, in complete independence of policy and without regard to the justice or injustices of the substance of the individual laws; by ready offering of individual service and friendship to all members of the public without regard to their wealth or social standing; by ready exercise of courtesy and friendly good humour; and by ready offering of sacrifice in protecting and preserving life.

6. To use physical force only when the exercise of persuasion, advice, and warning is found to be insufficient to obtain public cooperation to an extent necessary to secure observance of law and to restore order; and to use only the minimum degree of physical force which is necessary on any particular occasion for achieving a police objective.

7. To maintain at all times a relationship with the public that gives reality to the historic tradition that the police are the public and the public are the police; the police being only members of the public who are paid to give full-time attention to duties which are incumbent on every citizen, the interests of community welfare and existence.

8. To recognize always the need for strict adherence to police executive functions, and to refrain from even seeming to usurp the powers of the judiciary or avenging individuals or the state, and of authoritatively judging guilt and punishing the guilty.

9. To recognize always that the test of police efficiency is the absence of crime and disorder, and not the visible evidence of police action in dealing with them.

THE GROWTH OF CANADIAN POLICING
NINETEENTH CENTURY

With fur traders and gold seekers travelling to the North American continent in fairly large numbers, there was a growing need for keeping public order. This role fell largely to the soldiers who made up the militia in the vast expanse of what is now Canada. While there were police officers in place in certain locations, the presence of a military force was largely responsible for the maintenance of peace. This can be seen in the case of the Red River conflict which involved the Métis leader, Louis Riel (Marquis, 1993). In this instance, immigrants who had been brought to Lord Selkirk's settlement by the Hudson's Bay Company found themselves struggling for survival. When Selkirk's governor, Robert Semple, attempted to control the Métis, bloodshed was the inevitable result (Lunn and Moore, 1992).

A settlement, by its very nature, required a more stable approach to keeping the peace. This need was a positive influence in the growth of policing in Canada. In the western reaches this job was taken up by the North-West Mounted Police. In 1874, 300 members of the North-West Mounted Police left from Dufferin, Manitoba, to protect the territory north of Montana, which had become known to the Americans as "Whoop-Up Country." In 1885, the North-West Rebellion called for massive action on the part of the police and the military. This was followed by the first gold rush in 1898 on the Yukon River near Dawson, requiring the committed presence of an organized police force to maintain peaceful order. Again, the police were not alone in this enterprise. A special military unit known as the Yukon Field Force also protected the border and prevented any movement to annex the Yukon to the United States.

The North-West Mounted Police continued to operate as a police presence in the growing number of mining towns that sprang up across the territory. These towns were often unruly and filled with a transient population not entirely disposed to being respectful of the law. The challenge for police officers in these towns must have been enormous.

As towns became more settled and stable in their purpose and population, there were opportunities to introduce local government, again modelled on the British example. The mayor, as chief magistrate, held a commission as a justice of the peace and could dispense summary justice within the town. These justices of the peace had the authority to settle disputes on an informal basis, if possible. In some instances, those holding commissions as justices of the peace attempted to intervene in riotous situations and were fiercely resisted by the crowds (Marquis, 1993).

As cities in Canada incorporated, they became better able to deal directly with policing issues through the appointment of their own police constables. The main areas that attracted the attention of police constables included:

- civil disorder (e.g., sectarian clashes between Orangemen (English Protestants) and Irish Catholics);
- liquor violations (e.g., public drunkenness, taverns open after hours);
- waterfront disturbances;
- vagrancy;
- prostitution;
- labour unrest (e.g., on railroad construction lines);
- stray dogs and untended livestock; and
- other local bylaw infractions.

As these cities and towns grew, so did their need for more substantial police departments. In the early 1860s, Montreal had the largest police force in British North America with approximately 150 officers. Kingston, which was incorporated in 1838, did not appoint its own police force until 1841. Because there was such a strong emphasis on developing commercial stability in these early towns, it is not surprising that the maintenance of public order was given such a high priority. This is further reinforced by the fact that the mayors, aldermen, and appointed justices of the peace were frequently merchants or businessmen with an overriding interest in keeping the peace.

CONFEDERATION, THE *CONSTITUTION*, AND THE *CRIMINAL CODE*

When the Fathers of Confederation created the Dominion of Canada in 1867, they made some important decisions that would affect the type of policing enjoyed by the citizens of this new country. The union of New Brunswick, Nova Scotia, Canada East (Quebec) and Canada West (Ontario) would produce a nation with specific powers and responsibilities at various levels. Of major importance was the decision to give power over the criminal law to the federal government. Sir John A. Macdonald, as attorney general during the parliamentary debates on Confederation in 1865, expressed the view that the general government (i.e., the federal Parliament) should be responsible for making determinations about criminal law, including types of crime and punishment (see Friedland, 1984). Macdonald argued that it was important to have consistent criminal law applied equally in every province. This was unlike the approach taken in the United States, where every state has the power to develop its own criminal code and to establish their own punishment for offences. As a result, the *BNA Act* (now called the *Constitution Act, 1867*), gave full authority to the federal government for criminal law and the procedures to be followed in criminal matters, under section 91(27).

By making the enactment of criminal law an important part of the new federal government's responsibility, the Fathers of Confederation were intentionally distinguishing themselves from their American neighbours. Another decision that further highlighted our differences from the U.S. approach to criminal law was the adoption in 1893 of a code of criminal law and procedure developed for the British Colonial Office (Friedland, 1984). During the 19th century, model criminal codes were being designed and refined for use in the British Colonies, including Jamaica, Australia, New Zealand, the Gold Coast, and other colonial locations. Basically, the criminal law would consist of the newly enacted *Criminal Code of Canada*, along with other statutes that might apply, as well as the common law in each of the provinces as of an established date (Mewett and Manning, 1985). By centralizing the responsibility for the making of criminal law and procedure with the federal government, and by accepting the best efforts of the British jurists with the adoption of a code of criminal law, Canada's earliest legislators prepared the ground for a very English approach to law enforcement that has guided the development of policing in this country.

The administration of justice, or the actual mechanics of applying the law, was seen as a responsibility of the provinces. This assignment of power is set out in section 92(14) of the *Constitution Act, 1867*. It includes an expectation that overall responsibility for law enforcement will fall to the provinces. As a result, provincial police forces were introduced to assume this task. The first provincial force was created in 1870 in Quebec. Its main responsibility was to maintain order in the courts and provide safe escort for prisoners. When Manitoba joined Confederation in July 1870, they began work on the development of a provincial police force later that year. This force existed until 1932 when the RCMP assumed responsibility for provincial policing under contract to the Manitoba government. British Columbia, which became part of Canada in 1871, already had a police force that was the combination of two earlier services (Vancouver Island and Fort Langley). Upon joining Confederation this force became known as the British Columbia Provincial Police. The early origins of the present Ontario Provincial Police (which was formally created as the Ontario Provincial Police Force in 1909) can be seen in 1875 with the enactment of a statute providing for the appointment of a Detective for the Government of Ontario, under the Department of the Attorney General.

Confederation and the creation of a national capital in Ottawa brought forward the need for a national police force. To address this need the Dominion Police were created in 1868. Originally, this force consisted of two officers: one in Ottawa and one in Montreal. Their main objective was to protect federal property, including naval yards and parliamentary buildings. The focus of the Ottawa police continued to grow with its members enforcing laws with a national scope, for example, counterfeiting and trafficking laws. This office was also responsible for developing a national fingerprint bureau and increased its scope of operation to address several matters of national interest (Marquis, 1993; Talbot, Jayewardene and Juliani, 1985).

CANADA'S CENTURY

Sir Wilfrid Laurier, prime minister from 1896 to 1911, said that the 20th century would belong to Canada. The truth of this observation may be difficult to accept; however, the course of the present century has seen considerable growth and development in this country, especially in the area of policing. The movement away from total reliance on British institutions and influences has progressed in an orderly but persistent manner, and we have arrived at a point in time where Canada takes a proud and independent place in the world of nations. The experiences of two world wars, exposure to the threats of the Cold War in Europe, and the impact of the postmodern period have all left significant marks on our institutions and have contributed to further developments in the field of policing in Canada.

Some important events took place at the beginning of this century, prior to the spectre of the First World War. For example, in 1900 the Edmonton police department became the first in Canada to appoint a woman as constable. While Mrs. Emma Robinson was a part-time constable, this mark of achievement was quickly enhanced when the same police force in 1909 appointed the first Native police officer, Alex Decoteau, a Cree from the Red Pheasant Reserve near North Battleford, Saskatchewan. The Edmonton police department went on to set another record in 1913 when it appointed Annie Jackson as the first full-time female constable in Canada (Mair, 1992).

The creation of the Ontario Provincial Police Force (OPP) in 1909 has been noted above. This was an important step in the development of a distinctive model of provincial policing in Canada (Higley, 1984). As discussed earlier in this chapter, the responsibility for the administration of justice, including law enforcement, is seen to be a function of the provincial governments. When Alberta and Saskatchewan joined Confederation in 1905, both provinces elected to contract with the Royal North-West Mounted Police (RNWP) to provide this service and, therefore, did not immediately develop their own provincial police capability. This situation was altered in 1917 as outlined below.

The growth in Canada's population was huge, and this resulted in a concentration of people in the urban areas. Also, the expansion of the country into the Prairies caused an entirely new type of immigration to take place. The government made an effort to attract non-Anglo-Saxon settlers to the West who would devote themselves to farming and not settle into established urban communities. To help this take place, the government placed great importance on the construction of the national railway system. The construction of the railway, of course, created a need for the protection of building materials and the policing of the work crews labouring on the new railway lines. The Canadian Pacific Railway police were especially active during this time.

The annual immigration rates in Canada reached a peak in 1913 with approximately 400 000 people arriving on our shores. At the western edges of the country, immigration was also growing. Large numbers of immigrants from China were joining the work crews responsible for the construction of the Canadian Pacific Railway. These waves of immigrants from non-Anglo-Saxon centres created challenges for local, municipal, provincial and federal police agencies in dealing with racism and ethnic skirmishes which began to take place with some degree of predictability. The local police were often reluctant to become involved in these matters and it was not uncommon for the federal police to be asked to resolve such disputes (Talbot, Jayewardene and Juliani, 1985).

Other issues which the police had to deal with increasingly at the dawn of the new century included the following:

- temperance movement against the production and consumption of alcohol;
- pressure to introduce legislation to prohibit work on the Lord's Day;
- demands for legislation to limit or restrict the sale and availability of narcotics;
- opposition to the existence of prostitution and the White Slave Trade; and
- huge growth in urban centres like Calgary, Edmonton, Regina, and Saskatoon.

At the turn of the century, police officers were still expected to carry an enormous burden of responsibility that included many areas of activity beyond simple law enforcement. There was an tendency to have these officers provide all kinds of inspection functions that made their jobs extremely busy. It should also be noted that they were not richly rewarded for their efforts. Around 1900, working conditions for police constables were fairly poor. Station houses were not shining examples of modern construction and comfort, and officers typically worked 12 hours a day, 7 days a week. In terms of salary, a monthly income of approximately $70 could be considered the norm. Furthermore, training and instruction for new recruits were almost non-existent.

Sir Wilfrid Laurier in conversation with an officer of the law.

EARLY WARNING SIGNALS

In Sudbury, Ontario, it is possible to see an example of a situation that would continue to complicate policing up to the present. Within this single jurisdiction, there existed three police services all attempting to maintain their own position of authority: the Sudbury Police, and separate detachments of the RCMP and the OPP (Talbot, Jayewardene and Juliani, 1985). Such competition among police agencies would make life difficult for political masters at all levels of government and would be the source of much study and debate.

The growth of municipal policing in this century would not be without its problems. There were many who charged that the municipal police forces were hotbeds of corruption, patronage, inefficiency, and political interference. In 1909, the Cannon Commission was appointed to inquire into and report on such allegations within the Montreal police department. Opponents of municipal police departments included the social and moral reformers (often aligned with religious groups), civic politicians who wanted to impose greater control on the police chiefs, and the local press who delighted in accounts of police failure or folly.

The police of the early 1900s were confronted with increasing instances of labour unrest. The hard work and poor conditions of workers across Canada lead to considerable union movement activity that often resulted in strikes. The expectation was that the police would provide protection to people, property, and business when such events occurred. The Winnipeg Street Company Strike provides a stark example of this in 1906, followed by the devastating Winnipeg General Strike in 1919.

In 1904, the North-West Mounted Police became the Royal North-West Mounted Police (RNWMP) to acknowledge their significant contributions to the British Crown. During this early period there was some speculation that this force would be disbanded. Because the federal Liberal government was seen as a strong supporter of provincial and local rights, it was thought that they might dismantle the RNWMP. This would serve two purposes. First, it would allow for the faster growth of local and provincial police forces. Second, it would permit the federal government to reduce its expenses for the maintenance of this widely deployed police force. However, when Commissioner Herchmer (an appointee of the previous Conservative government) left his position to command a contingent of soldiers during the Boer War (1899–1902), the Liberal government was able to appoint its own head of the RNWMP and begin to transform the political makeup of the force. As we will see, the First World War brought about a number of other changes that would alter the nature of policing in Canada.

Of great importance to the development of professional policing in Canada was the creation in 1905 of the Chief Constables' Association of Canada (CCAC). This group, which is now known as the Canadian Association of Chiefs of Police (CACP), was founded in Toronto with an original executive committee made up of representatives from the Dominion Police and the municipal police departments of Quebec, Westmount, Guelph, and Winnipeg. When this body met in 1906, they discussed issues that would be relevant at any policing conference today, including new technology, accountability, police-community relations, training standards, and criminal law reform. They were also informed by presentations on police systems in place in Manitoba, New Brunswick, Ontario, and Quebec (Marquis, 1993).

ALFRED CUDDY—AN EXAMPLE OF POLICING EXCELLENCE

Perhaps the best illustration of the refinement reached by the police profession at the beginning of the 20th century can be found in the person of Alfred Cuddy. His impressive career as a leading "tramp" police officer has a breadth and depth of experience that is summarized below:

- born in Ireland with experience in the Royal Irish Constabulary;
- became a member of the Toronto City Police, 1882–1915;
- elected President of the Chief Constables' Association of Canada, 1915–1916;
- reorganized and directed the Calgary police, 1915–1919;
- appointed Commissioner of the Alberta Provincial Police, 1919;
- managed the Criminal Investigation Division of the OPP, 1922; and
- reorganized the Windsor police, 1927.

FIRST WORLD WAR (1914–1918)

One of the most important impacts of this war was the immediate requirement to supply able-bodied men for the battle overseas. As a result of this pressing need, existing police forces were depleted as officers volunteered to fight in this conflict. In Alberta and Saskatchewan, which were policed by the RNWMP under contract to these provincial governments, a decision was made that the federal force could no longer serve in this capacity. Therefore, in 1917 the RNWMP contracts were withdrawn and both provinces established their own provincial police forces. The Saskatchewan Provincial Police continued until April 1, 1928, and the Alberta Provincial Police continued until April 1, 1932.

The federal *War Measures Act* basically suspended typical civil liberties across Canada, and this gave police services with substantial powers. Of course, it was seen that these powers were warranted in order to prevent sabotage, treason, illegal alien activity, and generally preserve the stability of the national, provincial, and municipal governments. There was also concern over the growing socialist movements that were seen as the by-product of the Bolshevik Revolution in Russia. Fears that our democratic institutions were threatened by these forces were everywhere. Interestingly, this was also the period which saw the beginnings of the police union movement in Canada (Marquis, 1993).

SECOND WORLD WAR (1939–1945)

The beginning of this second global conflict revived the need for soldiers and drained the resources of existing police services. Again, there would be the imposition of the *War Measures Act* limiting normal civil liberties in Canada and providing more extensive powers to the police. Once again, there would be serious concerns about the safety of the people and property of the nation, and about the stability of the governments at all levels in the face of possible sabotage, subversion, and espionage. During this war, some 24 000 Japanese-Canadians were removed from their homes along the west coast and sent to internment camps under the supervision of the RCMP (as it became known in 1920).

As Marquis (1993) points out, the level of communication and cooperation among police services increased substantially during the war years. This period also witnessed a growth in private industry security services. Efforts were made to ensure that the stability of domestic industry was preserved and that citizens' morale on the home front was maintained in the face of great fear and anxiety. Military police were in evidence at troop installations across Canada, and they worked closely with the local police to maintain tranquillity. There was often the need for both authorities to search for and discipline deserters, or those in violation of conscription laws. The country was also subject to major developments in the area of civil defence and disaster planning, which created an enormous need for auxiliary police officers. In British Columbia, for example, the police coordinated a corps of civil defence volunteers numbering about 20 000 (Marquis, 1993).

Of course, the war effort brought greater attention to the potential value of women in policing. Although not foremost in the minds of police leaders in the 19th century, the capacity of women to take on increased levels of responsibility and authority was now becoming an unavoidable issue. A number of lobby groups made efforts to introduce women into the police profession. These early efforts resulted in some women gaining access as secretarial or support staff. However, a number of police forces established auxiliary volunteer police units that had women members. Those women who were employed directly by police forces had assignments in vice, juvenile crime, the detective squad, but not in uniform patrol.

While the production of the automobile for domestic use slowed during the years of the war effort, it is interesting to note that in 1940 there were nearly 1.5 million vehicles registered to Canadian drivers. This meant that serious thought had to be directed at the public safety issues resulting from this number of vehicles moving around the country. Police officers spent a great deal of energy developing regulations for traffic safety, including the design and engineering of safer highways, and the proper education of the public about the rules of the road.

COLD WAR

The years following the Second World War saw a period of substantial development in Canada. Many tragedies had befallen families who lost loved ones, or suffered the terrible damage of war. The spectre of conflict between the Allies of the Western world and the powerful Soviet Union clouded the euphoria of the victory in Europe. However, the sense of purpose that drove the postwar years was uplifting and productive. In spite of the potential for nuclear devastation, which had a gruesome preview in Hiroshima and

Nagasaki, Canadians were fuelled with a large sense of optimism and hope that drove postwar reconstruction.

In the context of policing, the period of the 1950s, 1960s, and 1970s (when the so-called Cold War was at its most intense) saw important advances in the professionalism and sophistication of law enforcement in Canada. With Newfoundland joining Confederation in 1949, the country reached its present structure of ten provinces and two territories. In the same year, the Supreme Court of Canada became the final court of appeal for civil and criminal cases. Previously such final appeals were referred to the Judicial Committee of Privy Council in Great Britain. Following the Second World War, there was a strong push for national identity that resulted in this kind of self-determination (Snell and Vaughan, 1985).

This was also a period that saw the growth of the RCMP, not only as a provincial police force under contract to individual provincial governments, but as a municipal police presence. By 1968, the RCMP maintained about 137 policing contracts with separate municipalities across Canada. This number would fluctuate over the next few years; however, their combined role as a federal, provincial, and municipal police service remained constant. Of particular importance following the Second World War was the RCMP's responsibility for providing security and intelligence services. Given the alarm raised by the presence of a powerful, hostile, and imperialist nation in the form of the Soviet Union, given the many nations equipping themselves with weapons of mass destruction, and given the increase in international terrorism, there was a perceived need to provide sophisticated counter-intelligence, counter-espionage, and counter-terrorist capabilities. The RCMP, as the lead federal law enforcement agency, took a clear role in this regard. However, the extensive involvement of the RCMP in typical policing matters, and their further activities for the protection of national security and the prevention of subversion and sabotage led several Royal Commissions and other inquiries to investigate the appropriate role of this police force.

The postwar period also saw a change in the patterns and policies of immigration. Because so many people had been displaced by the tragedy of global war, Canada became more welcoming in its acceptance of new arrivals, not only from Europe, but from Asia and Africa. The earlier immigrants had been largely unskilled or subsistence farmers, settling into concentrated urban enclaves or isolated rural areas. The more recent immigrants were generally skilled and included many professionals who would seek employment in the expanding urban areas. With this major change in the immigrant population, municipal police began to learn that they would require a special understanding in order to address these new Canadians. This learning was gradual, often requiring considerable external prodding and prompting, as we shall examine in more detail in subsequent chapters. However, the expanding cultural, racial, and ethnic diversity of Canada would constitute a major challenge for police services in the last half of the 20th century.

Attention was also being paid to the unique needs of the First Nations people across Canada. The RCMP implemented a program of special band constables that would permit a degree of self-policing on the reserves. In Ontario, the OPP established a similar program of Indian policing that resulted in band councils being able to select their own members to be trained, equipped and supervised by the OPP to deliver policing services on the many reserves in the province (Higley, 1984).

One significant event that shocked the entire nation during this period occurred as a result of activities taking place in the late 1960s. French-Canadian nationalism was extremely strong in Quebec with both legitimate and illegal aspects. The most radical elements of this movement engaged in terrorist activities, including the planting of bombs near radio stations, military installations, and government facilities. The acts of sabotage organized by the Front de Libération du Québec (FLQ) escalated quickly reaching a peak in 1970 with the kidnapping of British diplomat James Cross, and the kidnapping and brutal murder of Quebec's Minister of Labour, Pierre Laporte (Vastel, 1990). The resulting "October Crisis" witnessed a period of intense public fear combined with considerable military and police activity as the federal Trudeau government invoked the *War Measures Act*, which suspended normal civil liberties and allowed the police to exercise extensive powers of detention, arrest, and control. While it is not clear that the political reaction to this crisis was warranted, the event produced a climate of fear that has had lasting effects on Quebeckers (Anastaplo, 1975).

Such events highlighted a number of issues that required the attention of police decision makers across Canada. The presence of terrorists within our borders caused an intense focus on policing and public safety. The need for police to have better intelligence about the activities of such groups as the FLQ was obvious. Cooperation between police and other agencies resulted in some important exchanges that would grow into useful networks. The creation of the Criminal Intelligence Service of Canada (CISC) in 1970 is one good example of such an effort where the gathering, analysis, and dissemination of various kinds of criminal intelligence was shared among police agencies.

Protest movements of the 1960s, anti-Vietnam demonstrations, and organized campus violence all created enormous difficulties for police services in Canada. Even though the intensity of these disruptions were not as severe as they were in the United States, Canada was close enough to the flame to feel its heat. The demonstrations on American campuses inspired similar events in Canada, and several organizers migrated to this country to mobilize support for their cause. While we did not witness the same level of brutality as seen in the U.S. battles between the police and demonstrators at the 1968 Democratic Convention in Chicago or at the campus of Kent State University, we were also not immune to serious outbreaks of civil disobedience that revealed our police services to be unprepared to deal effectively with these disruptions.

Another important component of these postwar years was the presence of organized crime. The concerns expressed around gambling, corruption, prostitution, illicit drug trafficking, and other illegal activities were real. Police organizations at all levels invested much effort in dealing with the challenges of organized crime, including the growing threat of motorcycle gangs. Many police agencies established specialized units to confront this category of criminal activity, and again, cooperation among police services was seen as a positive weapon in this particular fight (Marquis, 1993).

Because Canada was becoming increasingly industrialized with reliable transportation routes linking the various centres of commercial and economic activity, there was huge growth in the number of motor vehicles travelling around the nation. Dealing with these vehicles, the problems of drinking and driving, and other infractions became another important focus of police activity. The investigation, reconstruction, and enforcement procedures relating to motor vehicles led police to realize that more could be accomplished through conscientious programs of prevention and driver education.

The whole concept of prevention, while not new, took on greater importance in this period as police organizations realized that they were being overwhelmed by demands for service. This lead to inventive crime prevention programs, the growth of volunteer police auxiliary programs, and increased attention to the needs of victims of crime. As the complexities of living in Canadian society increased, so too did the challenge of providing adequate policing. The gradual rise in crime rates in this period and the never-ending demands by the public for more and better services from their police officers led to substantial reliance on a well-organized, well-funded law enforcement capability. However, such growth in the demand and number of officers required to provide service could not continue without careful planning and examination (Doob, 1993). The period of reform and adaptation that brings us up to the present is considered next.

POSTMODERN ERA AND NEW REFORMS

The postmodern era may be considered as the period beginning in the 1980s and extending to the present time. Its main feature is the collapse of Marxism, especially the demise of its most visible expression in the former Soviet Union (Pangle, 1992). The political, social, and economic thought of Karl Marx and the ideologies developed by his many and varied followers characterized the extension of "modern" political thought. The people's democracies that grew in Russia, China, Cuba, and other countries were designed to realize the ideals of Marxist thought and create governments that would be stable and effective. The Western liberal democratic tradition attempted to combine democratic principles with human rights and may be seen in opposition to the totalitarian regimes that developed elsewhere. The fall of Marxism signaled the "victory" of the West and began the present search for modes of good government. The destruction of the Berlin Wall did not provide answers to the very difficult questions about how we should be governed, but it did establish that the global order would not subscribe to the kind of regime which Marx and his successors described in their writings. However, since this textbook is not designed as a primer on political theory or political science, it should suffice to indicate that the postmodern age is one of great complexity that requires us to rethink some of our most fundamental ideas about who we are and what we expect to accomplish in terms of our most basic aspirations. The postmodern era involves a reaction to modern theories of government, philosophy, science, technology, and other endeavours. It is a skeptical resistance to all forms of received wisdom.

What the postmodern era has driven home with relentless force is the persistence of change in our society. There is a strong recognition that the changes we face are not only serious, they are continuous (Wheatley, 1994). This has had an important impact on a number of our institutions, including police organizations in Canada. There is a great deal to be learned from the kinds of changes that police services are being asked to make as they seek different ways to structure themselves within a rapidly changing environment that does not easily accept the *status quo* as an option.

The remainder of this textbook tries to give some practical context for the kinds of influences that are now affecting police organizations in Canada, and looks closely at the various ways of delivering policing services. This will be done in order to assist the learning of those who are about to pursue a career in policing or to encourage those already involved in policing to re-evaluate their understanding of this activity.

CONCLUSION

We have seen that Canadian policing has grown from a blending of traditions that are essentially European and primarily English. We have also seen that the Canadian experience in policing is directly related to the experiences of those who came to Canada from a vast range of migration, which includes Asia, Africa, and Europe. The development of our police has been closely tied to our history and derives from traditions of law enforcement that include influences distinguishing us from the American policing experience. The growth of Canada, from the earliest times until the present, has been one based on democratic principles, with a priority on "peace, order, and good government." Our police organizations have largely served to meet those priorities with a fair degree of success. While the history of Canadian policing is a story that has not been fully explored, and while it is not without certain negative elements, it is reasonable to suggest that the people of Canada have been served well by police agencies that respect the basic principles of our society and contribute to our well-being and sense of order.

QUESTIONS FOR CONSIDERATION

1. Police services in Canada have a strong relationship to the federal government which is responsible for the establishment of criminal law and procedure. This is different from the approach taken in the United States where each state has the power to make its own criminal law. What are the advantages and disadvantages of these two approaches?
2. The approach to policing that Sir Robert Peel applied in the City of London placed an emphasis on the police being part of the community which they served. Another approach has officers operating more in keeping with a military model where officers are assigned to "detachments" and are called out when they are required to respond to calls. Examine these two approaches and apply them to various police services in Canada.

3. Canada has had a policy of multiculturalism with regard to the immigrants who came to this country. This policy placed value on those people retaining their ethnic, religious, and cultural heritage within the context of Canadian society. The United States has had a policy of immigration known as the "melting pot," where it is expected that people will assimilate American values and traditions and blend with the dominant culture. These two approaches have created different countries with different approaches to policing. What are some of these differences? What are the advantages and disadvantages of both approaches?
4. Policing in Canada happens at the federal, provincial, and municipal levels. What are the different police services that have developed at these various levels? What are their similarities and differences?
5. What are some of the major changes in the 19th and early 20th century that have had a lasting impact on the development of policing in Canada?

REFERENCES

Anastaplo, George. (1975). *Human being and citizen: essays on virtue, freedom and the common good*. Chicago: The Swallow Press.

Cooper, H.S. (1981). "The evolution of Canadian police." In McGrath, William T. and Michael Mitchell (eds.). *The police function in Canada*. Toronto: Methuen.

Critchley, T.A. (1967). *A history of police in England and Wales 900–1966*. London: Constable & Co.

Doob, Anthony N. (ed.). (1993). *Thinking about police resources*. Toronto: Centre of Criminology, University of Toronto.

Forcese, D.P. (1992). *Policing Canadian society*. Toronto: Prentice Hall Canada.

Friedland, M.L. (1984). *A century of criminal justice: perspectives on the development of Canadian law*. Toronto: Carswell Legal Publications.

Guth, DeLloyd J. (1994). "The traditional common law constable, 1235–1829: from Bracton to the Fieldings to Canada." In MacLeod, R.C. and David Schneiderman (eds.). *Police powers in Canada: the evolution and practice of authority*. Toronto: Published in association with the Centre for Constitutional Studies, University of Alberta by the University of Toronto Press, pp. 3–23.

Higley, Dahn D. (1984). *O.P.P.: the history of the Ontario Provincial Police Force*. Toronto: Queen's Printer.

Kelly, William and Nora Kelly. (1976). *Policing in Canada*. Toronto: Macmillan of Canada.

Kent, J.R. (1986). *The English village constable 1580–1642*. Oxford: Clarendon Press.

Lunn, Janet and Christopher Moore. (1992). *The story of Canada*. Toronto: Lester Publishing and Key Porter Books.

Mair, A.J. (1992). *E.P.S. the first 100 years: a history of the Edmonton Police Service*. Edmonton: Edmonton Police Service.

Marquis, G. (1993). *Policing Canada's century: a history of the Canadian Association of Chiefs of Police*. Toronto: Published for The Osgoode Society by the University of Toronto Press.

Mewett, A.W. and M. Manning. (1985). *Criminal law. 2nd ed.* Toronto: Butterworths.

Pangle, Thomas L. (1992). *The ennobling of democracy: the challenge of the postmodern age*. Baltimore: The Johns Hopkins University Press.

Reith, C. (1948). *A short history of the British police*. London: Oxford University Press.

Sewell, J. (1985). *Police: urban policing in Canada*. Toronto: James Lorimer & Company.

Snell, James G. and Frederick Vaughan. (1985). *The Supreme Court of Canada: history of the institution*. Toronto: Published for the Osgoode Society by the University of Toronto Press.

Stansfield, R.T. (1996). *Issues in policing: a Canadian perspective*. Toronto: Thompson Educational Publishing.

Stenning, P. (1981). *Police commissions and boards in Canada*. Toronto: Centre of Criminology.

Talbot, C.K., C.H.S. Jayewardene and T.J. Juliani. (1985). *Canada's constables: the historical development of policing in Canada*. Ottawa: Crimcare Inc.

Vastel, M. (1990). *The outsider: the life of Pierre Elliott Trudeau*. (Translated by H. Bauch). Toronto: Macmillan of Canada.

Wheatley, Margaret J. (1994). *Leadership and the new science: learning about organization from an orderly universe*. San Francisco: Berrett-Koehler Publishers.

White, W.L., R.H. Wagenberg and R.C. Nelson. (1994). *Introduction to Canadian politics and government. 6th ed*. Toronto: Harcourt Brace Canada.

TOWARD MORE LEARNING

For anyone wishing to learn more about the history of policing in Canada or about the beginnings of policing in general and some related topics, there are a number of good works available. The outline below pinpoints specific readings.

GENERAL HISTORY OF POLICING IN CANADA

Kelly, William and Nora Kelly. (1976). *Policing in Canada*. Toronto: Macmillan of Canada.

> This is a well-written and well-researched summary of the development of Canadian policing and is fairly easily found.

Marquis, G. (1993). *Policing Canada's century: a history of the Canadian Association of Chiefs of Police*. Toronto: Published for The Osgoode Society by the University of Toronto Press.

> This book was written to commemorate the founding and growth of the Canadian Association of Chiefs of Police (originally, the Chief Constables' Association of Canada). It is richly detailed and thoroughly researched by an academic historian. The story of the CACP mirrors the development of policing in Canada and provides a very good basis for a deeper understanding of this topic.

Talbot, C.K., C.H.S. Jayewardene and T.J. Juliani. (1985). *Canada's constables: the historical development of policing in Canada*. Ottawa: Crimcare Inc.

> Another good source of detailed background on the origins of policing in Canada. This book also has a good listing of references to other primary and secondary sources for the reader to pursue.

HISTORY OF THE RCMP

There are several sources of historical background on this police force which has been such a significant part of Canadian history. The items listed below are just the beginning.

Dempsey, H.A. (1974). *Men in scarlet*. Calgary: McClelland and Stewart West.

Kelly, William and Nora Kelly. (1976). *Policing in Canada*. Toronto: Macmillan of Canada.

HISTORY OF THE OPP

Higley, Dahn D. (1984). *O.P.P.: the history of the Ontario Provincial Police Force*. Toronto: Queen's Printer.

> This book, written by a retired Chief Superintendent of the OPP, is an excellent source of historical information about this provincial police service. It is extremely detailed and is illustrated with numerous photographs that capture the growth of a substantial and modern police service.

HISTORY OF OTHER CANADIAN POLICE SERVICES

There are several good histories prepared on the many individual police services across Canada. This is particularly true of the older organizations which have celebrated anniversaries of note. However, the reader is encouraged to refer to Appendix III of this book to locate some Web sites for individual police services which frequently have some useful historical background on the growth and development of that particular service (e.g., the home page for the Peel Regional Police has a good outline available).

HISTORY OF IMPORTANT CANADIAN INSTITUTIONS RELATED TO POLICING

Snell, James G. and Frederick Vaughan. (1985). *The Supreme Court of Canada: history of the institution*. Toronto: Published for the Osgoode Society by the University of Toronto Press.

This book provides a very thorough history of the development of the Supreme Court of Canada and accounts for its increasingly important role in the context of policing in Canada. The changes in the court from the time of Confederation until the introduction of the *Canadian Charter of Rights and Freedoms* in 1982 is extremely relevant to those who wish to learn more about policing in Canada.

HISTORY OF POLICING IN ENGLAND

Critchley, T.A. (1967). *A history of police in England and Wales 900–1966*. London: Constable & Co.

This provides a thorough study of the development of policing in England and Wales over a period of some 1000 years. It is a valuable guide to the basic formation and structure of policing that have influenced its growth in Canada.

Reith, C. (1948). *A short history of the British police*. London: Oxford University Press.

An excellent study which continues to provide a good background on the historical development of the British police. It is well written with substantial references to other important sources.

HISTORY OF POLICING IN THE UNITED STATES

Peak, K. J. (1997). *Policing America: methods, issues, challenges*. *2nd ed*. Upper Saddle River, N.J.: Prentice Hall.

This is an excellent introductory textbook that provides a good deal of concise information on the whole topic of policing in America. It is aimed at the under-graduate student and has a very good chapter entitled, "Historical Development" that traces some of the English roots of policing in North America, as well as the specific development of American policing. It is highly recommended as a companion to this textbook.

Smith, B. (1960). *Police systems in the United States. 2nd ed.* New York: Harper and Row.

A reliable source of historical information that was extensively revised for the second edition. This textbook examines the growth of policing in the United States from a thematic perspective that considers elements of a complex police system, including crime, traffic, rural and suburban police, urban police, state and federal police, organization, and central services.

CHAPTER TWO

THE CONTEXT OF POLICING

LEARNING OBJECTIVES

1. Identify aspects of the social context of policing in Canada
2. Identify aspects of the political context of policing in Canada
3. Explain aspects of the legal context of policing in Canada
4. Explain aspects of the technological context of policing in Canada
5. Describe the key goals and objectives of police in Canada

INTRODUCTION

In order to best understand the rich and varied history of policing in Canada and to further understand the kinds of police services we enjoy today, we need to see policing in its proper contexts. This chapter is designed to offer a snapshot of the current social, political, legal, and technological contexts as they relate to Canadian policing, and will not be overly detailed. It is often very difficult to separate these issues into neat categories as they tend to be closely interrelated and highly dependent on one another. This chapter will underline some of the major themes guiding our individual and institutional activities, and will stake out some of the boundaries within which our police agencies function.

An effort has been made to bring together a number of perspectives on the various contexts noted above. Since this textbook is intended to be of assistance to the student whose primary interest is in policing, the material presented here does not begin to do justice to any of the critical theories dealing with these areas. For the present purpose, we will sketch a general picture of the contexts of modern policing in Canada and provide some suggestions for those wishing to make further investigations in order to add depth to their understanding.

Again, Canada is essentially a product of many diverse and unique influences. We have a national Constitution that places a high priority on "peace, order, and good government." We are a country that shares a long and tranquil border with the most powerful nation in the world (Holmes, 1981). We have developed institutions and structures that assist us in organizing our public lives in a relatively satisfactory manner. All of this has contributed to the growth of police services in Canada, which may be seen as sharing certain fundamental goals and objectives that are consistent with the larger context of Canadian life. What police do in Canada is fundamentally guided by these basic goals and objectives. This chapter will briefly consider those aspects and offer guidance on future readings.

THE SOCIAL CONTEXT OF CANADIAN POLICING

Canadian society is composed of elements which make it different from other nations. There are aspects of social life in Canada that are the result of many years of social policy and practice shaping our society into something quite distinct. This particular social context has had both a direct and an indirect impact on the kind of policing we receive. However, the social context should not be seen in isolation from other areas explored in this chapter. The social dimension is but one facet of the larger framework that constitutes the Canadian identity.

What do we mean when we speak about the social context? Basically, this refers to the formal and informal arrangements in place for structuring and guiding the way in which members of a society interact. It has been said that human beings are, by nature, *social* animals. That means to say that we naturally desire the company and companionship of others, and we incline toward groupings of individuals for some shared purpose. The family, of course, is the basic social unit with which we are generally familiar. Beyond the family, there are many other social units that guide our daily lives, such as clubs, religious organizations, benevolent societies, charitable organizations, sports associations, fraternities and sororities, and professional associations. What is perhaps characteristic about Canada, with its long history of multiculturalism, is the great diversity and range of these types of social groupings.

Canada may be further characterized in its social context by a single distinguishing birthmark: the concept of "two solitudes." This refers to the long-standing coexistence of both French and English cultures in Canada. The social development of Canada has been substantially influenced by these two different heritages. There are characteristics of French-Canadian society that have resulted in a distinctive set of social groupings and arrangements, especially in Quebec. The religious, linguistic, cultural, and other differences found in the French-Canadian presence have contributed to a social fabric that is easily contrasted with the rest of Canada (Forsey, 1974; McRoberts and Posgate, 1980; McWhinney, 1979).

However, other areas in Canadian society are not without their own social distinctions. Of particular importance is the existence of a strong network of First Nations people throughout Canada. The various provinces and territories contain distinctive peoples who have an increasingly direct and special impact on the policing services they receive. All of the influences from the many different parts of the country contribute to the richness of Canada's social dimension. These are important pieces in the puzzle of society. If society is considered the highest level of human interaction, we must look at things like religion, morality, ethics, economics, sexuality, culture, politics, and other aspects of the lives of people engaged with one another. There are many complex relationships that develop as a result of our social arrangements and provide a focus for serious study known as sociology. The study of individuals in society is wonderfully interesting. It is also profoundly important to the topic of policing.

DEMOGRAPHIC INSIGHTS

Someone wishing to study any particular society must have an understanding of its basic components. This is where demographics comes into prominence. This is literally the

Police ambulance (circa 1905)

tracing of people within society. Demographics allows us to look at the numbers of people in different categories, which provides a better perspective on the social order. Demographics also permits us to consider the makeup of a society and to make some predictions about its growth and development. In Canada, demography can tell us a great deal about policing and the social trends that will affect its future.

An excellent source of demographics on Canadian society is Statistics Canada, which is a federal government agency that regularly tracks and publishes figures on a wide range of socio-economic and other indicators. We can determine, for example, that a large proportion of Canadians live in concentrated urban settings. We can also see that Canada has an aging population that will directly affect our law enforcement needs and priorities. What follows is a brief overview of some of the most significant demographic trends that reflect Canadian society (Normandeau and Leighton, 1990). It is important to remember here that the police themselves are drawn from the ranks of citizens who inhabit this country, and therefore, the social characteristics of the nation are directly relevant to the type of persons who become police officers. This is related to the notion of multiculturalism which will be discussed below in this chapter and will be addressed in more detail in Chapter 5 ("Becoming a Police Officer in Canada").

THE MULTICULTURAL SOCIETY

The present makeup of Canadian society has a rich diversity largely due to the presence of Native inhabitants and the descendants of the French and English settlers who altered the landscape to suit their needs. These founding peoples were soon joined by others who originated in Europe, with immigration patterns shifting to Asia and Africa as time progressed. Figure 2–1 indicates the sources of immigration to Canada and reveals that we are a country of immigrants.

For police organizations, the impact of Canada's particular approach to multiculturalism encourages a focus on activities that will improve the effectiveness of police in promoting tolerance and understanding between themselves and the visible minority community, including Aboriginal peoples (Ontario. Ministry of the Solicitor General and Correctional Services. Police-Race Relations Monitoring Board, 1996). The existence of a fully multicultural society places special demands on police resources for recruitment and outreach, training and learning programs, promotional policies, and police-community relations. Many police services have substantial cross-cultural training programs and also use representative multicultural advisory panels to assist in engaging the widest spectrum of the community in the policing enterprise.

There will be a continuing need to ensure that the criminal justice system and, in particular, the front-line police officer are in tune with the expectations and requirements of Canada's diverse population. The increased vulnerability of certain members of society (e.g., women) to particular kinds of crime due to language or other cultural barriers will need to be addressed. The continued potential for ethnic and racial violence that is the product of tensions transplanted from other homelands will require specialized forms of

FIGURE 2-1

IMMIGRANT POPULATION BY PLACE OF BIRTH, 1991*

	(thousands)
All places of birth	4342.9
United Kingdom	717.7
Southern Europe	711.6
Western Europe	431.5
Eastern Europe	420.5
Eastern Asia	377.2
Southeast Asia	312.0
United States	249.1
Caribbean and Bermuda	232.5
Southern Asia	228.8
Africa	166.2
South America	150.6
Western Asia and Middle East	146.8
Other Northern Europe	83.4
Central America	68.8
Oceania and other countries	46.3

*Based on data from a 20% sample of the population. Non-permanent residents are not included in this table.

Source: Reproduced by the authority of the Minister of Industry, 1997, Statistics Canada, "Immigration and Citizenship," cat. no. 93–316.

police intervention. This can be clearly seen in some of the activities undertaken by the Criminal Intelligence Service of Canada (CISC) in dealing with organized crime (Canadian Association of Chiefs of Police, 1991). The notion that official multiculturalism is perhaps a negative policy in terms of dealing with the future health of Canada has been expressed in some quarters (Hann and Asbury, 1992).

THE AGING SOCIETY

Another distinctive aspect of the social context within which the police must operate in Canada relates to the age of the population. Demographic trends show that our population is rapidly aging. By the year 2000 there will be a substantial number of citizens who are over the age of 65. The chart in Figure 2–2 compares relevant population projections for the years 1996 and 2016.

From a law enforcement standpoint this social demographic trend means that there will be a heightened need for police to be concerned with seniors' fear of crime, which is a common feature of seniors' satisfaction with a police service. There will also be an immediate and continuously growing concern for the vulnerability of the elderly. The exploitation of

FIGURE 2-2

POPULATION PROJECTIONS BY AGE GROUPS, 1996 AND 2016*

	1996 (thousands)	2016 (thousands)
All ages	29 963.7	37 119.8
0–4	1 991.5	2 052.8
5–9	2 036.9	2 072.2
10–14	2 035.2	2 105.7
15–19	1 996.3	2 194.8
20–24	2 027.0	2 378.2
25–29	2 217.5	2 482.2
30–34	2 615.4	2 541.4
35–39	2 657.3	2 530.4
40–44	2 377.8	2 509.9
45–49	2 146.6	2 569.5
50–54	1 667.4	2 791.4
55–59	1 327.3	2 688.7
60–64	1 209.4	2 308.2
65–69	1 129.7	1 971.6
70–74	980.4	1 420.6
75–79	704.9	989.8
80–84	471.7	714.1
85–89	245.8	466.5
90 and over	125.4	331.7

*Figures represent the medium-growth projection and the reference date is July 1.

Source: Reproduced by the authority of the Minister of Industry, 1997, Statistics Canada, CANSIM, matrix no. 6900.

seniors can take the form of elder abuse, including physical, mental, or sexual harm to the elderly, as well as fraud involving the elderly and the misuse of their financial assets. Police organizations have begun to take stock of these kinds of needs because they are able to see that this portion of society will be a growing consumer of their services (Plotkin, 1996).

THE FAMILY IN CANADIAN SOCIETY

The presence of two-income families in Canada is quite common, with both spouses in the work world and committing a significant portion of their energy to earning a living. However, there is also a growing number of single-parent families, typically headed by women who are both young and never-married. These types of trends are important to police organizations as they plan their resources and consider the functions they will perform on behalf of society. Clearly, these trends operate in different ways to direct police operations and require special approaches to ensure public safety and security. The income levels of these families will affect the police in very different ways and will require different solutions to the challenges they pose.

The New Skilled Worker in Society

While Canada began as an agricultural or agrarian society where any required skills were fairly simple and straightforward, it developed into an industrial society where unskilled labourers could often find gainful employment by simply mixing their labour with the products being made for sale or distribution. The worker today, however, must be increasingly skilled in a number of areas that place high demands on literacy, numeracy, and capacity for flexibility (Ogden, 1993). As the new millennium approaches, we are frequently being warned that the successful worker of tomorrow will be the "knowledge worker" (Drucker, 1994). Not only will the requirement for this new kind of worker have an impact on immigration patterns and trends in Canada, it will also influence police services, causing them to address and respond to the needs of a changing society. With more and more jobs being directed to the higher end of the knowledge scale, there will likely be fewer employment opportunities at the lower end of this scale. This trend will result in more potential for disruption as the previously strong base of lower-end employment begins to weaken. Police organizations will increasingly be called upon to deal with this fundamental shift in society's priorities and it can probably be assumed that labour and workforce unrest will be an important feature of this change.

Canada's Changing Workforce

The extent of some of the changes that have occurred over the last century in Canada with regard to the workforce can be seen in the table of historical statistics presented in Figure 2–3.

What is particularly interesting here is the change in the percentage of labour devoted to agricultural versus non-agricultural pursuits. Where a substantial 40.2% of the population at the beginning of this century were engaged in farming or related functions, in 1995 that percentage had tumbled to only 3.2%. This is a dramatic decrease in the focus of our labour force. Also significant in these statistics is the huge growth in the number of women who have joined the workforce over this period.

Important Social Movements in Canada

Throughout human history, significant changes have occurred as a result of social movements that have operated to create some kind of reform in the *status quo*. These types of movements often begin life as marginal forces with very little power and few resources, yet transforming themselves into compelling causes that lead to substantial change. Examples of such forces include:

- the temperance movement;
- the labour movement;

FIGURE 2-3

CHANGES IN CANADA'S WORKFORCE

	Early 1900s	1990s
Total Population	5 371 315 (1901)	29 606 100 (1995)
rural population	3 357 093 (1901)	6 390 000 (1995)
urban population	2 014 222 (1901)	20 907 000 (1995)
Labour Force	1 782 832 (1901)	13 506 000° (1995)
% of population		
of working age	43.9% (1901)	58.6% (1995)
agricultural pursuits	716 000 (40.2%) (1901)	431 000 (3.2%)(1995)
non-agricultural pursuits	1 065.972 (59.8%) (1901)	13 075 000 (96.8%)(1995)
Workforce and Gender		
male	1 544 050 (1901)	7 397 000° (1995)
female	232 571 (1901)	6 109 000° (1995)
Average Yearly Earnings		
manufacturing and others		
— hourly workers	$375 (1905)	$34 184 (1996)
supervisory and office		
employees — salaried		
workers	$848 (1901)	$46 979 (1996)
Union Membership	133 000 (1911)	4 780 000 (1995)

°This is the number employed. Official number of unemployed is about 1 500 000, not including those who have stopped looking for work.

Source: Reproduced by authority of the Minister of Industry, 1997, Statistics Canada, "Historical Statistics of Canada," cat. no. 11-516, and "Historical Labour Force Statistics," cat. no. 71-201.

- the women's movement;
- the environmental movement;
- the anti-abortion movement;
- the gay and lesbian rights movement;
- the anti-nuclear movement; and
- the Quebec independence movement.

The police, as the agency of the state most visibly tasked with public order maintenance, are called upon to respond to such movements when necessary. The control aspect of policing is most evident when police organizations are directed to impose order in public confrontations with such movements. There is often a debate about the legitimacy of such control and the lines of discussion place considerations of peace, order, and good government against proponents of civil liberty, individual autonomy, and the protection of human rights (McMahon and Ericson, 1984).

THE POLITICAL CONTEXT OF CANADIAN POLICING

Canada's political institutions are based on a fairly common understanding of representative government. Elements of the Canadian political environment that can be easily identified include:

- a system of free elections;
- universal suffrage where all citizens have the right to vote;
- the application of the principle of majority rule;
- protection of minorities;
- accountability of elected officials;
- a government operating openly through wide discussion; and
- responsiveness to informed public opinion.

Representative institutions can only be truly effective or democratic when, in theory, everyone can take part in the system (Hill, 1974). In order to bring the full benefits of representative government to the most practical level, Canada has implemented a high degree of local self-government. Perhaps one of the best places to look for such a form of democratic representation is at the municipal level. This is where most people are directly engaged in the political life of their country. This is also where the most immediate level of policing is typically assigned (Marquis, 1993).

All governments are, in many ways, experiments in human relations. This is particularly true in the case of Canada, which is not only of comparatively recent vintage but is a judicious blending of British, American, and other influences. This unique political context, which places a high priority on institutional examination and scrutiny, has a direct and immediate impact on the kind of policing that we expect and receive. This is borne out by the kind and number of inquiries, investigations, and Royal Commissions which have been established over the years to examine our policing arrangements, and the informed questioning of their propriety and practices (Roach, 1995; Sunahara, 1990).

Canada, as a state, has a federal system of government that is made up of a strong body in Ottawa, along with 10 provincial governments (Newfoundland, Prince Edward Island, New Brunswick, Nova Scotia, Quebec, Ontario, Manitoba, Saskatchewan, Alberta, and British Columbia), and two territories (Northwest Territories and the Yukon). This form of government has been important to the growth of our policing services, as discussed in Chapter 1. The unifying national perspective created by this form of government and the fact that we have a single, unified approach to criminal law and procedure are particularly relevant in this context. With a strong federal government comes an overall approach to policing that is guided by the elected officials who represent the various federal ridings across Canada, and that is also guided by the judges who preside over the various courts with jurisdiction in matters relating to criminal law and procedure. While the system of government known as federalism has shifted, transformed, and been modified over the life of this country, generating both defenders and critics, it has operated fairly effectively in creating a system conducive to consistent policing practices (Meekison, 1977).

Within a solid constitutional framework, the political life of Canada is guided in a form that is highly predictable and stable. The cycle of elections that brings our elected officials into power follows a regular routine. There is an organized system of political parties which brings individual candidates to our attention. There has always been some criticism of the party system and this continues to be the case as when we see dramatic shifts in the fortunes of political parties. (For example, the surprising reduction in popular support for the federal Progressive Conservative party during the election in 1993 brought the Liberal Party into office under the leadership of Jean Chrétien.) The strength of the Canadian Constitution is such that it provides a relatively clear and deliberate outline of the division of powers within the country and ensures that there are special guarantees that protect our individual rights and freedoms, as well as our parliamentary form of government and the institutions that result from this form of government.

The process of government, which is all part of the political context, is comprised of the following key components:

- the executive (prime minister and Cabinet);
- the bureaucracy;
- the legislature; and
- the judiciary.

THE EXECUTIVE

The executive level of government in Canada is made up of the office of the prime minister and the members of Cabinet. It is at this level that the most important decisions about the policies and programs that will guide the lives of Canadians are developed (Hockin, 1977). The prime minister is responsible for making key appointments of lieutenant governors of the provinces, judges who will preside over courts, and many other key positions on agencies, boards, and commissions that make decisions that affect our lives, our liberties, and our well-being. Cabinet is responsible for setting the agenda for what is going to happen during their government's term in office, including the legislation that will be introduced into the House of Commons for debate and possible passage. Most relevant to the issue of policing in Canada is the fact that the federal Cabinet contains two ministers whose activities will have a direct bearing on law enforcement in the country: the Solicitor General of Canada and the Minister of Justice (who is also the Attorney General of Canada). These two Cabinet posts are occupied by elected officials whose mandates include the federal direction of policing and the development, drafting, and prosecution of statutes that will establish the criminal law in Canada. A similar executive level exists in each of the 10 provinces with the prime minister's role being taken by the premier, who is the leader of the party winning the largest number of seats in the legislature. Like the federal government, each province has a Cabinet which is comprised of those elected members selected by the premier to take responsibility for the various ministries which provide policies, programs, and services to the public.

THE BUREAUCRACY

The bureaucracies that exist at the federal, provincial, and municipal levels are sizable. Their importance is central to the effectiveness and efficiency of the policies and programs set by government. Again, at the federal level, there are two federal departments whose bureaucrats most directly affect the practice of policing in Canada: the departments of the Solicitor General and Justice. These will be discussed in more detail in Chapter 3; however, it is worth noting that the Solicitor General's department includes the following areas: the Royal Canadian Mounted Police (RCMP), the Canadian Security Intelligence Service (CSIS), and other agencies that have functions relating to policing in Canada. These federal departments are further supported by provincial government agencies, which apply the policies and programs within their jurisdictions as well as any additional initiatives that the provincial legislatures are empowered to introduce. At the municipal level there are several layers of bureaucracy whose activities directly affect the delivery of police services.

THE LEGISLATURE

The federal Legislature is where the drama of national politics in Canada is takes place. The House of Commons in Ottawa is the stage for matters of national debate and where our elected representatives make determinations about the laws that will guide our lives, our activities, and our futures. Currently, there are 301 seats in the federal Legislature recently increased from 295. All of the individuals elected to those seats represent a significant portion of the Canadian public. All bills introduced into the House of Commons must be debated and discussed prior to passage and this is where the democratic process operates to ensure that Canadians have the benefit of representation. Each of the provinces has a similar structure in the form of a provincial legislature. Elected representatives at that level have an opportunity to deliberate on matters under provincial jurisdiction in order to provide good government. The division of powers between the federal and provincial governments was established by the *Constitution Act, 1867*, and the Supreme Court of Canada may be appealed to when there is disagreement over the interpretation of jurisdiction (Russell, 1982).

THE JUDICIARY

The judiciary is the last part of the overall structure of Canada's political system. It is composed of the judges who are placed in highly sensitive positions of authority and trust. These persons carry an expectation that they will make independent decisions according to the rule of law, consistent with the rules of procedure established over many years of practice, and consistent with the enormous body of jurisprudence that has been crafted over the years. The burden of such huge expectations is enormous, and Canada has been blessed with fine examples of judicial leadership, scholarship, and stability with very few exceptions (Kaplan, 1996). The impact of the judiciary on matters that relate directly to policing in Canada has increased substantially since the introduction of the *Canadian Charter of Rights and Freedoms*, and warrants careful and continuous study (Manning, 1983; McDonald, 1982; Milne, 1982; Russell, 1982; Strayer, 1983). The judiciary is part of the political structure that guides our lives in Canada, and is integral to the democratic institutions that have been established in this country. However, the specific elements of this structure are best considered as part of the legal context of policing in Canada and are presented in the following section.

POLITICS, REFORM, AND PUBLIC ADMINISTRATION

It is often suggested that the police are apolitical or non-political. It is also argued that the police should be as removed from politics as possible in order to ensure that the law is administered in the most independent manner. While it is important that the police be insulated from partisan politics that could influence their ability to deliver services in an impartial way, the police are, by their very nature, profoundly tied to the political workings

Metropolitan Toronto Police Museum and Discovery Centre

Toronto Police Mounted Unit outside Hart House, University of Toronto (circa 1910)

of society. The challenge of maintaining police independence from undue political interference while ensuring that the police operate in ways that are fully accountable to the public is one that has never been completely or adequately addressed (Stenning, 1994).

Within the context of the political structures in which policing operates, there is much to be learned by studying the workings of the various reform efforts taking place at the provincial/municipal levels in Canada. The mechanics of local government have become quite complex and, since a great deal of policing effort is placed at this level, it warrants better understanding. Municipalities are creations of the provinces in which they reside and the statutory arrangements made for their administration, management, and structure have an important bearing on the nature of policing that will be provided in those jurisdictions.

Canada has recently witnessed fairly active interest in the process of consolidating or amalgamating municipalities. This interest has largely been driven by an apparent conviction that savings could be realized at the local government level. The best evidence to date suggests that such savings are not substantial, and that governments should look for other reasons to justify this type of controversial activity (Sancton, 1996). Because a police organization typically consumes a large portion of the municipality's annual budget, frequently employs a significant number of people, and has a highly visible profile within the local community, it is not surprising that there is great interest in making these services as efficient and economical as possible. As a result, there is very little hope that police agencies will be able to avoid being drawn into debates at the political level when reforms are being contemplated. The control of municipal police budgets is an intensely political issue and has been the focus of study in recent years (McKenna and Evans, 1994).

Whenever there is activity in the area of municipal or local government reform, the question of how to deal with arrangements for public safety, law enforcement, crime prevention, and other related topics is usually near the top of the agenda (Ontario. Greater Toronto Area Task Force, 1996). As all levels of government across Canada intensify their search for better ways of providing service to the public, police organizations will be drawn into the political arena to account for their resource requirements and to join in the quest for alternative delivery mechanisms (Doob, 1993; Lindquist and Sica, 1995).

THE LEGAL CONTEXT OF CANADIAN POLICING

Because police officers operate in the service of the law, it is very important that we have a good understanding of the legal context of Canadian policing. The administration of justice rests upon laws that are developed and passed by our federal Parliament and provincial legislatures. Therefore, it is essential that there be a clear recognition of the key features of the legal system in Canada. Police officers are governed both by statutes and by common law. Under common law, police are accorded extensive powers to maintain the peace, protect property, and generally prevent crime. They are also given special powers of arrest, search, and seizure under a combination of common law and statute. The 10 provinces have individual statutes which outline the duties and responsibilities of police officers (MacIntosh, 1989). The control of the federal government over criminal law is set in the Constitution. Of major importance, in terms of the Canadian legal context for police officers, is the existence of the *Criminal Code of Canada*. This document undergoes constant change through case law or legislative amendment and forms the basis for a great deal of what police officers do on a regular basis. Therefore, it warrants special attention and study (Friedland, 1984; Parker, 1981; Watt and Fuerst, 1996).

The central authority within Parliament (i.e., Cabinet) has a responsibility to construct balance in the courts to ensure that regional, ethnic, gender, linguistic, and other factors are maintained in judicial appointments. It is also intended that there be a high degree of independence accorded to the administration of justice. To ensure that due process of law is observed, the political considerations that may enter to the arena of justice are meant to be kept to a minimum. There is some argument that this does not happen and that there is far too much politics involved with the administration of justice.

Courts in Canada exist at both the federal and provincial levels. It has already been noted that the *Constitution Act, 1867,* gave the federal Parliament exclusive jurisdiction over criminal law and the regulation of criminal procedure. It has also been noted that each of the provinces is responsible for maintaining its own civil and criminal courts and have the power to make laws in relation to the administration of justice within their boundaries.

FEDERAL COURTS

The Supreme Court of Canada is the highest court of appeal in matters both criminal and civil. Basically, this court is comprised of eight judges and one chief justice who is referred to as the Chief Justice of Canada. These judges hear appeals in criminal and civil cases. The following types of criminal appeals may be heard by the Supreme Court of Canada:

- where an accused's acquittal on an indictable offence has been set aside by a provincial Court of Appeal;
- where a provincial Court of Appeal judge has given a dissenting opinion on a point of law; and
- where appeal involves a question of law and leave has been granted by the Supreme Court of Canada.

Also, there is the Federal Court of Canada. This is a specialized court which has two divisions: appellate and trial. This court deals with cases relating to federal law in such areas as tax, immigration, and admiralty.

PROVINCIAL COURTS

Basically, the court system in the provinces is made up of three levels:

- superior court, which may include a Court of Appeal and a trial division;
- county or district courts, and
- inferior courts, generally referred to as "provincial courts."

Provincial court judges are typically responsible for hearing cases dealing with breaches of provincial statutes and the less serious criminal offences. These judges also conduct what are known as preliminary hearings which serve to determine if there is enough evidence available to bring an accused person to trial. Depending on the seriousness of a criminal case, trials are held at the district/county level or at the superior court. In many provinces, the district/county courts have been merged with the provincial superior court.

THE IMPACT OF THE *CHARTER*

Of central importance in the legal context is the existence of the *Canadian Charter of Rights and Freedoms*, which was proclaimed in April 1982. This document, which forms part of the *Constitution Act, 1982*, is a significant piece of legislation that places some crucial limitations on the exercise of police powers (Stuart, 1994). The following topics are relevant in this context and result in numerous court decisions which serve to guide and direct police activity:

- police discretion;
- random vehicle stops;
- search and seizure;
- arrest; and
- police questioning and interrogation.

The *Charter* cases become extremely important to the police, and therefore, a good understanding of the *Charter* and the extensive case law that is growing around it is essential to the student interested in policing. Castel and Latchman (1996) provide clear details on how to go about doing research on the *Canadian Charter of Rights and Freedoms* and other related constitutional topics.

Stenning (1982) describes the difficulty in providing a complete picture of the legal context for policing in Canada in the following manner:

> By now, it will be apparent that he who ventures to generalize about the legal status of the police in Canada, and about its implications, does so at his peril. The police operate under a variety of statutes, which contain significantly different provisions respecting the status and accountability of the police. These statutory provisions, by themselves, leave many important questions unanswered. (p. 130)

THE TECHNOLOGICAL CONTEXT OF CANADIAN POLICING

Canada is, beyond question, a technological society (Grant, 1969). Because policing relies so heavily on the latest developments in technology it is important that we have a good understanding of this area. In dealing with the capacity of the police to offer front-line services that prevent crime, maintain order, preserve the peace, and uphold the law, police organizations have increasingly turned to the available technology to facilitate their efforts.

Computers (Archambeault and Archambeault, 1984), weapons, identification techniques, investigative aids, equipment, vehicles, database management, telecommunications, the Internet, and other applications of scientific techniques have greatly enhanced the capacity of police organizations to operate within a complex world. More discussion will be provided in other chapters; however, it is worth noting that developments in technology often present something of a two-edged sword for police agencies. When a significant breakthrough is made in the application of technology, there is the potential that it will be misused. For example, the development of sophisticated communications devices allows the criminal element to more easily track and monitor legitimate enforcement efforts. The explosion of interest in the powers of the Internet has caused police to be concerned about the presence of pornography, as well as racist and hate-motivated material in an electronic format that easily crosses borders and international boundaries.

With every new advance on the technological front there is some potential for its perversion to support and advance criminal activity. This has a bewildering effect on police agencies who must attempt to first understand the new technology, then establish possible applications for legitimate law enforcement purposes, and often must then wait for legislators to introduce statutes that will effectively allow the police to deal with inappropriate use of the technology in question. There is also the serious question of the cost of any new technology. It is essential that police organizations budget for the introduction of new technology; however, this involves more than the simple acquisition of equipment. There are questions around the purchase or leasing of hardware or software and the related aspects of installation and retrofitting of police facilities to accommodate the new technology. There are also issues relating to personnel training and safety. Finally, decision makers need to consider questions around technology adaptation, replacement and compatibility with existing systems and platforms.

In some areas, it is absolutely critical that matters of compatibility be examined in detail in order that different police jurisdictions are not introducing technologies that cannot interact with one another. The police have considerable difficulty with this challenge since the rate of technological change is increasing rapidly as society places a high priority on such innovation and as the criminal element, particularly at the more sophisticated levels, is quick to incorporate any new technology to their advantage (Normandeau and Leighton, 1990; Ogden, 1993).

Technology also has a tendency to distance police officers from direct and immediate contact with the public they are sworn to serve. There are some serious questions about the threat to individual liberties posed by a wholesale embracing of highly sophisticated means of surveillance and control being placed at the disposal of the police (Ellul, 1964). This "technological trap" needs to be recognized and understood if appropriate responses are going to be found that satisfactorily combine appropriate technical expertise with community-oriented service delivery (Ontario. Task Force on Policing in Ontario, 1974). Therefore, police leaders have a challenge in identifying and introducing techniques and technology that will not alienate front-line officers from the public that they are sworn to serve. The following observation of Cassels (1995) is valuable in this regard:

Technology must be selected, structured and implemented to support the basic organizational components of today's policing model. Police leaders must therefore change their emphasis from technology in the form of gadgets to technology that supports local neighborhood problem solving. (p. 113)

WHAT DO POLICE DO IN CANADA?

Within the context of the areas discussed above, police in Canada have a general mandate to deliver the following core functions:

- prevent crime;
- enforce the law;
- maintain public order;
- assist victims of crime; and
- respond to emergencies.

While the specifics of these core functions will differ quite substantially from province to province, and from one police service to another, there is a remarkable degree of similarity among the police organizations which serve the public safety interests of Canadians. Because the *Criminal Code of Canada* sets out a kind of template for the application of criminal law in the country there exists a high degree of consistency. While each province has responsibility for the administration of justice within their jurisdiction, and while there is scope for some variation in the application and enforcement of what are known as provincial offences, the consistent presence of criminal law in Canada makes for a fairly uniform police mandate.

FUNDAMENTAL GOALS AND OBJECTIVES OF CANADIAN POLICING

In order to best understand how individual police services perceive their fundamental goals and objectives, it is useful to turn to their "mission statements." If such a document exists, it will probably outline in fairly clear language the basic purposes that the organization intends to serve. Across Canada there are common themes to these statements that usually reflect most, if not all, of the following points:

- respect for, and observance of, the *Canadian Charter of Rights and Freedoms*;
- obligation to enforce the law;
- commitment to ensure the prevention and detection of crime;
- intention to serve and protect the public;
- commitment to reflect and respect the communities they serve, including a particular recognition of multicultural, racial, ethnic, and other factors;
- commitment to the preserve the peace;
- demonstration of respect for victims of crime; and

- commitment to public awareness and education on crime prevention, law enforcement, and other public safety issues.

In Ontario, for example, the *Police Services Act*, which came into force in 1990, has a "Declaration of Principles" that guides the delivery of police services throughout that province. This declaration contains all of the elements listed above and is further reflected in the "mission statements" which were prepared by many individual police services in Ontario to express a consistent theme and vision of their purpose (Hamilton et al., 1995). Across Canada, police services have built their organizational identities on some of the concepts outlined above and in subsequent chapters we will see this in much greater detail.

CONCLUSION

Having given some consideration to the social, political, legal, and technological contexts in which policing in Canada operates, it should be clear that there are enormous challenges facing those engaged in this profession. It has been said that changing the police is like bending granite. However, as police organizations have tried to keep pace with the staggering numbers of changes and developments in all of the areas noted above, it should be acknowledged that many police services in Canada have been responsible for making adjustments to accommodate and internalize many of these changes. One could suggest that, particularly in the area of new technology, police organizations are quick to anticipate the introduction and practical application of such innovations. It has been a hallmark of Canadian policing to be in the forefront of technological advances.

With the nature of policing so deeply penetrated by the social, political, legal, and technological contexts discussed in this chapter, it is little wonder that our law enforcement services are so clearly a reflection of the Canadian identity.

QUESTIONS FOR CONSIDERATION

1. Police organizations provide services which tend to control or constrain the activities of individuals. In a democratic society that places a high value on individual freedom, how are we able to justify such forces of control?
2. Has the social status of policing changed in the last century? What is the view of policing held by the average citizen?
3. Does the application of extensive technology serve the best interests of policing? What are possible limitations of technology in the delivery of police services?
4. Discuss how dramatic changes in the social, political, legal, or technological contexts could affect the delivery of police services in Canada.
5. Social movements have had a great impact on policing in Canada. Pick one of the major social movements identified in this chapter and discuss the ways in which policing has been affected by that movement.

6. Police services in Canada have similar goals and objectives. What distinguishes these goals and objectives from other public services? What are some of the similarities between police services and other public agencies?

REFERENCES

Archambeault, W.G. and Betty J. Archambeault. (1984). *Computers in criminal justice administration and management: introduction to emerging issues and applications.* Cincinnati: Anderson Publishing.

Bell, David and Lorne Tepperman. (1979). *The roots of disunity: a look at Canadian political culture.* Toronto: McClelland and Stewart.

Bellamy, David J., Jon H. Pammett and Donald C. Rowat. (1976). *The provincial political systems: comparative essays.* Toronto: Methuen.

Brooks, S. (1993). *Public policy in Canada: an introduction. 2nd ed.* Toronto: McClelland and Stewart.

Canada. Solicitor General. Police and Security Branch. (1990). *Federal/Provincial/Territorial meeting on police policy issues.* Ottawa: Solicitor General Canada.

Canadian Association of Chiefs of Police. Organized Crime Committee. (1991). *Organized Crime Committee report.* [Ottawa]: Canadian Association of Chiefs of Police.

Cassels, D. (1995). "The role of technology on crime and policing." In *Management challenges in 21st century policing: conference proceedings.* Ottawa: Centre for Police Management and Research (Straffordshire University, U.K.) and Canadian Research Institute for Law and the Family (University of Calgary), and the Solicitor General Canada.

Castel, Jacqueline R. and Omeela K. Latchman. (1996). *The practical guide to Canadian legal research. 2nd ed.* Toronto: Carswell.

Ceyssens, P. (1994). *Legal aspects of policing.* Toronto: Carswell.

Doern, G. Bruce and Peter Aucoin (eds.). (1979). *Public policy in Canada: organization, process, and management.* Toronto: Macmillan of Canada.

Drucker, Peter F. (1994). "The age of social transformation." *The Atlantic Monthly*, November, pp. 53–80.

Dyck, R. (1993). *Canadian politics: critical approaches.* Toronto: Nelson Canada.

Ellul, J. (1964). *The technological society.* (Translated by John Wilkinson). New York: Vintage Books.

Ellul, J. (1990). *The technological bluff.* (Translated by Geoffrey W. Bromiley). Grand Rapids, Michigan: William B. Eerdmans Publishing.

Forsey, Eugene A. (1974). *Freedom and order: collected essays.* Toronto: McClelland and Stewart.

Friedland, Martin L. (1984). *A century of criminal justice: perspectives on the development of Canadian law.* Toronto: Carswell Legal Publications.

Grant, G.P. (1965). *Lament for a nation: the defeat of Canadian nationalism.* Toronto: McClelland and Stewart.

Grant, G.P. (1969). *Technology and empire: perspectives on North America.* Toronto: House of Anansi.

Grant, G.P. (1986). *Technology & justice*. Toronto: House of Anansi.

Guy, J.J. (1995). *How we are governed: the basics of Canadian politics and government*. Toronto: Harcourt Brace & Co. Canada.

Hamilton, Mr. Justice John F. et al. (1995). *The 1996 annotated Ontario Police Services Act*. Toronto: Carswell.

Hann, Robert G. and Kathryn Asbury. (1992). *Change is the environment: Ontario region environmental scan: submitted to Ontario region, Ministry of the Solicitor General Canada*. Ottawa: Solicitor General Canada, Intergovernmental Affairs Regional Office.

Higgins, Donald J.H. (1977). *Urban Canada: its government and politics*. Toronto: Macmillan of Canada.

Hill, Dilys M. (1974). *Democratic theory and local government*. London: George Allen & Unwin Ltd.

Hockin, T.A. (1976). *Government in Canada*. Toronto: McGraw-Hill Ryerson Ltd.

Hockin, T.A. (ed.). (1977). *Apex of power: the Prime Minister and political leadership in Canada. 2nd ed.* Scarborough: Prentice Hall Canada.

Holmes, John W. (1981). *Life with uncle: the Canadian-American relationship*. Toronto: University of Toronto Press.

Kaplan, William. (1996). *Bad judgment: the case of Mr. Justice Leo A. Landreville*. Toronto: University of Toronto Press for the Osgoode Society for Canadian Legal History.

Lindquist, E. and Tammy Sica. (1995). *Canadian governments and the search for alternative program delivery and financing: a preliminary survey*. Toronto: KPMG Centre for Government Foundation.

MacIntosh, Donald A. (1989). *Fundamentals of the criminal justice system*. Toronto: Carswell.

Macpherson, C.B. (1965). *The real world of democracy*. Toronto: CBC Enterprises.

Manning, M. (1983). *Rights, freedoms and the courts: a practical analysis of the Constitution Act, 1982.* Toronto: Emond-Montgomery.

Marchak, M.P. (1975). *Ideological perspectives on Canada*. Toronto: McGraw-Hill Ryerson Ltd.

Marsden, L.R. and E.B. Harvey. (1979). *Fragile federation: social change in Canada*. Toronto: McGraw-Hill Ryerson Ltd.

McDonald, David C. (1982). *Legal rights in the Canadian Charter of Rights and Freedoms: a manual of issues and sources*. Toronto: Carswell Legal Publications (Western).

McKenna, Paul F. and D.G. Evans. (1994). "Balancing police budgets and decision making: an experiment in disentanglement." *Canadian Public Administration*, 37(4), pp. 598–613.

McMahon, Maeve W. and Richard V. Ericson. (1984). *Policing reform: a study of the reform process and police institution in Toronto*. Toronto: Centre of Criminology, University of Toronto.

McRoberts, Kenneth and Dale Posgate. (1980). *Quebec: social change and political crisis*. Toronto: McClelland and Stewart.

McWhinney, E. (1979). *Quebec and the Constitution 1960–1978*. Toronto: University of Toronto Press.

Meekison, J.P. (ed.). (1977). *Canadian federalism: myth or reality. 3rd ed.* Toronto: Methuen.

Milne, D. (1982). *The new Canadian constitution*. Toronto: James Lorimer & Company.

Normandeau, André and Barry Leighton. (1990). *A vision of the future of policing in Canada: police-challenge 2000: background document*. Ottawa: Solicitor General Canada, Police and Security Branch.

Ogden, Frank. (1993). *The last book you'll ever read: and other lessons from the future*. Toronto: Macfarlane Walter & Ross.

Ontario. Greater Toronto Area Task Force. (1996). *Greater Toronto: report of the GTA Task Force*. Toronto: Queen's Printer.

Ontario. Ministry of the Solicitor General. (1991). *Future trends in society: an Ontario perspective*. Toronto: The Ministry.

Ontario. Ministry of the Solicitor General. Strategic Planning Committee on Police Training and Education. (1992). *A police learning system for Ontario: final report and recommendations*. Toronto: The Ministry.

Ontario. Ministry of the Solicitor General and Correctional Services. Police-Race Relations Monitoring Board. (1996). *Good beginnings: a catalogue of police-race relations initiatives in Ontario*. Toronto: The Ministry.

Parker, Graham. (1981). "The origins of the Canadian Criminal Code." In Flaherty, David H. (ed.) *Essays in the history of Canadian law*. Toronto: Published for the Osgoode Society by University of Toronto Press.

Plotkin, Martha R. (1996). "Improving the police response to domestic elder abuse victims." *Aging*, 367, pp. 28–33.

Roach, Kent. (1995). "Canadian public inquiries and accountability." In Stenning, Philip C. (ed.). *Accountability for criminal justice*. Toronto: University of Toronto Press.

Russell, Peter H. (1982). *Leading constitutional decisions. 3rd ed*. Toronto: Carleton University Press.

Sancton, A. (1996). "Reducing costs by consolidating municipalities: New Brunswick, Nova Scotia and Ontario." *Canadian Public Administration*, 39(3), pp.267–289..

Stenning, P.C. (1982). *Legal status of the police: a study paper prepared for the Law Reform Commission of Canada*. Ottawa: Law Reform Commission of Canada.

Stenning, P.C. (1994). "Police and politics: there and back and there again?" In MacLeod, R.C. and David Schneiderman (eds.). *Police powers in Canada: the evolution and practice of authority*. Toronto: Published in association with the Centre for Constitutional Studies, University of Alberta by University of Toronto Press, pp. 209–240.

Strayer, B.L. (1983). *The Canadian constitution and the courts: the function and scope of judicial review. 2nd ed*. Toronto: Butterworths.

Stuart D. (1994). "Policing under the Charter." In MacLeod, R.C. and David Schneiderman (eds.). *Police powers in Canada: the evolution and practice of authority*. Toronto: Published in association with the Centre for Constitutional Studies, University of Alberta, by University of Toronto Press, pp. 74–99.

Sunahara, D.F. (1992). "Public inquiries into policing." *Canadian Police College Journal*, 16(2), pp. 135–156.

Volti, R. (1995). *Society and technological change. 3rd ed*. New York: St. Martin's Press.

Walinsky, A. (1995). "The crisis of public order." *The Atlantic Monthly*, July 1995, pp. 39–54.

Watt, The Honourable Mr. Justice David and Michelle K. Fuerst. (1996). *The annotated 1997 Tremeear's Criminal Code*. Toronto: Carswell.

White, Walter L., Ronald H. Wagenberg, and Ralph C. Nelson. (1994). *Introduction to Canadian politics and government. 6th ed*. Toronto: Harcourt Brace Canada.

TOWARD MORE LEARNING

SOCIAL CONTEXT OF CANADIAN POLICING

Marsden, L.R. , and E.B. Harvey. (1979). *Fragile federation: social change in Canada*. Toronto: McGraw-Hill Ryerson Ltd.

Though somewhat dated, this publication offers an excellent survey of social change in Canada and provides a sound theoretical basis for its study. The authors also include an extensive bibliography of useful earlier sources.

Statistics Canada has a regular feature on its Web site dealing with current social demographic trends, as well as analytical reports on various topics that may relate to policing and its social context. See Appendix III for Web site information on Statistics Canada and its various services and publications.

POLITICAL CONTEXT OF CANADIAN POLICING

Guy, J.J. (1995). *How we are governed: the basics of Canadian politics and government*. Toronto: Harcourt Brace & Co. Canada.

This recent publication provides detailed and well-organized background on the fundamentals of Canadian politics. Of additional value are the appendices which contain some useful pieces of legislation such as the *Constitution Act, 1867* (also known as the *British North America Act*), the *Canadian Charter of Rights and Freedoms*, and the *Canadian Bill of Rights*.

White, Walter L., Ronald II. Wagenberg, and Ralph C. Nelson. (1994). *Introduction to Canadian politics and government. 6th ed*. Toronto: Harcourt Brace Canada.

A reliable and clearly written textbook that offers good coverage of the topic in a format aimed at the community college or undergraduate level. Also contains useful references and suggested readings.

In addition to textbooks and other academic works, a regular reading of local and national newspapers and current affairs magazines will provide additional insight into the political context.

Also, government Web sites across Canada often contain topical information that is pertinent to policing issues. See Appendix III for some suggested Web sites that may contain helpful and current background information.

LEGAL CONTEXT OF CANADIAN POLICING

Castel, Jacqueline R. and Omeela K. Latchman. (1996). *The practical guide to Canadian legal research. 2nd ed*. Toronto: Carswell.

In order to understand the complexities of legal research that is so important to policing, it is useful to have access to this kind of publication which takes the reader though the basics. The authors provide a systematic overview of Canadian legal research, including the common law system. They deal with the full range of tools that are available to ensure that the most up-to-date information is acquired on case law and statute law and provide a step-by-step guide to using computer-based research tools, such as legal databases and CD-ROMS.

Ceyssens, P. (1994). *Legal aspects of policing*. Toronto: Carswell.

This definitive publication is a loose-leaf service that is continuously updated to provide comprehensive and current information on the legal status of police officers in Canada. This work includes extremely valuable appendices containing the relevant provincial statutes that relate to policing, including statutes relating to the RCMP.

N.B.: As new legislation is frequently introduced which may significantly amend the statutes that pertain to policing in various jurisdictions, it is important that the reader ensure that the most current form of any statute is being referenced.

Gall, Gerald L. (1995). *The Canadian legal system. 4th ed.* Toronto: Carswell.

A recent update of a valuable work that provides coverage on all elements of the Canadian legal system. Detailed treatment of the role and hierarchy of the courts, including a separate and distinct section of the legal system in Quebec.

MacIntosh, Donald A. (1989). *Fundamentals of the criminal justice system*. Toronto: Carswell.

A good primer on Canada's legal system, the nature and purpose of criminal law in Canada, the role of the police and lawyers within this system, and numerous other relevant topics that deal with the application of criminal law within the context of the *Charter*.

Stenning, P.C. (1982). *Legal status of the police: a study paper prepared for the Law Reform Commission of Canada.* Ottawa: Law Reform Commission of Canada.

This is a highly regarded study that provides a thorough review of the origins and development of the office of the police constable both in Canada and England. The book sets out useful detail with regard to the legal context of policing in Canada and contains a valuable bibliography of references used in Professor Stenning's research. An important resource for the serious student.

Watt, The Honourable Mr. Justice David and Michelle K. Fuerst. (1997). *The annotated 1997 Tremeear's Criminal Code*. Toronto: Carswell.

This is essential reading for the student who wants to understand the legal context of policing in substantial detail. The authors are highly competent to provide expert commentary on recent Supreme Court of Canada and provincial Court of Appeal decisions. The most current text of the *Criminal Code of Canada* is provided, as well as current provisions of related statutes: *Canada Evidence Act, Canadian Charter of Rights and Freedoms, Food and Drugs Act, Narcotic Control Act,* and *Young Offenders Act.*

Review of the reports of criminal cases in Canada is often a very good way of understanding the legal context of Canadian policing. Annual reviews of important criminal cases is useful. The various law schools and other legal research centres should have resources that the student can access to obtain current information on developments in criminal law and procedure that would affect policing.

TECHNOLOGICAL CONTEXT OF CANADIAN POLICING

Ogden, Frank. (1993). *The last book you'll ever read: and other lessons from the future.* Toronto: Macfarlane Walter & Ross.

This is an excellent source of information on the broadest range of technological and other changes that will confront us in the near future. Ogden is a well-respected Canadian futurist who monitors worldwide trends and technological breakthroughs. This book covers a wide range of topics, including the process of change, the transition in the work force, medicine and biotechnology, communications, education, and a number of other interesting areas that will affect our lives.

FUNDAMENTAL GOALS AND OBJECTIVES OF CANADIAN POLICING

The annual reports, mission statements, and other high-level documents prepared by individual police services across Canada will provide the reader with substantial insight into the basic focus of police organizations. These items may be acquired directly from the police service, or, in many instances, they will be readily available from local public libraries, universities, community colleges, or resource centres.

Also, see Appendix III, which provides details on Web sites for specific police departments. These Web sites frequently contain a home page that outlines the vision, mission statement, mandate, goals and objectives of the police service.

CHAPTER THREE

POLICE JURISDICTIONS IN CANADA

LEARNING OBJECTIVES

1. Identify three main jurisdictions of policing in Canada
2. Identify three jurisdictions in Canada that deliver their own provincial police services
3. List examples of private police organizations in Canada
4. Explain the key characteristics of First Nations policing in Canada
5. Describe major similarities and differences between public and private policing in Canada

INTRODUCTION

In Chapter 1 of this textbook, the origins and beginnings of policing in Canada were considered in some detail. A number of the jurisdictional issues which developed as a result of the country's growth were touched on, particularly at the municipal level. In Chapter 2 we looked at the context of Canadian policing, including several social, political, legal, and technological aspects. Policing in Canada was seen as operating in a unique environment that produced significantly consistent goals and objectives for the providers of this important service.

In this chapter we will look closely at various police jurisdictions in order to learn more about these different spheres of operation. By considering the individual parts of Canadian policing, we hope to have a better understanding of the entire picture. This chapter will begin at the national or federal level and move to the local or municipal level. Also, there will be some discussion of special categories of policing in Canada, including the emerging role of private security.

The purpose of this chapter is to provide a reasonably complete picture of all levels of Canadian policing, including those elements that are not well understood or recognized

by the public at large. This thorough understanding of the full spectrum of police jurisdictions is designed to provide the reader with an informed perspective on the current state
of policing across the country.

FEDERAL POLICING

Within the federal form of government that Canadians now enjoy, it makes sense to begin
a sketch of police jurisdictions at the top of this system. Because the Solicitor General of
Canada is in charge of a portfolio that includes the Royal Canadian Mounted Police
(RCMP), this department is the first to be considered in this examination.

The Solicitor General of Canada is the federal Cabinet minister appointed to oversee the following areas of public service:

- Royal Canadian Mounted Police (RCMP);
- Canadian Security Intelligence Service (CSIS);
- Correctional Service of Canada; and
- National Parole Board.

The Ministry of the Solicitor General of Canada includes a department (created in
1966) that forms the basis of the bureaucracy supporting the development, implementation
and review of policies and programs designed to meet the minister's overall mandate
(Canada. Solicitor General, 1996). This department functions to provide strategic leadership
on a national basis for policing, law enforcement, corrections and prisoner release. It is
further instrumental in the process of realizing First Nations policing in Canada by way
of tripartite agreements (along with provincial/territorial and First Nations entities).

In total this ministry has a budget of $2.5 billion and over 32 000 employees (Canada.
Solicitor General, 1996). To achieve its goal of protecting the public and maintaining a just,
peaceful, and safe society, the ministry has recently undertaken some important initiatives
including the following:

- completion of 32 First Nations policing agreements;
- completion of a national system designed to identify high-risk offenders;
- consultations on the establishment of a national DNA databank (Canada. Solicitor
  General, 1996a); and
- consultations on improvements for the management and sharing of criminal justice
  information.

The Ministry of the Solicitor General has also had to streamline some of its activities
in order to realize budget savings. These efforts have included the closing of a number of
regional offices for the ministry, and the termination of funding to centres of criminology
in Canadian universities. However, as a result of its efforts at strategic planning, the ministry has identified the key issues which it will pursue over the next few years:

- organized crime;
- effective management of justice information;
- justice for Aboriginal people;
- crime prevention; and
- violence in Canadian society.

THE ROYAL CANADIAN MOUNTED POLICE (RCMP)

Broadly speaking, the RCMP may be employed in or outside Canada in any manner prescribed by the Governor General in Council (i.e., the federal Cabinet). Specifically, the RCMP, as a federal police service, operates to enforce federal laws, including the *Criminal Code of Canada*, the *Narcotic Control Act,* the *Young Offenders Act*, and the *Indian Act*, among others. The RCMP also provides enforcement of federal statutes such as the *Canada Shipping Act*, customs and excise legislation, as well as offering protection of federal property (e.g., the prime minister's official residence at 24 Sussex Drive, Ottawa).

The RCMP is lead by a commissioner, who is appointed by the federal Cabinet (i.e., the Governor General in Council) according to the provisions of the *Royal Canadian Mounted Police Act*. The Commissioner of the RCMP has a status in the federal public service similar to a deputy minister and reports to the Solicitor General of Canada. The commissioner is authorized to appoint members to the RCMP as required.

The RCMP is divided into 13 regional divisions across Canada. Each of these divisions is further arranged into subdivisions, which are broken down into individual detachments. (Because these smaller units are prone to change and modification, it is not seen as useful to fix precise numbers around these elements.) Given the RCMP's significant attachment to the nation's business and their role in providing security for the people, possessions, and property attached to the federal function, it is not surprising that this police service has headquarters in the nation's capital—Ottawa. Of special importance to the national mandate of the RCMP is the operation of the following areas, collectively known as the "National Police Services":

Peter Bregg/Maclean's

RCMP officers in red serge (June 1992, Ottawa)

- Canadian Police Information Centre (CPIC);
- Canadian Police College (CPC);

- Criminal Intelligence Service of Canada (CISC);
- Criminal History and Fingerprint Repositories; and
- Forensic Laboratory Services.

BRIEFING NOTE

In 1998, the RCMP will be celebrating its 125th anniversary. With the authorization of the creation of the North-West Mounted Police in 1873, the RCMP began its long and distinguished history of service to Canada. Planning for this celebration is already underway, with the theme:

"A Proud History...A Challenging Future."

CANADIAN POLICE INFORMATION CENTRE (CPIC)

Across Canada, it is essential that police, courts, and corrections personnel have a method for identifying individuals with whom they must deal. Quick and reliable information is of primary importance in order to provide public and officer safety, as well as for investigative purposes. Courts require this kind of information in order to verify that they are holding the correct individual for the correct reasons. Finally, penitentiaries and correctional institutions need this information to reference an individual's criminal history and prior records for proper offender classification and case management. Overall, this source of information is crucial to supporting the whole system of justice in Canada (Campbell, 1996).

The main source of this information is a national database in Ottawa, which is managed by the RCMP. The Canadian Police Information Centre (CPIC) is an integrated, automated system that provides detailed information on criminals and crime. This system has been operational since 1972 and is accessible by all police organizations across Canada through computer terminals with telecommunications linkages. Presently, there are approximately 2500 points of access to CPIC, which includes nearly 1300 federal, provincial, and municipal police departments.

CPIC contains electronic data organized under the following files:

FILE NAME	DATA INCLUDED
Vehicle	Vehicles stolen, abandoned, or wanted in connection with a crime; stolen licence plates, validation stickers, Vehicle Identification Number (VIN) plates, and parts.

continued

FILE NAME	DATA INCLUDED
Persons	Persons wanted by the police; charged persons, parolees, persons prohibited from possessing weapons, or driving; missing persons; body marks or scars, descriptions of clothing; unidentified bodies, or body parts, etc.
Property	Guns, stolen property, and securities (e.g., stocks and bonds), etc.
Marine	Stolen and/or abandoned boats, motors, or other watercraft.
Criminal Record Synopsis	Abridged version of criminal records supported through the submission of fingerprints. This file is maintained by Identification Services personnel in the National Police Service program of the RCMP, Ottawa.
Dental Characteristics	Dental records of individuals are stored in this file, as a sub-category of the Persons File. It is intended to assist police personnel in the identification of human remains, comatose victims, or those persons suffering from amnesia.
Criminal Records	Complete criminal records may be accessed from this file which is maintained by RCMP Identification Services.
Inmate File	Individual information on those under the control of Correctional Services Canada, both incarcerated and on parole.
Wandering Persons Registry	Individuals who have been registered with the Alzheimer's Society of Canada national office. This file is intended to assist police in the identification and return of persons suffering from Alzheimer's disease.

CPIC also permits access to motor vehicle information maintained by every province in Canada. It is further connected with the National Crime Information Center (NCIC) in the United States, as well as with individual state databases through an interface known as the Automated Canadian United States Police Information Exchange System (ACU-PIES). This system is maintained by INTERPOL Ottawa (see more detail below) which is part of the RCMP's international mandate.

CANADIAN POLICE COLLEGE (CPC)

A course identified with the "Canadian Police College" first appeared in 1938. However, it was not until January 1966 when a Federal-Provincial Conference on Organized Crime recommended the development of a national college for police officers that an institution known as the Canadian Police College truly came into being. It was intended that courses offered at this facility would concentrate on police management, administration, and specialized investigations. In 1973, the Treasury Board of the federal government endorsed the establishment of a Canadian Police College under the auspices of the RCMP, and the present facilities were constructed in Ottawa in 1976. Increasingly, the Canadian Police

College is beginning to use alternative approaches to the delivery of education and learning to its clientele, including consideration of the importance of the Internet. It has also begun a cost-recovery approach to the delivery of the more that 30 different courses which it offers to the police community. CPC also welcomes police representatives from other countries to attend its programs, which gives the College an international reputation.

Of some considerable importance to the student of law enforcement in Canada, CPC also maintains the Canadian Police College Library which has a large collection of materials in a variety of formats, including CD-ROM, videotape, and print. Some of the topics that are covered in this collection include:

- law enforcement and criminology;
- techniques of investigation;
- special enforcement areas (e.g., drugs, white collar crime);
- organizational development and management;
- history and growth of the RCMP; and
- training and development of police personnel.

CRIMINAL INTELLIGENCE SERVICE CANADA (CISC)

The Criminal Intelligence Service Canada (CISC) is an agency that facilitates cooperation among criminal intelligence units within Canada's law enforcement community in order to combat the growth of organized crime. CISC is made up of a central bureau located in Ottawa and a network of nine provincial bureaux located in each province (with the exception of Prince Edward Island, which is included in the operation of the Nova Scotia bureau).

Membership in CISC includes federal, provincial, and municipal or regional police services across Canada with full-time intelligence units. Currently the organization includes:

- Royal Canadian Mounted Police (RCMP);
- Sûreté du Québec;
- Ontario Provincial Police;
- Royal Newfoundland Constabulary; and
- 85 municipal/regional police departments.

The various intelligence units linked within CISC contribute primary data to their respective provincial bureaux for further analysis and dissemination. This data is relevant to organized crime and other significant criminal activities within Canada.

The Central Bureau, in Ottawa, takes its overall direction from an executive committee which is made up of representative chiefs of police and commanding officers from the RCMP across Canada. The executive committee is chaired by the RCMP commissioner. This group meets annually to review CISC's operation and to formulate goals and priorities. In 1996, CISC assessed its efforts in the following areas of organized crime (CISC, 1996):

- Asian organized crime;
- Eastern European organized crime;
- Italian organized crime;

- Aboriginal organized crime;
- outlaw motorcycle gangs;
- Colombian organized crime;
- proceeds of crime and money laundering;
- counterfeit activity; and
- computer/telecommunications crime.

CANADIAN POLICE RESEARCH CENTRE (CPRC)

In partnership with the Canadian Association of Chiefs of Police (CACP) and the National Research Council of Canada (NRCC), the RCMP is involved in a national program of research, development, assessment, and implementation of projects that will benefit law enforcement and general public safety. It offers an opportunity for specialized enterprises to be fostered for the purpose of practical application in this area.

The CPRC is staffed by members of the RCMP and the NRCC, and encourages the support and assistance of the Canadian law enforcement community and the security sector for its overall guidance. The CPRC is committed to ensuring that technology is developed for the greater benefit of the policing community and the public at large. It objectives are basically to:

- develop the most reliable equipment for the benefit of the police community;
- ensure that new technology is affordable; and
- develop partnerships with appropriate industry in Canada as well as within the international community.

INTERPOL OTTAWA

In 1949, the federal Minister of Justice identified the RCMP as the National Central Bureau (NCB) for the International Criminal Police Organization (ICPO), also known as INTERPOL. This is an official intergovernmental organization made up of 150 member countries with headquarters in Lyons, France. The aims of INTERPOL are as follows (RCMP, 1990):

> To ensure and promote the widest possible mutual assistance between all criminal police authorities within the limits of the laws existing in the different countries and in the spirit of the "Universal Declaration of Human Rights," and

> To establish and develop all institutions likely to contribute effectively to the prevention and suppression of ordinary law crimes. (p. 1)

As the Canadian link with this organization, INTERPOL Ottawa undertakes functions in order to:

- collect documents and information from various sources dealing with international law enforcement and forward this material to other NCBs and the INTERPOL General Secretariat;

- ensure that police inquiries and operational assistance requested by the NCBs in other countries are carried out, and to provide a response to other NCBs requests for information and criminal history checks;
- transmit requests for international investigative assistance originating with Canadian police departments or the justice system to other NCBs; and
- send delegates to participate in INTERPOL General Assembly sessions and ensure that the implementation of General Assembly resolutions.

The value of this kind of international connection for law enforcement agencies in Canada, through the RCMP, is that it provides access to significant assistance in a number of important areas of investigation, including:

- offences against persons and property: hostage-taking, kidnapping, murder, unlawful interference with civil aviation, terrorism, weapons and explosives offences, theft and other illicit dealings relating to property of all types including cultural property and stolen art;
- economic and financial crime: counterfeiting of currency and other legal documents, forgery, anti-rackets and fraud of various kinds, including computer crime; and
- drug trafficking: the illegal cultivation, processing, transportation and sale of drugs, narcotics, or other controlled substances.

INTERPOL operates through a budget that results from the contributions made by member states. It uses a number of means for communicating with its member countries including police communications networks, phototelegraphy, telephone, facsimile, telex, and Morse code. INTERPOL conducts special meetings, conferences, and symposiums to deal with ongoing investigations, and to discuss police methods and techniques of interest. It also offers an information exchange and research centre for documentation, training, and cooperation in technical areas. INTERPOL's official publication is the *International Criminal Police Review*, which is published every other month in the organization's four official languages (English, French, Spanish, and Arabic).

Through a network of RCMP liaison officers, posted at 19 embassies or high commissions throughout the world, the Foreign Services Directorate is able to provide assistance to law enforcement organizations in Canada when they are seeking information on criminal activity in foreign countries. Such assistance may involve locating witnesses or victims outside of Canada, or the apprehension of suspects who have fled Canadian jurisdiction. This directorate also provides help to foreign countries in the conduct of inquiries in Canada, as long as the offences would be in violation of Canadian federal law, or if the offences were committed within Canada.

CANADIAN SECURITY INTELLIGENCE SERVICE (CSIS)

As a direct result of the recommendations of the McDonald Commission in 1981, the Canadian Security Intelligence Service came into existence with the passage of the

Canadian Security Intelligence Service Act, 1984 by the federal Parliament. The purpose of this organization was to satisfy two fundamental and related needs: protecting Canadians and their governments against foreign attempts to employ secret and/or coercive methods for the promotion of their interests in this country; and ensuring that the elements of Canadian democracy are safeguarded from efforts to destroy, disable, or diminish those elements (McDonald, 1980). The creation of CSIS also amounted to the disbandment of the RCMP's Security Service and put in its place a civilian agency that would provide intelligence services to the Canadian government and its citizens.

BRIEFING NOTE

Intelligence services in Canada got their start when Sir John A. Macdonald, as the last Attorney General of Upper Canada, formed the Western Frontier Constabulary in 1864. This small intelligence unit observed, and reported on, activities along the borders of Upper Canada that related to the Civil War in America (Canada. CSIS, 1990).

With substantial public oversight controls on the operation and activities of CSIS, this organization has a mandate to function in the following areas:

- espionage and sabotage;
- foreign-influenced activities; and
- political violence and terrorism.

Originally, CSIS also had a mandate to deal with subversive activities; however, the difficulty of establishing what actually constitutes subversion has made this element less central to the workings of the organization. In the context of its day-to-day activities, CSIS relies on the application of an intelligence cycle that generates useful information pertaining to the security of Canada and Canadians. This type of information is, of course, valuable to law enforcement agencies, as well as to various government ministries and officials. This intelligence cycle has the following components:

- planning;
- collection;
- analysis; and
- dissemination.

PLANNING This element is essential to the whole intelligence process from initial threat identification to a final analysis of that threat. Placing the threat into its proper context requires information on other threats and trends that may have an impact on the original threat. Planning allows priorities to be established and appropriate resources to be allocated, and ensures that new information is brought into the intelligence cycle as it becomes available or relevant.

COLLECTION Information of many kinds drives the intelligence process and may be gathered from a wide range of sources, including newspapers, books, academic journals, and scholarly studies. Primary data may come from other sources including interviews, physical or electronic surveillance or other intelligence organizations.

ANALYSIS Careful analysis that is informed by an understanding of public policy and a sensitivity to local, national, and international trends will provide a firm basis upon which to make assessments of available data. These assessments may then be assembled in a format that can be effectively disseminated. This function has three subsets: operational (i.e., specific and short-term) analysis; strategic (i.e., global and long-term) analysis; and supporting analysis (a review of public sources to supplement and extend the first two categories, planning and collection).

DISSEMINATION This area involves the delivery of an intelligence product to appropriate clients, primarily the Government of Canada. Additional beneficiaries of this intelligence resource include officials in various departments of federal, provincial, territorial, or local governments, and, of course, law enforcement agencies throughout Canada.

THE MINISTER OF JUSTICE AND ATTORNEY GENERAL OF CANADA

The Department of Justice within the Government of Canada has been modified over the years as a result of the introduction of the *Canadian Charter of Rights and Freedoms* (1982), the recognition of First Nations treaty rights in the *Constitution Act, 1982*, and several judicial decisions. The connection between law and public policy is now closer than ever and, therefore, it brings the minister responsible for justice issues (who is also the Attorney General) into direct contact with matters that pertain to policing in Canada.

The Minister of Justice is the member of Cabinet who deals with legal matters and is, in fact, the legal advisor to the federal government. This Cabinet member plans, develops, and implements government policies pertaining to the administration of justice in Canada's federal jurisdiction. The Attorney General of Canada is known as the chief law officer of the Crown (i.e., the government) and is responsible for providing legal advice and guidance to government departments and agencies, as well as supervising all litigation brought by, or against, the Government of Canada (including the Crown or any federal department). Historically, the Minister of Justice and the Attorney General are the same individual. Because of this broad responsibility for matters of vital interest to law enforcement and policing, it is not difficult to understand the importance of this minister and this minister's departmental obligations. Of central importance is the Department of Justice's mandate to draft legislation and regulation under federal authority. This includes all statutes and regulations that pertain to the operation of law enforcement and police organizations in Canada. This department prepares amendments to such federal statutes as the *Criminal Code of Canada*, the *Narcotic Control Act*, the *Young Offenders Act*, and other important pieces of legislation that have a direct bearing on the activities of police officers in Canada.

Within this department, the Criminal and Social Policy Sector, as well as the Criminal Law Branch, offer legal advice in the area of criminal law and the application of criminal law power in the context of federal laws and regulations. These specialists also provide assistance on the application and interpretation of criminal law. The Criminal Law Branch has a responsibility for litigation relating to drugs and the proceeds of crime and provides appropriate advice on extradition and interjurisdictional legal assistance.

The Minister of Justice holds responsibility for more than 40 federal statutes (including the *Criminal Code of Canada*, the *Young Offenders Act*, the *Canadian Human Rights Act*, and the *Access to Information Act*). While the Department of Justice does not establish policy on matters dealing with policing, corrections, and parole, which fall under the mandate of the Solicitor General of Canada, there is considerable overlap and connection between these important policy fields which form the Canadian justice system.

PROVINCIAL POLICING

In Canada, there are only three jurisdictions that continue to provide their own provincial police service:

- Quebec;
- Ontario; and
- Newfoundland.

In Chapter 1 we considered some of the details which lead to this development. The reader will note that it is extremely difficult to arrive at completely accurate figures on the actual number of police services in any given jurisdiction. This is a real sign of the dramatic changes which are facing police organizations in Canada today. The most recent Statistics Canada reports for Ontario, for example, have now been made obsolete by takeovers of municipal police services by the OPP, amalgamations of municipal police services, or some other form of restructuring.

QUEBEC—SÛRETÉ DU QUÉBEC (SQ)

The Sûreté du Québec was created in 1870 under the name "Police provinciale du Québec." In 1922 the name was again changed to "Sûreté provinciale du Québec." The Quebec *Police Act* of June 1968 gave this service its present name. Police services are provided out of 112 detachments which fall into 9 districts. The Sûreté du Québec ensures public security in 1368 municipalities and territories and cooperates with police services offered in an additional 231 municipalities through the provision of operational support and logistics. It is the only service that has jurisdiction throughout the province of Quebec.

This police service is lead by a director general, who is under the authority of the Minister of Public Security. This minister of the provincial government is responsible for the maintenance of peace, order and public security throughout the entire territory of Quebec. The philosophy of this police service recognizes that the active participation of the community, in all its diversity, is essential to the achievement of its mandate. As a result, it utilizes a variety of approaches and methods for ensuring the participation of citizens. This is intended to lead to an ongoing dialogue that addresses community needs and the legal requirements placed on the police service.

ONTARIO—ONTARIO PROVINCIAL POLICE (OPP)

Formed in 1909, the Ontario Provincial Police (OPP) has a long history of providing police services within the province of Ontario. The mandate of the OPP has changed somewhat over its many years of existence; however, it has continued to grow with the demands of the province, and its development mirrors much of the transformations which have occurred over this century (Higley, 1984). Basically, the OPP provides a generalist policing service throughout the province of Ontario. Its jurisdiction includes about 993 000 square kilometres of land, as well as nearly 174 000 square kilometres of waterways.

Currently the OPP is based in Orillia, Ontario, in new headquarters facilities that were officially opened in 1995. The OPP is lead by a commissioner whose powers, duties, and responsibilities are detailed in the *Police Services Act*. This position reports to the Deputy Solicitor General and Deputy Minister of Correctional Services within the Ministry of the Solicitor General and Correctional Services, giving the commissioner a status similar to that of an assistant deputy minister within the Ontario Public Service. The commissioner is responsible for a large deployed organization that includes 6 regions and 8 bureaux, with approximately 6000 uniformed and civilian staff members.

There will be more discussion of the OPP in Chapter 10 dealing with innovations; however, this organization is responsible under the *Police Services Act* as follows:

- police those municipalities which are not required by statute to maintain their own police service, or which have contracted this service from the OPP in lieu of establishing or maintaining their own police service;
- respond to municipal police service requests for special assistance in emergencies;
- provide traffic control on all 400 series and King's highways, including those parts that are within the jurisdiction of municipal police agencies;
- provide police services in respect of all navigable bodies and courses of water in Ontario, excluding those that lie within municipalities designated by the Solicitor General;
- provide investigative services, on request, to the coroner's office, other provincial ministries, and municipal police services as stipulated by the *Police Services Act;* and
- perform other assigned duties such as the maintenance of a provincial firearms registry.

NEWFOUNDLAND—ROYAL NEWFOUNDLAND CONSTABULARY (RNC)

The Royal Newfoundland Constabulary has provincial policing jurisdiction in St. John's, Corner Brook, and Labrador City, and delivers services which are intended to accomplish the following:

- prevent crimes and other offences;
- provide assistance and encouragement in the prevention of crimes and other offences;
- assist the victims of crime;
- conduct criminal investigations into alleged breaches of the *Criminal Code of Canada*, the *Narcotic Control Act*, and other federal or provincial statutes;
- apprehend criminals and other offenders who may be lawfully taken into custody;
- lay charges, prosecute, and assist in prosecutions;
- execute warrants;
- process applications for firearms acquisition certificates (FAC); and
- issue certificates of conduct.

The Royal Newfoundland Constabulary is lead by a chief of police. Presently, a review of the delivery of police services in Newfoundland is taking place. This review will consider the costs of providing policing through the RCMP and the RNC. As of 1994, the statistical characteristics of the RNC were as follows:

FIGURE 3-1

STATISTICAL CHARACTERISTICS OF THE RNC

Municipality	Population	Total Personnel			Per Capita Cost
		Police	*Civilian*	*Other*	
St. John's	165 200	264	66	0	$100
Corner Brook	22 500	42	6		$126
Labrador City	11 400	23	4	15	$157

Source: Reproduced by authority of the Minister of Industry, 1997, Statistics Canada, *Selected Police Administration Characteristics of Municipal Police Departments*, 1994, cat. no. 85F0016XPB, page 1.

RCMP CONTRACTS WITH PROVINCIAL GOVERNMENTS

In all other provincial jurisdictions, the RCMP maintains a contract with individual provincial governments for the delivery of police services. These contracts typically have a number of similar features. At present, the RCMP has approximately 10 400 people engaged in the delivery of contract policing services throughout Canada. This number includes those RCMP members assigned to municipal policing contracts (see details discussed below). Contract policing through the RCMP generates nearly $700 million in revenue for the federal government.

As presented in Chapter 1, Canada became steadily more urbanized and industrialized in the years following the First World War. With this growth came a pressing need for organized and effective police services in municipalities. As a result of negotiations between the premier of Saskatchewan and the Commissioner of the RCMP in 1928, the RCMP assumed the responsibilities of the Saskatchewan Provincial Police under the terms of a contract which had the federal government assuming 60% of the costs and the province paying the remaining 40%.

When the Great Depression of 1929 seized Canada, the RCMP became a contract

Royal Canadian Mounted Police

RCMP logo

policing presence in most of the country. The burden of providing social assistance and relief to the many destitute Canadians during this period compelled the provinces to seek the financial aid offered by accepting RCMP contract policing substantially funded by the federal government. In 1932, the provinces of Prince Edward Island, New Brunswick, Nova Scotia, and Alberta each signed individual agreements for RCMP contract policing similar to the Saskatchewan model.

During the Second World War, the RCMP's provision of policing at federal, provincial, and municipal levels was extensive and laid the groundwork for the major commitment of this federal police service in many parts of Canada. Over time, the federal portion of the payment for the costs of these contract services has decreased. From an initial federal commitment of 60% the federal contribution has been gradually reducing its portion to 30%, as of 1990. Contracts that were renewed in 1992 set the provincial, territorial, or municipal portion at 70%, or, for municipalities with a population over 150 000, at 90%. Policing agreements were extended for a period of twenty years, with a provision for the review of service delivery costs every five years (RCMP, 1996).

MUNICIPAL AND REGIONAL POLICING

It has been noted that municipal policing has grown substantially over the last century (Marquis, 1993). Certainly the sheer number of those engaged in public police service delivery is highest at this level. If RCMP and OPP officers delivering municipal (i.e., contract) police services are included, municipal policing accounts for approximately 62% of all police officers in Canada (Statistics Canada, 1994).

Beginning in the 1960s and 1970s, there was a growing interest in the idea of regional policing. This involved the amalgamation of a number of local municipal police services into a larger entity based on regional boundaries. This approach to policing was particularly appealing to decision makers in Ontario (Fairweather, 1978). The first prime example of a regional police force in Ontario was the Niagara Regional Police, created in 1971. A special example is found in Metropolitan Toronto, which has a police service that was formed in 1957 by linking the 13 separate police departments within the City of Toronto, and the Boroughs (at that time) of Etobicoke, York, North York, East York, and Scarborough. Though technically not a regional government, it provides an excellent example of the successful amalgamation of various jurisdictional police services into one cohesive service.

In British Columbia, more recently, the issue of regionalized policing was studied in detail by Mr. Justice Wallace T. Oppal as part of that province's Commission of Inquiry on Policing in British Columbia. Mr. Justice Oppal's inquiry included a substantial amount of research on topics such as aspects of regionalized policing (Oppal, 1994). Based on this research, a number of clear incentives were seen for this approach to the challenge of policing:

- reduction of the costs of policing;
- elimination in the duplications and inefficiencies in municipal policing;
- ability to address the potential for corruption and unequal application of the criminal justice system;
- greater capacity to deal with shifts in population and related changes in policing needs in large urban areas;
- increased levels of cooperation and coordination among law enforcement agencies;
- increased capacity to delivery specialized police services (e.g., emergency response units, forensic identification services, underwater search and recovery, among others);
- greater consistency in the equitable delivery of service and greater equity in the distribution of the costs of policing; and
- increased capacity for human resource development from recruitment, selection, and orientation training to ongoing learning and development.

On the other hand, the concerns around regionalization of police services should also be considered. They can be summarized as follows:

- loss of local control;
- loss of resources;
- loss of local police identity;
- reduced effectiveness of community policing; and
- resistance within police services.

The report and supporting documentation prepared through Mr. Justice Oppal's inquiry provides a good survey of the experience with regionalized police services and offers some insight on the use of this particular approach for the delivery of these services (Oppal, 1994).

While there continue to be strong arguments in favour of local municipal policing, particularly in the context of the delivery of "community policing," there has been a considerable movement to larger police services that can effectively address the complex needs of a group of municipalities through the introduction of regional police services. However, a number of police experts have pointed out that police services can become too large to be effective (Lunney, 1995). With municipal governments in many provinces across Canada looking for ways to become more effective, efficient, and economical, the attention being paid to amalgamation, regionalization, cooperation, and coordination among individual municipal police services has grown substantially.

While the Yukon, the Northwest Territories, and Newfoundland are the only jurisdictions without specific municipal police services, those throughout the rest of Canada are in the process of such major change that it is virtually impossible to provide accurate figures on current breakdowns. Many jurisdictions are looking at municipal amalgamations with implications for police services, establishing contracts with the RCMP or, in Ontario, with the OPP for the delivery of municipal police services by way of contract. As these arrangements are being discussed and decided upon, the jurisdictional map of policing in Canada changes with great regularity, but little predictability. There is much to be learned by comparing experiences with other areas that have tackled the issue of amalgamation in order to determine possible benefits and adverse consequences of this course of action (Sancton, 1996).

POLICING IN THE TERRITORIES

Policing in the Yukon and the Northwest Territories is currently provided exclusively by the RCMP. The numbers of officers assigned has been identified by Statistics Canada as follows:

FIGURE 3-2

POLICE STATISTICS FOR THE YUKON AND NORTHWEST TERRITORIES

Location	Total Number of Police Officers	Population/Police Officer
Yukon	113	266
Northwest Territories	234	275

Source: Reproduced by authority of the Minister of Industry, 1997, Statistics Canada, *Juristat*, 16(1), cat. no. 85-002, p. 18.

SPECIAL CATEGORIES OF POLICING
FIRST NATIONS POLICE

Canada's First Nations, or Aboriginal, population is made up of four primary groups:

- status Indians;
- non-status Indians;
- Métis; and
- Inuit.

BRIEFING NOTE

On April 1, 1999, there will be a new territorial entity representing the Inuit community to be known as Nunavut. This jurisdiction will join the Yukon and the Northwest Territories as part of the Canadian political structure. There will be some jurisdictional responsibility for policing falling to this new level of government; however, as with the two existing territories, it is likely that the RCMP will have substantial involvement in the delivery of policing services.

Those who are identified as status Indians are organized into some 600 bands and live on approximately 2200 reserves throughout Canada. These reserves are primarily located in rural and isolated regions of the country.

It has been a challenge to approach the question of First Nations policing in a way that is both fair and appropriate. A number of inquiries and commissions have tended to the conclusion that the treatment of the First Nations people by Canada's criminal justice system (which includes police, courts, and corrections) has not been satisfactory (Sunahara, 1992). The inadequacy of the *status quo* with regard to policing for the First Nations is no longer in serious question; the concern now rests on arriving at suitable and substantial solutions (Ontario. Task Force on Race Relations and Policing, 1992).

In 1996, the federal government endorsed a new First Nations Policing Policy which supported the ongoing development of quality, effective, and culturally sensitive law enforcement services within those communities. As well as continuing to negotiate tripartite (i.e., federal, provincial/territorial, and band council) agreements, the federal government, through the Solicitor General's office, has established the following priorities:

- improve access to First Nations policing arrangements and extend their coverage within fiscal restraints;
- provide support to First Nations policing governing authorities and services to overcome organizational challenges;
- negotiate arrangements for policing consistent with federal self-government policy, and work with provincial/territorial jurisdictions to establish the legal basis for First Nations policing in those areas;
- support innovative developments in First Nations policing and assist in ensuring the conditions for their success;
- support and facilitate partnerships among provincial/territorial authorities, municipalities, police services and their respective communities to advance quality policing for First Nations, and other Aboriginal peoples, both on and off reserves; and
- improve the overall accountability and efficiency of the program of Aboriginal Policing and the First Nations Policing Policy.

The clear policy direction being endorsed and supported by the federal government, as well as through the provinces and territories, is one that moves toward large-scale self-policing for the First Nations and Aboriginal peoples (Canada. Solicitor General, 1996).

In Ontario, the OPP holds responsibility for working within the context of this national policy and has developed a plan that supports this overall policy goal. Agreements are provided for under the terms of the "Statement of Political Relationship and the Ontario First Nations Policing Agreement, 1991–1996" and are consistent with the following plan:

> The Ontario Provincial Police believes that First Nations Territories in the Province of Ontario should be policed by First Nations people. In partnership with the First Nations communities, and consistent with their aspirations and government policy, the Ontario Provincial Police is committed to facilitating a smooth transition to self-policing. (Ontario Provincial Police, 1996)

In other Canadian jurisdictions, the whole issue of First Nations, or Aboriginal, policing is being studied in great detail in order to develop appropriate approaches that will result in the delivery of the effective services that are suited to the needs of these communities (Oppal, 1994; Grant, 1992).

UNIVERSITY AND COMMUNITY COLLEGE POLICE

Over the last two decades there has been a substantial growth in the number and quality of police services offered to the people attending at, and employed by, the country's colleges and universities. Given the high concentration of people in these institutions of higher learning, and, given the need for substantial protection and security, it should not be surprising that this development has taken place. Furthermore, many of these institutions are located in Canada's larger urban centres and this places a significant onus of responsibility on the administrators to protect their staff, students, and facilities. Typically, these campus police officers have no special powers and must report serious occurrences to the local public police service. However, they frequently have a great deal of training and background that allows them to provide a high level of service within their area. Some of these officers are given special constable status, which provides them with certain specified powers that are frequently limited in time, application, and location.

TRANSPORTATION, WATERWAYS AND PARKS POLICE

The federal *Railway Act* permitted special constables to travel free of charge on company railroads (i.e., the Canadian Pacific, Canadian Northern, and Grand Trunk). As a category of private police, the railway police officials were involved with the Chief Constables' Association of Canada (now known as the Canadian Association of Chiefs of Police). With significant human and material assets, they were important to the stability of an important Canadian resource. Their job was primarily to prevent theft, damage, and vandalism, as well as to provide protection during strikes. Amendments to the *Railway Act* were introduced in 1918 to allow the railway companies the authority to have police constables appointed for the protection of their personnel, property, and materials (Marquis, 1993).

Ports Canada Police and the Canadian Coast Guard are two of the main services which offer forms of offshore protection. These organizations are under review by the federal government with a view to their possible privatization.

PRIVATE SECURITY (IN-HOUSE AND CONTRACT)

In the early 1970s in Canada, detailed knowledge about private policing, or private security, was extremely limited. In the public mind it had generally negative connotations which were the result of perceptions developed in the United States with regard to private detectives and strike-breaking security forces employed by private industry. Over the last 20 years, both the perception and the reality around private security has changed (Chaiken and Chaiken, 1987). These changes warrant some attention if there is to be an accurate understanding of the role of private policing in Canada and their relationship to the public police.

In looking at the development of private police, Stenning has determined that most Canadians when they are exposed to "policing" are, in fact, dealing with some form of private police. In public housing projects, in commercial centres, in parks, and various tourist attractions and shopping malls, the public are constantly interacting with security personnel who are in the employ of private police agencies (Stenning, 1989). While private police representatives have been present for a long time in Canada, it is only recently that the public police have begun dealing with them in a way that begins to resemble a partnership (Stenning, 1989). In tracing the evolution of this relationship it is important to recognize that a large of number of experienced and senior police officers have become responsible for the leadership of private policing organizations that are now competing with the public police for the public safety market.

In terms of the capacity for private police to offer a professional alternative to public policing, Stenning (1989) makes the following assertion:

> ...the current economies of policing leave little room for doubting that the growing ascendancy of private policing at the expense of public police services will continue. The fact here...is that the better private policing organizations are now able to provide policing services which are comparable in quality to those provided by public police organizations at considerably less cost and greater efficiency. (p. 184)

In Canada, a number of studies have begun to seriously examine the viability of assigning a number of functions to private police organizations. Of course, there is concern that standards and regulations are put in place to ensure that private police members operate in ways that are in the public interest. The need for proper selection, training, certification, discipline, and management of these services is understood, and most provinces have some form of legislation that guide the licensing and operation of private investigators and security personnel (Ontario. Ministry of the Solicitor General and Correctional Services, 1996; Oppal, 1994).

One recent example of the blending of public police experience and private policing enterprise can be found in the creation of KPMG Investigation and Security Inc. (KPMG ISI). As the country's largest professional services firm, KPMG has a strong reputation within public and private corporations in Canada, as well as an international network of affiliates. In 1995, a new practice was developed under the leadership of Norman Inkster, an ex-Commissioner of the RCMP. The purpose of this practice is to offer an extensive range of investigative and security services to businesses not only in Canada, but around the world. KPMG ISI is composed of former police officers, forensic accountants, and computer experts offering a full range of related services. The concentration of services is threefold:

- *risk management*—covering activities like fraud, infringement of intellectual property laws, false insurance claims, and theft of information;
- *investigation*—includes areas relating to forensic accounting, the tracing of assets, gathering of intelligence, business process reviews, and the study of various industries; and
- *prevention*—consulting with clients on executive protection, including risk assessment and precautionary measures.

A study undertaken by KPMG in 1995 discovered that losses due to fraudulent activity is responsible for losses of more than $120 billion in Canada (KMPG ISI, 1995a). Furthermore, this study revealed that approximately $1.3 billion is lost to false insurance claims every year in Canada. In order to investigate these types of fraudulent claims, police and other investigation departments are spending an additional $1 billion. The magnitude of these costs and the dwindling capacity of public police organizations to deal with these demands have contributed to the growth and viability of private police and security operations like KPMG ISI.

KPMG ISI also undertook a survey of chiefs of police in Canada in October 1995 dealing with their perceptions of white collar crime (KPMG ISI, 1995b). The results of this survey indicated a number of interested points:

- 69% of the respondents agreed that their departments were under-resourced;
- a majority of chiefs of police view fraud and other forms of white collar crime as significant problems for law enforcement;
- Canadian police services do not currently place a priority on fraud and white collar crime, and 94% of the police chief respondents indicated that their resources were devoted to crimes of violence;
- a lack of financial resources and trained personnel make it difficult for police chiefs to assign responsibility within their departments for the investigation of fraud and white collar crime; and
- the increasing complexity of fraud schemes and other white collar crimes has led to the need for Canadian business to turn to private resources for appropriate kinds of expertise.

The acceptance of a new model of policing that is concerned with a true partnership with the community, whether it is called community policing, problem-solving policing, or some other variant, will lead the public police to view their private policing counterparts as possible allies in the process of ensuring greater public safety. There has been some success in forging useful collaborations between these two areas of activity that will likely grow in the future (Greene, Seamon, and Levy, 1995).

CONCLUSION

There is great diversity across Canada in the delivery of police services when all possible jurisdictions are taken into account. We can see this diversity with the RCMP, as the federal police agency, engaged in contract policing at the provincial and municipal levels; with the trend to regionalization being pursued in the delivery police services that provide law enforcement to a collection of local municipalities; and with various jurisdictions seeking out new and creative ways of making their police services more efficient, effective, and, at the same time, less expensive to fund.

The dramatic growth in the area of private policing offers a range of options and opportunities that will be debated and modified over the next few years; however, it is clear that greater levels of cooperation and coordination will need to be pursued in the entire area of public safety. The jurisdictional issues will engage the public, the public police, governments (at all levels), and private security providers in detailed discussions that should benefit the goals of crime prevention, public order maintenance, and effective law enforcement.

The categories and sub-categories of police and quasi-police are presently unclear. Legislation to ensure that the areas of activity assigned to these two distinct groups is important, but should not diminish the public's capacity to have the fullest range of services at their disposal for the best protection of their communities. Regulations for the selection, training, equipment, liability, and evaluation of police personnel in the public and private realms need to be improved and tailored to the highest standards necessary for the public interest. Certainly, the wide range of opportunity within the area of policing, broadly defined, is both a challenge and an incentive for policy makers, practitioners, and the public.

QUESTIONS FOR CONSIDERATION

1. What were some of the important considerations for the RCMP in providing provincial police services, especially during the war years?
2. Examine the growth of regional policing in Ontario, beginning in the 1960s and 1970s and explain its apparent popularity.
3. What would be the possible impact on policing in Canada if Quebec separated?
4. Examine the development of First Nations self-policing in Canada. What are some of the benefits of this approach? What are the possible adverse consequences of this approach?
5. Why has there not been a trend to promote the establishment of police services at the county level in Canada?

REFERENCES

Campbell, Mr. Justice Archie. (1996). *Bernardo Investigation Review: report of Mr. Justice Archie Campbell*. Toronto: Ontario Ministry of the Solicitor General and Correctional Services.

Canada. Criminal Intelligence Service Canada. (1996). *CISC annual report on organized crime in Canada*. Ottawa: CISC.

Canada. Canadian Security Intelligence Service. (1990). *The Canadian Security Intelligence Service: helping to protect Canada and its people*. Ottawa: CSIS.

Canada. Solicitor General Canada. (1996). *Outlook*. Ottawa: Solicitor General of Canada.

Canada. Solicitor General Canada. (1996a). *Establishing a national DNA data bank: consultation document*. Ottawa: Minister of Supply and Services Canada.

Chaiken, Marcia and Jan Chaiken. (1987). *Public policing: privately provided*. Washington, D.C.: National Institute of Justice.

Cunningham, William C. and Todd H. Taylor. (1985). *Private security and police in America: the Hallcrest report I*. Boston: Butterworth-Heinemann.

Fairweather, S.C. (1978). *A review of regionalized policing in Ontario*. Toronto: Ontario Police Commission.

Grant, Alan. (1992). *Policing arrangements in New Brunswick: 2000 and beyond*. [Fredericton, N.B.]: Published under the authority of the Department of the Solicitor General, Province of New Brunswick.

Greene, Jack R., Thomas M. Seamon, and Paul R. Levy. (1995). "Merging public and private security for collective benefit: Philadelphia's center city district." *American Journal of Police*, 14(2), pp. 3–20.

Higley, Dahn D. (1984). *O.P.P.: the history of the Ontario Provincial Police Force*. Toronto: The Queen's Printer.

KPMG Investigation and Security Inc. (1995a). *1995 Fraud survey report*. Toronto: KPMG ISI.

KPMG Investigation and Security Inc. (1995b). *1995 Chiefs of police survey*. Toronto: KPMG ISI.

KPMG Investigation and Security Inc. (1996). *1996 Fraud survey report*. Toronto: KPMG ISI.

Marquis, Greg. (1993). *Policing Canada's century: a history of the Canadian Association of Chiefs of Police*. Toronto: University of Toronto Press for the Osgoode Society.

McDonald, D.C. (1980). *Commission of Inquiry Concerning Certain Activities of the Royal Canadian Mounted Police*. Ottawa: Supply and Services Canada.

Murphy, Christopher. (1991). "The future of non-urban policing in Canada: modernization, regionalization, provincialization." *Canadian Journal of Criminology (Police and Society in Canada)*, 33(3/4).

Normandeau, André and Barry Leighton. (1990). *A vision of the future of policing in Canada: police-challenge 2000: background document*. Ottawa: Solicitor General Canada.

Ontario. Ministry of the Solicitor General and Correctional Services. (1996). *Review of police services in Ontario: a framework for discussion*. Toronto: The Ministry.

Ontario. Task Force on Race Relations and Policing. (1992). *The report of the Race Relations and Policing Task Force*. Toronto: The Task Force.

Ontario Provincial Police. (1996). *Annual report, 1994*. Orillia: Ontario Provincial Police.

Oppal, Mr. Justice Wallace T. (1994). *Closing the gap: policing and the community: the report*. [Victoria, B.C.]: Commission of Inquiry, Policing in British Columbia.

Royal Canadian Mounted Police. (1990). *The International Criminal Police Organization: INTERPOL Ottawa: Canada's law enforcement link with the world*. Ottawa: Published by the Royal Canadian Mounted Police Public Affairs Directorate for INTERPOL Ottawa.

Royal Canadian Mounted Police. (1996). *Partners in policing: the Royal Canadian Mounted Police contract policing program*. Ottawa: RCMP

Sancton, Andrew. (1996). "Reducing costs by consolidating municipalities: New Brunswick, Nova Scotia and Ontario." *Canadian Public Administration*, 39(3).

Statistics Canada. Canadian Centre for Justice Statistics. (1996). *Selected police administration characteristics of municipal police departments, 1994*. Ottawa: Statistics Canada.

Statistics Canada. Canadian Centre for Justice Statistics. (1996a). "Police personnel and expenditures in Canada, 1994." In *Juristat*, 16(1).

Stenning, Philip C. (1989). "Private police and public police: toward a redefinition of the police role." In Loree, Donald J. (ed.). *Future issues in policing: symposium proceedings*. Ottawa: Canadian Police College.

Sunahara, David F. (1992). "Public inquiries into policing." *Canadian Police College Journal*, 16(2), pp. 135–156.

TOWARD MORE LEARNING

FEDERAL POLICING

Solicitor General Canada

Hornick, Joseph P. et al. (1996). *A police reference manual on crime prevention and diversion with youth*. Ottawa: Canadian Institute for Law and the Family and Solicitor General Canada.

The Ministry of the Solicitor General Canada has collaborated on the production of this publication with a number of academics and authorities responsible for crime prevention programs and related topics. This is a joint venture with the Canadian Institute for Law and the Family, which is a non-profit research organization based at the University of Calgary. It offers detailed assistance to the police practitioner in all jurisdictions with regard to dealing with youth violence.

Canadian Police College

The Web site for CPC is: www.cpc.gc.ca. It includes an overview of the college, course calendar and schedule, recent reports and an electronic version of the CPC newsletter. Back issues of the *Canadian Police College Journal* provide an excellent source of information on the academic research in Canadian policing, as well as several important practical studies undertaken in cooperation with police services in Canada.

Criminal Intelligence Service Canada

Criminal Intelligence Service Canada. *Annual reports*. Ottawa: CISC.

Each annual volume provides extensive details on the operation of this national body and pinpoints areas of activity in relation to its mandate.

Canadian Security Intelligence Service

Canada. Special Committee of the Senate on the Security Intelligence Service. (1983). *Report of the Special Committee of the Senate on the Security Intelligence Service: delicate balance: a security intelligence service in a democratic society*. Ottawa : Supply and Services Canada.

This publication offers some historical perspective on the movement in Canada toward the establishment of CSIS and the Royal Commission and Commission of Inquiry which triggered that movement. The report summarizes a great deal of useful information that provides a thorough background on this important security service. There is strong support for an open approach to security intelligence and a requirement that accountability mechanisms be put in place to ensure the proper governance and oversight of this process.

Canada. Security Intelligence Review Committee. (1985–present). *Annual report*. Ottawa: SIRC.

The annual reports of the official body which oversees the operation and administration of the Canadian Security Intelligence Service (CSIS) are extremely helpful in getting an in-depth understanding of the organization and the issues and matters which most closely concern security intelligence in Canada.

Canadian Police Research Centre

The annual reports of this organization provide a fascinating insight into the types of projects which are being advanced through the work of CPRC. The most current report (1995–1996) includes details on activities in three main categories: health and safety (protecting the police in hazardous situations); operational effectiveness (fighting crime, gathering information, intelligence and evidence); and protecting the public (traffic, custody, and crime prevention).

Department of Justice

Canada. Department of Justice. (1996). *Safer communities: a Parliamentarian's crime prevention guide*. Ottawa: Dept. of Justice.

This item published by the Department of Justice Canada is designed as a reference tool for Canadian Parliamentarians; however, it has been made available through the Internet or by ordering through a supplier. The guide deals with crime facts in Canada, the costs of crime, and a variety of means for creating safer communities in Canada. It gives detailed background on special topics: children, youth, women, seniors, vulnerable minorities, and violence in the home. The publication contains a very helpful "Community Crime Prevention Checklist" and other worthwhile appendices. The Dept. of Justice Web site is: http://www.jc.ca.

PROVINCIAL POLICING
British Columbia

Oppal, Mr. Justice Wallace T. (1994). *Closing the gap: policing and the community: the report*. 3 volumes. [Victoria, B.C.]: Commission of Inquiry, Policing in British Columbia.

This thorough study of policing in British Columbia is worthy of consideration by anyone wishing to gain a complete picture of current issues facing this jurisdiction. In three volumes, Mr. Justice Wallace T. Oppal's Commission of Inquiry has examined several aspects of this province's law enforcement situation. The contents of these volumes are as follows:

Volume I

- the governance of policing in British Columbia;
- community-based policing;
- regionalization of policing services; and
- human resources management.

Volume II

- use of non-police personnel;
- Aboriginal policing;
- high-risk policing;
- complaints and discipline; and
- the role of the RCMP in policing the province.

Volume III

- sources;
- submitters' list;
- bibliography;
- cases; and
- police officer survey.

Ontario

Ontario. Ministry of the Solicitor General and Correctional Services. (1996). *Review of police services in Ontario: a framework for discussion*. Toronto: The Ministry.

In 1995, the Solicitor General and Minister of Correctional Services for Ontario, the Honourable Robert Runciman, began a comprehensive review of police services. This review was designed to be an extensive examination of the following topics:

- equitable financing of police services;
- alternative sources of revenue for police services;
- structure and organization of police services;
- policing functions;
- civilian governance of police services; and
- oversight of police services.

In order to generate discussion around these topics and to stimulate thinking among the policing stakeholders, the ministry issued the above-noted document.

New Brunswick

Grant, Alan. (1992). *Policing arrangements in New Brunswick: 2000 and beyond.* [Fredericton, N.B.]: Published under the authority of the Department of the Solicitor General, Province of New Brunswick.

This study was undertaken by Prof. Grant in order to examine the current policing arrangements in the province of New Brunswick. As a result of this review, it would be feasible to develop a basis for modifying these arrangements and provide policy advice for policing New Brunswick in the 21st century.

SPECIAL CATEGORIES OF POLICING

First Nations Policing

Rolf, C.H. (1991). *Policing in relation to the Blood Tribe report of a public inquiry, Volume 1: findings and recommendations.* Edmonton: Government of Alberta.

In 1988, concerns about police handling of the deaths of Blood Tribe members was communicated by the Chief to the Alberta premier. As a result, an inquiry began under Assistant Chief Judge Rolf. This inquiry examined a number of suspicious deaths and the conduct of the police. It also examined issues relating to a confrontation involving members of the Blood Tribe, the RCMP, and members of the Town of Cardston, and considered various policies that guided the inter-relationships between the Blood Tribe and the federal and provincial governments. This publication details the findings and recommendations of that inquiry.

Hamilton, Mr. Justice Alvin C. and Associate Chief Judge C. Murray Sinclair. (1991). *Report of the Aboriginal Justice Inquiry of Manitoba, Volume 1: the justice system and aboriginal people.* Winnipeg: The Queen's Printer.

The Manitoba Aboriginal Justice Inquiry began in reaction to the murder of Helen Betty Osborne in The Pas in 1971, and the police shooting of John Joseph Harper in Winnipeg in 1988. These two events lead to an inquiry which made some important recommendations around the police handling of occurrences involving First Nations people.

University and Community College Police

A number of campus police organizations have developed very sophisticated and instructive Web sites to assist visitors in understanding their mission, mandate, goals and objectives, as well as to provide information for people who may wish to seek a career in this form of law enforcement. Many of these Web sites contain helpful tips on personal safety and provide contact numbers and information for other on-campus services (e.g., campus security escorts, campus sexual assault centres, and lost property reporting). See Appendix III for a listing of these Web sites.

Private Security (In-house and Contract)

Many of the major private security firms have established interesting Web sites that provide a full array of information on the services which they offer. It is useful to review these sources in order to gain a deeper appreciation of the professional level at which many of these organizations are now operating. See Appendix III for a listing of possible locations.

> Organizations have begun to develop in Canada that represent the interests of our growing private security sector. One example of this increased commitment to professionalism is to be found in the Canadian Society for Industrial Security (CSIS) which is based in Ottawa. This organization has representatives across Canada and organizes a number of workshops, conferences, and seminars to discuss topics and matters of interest and importance to their membership. The organization also publishes a periodical, *Canadian Security,* which has topical articles dealing with this sector. CSIS has conducted public opinion surveys (through Angus Reid) in relation to the acceptance of private security in Canada. See Appendix III for details on contacting this organization.

Cunningham, William C., John J. Strauchs, and Clifford W. Van Meter. (1990). *Private security trends: 1970–2000: the Hallcrest report II.* Boston: Butterworth-Heinemann.

This publication takes another look at the key trends and issues affecting the private security sector following the important study published in 1985, under the auspices of the U.S. National Institute of Justice. It is a definitive source of statistical information on this area of study and business.

Stenning, Philip C. (1989). "Private police and public police: toward a redefinition of the police role." In Loree, Donald J. (ed.). *Future issues in policing: symposium proceedings.* Ottawa: The Canadian Police College.

Prof. Stenning has written extensively on the topic of private policing and, along with Clifford Shearing, is acknowledged as a leading authority in this area. The essay which Prof. Stenning contributed to this symposium provides a good overview of the development of private policing in Canada and indicates that private policing is becoming more widely accepted in the public realm as a viable alternative to public police. It is also evident that the level of skill in many private police organizations is substantial as private policing has been successful in attracting some extremely senior police executives who have transformed their investigative, administrative, and operational skills into efficient business enterprises.

CHAPTER FOUR

BECOMING A POLICE OFFICER
IN CANADA

LEARNING OBJECTIVES

1. Identify elements that qualify policing as a profession
2. Identify key knowledge, skills, and abilities required for employment as a police officer in Canada
3. List ways in which police organizations can value and reflect diversity in their service delivery
4. Explain reasonable physical expectations for police work in Canada
5. Identify normal stages for the recruitment of police personnel in Canada

INTRODUCTION

Nothing is of more immediate importance to someone seeking a career in policing than the precise steps that must be followed in order to secure employment in a police organization. These are some of the first questions that may come to mind:

- What are the basic qualifications to be considered for employment in a police service?
- What tests will I have to take?
- What are the physical requirements?
- What are the educational requirements?
- Does it matter if I have a criminal record?
- How long will I have to wait to hear if I'm accepted?
- How often can I apply?

Because policing is seen as a good career option that continues to have fairly high salary levels and offers relatively stable prospects for continuing appointment, it attracts a large number of qualified applicants.

Over time, police recruitment practices have changed, expectations have evolved, and the legal framework within which police organizations must operate have been modified to reflect demonstrated knowledge, skills, and abilities (KSAs) and sound human resources practices. This chapter will consider whether or not policing can be truly considered a "profession" and will look at some things that can be done to prepare for employment in a police organization. Then there will be an examination in some detail about the KSAs that are seen to relate directly to police work and we will look at what the immediate future holds in this regard. The need to subscribe to the notion of continuous learning will be underlined and presented in anticipation of a more detailed treatment of an organizational learning model in Chapter 10.

Taking stock of the physical demands of the job of a police constable introduces some complex issues. Of course, it is important that physical strength and endurance are considered in the recruitment of police officers; however, it should not be overrated. Considerations around technology, weapons, equipment, teamwork, and other elements make precise physical standards difficult to justify if they are set too high. The work that has been done to arrive at job-specific physical requirements will be discussed later in this chapter.

PROFESSION OR VOCATION?

The characteristics of a profession have been studied in a number of areas and policing is frequently being challenged to recreate itself in ways which are consistent with a professional model (Brodeur, 1992). The professional model may include these characteristics:

- specialized knowledge and technical expertise;
- clearly delineated and stable membership;
- an overcoming of personal attitudes and their replacement with established professional perspectives that are widely shared within the membership; and
- public recognition and acknowledgment that the field of endeavour is a profession.

If one considers the criteria outlined above, it is certainly possible to make the case for the professional status of police. Clearly the kind and quality of training and learning that police officers require make policing eligible according to the first point relating to special knowledge and technical expertise. This point will be further detailed in Chapter 7 ("Assignment to Duty"). Given the stable tenure of most police officers who enter the field of police as a lifelong career and frequently embark on second careers which are in a similar or related field, the second criterion of a clearly delineated and stable membership appears to be substantially satisfied. The establishment of a coherent set of attitudes and values in the context of policing may be consistent with the third criterion of a professional model; however, it has also been the source of serious concern in some academic circles (Ellis, 1991). There have been many who would argue that policing creates a subculture that frequently operates in opposition to the highest professional interests of its members. In terms of the fourth criterion relating to public perception, there is perhaps some level of doubt as to whether or not the field of policing is viewed as a profession. It may be part of the belief that the work of a police officer is on a footing somewhat below that of other professions (e.g., lawyers, doctors, chartered accountants, or engineers) because of the high degree of unionization within police departments, the strict hierarchical nature of the police rank structure, and, finally, the fact that individuals may qualify for entrance into the field of policing without any formal university preparation that is uniquely directed at this field of endeavour.

BEGINNING THE PROCESS

In order to properly begin the process of seeking employment in a police organization, it is best to have a clear personal plan. Many candidates embark on a career in policing without really understanding what the true nature of this job will be, and whether or not they are truly suited to this type of work. In order to make the best career decision possible, there is some preliminary thinking that should be done well in advance of any application. One of the first points to ponder is whether or not you meet the most basic qualifications for employment in a police organization, namely:

- Canadian citizen (or landed immigrant status);
- minimum age (usually 18 or 19);
- physically fit, with height and weight in proportion;
- good moral character and habits; and
- successful completion of at least four years of secondary school (or its equivalent).

BRIEFING NOTE

You may be assigned to any part of the City of Vancouver to work in all kinds of conditions and with all types of people. Some buildings you will enter will be structurally unsafe and unsanitary. You may be required to search people who are dirty, neglected, or injured. You will come into contact with persons drunk, high on drugs, mentally unstable or agitated, and persons covered with blood, vomit, or other bodily fluids. You will see dead persons who have suffered a violent death, or bodies who are decomposed. You will encounter children who because of their living environment, have no hope. You will meet others who have simply given up hope. Regardless of social status, religion, race, or lifestyle, you will endeavour to treat all persons equally. Some members of the public will be hostile towards you because you are a Police Officer and will express their anger in words or actions. You will strive to behave professionally in the face of provocation.

Source: Vancouver Police Department. *"Making a difference every day": a policing career in the City of Vancouver* (Revised 97/12/22), p. 4. Used with permission.

MYTH VS. REALITY

Many people have formed an impression of police work from sources which are not fully accurate or truly representative of the realities of the job. Most individuals rarely come into direct contact with police officers in any way that would provide them with a deep insight into the true nature of this work or the demands which it places on those who deliver the range of services typically provided by a police department. However, we do see the exaggerated presentation of police work in the entertainment industry creating a myth about the excitement, danger, brutality, and autonomy of police officers which is not helpful in developing a full understanding. Also, the media have been successful in bringing to public attention the most dramatic and traumatic aspects of police work with an intense concentration on officers who have been the subject of disciplinary proceedings for criminal conduct or breaches of internal policies and procedures. There is a great deal that can be done to ensure that a better comprehension of policing is arrived at by those who are thinking about career opportunities in this field. Replacing some of the common myths with a realistic view is one of the earliest tasks that should be taken up by any prospective candidate.

DOING YOUR HOMEWORK

Many police services now maintain detailed Web sites on the Internet that can be searched for useful background information not only on the department's individual recruitment standards and practices, but also on the history and development of the police service. This is a good source of data to provide current details that will help in better knowing the various demands of the work of policing (see Appendix III for a listing of police Web sites).

Another good source of information on police departments is to be found in their published annual reports. These documents normally provide fairly up-to-date details on the organizational structure of the service, its mission, mandate, goals, and objectives, and the jurisdictional boundaries within which it operates. Annual reports also give good background on the new initiatives a police service has undertaken during the report year and statistics on its operations. These public documents are useful in getting an insight into the workings of a police organization, its character, and the direction it is

RCMP officer with new Canadian

Michael Stuparyk/Toronto Star

going in for the future. Some police departments, like the Belleville Police Service in Ontaro, are planning to place the entire text of their annual report on their Web site to provide broad access to this important document and reduce production costs through this electronic means of publishing.

KNOWLEDGE, SKILLS, AND ABILITIES

There has been a substantial amount of research undertaken in the last few years dealing with the precise knowledge, skills, and abilities (KSAs) required to effectively perform the duties of a police officer. In Ontario, two studies have recently been completed which offer a wealth of detail on the KSAs needed to fulfill the functions of a police officer (Ontario. Ministry of the Solicitor General, 1992a; Hay Management Consultants, 1993).

In Ontario, the Ministry of the Solicitor General's Strategic Planning Committee on Police Training and Education undertook a rigorous series of consultations within the police community and through the public in order to establish the future learning needs for police officers at all rank levels, including entry-level constables. This process involved doing detailed environmental scanning to assess the future issues that would be confronting police organizations in the next decade. As a result of this broad examination and research, the project applied a technique known as "functional job analysis" to develop strategic learning requirements for police constables. The functional job analysis component of this research identified 101 specific areas of knowledge, skills, and abilities that are necessary for the performance of the tasks typically assigned to a police constable. Any initial or recruit orientation program for police constables should properly address these areas in preparing candidates for assignment to probationary duty in a police organization (Ontario. Ministry of the Solicitor General, 1992a).

The research mandate of the Strategic Planning Committee on Police Training and Education went on to identify 20 areas that would be of "strategic" importance to police organizations in the future in terms of greater emphasis or enhancement or as additional new KSAs. These 20 areas of strategic learning are listed below:

- communication skills;
- interpersonal and sensitivity skills;
- knowledge of human behaviour;
- ability to accept and work with community diversity;
- ability to serve victims;
- ability to initiate, promote, and facilitate community policing;
- ability to use policing-related technology;
- analytical skills and problem-solving ability;
- knowledge of political systems and processes;
- knowledge of crime prevention strategies;
- personal and organizational development skills;
- knowledge of other agencies;

- team-building skills;
- ability to use crime trend information;
- ability to apply basic police authorities and knowledge of case preparation;
- ability to act ethically and professionally;
- ability to maintain a reasonable level of physical fitness and well-being;
- ability to use force appropriately;
- officer safety skills; and
- conflict avoidance, resolution and mediation skills.

The final report provides further definitional detail on the content of those KSAs for strategic learning requirements (Ontario. Ministry of the Solicitor General, 1992a). What should become immediately apparent is the wide array of capabilities the modern police officer is expected to possess in order to satisfactorily meet the demands and requirements of this job. Clearly, the future of policing in Canada relies heavily on being able to attract extremely talented and competent individuals. In order to be effective, police recruitment policies, practices, and procedures must draw from the largest range of potential candidates in order to meet the high standards that are being established for police personnel.

Across Canada, these KSAs will not alter too dramatically since there is a great deal of consistency across police jurisdictions with regard to what police are expected and empowered to do in the line of duty. This is the case because of the overall importance of the *Criminal Code of Canada*, as well as other significant federal legislation that relates to the criminal law (e.g., the *Young Offenders Act*, the *Narcotic Control Act*, and the *Charter*).

The Police Constable Selection Project in Ontario also established a number of competencies that would be required for officers at the entry level. This project was designed to define the minimum requirements for each of the competencies identified as being essential for the position of police constable. Furthermore, this group was tasked with assessing and evaluating selection tests, methods, and procedures employed by police services in Ontario to determine their accuracy, predictive value, and overall fairness. Finally, this group distilled its review and research in the form of recommendations for a new constable selection process for Ontario that represented "best practices" while still meeting the principles of cost-effectiveness. This work resulted in the identification of eight essential competencies that should be required for selection to the position of a police constable:

- *analytical thinking*—demonstrate logical cause-and-effect thinking; systematically identify patterns or connections between situations, persons, or events; identify key elements in complex situations;
- *self-confidence*—believe in one's own abilities, opinions and judgments; understand one's own strengths and limitations; and handle failures constructively;
- *communication*—communicate in a manner that demonstrates understanding and responsiveness to the concerns, motivations, feelings, and behaviour of others; use non-racist, non-sexist language; demonstrate verbal and written communication skills needed for self-expression and the clear and accurate presentation of information;

- *flexibility/dealing with diversity*—adapt to, and function effectively in, a variety of situations, individuals, groups, and changing circumstances; work effectively with a wide cross-section of the community representing diverse backgrounds, cultures, and socio-economic conditions; able to acknowledge and adapt to underlying problems/issues;
- *self-control*—control one's emotions in the face of provocation, opposition, or hostility; able to work under stressful conditions and apply constructive approaches in dealing with these situations;
- *relationship building*—develop and maintain a network of contacts, inside and outside of school, work, community, etc. including individuals, organizations, and groups who can provide information, advice and support in the achievement of interpersonal or work-related goals;
- *achievement orientation*—focus on the attainment of successful outcomes by always striving for improved performance, demonstrate commitment to the accomplishment of self-directed or organizational goals and/or standards; and
- *physical skills and abilities*—meet the requirements of a general fitness, strength, and endurance assessment, with modifications for male and female applicants. Physical ability testing would relate directly to job performance.

STAGES ALONG THE WAY TO RECRUITMENT

The Ontario Constable Selection Project proposed an eight-stage process to identify and recruit suitable candidates for police service:

STAGE ONE: RECRUITMENT STRATEGIES AND PLANS

The report suggested that police services develop specific recruitment strategies that would serve to recruit a broad range of applicants and identify long-term organizational staffing needs. These strategies could effectively target candidates with a higher potential for recruitment and apply more user-friendly approaches to the recruitment process.

STAGE TWO: RECRUITMENT, JOB AWARENESS, AND SELF-SELECTION

Police services should develop standardized recruitment literature that clearly focuses on the minimum requirements. It is essential that potential candidates have a complete picture of the work of a police constable and the steps which they will have to follow in making their application for employment. It was further recommended that applicants would benefit by having access to a knowledge questionnaire relating to police work that potential applicants could self-administer. Also, a personal competency assessment tool could be provided so that candidates might better understand their own potential for success in this career. In many instances, individuals might screen themselves out of the process on the basis of this self-assessment.

STAGE THREE: APPLICANT SUBMISSION

It was suggested that a single, standardized application form be developed for use across the province. This form would allow all applicants to complete a consistent document that was in adherence with the provincial *Human Rights Code* and other relevant legislation (e.g., the *Freedom of Information and Protection of Privacy Act*). This standardized approach to application would facilitate the establishment of a centralized registry of applicants that would greatly streamline the work of individual police departments in seeking out and securing qualified candidates. There was also thought given to the number of times a person could apply for consideration. In the case of Ontario, the provincial Ombudsman determined that one application per year is reasonable and fair; however, two unsuccessful applications should disqualify any individual from further consideration by a police service.

STAGE FOUR: ASSESSMENT

There was support for the preparation of educational literature and practice documents which could be provided to qualified candidates *before* the administration of tests. These items would be designed as guides for the assistance of applicants and to reduce test bias for those unaccustomed to being tested. A great deal of attention should be paid to the selection, training, and certification of personnel who would administer these tests. The project highlighted the need for fully competent individuals being engaged in this important step in the process, as well as the potential for the establishment of regional and local testing teams that could undertake fair and impartial testing on behalf of police services within their area.

The research conducted by this project indicated that the General Aptitude Test Battery (G.A.T.B.) was a valid and reliable testing mechanism that can be effectively applied in the process of police constable selection. However, there was a recommendation that reading, writing, and spelling tests that would be job-relevant need to be developed and incorporated into the new selection system. The significant concern in this context is that any such tests

BRIEFING NOTE

The G.A.T.B. is designed to measure aptitude in the following areas:

- *arithmetic skills*—the test measures a person's basic understanding of the operations of addition, subtraction, division, and multiplication;
- *problem-solving skills*—the exercise measures an individual's ability to solve mathematical problems;
- *spatial aptitude*—the test measures a person's ability to select the shape that a flat object will take when it has been folded in a predetermined way; and
- *verbal skills*—the exercise measures a person's ability to understand relationships between words.

be valid, reliable, user-friendly, and operate to minimize bias or adverse impact. Finally, there was strong support for providing applicants with details about their success or failure at all of the tests administered in this process. The provision of honest and constructive feedback was seen as being valuable for everyone involved in the aptitude testing stage.

Assessment elements need to be carefully developed to match the identified competencies established for the position of police constable. The key components would include:

- *job-relevant simulations*—exercises that capture the substance and diversity of the job. A number of simulations should be developed in order to avoid too much familiarity on the part of applicants.
- *personality tests*—such instruments are necessary to prevent the selection of individuals with disordered personalities. The second Minnesota Multiphasic Personality Inventory (MMPI-2) and the 16 PF have been identified as suitable tests in this regard; however, a certified psychologist is the only person qualified to analyze these test results (Hargrave and Berner, 1984; Lowman, 1989; Trompetter, 1993).
- *physical skills and ability testing*—many studies have been done in this area in order to ensure that physical requirements and tests are directly job-related.

STAGE FIVE: LOCALLY FOCUSED INTERVIEW

It is recommended that local interviews be conducted by a panel of at least two members who are trained and certified for this purpose. These interviews should follow a structured series of questions with scoring templates that assist the interviewers in making consistent evaluations of applicants based on local organizational requirements and actual job performance.

STAGE SIX: BACKGROUND/REFERENCE CHECK

Again, the requirement at this stage is for consistent, relevant, and reliable information that is directly tied to the behaviour of the candidate. Standardized questions, procedures, and documentation are important at this stage. As with those who are tasked with the administration of tests, the personnel assigned to doing background investigations should meet established selection, training, and certification criteria.

STAGE SEVEN: FINAL SELECTION

There should be detailed guidelines on the criteria to be applied when making final recruit selection decisions. Some attention should be paid to the selection, training, and certification of personnel making these final selection decisions on behalf of the police organization, and all final decisions should be accompanied by documentation containing the rationale for those decisions.

STAGE EIGHT: PROBATIONARY EMPLOYMENT

Having been successful up to this stage, the probationary constable should be able to complete whatever recruit orientation is required for assignment to duty. While operating

BRIEFING NOTE

Individuals seeking a career in law enforcement in Ontario have been found, on average, to apply to five or six police departments. This results in more than 20 000 applications being received, processed, and evaluated by police services at an annual cost of nearly $8.8 million.

under the terms of the probationary period, the police constable should be assigned to a coach officer/supervisor who will be properly trained to assist the new recruit in meeting a standardized performance management process that will guide, evaluate, and facilitate the growth of the police constable in the complete range of required competencies.

A number of police services across Canada have put a great deal of effort into the development of packages that will assist potential applicants in understanding what will be required of them on the job and also in going through a relatively lengthy selection process. Because of the importance of the decision being made and the investment in terms of training, development, equipment, and support, police organizations take this responsibility very seriously (Vancouver Police Department, 1996).

PHYSICAL EXPECTATIONS

A considerable amount of study and effort has gone into the process of determining the best physical fitness tests to find suitable candidates for the work of policing. Of course, this is rather difficult given the extremely broad range of assignments which may fall to any individual officer (see Chapter 7—"Assignment to Duty"). However, the kinds of physical expectations currently in place have some common themes that apply quite extensively to policing across Canada.

In the area of physical fitness, it is possible to include medical considerations and visual acuity. Many police services have set fairly clear minimum standards in this regard to ensure quality applicants for police service. Because the physical demands of police work may be quite high, police organizations want potential applicants to arrive with sufficient aptitude to deal with these demands. Many recruitment brochures point out that the police constable may be expected to chase suspects on foot, drive police vehicles safely at high speeds, and patrol on foot or bicycle. Furthermore, officers carry a great deal of equipment with them for their own and the public's protection. This equipment includes a firearm, which requires significant levels of proficiency.

One test that has been developed to evaluate physical fitness is the Peace Officers Physical Abilities Test (P.O.P.A.T.). This is a timed obstacle course which includes a mobility run, a pull station with an 80-pound weight on a pulley, squat thrusts, a standing vault, and weight carry. During the same day as these tests are administered, the candidate is required to do a timed run (2.4 kilometres or 1.5 miles in 12 minutes) and a swim test (Coutts, 1990). Frequently, candidates can get assistance on developing their strength and skill for these tests through the local YMCA. Details of the exact tests are typically available through the police service. It is important to note that specific requirements vary by age and gender; however, these tests have been examined to ensure that they are a fair and suitable means of assessing fitness for duty in a police organization.

OTHER CONSIDERATIONS

Some police services use a variety of other means to assist them in selecting the best candidates for recruitment. Among those tools are the following:

- *polygraph tests*—this normally involves an interview conducted by a certified polygraph operator who will assess a candidate's truthfulness regarding personal history and qualifications;
- *assessment centres*—in these circumstances, applicants are placed into situations that involve role-playing related to the work of a police constable. Trained officers observe, record, and assess the behaviour and skills demonstrated by the applicant during the exercise (including such qualities as intelligence, integrity, problem solving, tolerance of stress, learning ability, initiative, decisiveness, oral and written communication skills, interpersonal sensitivity, powers of observation, and personal impact); and
- *medical examinations*—this element is completed to ensure that the candidate has the basic medical soundness to undertake the requirements of the police constable's job, and includes visual acuity tests to the standard legally established in that jurisdiction. Some police services have set up separate processes for those possible candidates whose eyesight does not meet the entry standards, but who wish to consider surgery to correct their deficiencies. The procedure known as excimer laser surgery can correct some vision deficiencies; however, it is expensive and amounts to a very significant decision on the part of the applicant (Vancouver Police Department, 1996).

VALUING DIVERSITY

Police departments have become increasingly aware of the need to reflect the diversity of the communities that they serve. This is good business practice on a number of fronts, including the operational necessity of having individuals within your organization who can deal with and understand a portion of your clientele. Much has been done in the past

Days of Action protest (October 1996, Toronto)

Peter Bregg/Maclean's

few years in making the recruitment, selection, and orientation process more welcoming for all variety of potential candidates. This idea is reflected in the overall mission statements of many police departments in Canada. Of course, policies that encourage this inclusive approach to recruitment and retention of a broad range of police officers must be followed by practices which realize those policies. In order to ensure that this is occurring, many police organizations have established units within their human resources area to monitor and report on progress in this regard. Consideration has been given to encourage applications from particular categories of police candidates including:

- women;
- visible ethnic minorities; and
- civilians.

WOMEN IN POLICING

The study of women in policing has been undertaken from a number of perspectives which often includes serious academic evaluation of their recruitment, training, assignment to duty and success within the organizational hierarchy of police departments. The movement to recruit and promote a greater number of qualified women within police services in Canada has developed over the last 25 years; however, there is clearly a recognition that more needs to be accomplished in this strategic area of human resource management.

Women entered the operational levels of police organizations in the 1970s are now beginning to reach a stage where they should be eligible for promotion to the most senior ranks and be given an opportunity to apply their skills at the highest levels of assignment. The de-emphasis on physical strength as a key aspect of police competence has been of some assistance in removing a potential bias against women in policing (Cuadrado, 1995). A more realistic understanding of the value of negotiation and dispute resolution skills has also contributed to the greater acceptance of women in policing. Evaluations that have studied the effectiveness of women police officers in operational settings have tended to find that they are just as capable as their male counterparts (Morash and Greene, 1986).

VISIBLE ETHNIC MINORITIES IN POLICING

The recruitment of individuals who reflect the communities which police organizations serve has been developing considerably across Canada. With significant demographic change in the composition of Canada's population, police organizations have been making efforts to ensure that their policies, programs, and practices bring forward a better cross-section of candidates for careers in policing. Attention has been drawn to this issue throughout Canada by a number of important commissions and inquiries which have examined these matters in detail and have made substantive recommendations to governments on ways to improve the representation of visible ethnic minorities within police departments. It was generally the case that police services which had established an active program targeting the recruitment of specific groups of people were more successful in their efforts than those organizations which relied on traditional methods (Ontario. Race Relations and Policing Task Force, 1989).

CIVILIANIZATION IN POLICING

Many of the studies which looked at the issues of women and visible ethnic minorities in policing also came to the conclusion that much of what was being done by police officers could be effectively assigned to civilians within those departments. There has been a growing recognition not only of the need for greater civilianization in policing, but the positive benefits which may result from such initiatives. Criteria have been established to help police services determine if a specific function or range of functions requires a fully trained, sworn police officer. Often there is some consideration given to the potential for cost savings by having a civilian member undertake a particular function. This may not be easily accomplished, particularly in those areas like computer programming, financial management and accounting, forensic identification, senior management, or specialized technical assignments, where highly developed skills and knowledge are required of the incumbent.

TRAINING, EDUCATION, AND LEARNING

A substantial amount of research has been conducted on the need for a university degree for police officers and its impact on successful job performance. The evidence to date seems to indicate that it is nice, but not necessary. The formal content of these studies has routinely shown that police officers who possess a university degree do not, as a class, perform to any higher standard of service. There are many arguments which can be made to support the value of having people with the discipline required to pursue and successfully complete the requirements of a university program; however, it is clearly not a means of guaranteeing the selection of ideal police constable candidates.

Once someone has passed through the extensive testing and interviewing stages in the selection process, there still remains the formal training undertaken at some form of police academy. These programs vary across the country; however, their main purpose is to provide those selected with a foundation of theory, practical knowledge, and skill that will allow them to move into a field assignment under the direct guidance and supervision of a coach officer. These programs have been established with an emphasis on practical information that relates to the specific police service and jurisdiction within which the new recruit will function. Because the development of proficiency as police constable may take up to five years to achieve, it is critical that recruit training focus on the essential elements of the job, and also that training, education, and development continue throughout the officer's career.

Various approaches can be taken in the delivery of initial police training. Normandeau and Leighton (1992) identified four basic models:

- traditional model that separates police education and training from the mainstream of adult education. Police recruits who have met the basic educational requirements for the position of constable attend orientation, in-service, and advanced training courses at a separate police training facility (e.g., RCMP training academy in Regina and the Ontario Police College);

- police training programs, designed for specific areas of activity, are delivered for police personnel out of a local university. Academic staff may provide instruction on topics like management and administration, social sciences, and other areas, while police instructors concentrate on recruit orientation and operational policies and procedures. This model may also include members of the local bench and bar providing instruction on the criminal law and related topics. This approach is being applied at the Saskatchewan Police College, functioning out of the University of Regina, and the Atlantic Police Academy which is part of Holland College, on Prince Edward Island;
- institutional approach that brings together all elements of the criminal justice system for a broadly based exposure. This type of model is in place at the Justice Institute of British Columbia which was formed in 1978 as a unique post-secondary educational institution. Its purpose is to enhance justice and public safety by developing and delivering training programs for practitioners in all areas of the justice system; and
- a fully integrated model which places police training within the adult learning mainstream. This approach is being used in Quebec where potential candidates are enrolled in a provincially sponsored community college program which offers courses in policing, criminology, law, and other relevant topics. Successful graduates of this program then proceed to a course of instruction out of the Quebec Police Institute in Nicolet.

In British Columbia, the approach to recruit training follows a "block" format to prepare individuals who have been hired by a municipal police department and are sworn officers of their department. These blocks of training are outlined below:

Block I

- Basic police training at the police academy—duration: 12 weeks

Block II

- Training under a field trainer at the police department—duration: 9 weeks

Block III

- Further police training at the police academy—duration: 8.5 weeks

  Upon successful completion of Block III, police constables are considered to be "qualified" and can return to their departments to work without the supervision of a field trainer.

Block IV

- Requalification training at the police academy following one year of service

Block V

- Requalification training at the police academy after two years of service as a "Qualified Municipal Constable"—duration: 1 week.

  Successful completion of this block results in the individual being designated a "Certified Municipal Constable."

In many jurisdictions the process for training police recruits has undergone a great deal of study and analysis. Typically jurisdictions share certain characteristics that produce capable recruits who have some combination of knowledge, skills, and abilities which allow them to function with a trained coach or field officer during an initial period of probation. Frequently, an individual police department will introduce an additional period of recruit orientation that is tailored to meet the department's specialized operational, corporate or human resources needs. This is the case within the Metropolitan Toronto Police Service where new recruits are assigned to 14 weeks of further training before they are assigned to field operations. Some of the topics dealt with during this period of additional orientation in Metropolitan Toronto are listed below:

- defensive tactics;
- Force rules and regulations;
- *Highway Traffic Act*;
- *Criminal Code of Canada*;
- domestic violence and victims' services;
- ethics and problem solving;
- team building;
- human relations;
- community policing;
- firearms training (on the range);
- forensic identification services;
- crime scene management;
- radar operation;
- computer training (including mobile display terminals); and
- directing traffic.

CONCLUSION

The process of becoming a police officer in Canada is one that requires a great deal of dedication and determination on the part of the applicants, as well as on the part of the organizations who are looking for the very best candidates to become part of their service. Without suggesting that the police recruitment process in Canada has reached a stage of perfection, there can be little doubt that a great deal of intelligence and effort has been invested in bringing the policies and procedures in this area up to a much higher standard than was the case only a decade ago.

In the areas of police constable training and development, a wealth of research and study has been invested in making certain that police executives and their civilian governing authorities are aware of the state of the art in this regard. The key decision makers who determine police budgets know that the training, education, and development of police officers is an investment that has a direct impact on the organization's effectiveness and well-being. With a broadening of exposure to the techniques and expertise that exist within the larger adult learning community, police organizations are beginning to deal more effectively with the challenge of training to high levels of KSAs required for proper policing in the future.

With women, visible ethnic minorities, and civilians playing a more prominent role in the human resource planning of police services, there will be further change and evolution in the manner in which these services deliver their programs, and there will be transformations in the kinds of opportunities and assignments available for individuals within these departments.

QUESTIONS FOR CONSIDERATION

1. Can policing be considered a true profession?
2. What are some of the important considerations someone should bear in mind before applying for a position as a police officer in Canada?
3. What are the arguments in favour of having strict visual acuity requirements for police officer recruitment? Are there considerations which would suggest that these requirements be reviewed?
4. What are the benefits of having an employment outreach plan for a police service that aims at attracting a wide range of applicants, including women, visible ethnic minorities, and other groups?
5. Which of the four models of police recruit training outlined in this chapter is the most effective for preparing police officers for assignment to duty in Canada today?
6. What are some possible barriers for women in policing? How might these barriers be overcome or eliminated?
7. Civilianization has been part of policing for many years. What, if any, are the limits to the use of civilians in a modern police department?
8. Discuss the various types of tests and interviews that are used by police services in screening candidates. What are the advantages and disadvantages of these different approaches?

REFERENCES

Bloch, P. and D. Anderson. (1974). *Policewomen on patrol: final report: methodology, tables and measurement instruments*. Washington, D.C.: Urban Institute.

Brodeur, Jean-Paul. (1992). "Professionalism and community policing." In *Managing diversity and change: a training strategy*. Regina: Police Educators Conference Board of Canada.

Buckley, Leslie B. and Petrunik, Michael G. (1995). "Socio-demographic factors, reference groups, and the career orientations, career aspirations and career satisfaction of Canadian police officers." *American Journal of Police*, 14(2).

Coutts, Larry M. "Police hiring and promotion: methods and outcomes." *Canadian Police College Journal*, 14(2).

Cuadrado, Mary. (1995). "Female police officers: gender bias and professionalism." *American Journal of Police*, 14(2).

Doerner, William G. (1995). "Officer retention patterns: an affirmative action concern for police agencies?" *American Journal of Police*, 14(3/4).

Ellis, Reginald T. (1991). "Perceptions, attitudes and beliefs of police recruits." *Canadian Police College Journal*, 15(2).

Hale, D. (1992). "Women in policing." In Cordner, G. and D. Hale (eds.). *What works in policing: operations and administration examined*. Cincinnati, Ohio: Anderson Publishing.

Hargrave, G.E. and J.G. Berner. (1984). *POST psychological screening manual*. Sacramento, Calif.: California Commission on Police Officer Standards and Training.

Hay Management Consultants and Dennis Strong & Associates. (1993). *Police constable selection: community recruiting—selecting constables for the future: phase II final report recommended design of the new selection system*. [Toronto: Ontario Ministry of the Solicitor General and Correctional Services].

Horn, William G. (1975). *A study of police recruit training programs and the development of their curricula*. Unpublished doctoral dissertation, Michigan State University.

Krimmel, John T. (1996). "The performance of college-educated police: a study of self-rated police performance measures." *American Journal of Police*, 25(1).

Lowman, R.L. (1989). *Pre-employment screening for psychopathology: a guide to professional practice*. Florida: Professional Resource Exchange.

McKenna, Paul F. (1990a). "New demands mean police need improved training and education." *Carswell Police News*, 117.

McKenna, Paul F. (1990b). "To understand and cope: issues of multiculturalism and race in policing." *Carswell Police News*, 119.

McKenna, Paul F. (1990c). "Computers and word processors facilitate all phases of police training." *Carswell Police News*, 120.

McKenna, Paul F. (1990d). "Training police in a Charter-driven world." *Carswell Police News*, 121.

McKenna, Paul F. (1990e). "Firearms training is an ongoing need in modern policing." *Carswell Police News*, 122.

Morash, Merry and Jack R. Greene. (1986). "Evaluating women on patrol." *Evaluation Review*, 10(3).

Naismith, Clive et al. (1987). *A report on the constable training program: submitted by the Training Study Group*. Toronto: Ontario Police Commission.

Nelson, E.D. (1992). "Employment equity and the Red Queen's hypothesis: recruitment and hiring in western Canadian municipal police departments." *Canadian Police College Journal*, 16(3).

Normandeau, André and Barry Leighton. (1990). *A vision of the future of policing in Canada: police-challenge 2000: background document*. Ottawa: Solicitor General Canada.

Ontario. Ministry of the Solicitor General. Strategic Planning Committee on Police Training and Education. (1992a). *A police learning system for Ontario: final report and recommendations.* Toronto: The Ministry.

Ontario. Ministry of the Solicitor General. Strategic Planning Committee on Police Training and Education. (1992b). *Report on high impact learning methodologies.* Toronto: The Ministry.

Ontario. Ministry of the Solicitor General. Strategic Planning Committee on Police Training and Education. (1992c). *Report on police training and education in other jurisdictions.* Toronto: The Ministry.

Ontario. Ministry of the Solicitor General. Strategic Planning Committee on Police Training and Education. (1992d). *Report on consultations with the community on future policing and police training issues.* Toronto: The Ministry.

Ontario. Ministry of the Solicitor General. Strategic Planning Committee on Police Training and Education. (1992e). *Report on Ontario police community initial consultation.* Toronto: The Ministry.

Ontario. Ministry of the Solicitor General. Strategic Planning Committee on Police Training and Education. (1992f). *Report on private sector learning initiatives.* Toronto: The Ministry.

Ontario. Ministry of the Solicitor General. Strategic Planning Committee on Police Training and Education. (1992g). *Report on strategic learning requirements for police personnel.* Toronto: The Ministry.

Ontario. Ministry of the Solicitor General. Strategic Planning Committee on Police Training and Education. (1992h). *Report on the evaluation of adult learning in the workplace.* Toronto: The Ministry.

Ontario. Ministry of the Solicitor General. Strategic Planning Committee on Police Training and Education. (1992i). *Report on evaluating learning systems.* Toronto: The Ministry.

Ontario. Ministry of the Solicitor General. Strategic Planning Committee on Police Training and Education. (1992j). *Report on consultation with the police community on police specialties in the future.* Toronto: The Ministry.

Ontario. Ministry of the Solicitor General. Strategic Planning Committee on Police Training and Education. (1992k). *Report on future policing issues in Ontario.* Toronto: The Ministry.

Ontario. Ministry of the Solicitor General. Strategic Planning Committee on Police Training and Education. (1992l). *Report on relationship between higher education and police learning requirements.* Toronto: The Ministry.

Ontario. Task Force on Policing in Ontario. (1974). *The Task Force on Policing in Ontario: report to the Solicitor General.* Toronto: Solicitor General of Ontario.

Ontario. Task Force on Race Relations and Policing. (1992). *The report of the Race Relations and Policing Task Force.* Toronto: Solicitor General of Ontario.

Ontario. Task Force on the Racial and Ethnic Implications of Police Hiring, Training, Promotion and Career Development. (1980). *Policing in Ontario for the eighties: perceptions and reflections: report of the Task Force on the Racial and Ethnic Implications of Police Hiring, Training, Promotion and Career Development.* Toronto: Solicitor General of Ontario.

Shusta, Robert M. et al. (1995). *Multicultural law enforcement: strategies for peacekeeping in a diverse society.* Englewood Cliffs, N.J.: Prentice Hall.

Skiff, Dana Allen. (1976). *An approach to designing a police recruit training program reflecting the readiness to learn and the developmental tasks of the police recruit.* Unpublished thesis, Boston University, School of Education.

Trompetter, P.S. (1993). "Pre-employment psychological screening of violence-prone peace officer applicants." *The Journal of Criminal Law Enforcement,* 27(1): 16–19.

Vancouver Police Department. (1997). *"Make a difference every day": a policing career in the City of Vancouver.* Vancouver: Vancouver Police Department.

Walker, S. Gail. (1993). *The status of women in Canadian policing: 1993*. Ottawa: Solicitor General Canada.

Worden, Robert E. (1990). "A badge and a baccalaureate: policies, hypotheses, and further evidence." *Justice Quarterly*, 7(3).

TOWARD MORE LEARNING

One means of getting specific information on the recruitment policies and practices of an individual police service is to seek out their Web site. A growing number of departments are putting lots of detail in these locations to help potential candidates understand the minimum and special requirements for application. See Appendix III for a listing of Web sites that will help you locate departments you may be interested in contacting.

Also of value for background purposes are the annual reports of individual police services. These can be requested directly from the police department itself or acquired through a local public, university, or community college library.

Stansfield, Ronald T. (1996). *Issues in policing: a Canadian perspective*. Toronto: Thompson Educational Publishing.

A chapter of this recent work is focused on the training of police officers in Canada, and considers three basic types of police training systems: open, closed, and hybrid. The author applies some of the concepts of "spectrum psychology" to evaluate the appropriateness of current approaches to police training and finds them lacking in certain important areas of inclusiveness, empathy, and accountability.

Ontario. Ministry of the Solicitor General. Strategic Planning Committee on Police Training and Education. (1992). *A police learning system for Ontario: final report and recommendations*. Toronto: The Ministry.

This report contains the most extensive, recent study of police learning in Canada and holds a great deal of information that is of direct value to anyone wanting to better understand the learning requirements of a police constable. Additionally, the final report summarizes similar findings for other levels within a typical police department. In presenting a conceptual framework to lead the process of police learning, this report offers extensive guidance that is based on solid academic research, comparative analysis, and broadly based consultation.

CHAPTER FIVE

LEADERSHIP AT EVERY LEVEL:
FUNDAMENTALS
FOR POLICING

LEARNING OBJECTIVES

1. Identify a conceptual framework for understanding "leadership"
2. Describe ten aspects of leadership that deal with interaction with people
3. Describe six aspects of leadership that deal with managing information
4. Explain the ethical dimension of policing

INTRODUCTION

Much has been written on the topic of leadership (Bothwell, 1983; Burns, 1975; Janis, 1989; Larson and Mingie, 1992; Lunney, 1989; McKenna and Evans, 1995). Typically, there is some effort to distinguish leadership from management and to indicate that leadership is something that requires very special skills in areas that affect the effectiveness of senior executives. As this textbook is intended for those considering a career in policing in Canada, it may seem unusual to devote an entire chapter to a topic that appears to relate only to the upper layers of the organizational chart. However, the clear message that is intended here is simple: leadership qualities can be developed and displayed at all levels of an organization. The skills of leadership are not completely mysterious and can be refined by anyone with a clear understanding of those skills. This chapter is aimed at providing the basis for such an understanding, along with an encouragement to work toward their application within a Canadian policing context.

We will examine some of the existing literature on leadership and make connections between that literature and the field of law enforcement. In order to broaden the base of this understanding this chapter will reference a wide range of sources that offer insight into this important topic.

Also of critical significance to anyone attempting to build their own capacity for leadership within a police organization is the issue of ethics. In this chapter we will also consider the ethical dimension of policing and offer some helpful guidance on the construction and care of good character.

WHAT IS LEADERSHIP?

There are practically as many definitions of leadership as there are people who have taken the time to ponder its qualities and characteristics. What this presentation does *not* propose to do is offer a definitive outlook on this difficult topic. Instead, it will be more valuable to suggest some elements that can be used to help guide the growth of a personal approach to leadership and offer a conceptual framework within which to operate. The important message to be drawn from this treatment of the subject is that leadership is vitally important in the area of policing, and that with a clear notion of key aspects of leadership development everyone can work toward greater effectiveness in their working life.

Very simply put, leadership implies the possession of the qualities of a leader. A leader is someone who is equipped to move people and events toward some goal or objective. Within this simple framework it is not difficult to see how leadership qualities can appear in any number of circumstances and not necessarily only at the executive level.

RCMP Peacekeepers UN (July 1994, Ottawa)

Peter Bregg/Maclean's

LEADERSHIP SKILLS

As part of a review of leadership practices and skills, the Leadership Development Task Force under the auspices of the National Society for Performance and Instruction, an international human resources development organization based in Washington, D.C., prepared a preliminary report that divided the skills which they identified into two main categories:

- interactive/people managing skills; and
- information managing skills.

The task force proceeded to subdivide these two categories into specific areas of application which could be used as the basis for the design and delivery of programs to develop those skills within an organizational context (Hutchison et al., 1988). What follows is a summary of the task force's critical skills analysis.

INTERACTION WITH PEOPLE

INTERPERSONAL COMMUNICATIONS

This involves the content and quality of interactions among individuals or groups and can be directly observed or evaluated. Communication can take the form of face-to-face interaction or may be at a distance. It may include electronic or written communication and can be assessed in its immediate application or by its impact over time. It is important to emphasize that the recipient of the communication determines its effectiveness, not the originator of the communication.

NETWORKING

This relates to skill in undertaking exchanges between peers and colleagues that result in the sharing of information, advice, insight, resources, support and other elements which may be mutually beneficial. The extent of one's network of contacts can provide an indication of leadership potential while the ability to sustain and expand the reach of this network is also seen as being valuable.

LEADERSHIP

As a specific subset, leadership can be understood to be any behaviour which attempts to influence another person or group for the achievement of some defined end. A good leader may be found anywhere within an organization and has the capacity to coordinate group effort in working toward common goals and objectives.

NEGOTIATION SKILLS

This involves an ability to arrive at solutions which all participants can support and buy into as a result of discussion, deliberation, and consensus. It requires communication skills with a purpose and a capacity to reach an objective that transcends personal differences and disagreements.

CONFLICT MANAGEMENT

This skill allows someone to operate effectively in situations characterized by conflict. It implies that the people involved will be dealt with in ways that are respectful, but will still be motivated to move toward a resolution to the issues at hand. It includes an ability to honour the opinions and thoughts of others and maintain the dignity of the group and its parts while continuing to advance toward established goals and objectives. This may entail the need to develop alternative solutions that satisfy the broadest range of opinion within the group.

DELEGATION

This is a capacity to place trust in others so they can assume responsibility and have the capacity to undertake some action or task. Delegation is a strong force for positive motivation and should be done in ways that strengthen the skills of the person to whom activities are delegated. Effective delegation involves an ability to have the person fully understand the assignment being given and provide that person with the necessary tools to accomplish the delegated task.

PARTICIPATIVE MANAGEMENT

In practising good participative management, the individual is able to work effectively with groups and teams, exchange ideas and thoughts freely, and encourage involvement in the decisions and processes of the group. It also involves establishing levels of empowerment that provide clearly understood areas of responsibility, accountability, and capacity.

MOTIVATION

This calls for an ability to maintain one's own motivation in pursuit of established personal and/or organizational goals, as well as an understanding of the means by which other people may motivate themselves to turn their energies toward the attainment of shared goals and objectives. There is a clear understanding of the need for positive reinforcement and the delivery of meaningful, genuine, objective, and timely feedback tied to actual behaviour.

COACHING

Coaching involves applying skills in the areas of demonstrating, facilitating, guiding, instructing, and offering leadership by example. This skill is strongly related to good communication and should be guided by a performance plan that sets out specific behaviours for the person being coached. Coaching requires that the individual is able to encourage someone toward the development of an expected level of proficiency. It often involves inspiring and challenging improved performance over time and is normally based on the coach's high level of skill in the area of endeavour and a broad capacity for genuinely supportive, non-judgmental behaviour (Stowell, 1988).

MENTORING

Mentoring involves an ability to establish a sustained relationship with someone who possesses less skill or proficiency in order to move them toward higher levels of competence and confidence in a shared area of activity. This skill relies heavily on feedback and empathy to guide the person being mentored. It also requires that the mentor have strong listening skills, rapport, and be able to instill trust in order to foster a positive learning experience for all concerned.

MANAGING INFORMATION

SUBJECT MATTER CREDIBILITY

This category relates to a leader's skill in subject matter expertise. Credibility involves the assessment of peers, colleagues, superiors, subordinates and clients. This credibility could be established by writing in professional publications, instructing in the area of activity, making presentations on the subject, or being formally recognized for contributions in the field of policing. Increasing levels of responsibility and authority in the field of endeavour may also contribute to the perception of subject matter credibility.

PROBLEM SOLVING

The understanding and application of a problem-solving approach will follow an established pattern. There will be a more detailed discussion of this topic in Chapter 10 ("Leading Innovation in Canadian Policing"); however, problem solving normally follows a cycle characterized by scanning, analysis, response, and assessment. Skill in this area will be demonstrated by the formulation of appropriate, timely, cost-effective, and creative solutions to problems.

DECISION MAKING

This involves an ability to discriminate among a number of alternative solutions and select the solution that carries with it the greatest benefit and the least risk. It also implies an ability to take into account the possible constraints which can compromise the best decision that could be made if ideal circumstances were in place (Janis, 1989).

GOAL AND OBJECTIVE SETTING

Goal and objective setting requires an ability to determine and move toward group goals and objectives. This includes a capacity to clearly identify specific tasks that would be required for this purpose and to establish action plans for the completion of those tasks. It is related to consensus-building skills and operates in conjunction with time management capabilities and the ability to communicate clearly with colleagues.

PLANNING AND ORGANIZATION

The planning function involves an ability to design an anticipated future and to move effectively toward its realization. The process of planning involves an outline of the key issues to be addressed along with an analysis of a proposed direction, and the presentation of benefits and/or adverse consequences involved as well as assumptions, concerns, and resource implications of the plan. Frequently, planning is directly tied to the decision-making process and involves significant levels of consultation which must be factored into the timing of the planning process.

IMPLEMENTATION

This involves skill in putting into effect the actions which have been identified through the problem-solving process. Planning will normally establish an implementation strategy that will need to be followed, and perhaps revised, to address unforeseen issues or challenges. The skill required here is twofold: a capacity to follow an established schedule for action, and flexibility in order to identify the possible need for adaptation and/or modification of an existing plan to overcome difficulties or changing circumstances.

PROJECT AND TIME MANAGEMENT

Skills in various approaches that have been developed to guide a project from inception, through design and planning, to completion. It involves the management of people, time, resources, activities, and information in ways that are cost-effective and meet the expectations established for the project. Also required in this area of activity is an ability to prioritize and sequence related events in a way that will contribute to the efficient conclusion of the

Motorcycle traffic control (Toronto)

Peter Bregg/Maclean's

tasks involved in the project. An additional skill involves the recognition of, and respect for, the time constraints of others.

Another way to view the required elements of leadership is according to the following "Leadership Grid," which charts various qualities in terms of their specific focus:

FIGURE 5-1

LEADERSHIP GRID

Job-centred Qualities
- resourceful
- accomplishment-oriented
- decisive
- quickly processes new information

Team-centred Qualities
- leads peers and subordinates
- fosters environment that promotes growth
- deals with problems among team members
- attracts quality team members

Interpersonal Qualities
- develops and sustains strong relationships
- demonstrates compassion and sensitivity
- maintains personal composure
- deals directly with individuals and groups

Self-possessed Qualities
- balances personal life with work commitments
- demonstrates self-awareness
- makes people comfortable in a variety of settings
- demonstrates flexibility in changing situations

THE ETHICAL DIMENSION OF POLICING

The topic of ethics is central to any complete understanding about leadership in policing in Canada. There has been an enormous increase in the level of interest in this topic generally (Kernaghan, 1994a). With regard to the policing profession, it has never been more critical that the ethical dimension be fully and properly understood. Edwin Delattre (1994) presents this point in the following manner:

> The mission of policing can safely be entrusted only to those who grasp what is morally important and who respect integrity. Without this kind of personal character in police, no set of codes or rules or laws can safeguard that mission from the ravages of police misconduct. No one need choose to be a police officer or to bear the public trust; but those who do—no matter how naively and no matter how misguided their original expectations—must acquire the excellence of character necessary to live up to it. (p. 15)

With serious questions being raised in the public mind around standards of police accountability, with concerns about the use of force by police officers, and with serious debate over the proper use of police discretion, it is not surprising that the ethical dimension

FIGURE 5-2

DYNAMICS OF POLICE INTEGRITY

Dynamics of Police Integrity

External Forces Impacting Police Department

- Civilian Complaint Board
- Media
- Political Influence
- Community Demands
- Other Sectors, Criminal Justice System

Departmental Forces Impacting Police Personnel

- Promotion System
- Leadership, Chief/Commanders
- Reward Structure
- Departmental Values/Policies
- Accountability System
- Quality of Supervision
- Disciplinary System
- Inservice Training
- Entry-Level Training
- Selection/Hiring Process

Police Officer's Career

Personal Forces Impacting Police Personnel

- Economy/Personal Finances
- Diversity Issues in Department
- Family Values/Moral Literacy
- Experience with Aggressive Police Tactics
- Police Subculture
- Community Response to Police Activities and Presence
- Frustration with Criminal Justice System
- Peer Influence
- Alcohol/Drug Abuse

Graphic: Jennifer S. Novecio

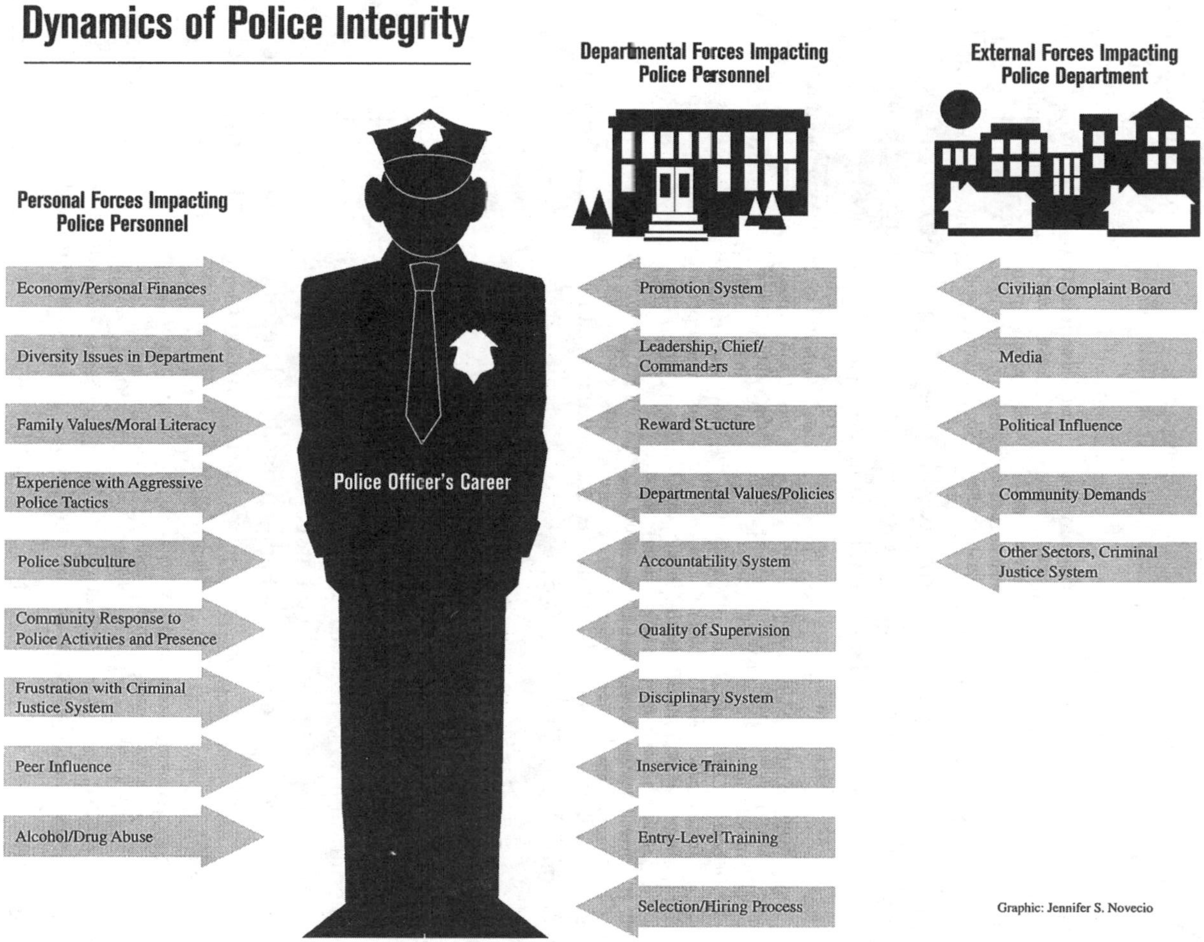

Adapted from: Gaffigan, Stephen J. and Phyllis P. McDonald. (_997). *Police integrity: public service with honor: a partnership between the National Institute of Justice and the Office of Community Oriented Policing Services.* Washington, D.C.: U.S. Dept. of Justice. p. 92. Used with permission.

of policing has become an important concern for police leaders. Many police departments are investing a significant effort in reviewing their training, education, and development programs in the ethics of policing to ensure that their members are fully versed in the highest standards of responsible service. Because many police departments are moving to flattened organizational structures, with fewer supervisors to manage across a wider span of responsibility, it is critical that individual officers have the character and moral stability to guide their own behaviour in accordance with those high standards.

Because police officers are held to incredibly high standards of behaviour and are subject to extensive internal and external oversight and scrutiny by a number of governing authorities and oversight bodies, it has been suggested that police departments should not be a mere microcosm of the society which they serve (Delattre, 1994). By being selective, police organizations attempt to ensure that they are attracting people who will operate at elevated ethical and moral levels. As Delattre (1994) says:

> A police department is selective—the more selective, the better. People born into a society do not have to meet eligibility requirements and standards, submit to background investigations, complete instructional programs, undertake probationary terms and field training, learn and perform in accordance with departmental policies, cooperate with internal investigations, or, ultimately, retire from service. Police do. In every good department, such features elevate the department and its sworn and civilian personnel beyond the norms for society as a whole. (p. 228)

Figure 5–2 offers a useful overview of some of the dynamics of police integrity and their effects on an individual officer's career.

CONCLUSION

Given the extreme importance of developing good leadership skills, it is essential that police organizations in Canada do whatever they can to ensure that they select candidates for recruitment who demonstrate leadership qualities or who show evidence of being capable of growing into competent, capable, and conscientious leaders in the future. Because police service is such a highly refined, and heavily empowered form of public service, it is critical that police officers learn from the outset that they have a special burden of trust and responsibility to protect the public good and to uphold the law in an ethical and professional manner.

With major changes facing the ways in which policing will be delivered in Canada in the years to come, it is important that those charged with the powers and obligations to provide that service have the best leadership available at all levels in their respective organizations. This challenge is profound and will offer great satisfaction to those who undertake it with purpose and resolve.

QUESTIONS FOR CONSIDERATION

1. What are some of the differences between management skills and leadership skills?
2. Identify some ways in which a police constable could refine their communication skills.
3. What would be the qualities that a police department should look for in selecting a coach officer for the guidance of new recruits?
4. What kinds of ethical questions should a police service be concerned about when interviewing applicants for police recruitment?
5. Discuss the personal, internal, and external aspects of police integrity. Should there be limits on the ethical standards set for police officers?
6. Are there differences in the levels of police corruption across Canada? How does Canada compare to other countries with regard to police corruption?
7. Discuss the issue of a police officer's right to a private life.

REFERENCES

Bothwell, L. (1983). *The art of leadership: skill building techniques that produce results*. Englewood Cliffs, N.J.: Prentice Hall.

Burns, James McGregor. (1975). *Leadership*. New York. Harper and Row.

Delattre, Edwin J. (1994). *Character and cops: ethics in policing. 2nd ed.* Washington, D.C.: The AEI Press, Publisher for the American Enterprise Institute.

Gaffigan, Stephen J. and Phyllis P. McDonald. (1997). *Police integrity: public service with honor: a partnership between the National Institute of Justice and the Office of Community Oriented Policing Services*. Washington, D.C.: U.S. Dept. Of Justice.

Hutchison, Cathleen et al. (1988). *The Leadership Development Task Force: preliminary report*. Washington, D.C.: National Society for Performance and Instruction.

Ingstrup, Ole. (1995). *The strategic revolution in executive development: what does it mean for you and your organization?* Ottawa: Canadian Centre for Management Development.

Janis, Irving L. (1989). *Crucial decisions: leadership in policymaking and crisis management*. New York: The Free Press.

Kernaghan, Kenneth. (1994a). "The emerging public service culture: values, ethics, and reforms." *Canadian Public Administration*, 37(4).

Kernaghan, Kenneth. (1994b). "Ethics: do they provide a core of stability in a changing world?" In *Perspectives on public management: values in the public service*. Ottawa: Canadian Centre for Management Development.

Kouzes, James. (1988). "Learning to lead." In Dixon, George. *What works at work: lessons from the masters*. Minneapolis: Lakewood Books.

Larson, Peter and Robert Mingie. (1992). *Leadership for a changing world: developing executive capability*. Ottawa: Conference Board of Canada and Canadian Centre for Management Development.

Lunney, Robert. (1989). "The role of the police leader in the 21st century." In Loree, Donald J. (ed.). *Future issues in policing: symposium proceedings*. Ottawa: The Canadian Police College.

MacDonald, Victor N. (1986). *A study of leadership and supervision in policing*. Ottawa: The Canadian Police College.

Manion, John L. (1989). *A management model*. Ottawa: Canadian Centre for Management Development.

McKenna, Paul F. and Donald G. Evans. (1995). "Leadership as learning: learning as leadership." *The Police Governor*, 5(2).

Schein, Edgar. (1985). *Organizational culture and leadership*. San Francisco: Jossey-Bass

Scissons, Ed. (1988). *Police leadership part I: inter-personal decision making*. Ottawa: The Canadian Police College.

Scissons, Ed. (1990). *Police leadership part II: organizational decision making*. Ottawa: Canadian Police College.

Stayer, Ralph. (1990). "How I learned to let my workers lead." *Harvard Business Review*, 68(6).

Stowell, Steven J. (1988). "Coaching: a commitment to leadership." *Training and Development Journal*, 42(6).

Teal, Thomas. (1996). "The human side of management." *Harvard Business Review*, 74(6).

Wheatley, Margaret J. (1994). *Leadership and the new science: learning about organization from an orderly universe*. San Francisco: Berrett-Koehler Publishers.

TOWARD MORE LEARNING

LEADERSHIP

Sashkin, Marshall. (1990). *The visionary leader: leader behavior questionnaire. 3rd ed.(Self)*. King of Prussia, Penn.: Organization Design and Development, Inc.

This is an excellent means by which individuals can begin to assess their leadership qualities. It is a questionnaire that is designed to produce information on your personal approach to the process of leadership. It contains 50 basic statements that describe leadership behaviours, characteristics, or the impact that a leader may have on an organization. By indicating how true each statement is for you, it is possible to measure your own leadership behaviours and characteristics. Dr. Sashkin's approach is based on the work and research of James McGregor Burns, who first identified leaders as those individuals who create visions that are capable of transforming both people and organizations. This questionnaire is also based on the writings of Warren Bennis, who spent a great deal of time and energy interviewing the chief executive officers of America's largest corporations. Other sources of insight for Sashkin were Dr. David McClelland of Harvard University and Dr. Elliot

Jacques, an organizational psychologist. These various sources have been combined into a very useful tool for developing a personal insight on your leadership capabilities and, as a result, finding appropriate ways for enhancing and directing those capabilities. The questionnaire may be accompanied by separate publication by Dr. Sashkin, entitled, *Becoming a visionary leader.* This booklet places the questionnaire into an appropriate context with other related historical models, provides a definition of "visionary leadership," and offers further explanation of the interpretive material in the *Leader Behavior Questionnaire.*

Copies of the *Leader Behavior Questionnaire* and *Becoming a visionary leader* can be acquired in Canada through:

Organizational Learning Resources
200 Edgeley Blvd., Unit 16
Concord, Ontario
Canada L4K 3Y8
Tel.: (905) 669-6759
Fax.: (905) 669-9132

ETHICAL DIMENSION OF POLICING

Delattre, Edwin J. (1994). *Character and cops: ethics in policing. 2nd ed.* Washington, D.C.: The AEI Press, Publisher for the American Enterprise Institute.

This is a superb book dealing with a wealth of issues related to the important topic of ethics and morality in the field of policing. Dr. Edwin Delattre is a professor of education and philosophy at Boston University and has written and lectured extensively to police officers. His experience with members of the police profession is evident in his many writings and he is a frequent lecturer at the FBI Academy in Quantico, Virginia. This book includes a useful appendix that provides "A Guide to the Further Study of Ethics in Policing" that offers suggestions for books and periodicals to assist the student who is interested in this topic to pursue their learning.

CHAPTER SIX

THE BASICS OF POLICE ADMINISTRATION

LEARNING OBJECTIVES

1. Identify the elements of a "system"
2. Apply a systems theory to policing in Canada
3. Explain key elements of the system of policing in a Canadian context
4. Explain the idea of police independence in Canada
5. Understand the advantages and disadvantages of the concept of unity of command
6. Describe the differences between police command and control and empowerment

INTRODUCTION

When looked at as a service that is in the "business" of providing crime prevention, law enforcement, public order maintenance, emergency response, and assistance to victims of crime, it is not difficult to understand that police administration is not far removed from the administration or management of *any* organization which provides a service to the public. As a result, police departments have become increasingly engaged in the process of looking beyond their own discipline for insight, guidance, and inspiration for making improvements in the ways they go about doing their job. Of course, it is always important to remember that police organizations have special characteristics which distinguish their activities and actions from other fields; however, in thinking about the improvement of human performance and interaction, there is much to be learned from the broadest understanding available (Martin, 1995).

This chapter will look at a systems theory of organization and will place Canadian policing into this framework. It will also consider the concept of accountability as it has developed in a Canadian context and examine the ways in which we have attempted to ensure that our police are fully accountable to the public which they are sworn to serve. The topic of police independence will be considered with some explanation about the tension that exists between accountability and independence in the context of modern policing.

The basic elements of hierarchy, span of responsibility, delegation of authority, empowerment, specialization, and chain of command will all be considered in some detail as they relate to the administration of police organizations in Canada. Because these elements form the fundamentals of police administration in Canada and are in a state of change, it is important to have a good understanding of their relevance and meaning to the business of policing. Some reference will be made to the literature that has developed in the area of organizational leadership and business management which should help guide the reader to a better understanding of current theory and practice that is informing police administrators and decision makers.

A SYSTEMS THEORY OF ORGANIZATION

In her book, *Leadership and the new science*, Margaret Wheatley (1994) makes a useful observation about where we are in our thinking about organizations:

> Our concept of organizations is moving away from the mechanistic creations that flourished in the age of bureaucracy. We have begun to speak in earnest of more fluid, organic structures, even of boundaryless organizations. We are beginning to recognize organizations as systems, construing them as "learning organizations" and crediting them with some type of self-renewing capacity. These are our first, tentative forays into a new appreciation for organizations. My own experience suggests that we can forego the despair created by such common organizational events as change, chaos, information overload, and cyclical behaviors if we recognize that organizations are conscious entities, possessing many of the properties of living systems. (p. 13)

What Wheatley is referring to above is the idea that organizations should be viewed as whole entities where the component parts are seen as operating together in an interdependent way, rather than as isolated, independent operations. This systems approach to organizations is not altogether new; however, it has been considerably refined over the last few years with new discoveries in the areas of quantum physics, chaos theory, and the study of self-organizing systems (Wheatley, 1994).

There is some immediate evidence that by viewing the organization as a system, it is far easier to understand ways to help people become more effective within the processes of that organization. By concentrating on the human element of organizations, it is possible to develop approaches to organizational life that make better use of all of the resources available to the organization. In policing, while this understanding has some important complications, many police services are beginning to see the value of taking a systems view of their "business." As a result, they are breaking new ground with regard to the delivery of service and the quality of life for their employees. There will be more attention paid to these kinds of innovative approaches in Chapter 10; however, it is worth noting that a systems approach to organizations has opened the door to major change in many police departments.

One major contributor to the concept of systems thinking is Peter Senge, the author of an important and influential book, *The fifth discipline*. He observes in a recent publication (1994) that:

> During the last few years, a new understanding of the process of organizational change has emerged. It is not top-down or bottom-up, but participative at all levels—aligned through common understanding of a system. This is possible because archetypes and other system-oriented tools have put system dynamics language into the hands of teams and on the walls of meeting rooms, where they can energize organizational learning at all levels. People are also exploring systems thinking in learning laboratories which fit their own cases and needs. (p. 89)

It is possible to look at most groupings of people and activities and see quite quickly how they are interconnected in ways that resemble a system. The family, for example, is a *system* where the behaviour, attitudes, actions, and beliefs of one member of the family will have an influence on the other members of the family. Not always will such family systems operate smoothly, but the impact of one part of the system on the others is fairly easy to see in the routines of daily life. We refer in common speech to such things as a subway system, or a mass transit system, knowing that the parts of the whole are designed to operate together in some manner that increases our convenience, efficiency, safety, or well-being. In the case of a mass transit system, we expect that the routes will be somehow interrelated to provide for easy access within the geographic area being served. There is some expectation that it will be possible to transfer from one part of the system to another with minimal difficulty. For example, having taken a street car along one portion of your route, you are then able to easily transfer to a bus to complete another portion of your trip. Clearly, one of the drawbacks of a system is that any serious malfunction or problem with one part of the system will likely be experienced, to some degree, across the entire system. Therefore, in our mass transit example, if there is a power failure on the subway line, this may cause delays and backups that will affect the other parts of the system, requiring some form of special response to overcome the initial slowdown.

In everyday life we often talk about systems. Consider the following examples:

- solar system;
- ecosystem;
- computer system;
- education system;
- human immune system;
- circulatory system;
- library system;
- water system; and
- criminal justice system.

What is also true about systems is that they are frequently made up of identifiable subsystems which operate within their own spheres of activity. For example, a mass transit system may be made up of a number of subsystems which operate along parallel and interconnected lines. These subsystems could include: highways, expressways, and toll roads; a network of surface buses; street cars, trolleys, or light rapid transit (LRT) vehicles; a subway; ferries, or other watercraft for the transport of people or vehicles; short take-off and landing (STOL) commuter aircraft; and any other mode of transport which could be part of the larger transit system.

When looking at systems or subsystems, it is valuable to consider the interrelationships that are affecting the component parts. In order to provide an efficient and effective system, attention should be paid to the best operation of the individual parts in relation to the whole. A highly efficient element of a system may not contribute to overall success if it does not operate smoothly with the other parts of the system. For example, a heart that pumps huge quantities of blood at an enormous rate is not going to be very useful if the arteries which carry that blood cannot handle this rapid rate, nor if the parts of the body which receive this blood cannot process it and dispense with waste at a similar rate. Systems are judged by the coordination and cooperation between the parts of that system. Everything needs to be placed in some kind of balance to make the system work properly. This requires constant monitoring.

In the computer world, the requirement for constant vigilance over the system is one reason why there is such an enormous demand for systems analysts. These are people whose skill is directed at examining the computer hardware, software, and networks in an organization and making judgments about their proper linkage and combination. The interdependence of an organization's computer network is most clearly highlighted when there is a problem, for example, when the system "crashes." In policing, it is possible to view the police department as a system of interdependent parts working together smoothly in order to deliver a professional service that is directed at public safety, law enforcement, crime prevention, public order maintenance, assistance to victims of crime, and emergency response. All the parts of the system need to be operating in a coordinated fashion for this wide-ranging service to be delivered in an efficient and effective manner. Figure 6–1, below, shows the basic component parts of any system that has some feedback mechanism, also known as a "closed-loop system."

In order to best understand how a system works, it is helpful to remember the component parts listed above. The *inputs* supply the system with whatever is required to undertake the *processes* that characterize the system. Once these inputs have been processed they become *outputs* that can be judged according to some standard, and the resulting *feedback* is folded back into the system for determining if the system is operating properly or if modifications are required.

CANADIAN POLICE ORGANIZATIONS AS SYSTEMS

In Canada, police organizations may be seen as fairly complex systems made up of a number of equally complex subsystems which must operate together in ways that require significant amounts of coordinated attention and expertise. Because we have already seen in

FIGURE 6-1

CLOSED-LOOP SYSTEM

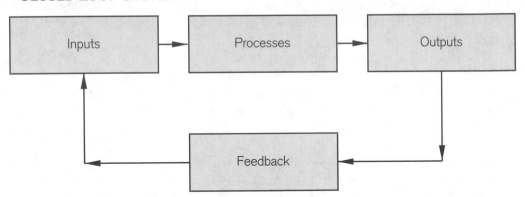

Chapter 2 that police organizations in Canada are part of a larger context that includes so-cial, political, legal, and technological elements, it is not difficult to begin to understand the complexities of modern police management in Canada. By applying the template of a systems theory to policing, however, it is possible to break these systems and subsys-tems down into component parts in order to look at their various inputs, processes, out-puts, and feedback mechanisms. As a result of this capacity to focus on the individual parts, it becomes easier to understand not only how the parts operate and to think about their effectiveness, but it is also possible to understand the whole as something resulting from the combination of these component parts. Although there will be more discussion on the value of "systems thinking" as applied to policing in Canada presented in Chapter 10, it is useful to consider the following representation of a system within which policing in Canada currently operates:

As presented in a very simple manner in Figure 6–2, police organizations in Canada are part of a large complex system, which can be called "society." In this instance, we have subdivided society into a series of smaller groupings that attempt to capture the range of subsystems with which a police organization in Canada will normally have to interact in some meaningful way. These groupings include all levels of government, the business realm, special interest groups (which may be funded by governments or private interests), the media (which may be seen as a particular offshoot of the business realm), a wide range of public and private institutions (which could include hospitals, schools, colleges, universities, agencies, boards, commissions, foundations, charities, etc.), and the private security sector (which, again, may be seen as a special category within the business subsystem).

There is meant to be some interrelationship between the various components of the system and the police. In making this representation more complete it may be helpful to think of the aspects of the criminal justice system, for example, as being embedded in the areas represented by both the federal and provincial governments. Clearly, the federal courts and corrections are included in that system, with the provincial courts and the

FIGURE 6-2

CANADIAN POLICING AS PART OF A SYSTEM

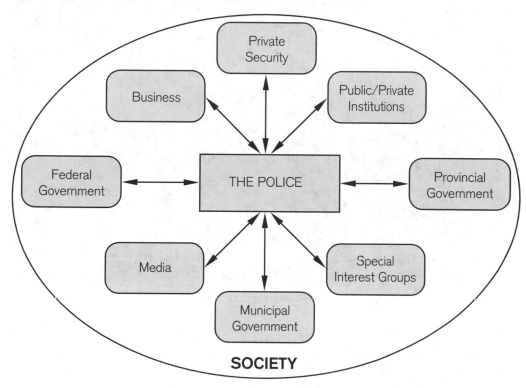

prisons as part of the system operating at that level of government. This representation is meant to capture some of the key elements of the larger system within which policing in Canada operates and to help understand that the police in this country by no means function in isolation. There will be more discussion about the topic of police independence later in this chapter; however, the emphasis in this presentation is on the interdependence of police organizations with other parts of society at large.

ACCOUNTABILITY

The notion of accountability is extremely important in the context of policing in Canada. In fact the effectiveness of any system of policing will hinge on the capacity of that system to have in place mechanisms or processes that ensure there is accountability for the delivery of this service. The concept of accountability can best be understood by going to any number of sources for guidance. One valuable source is the Royal Commission on Financial Management and Accountability (1979):

Chris Schwarz/Maclean's

Ontario Public Service Employees Union (OPSEU) demonstration (March 29, 1996, Toronto)

Accountability is the essence of our democratic form of government. It is the liability assumed by those who exercise authority to account for the manner in which they have fulfilled responsibilities entrusted to them, a liability ultimately to the Canadian people owed by Parliament, by the Government and, thus, every government department and agency. (p. 21)

In a recent work on accountability, Guy Leclerc and his colleagues (1996) note that it has drawn meaning and content from a number of areas and disciplines, including political theory, philosophy, religious studies, sociology, management, and public administration. What is valuable from a policing perspective is that, fundamentally, accountability rests upon two explicit elements: expectations and specific performance. Within the current climate of concern for clear accountability standards, there is renewed interest in performance measurement, that is, precise methods for evaluating what has been done to meet the specific responsibilities which have been assigned. An earlier study of management and accountability in the Ontario Government by Price Waterhouse (1985) frames the matter quite well, with an added note about the consequences of poor performance:

We regard the accountability structure or framework within government as the set of relationships through which

- responsibility and authority are delegated by one organization or person to another;
- a base of objectives, expectations and performance review is established for the exercise of that responsibility or authority;

- a rendering of account take place; and
- approval or discipline may ensue.

All four of these elements should be present for a true accountability relationship to exist. (pp. 2–3)

Basically, police organizations in Canada are accountable to the public. More specifically, within their precise area of jurisdiction, they are accountable to a local governing authority that is put in place for this purpose (Stenning, 1981). In some jurisdictions this will be a police services board, a committee of municipal council, a Minister of Justice or Solicitor General, or a board of commissioners of police. In any event, police organizations are part of a system that holds them to account for their policies, programs, procedures, personnel, purchases, priorities, and practices. The issue of accountability is one which has come under close scrutiny in recent years as citizens and the governments that represent them have begun to call for higher levels of feedback and justification from the public sector, including police services. In Canada, the accountability framework can be seen in two forms which, although they overlap in some applications, can be distinguished in terms of their purpose and processes:

- civilian governing authorities; and
- oversight of police activity.

CIVILIAN GOVERNING AUTHORITIES

Civilian governing authorities provide police departments with some forum for directing the overall goals and objectives of that department and constitute a link with the community that is being served (Hann et al., 1985). It can be viewed as the process of engaging the public in the formulation and implementation of broad policies that will guide the police service (Reiner, 1995). This form of police accountability has a long tradition in Canada. For example, municipal boards for police departments were established in Ontario as early as 1858. The style of civilian governing authority varies across Canada; however, the general thrust of what these authorities do is largely consistent. Whether these authorities are police services boards (as in Ontario), provincial police commissions, committees of council, boards of commissioners of police, or any other form, they all have some role to play in expressing the public interest in policing and taking part in the general good government of policing within their jurisdiction. Martin (1995) provides a useful overview of the role of governing authorities with respect to police accountability:

> One can summarize with the suggestion that, where boards impose accountability on the department, they do so in areas of administration and have been restrained, or otherwise held aloof, from more specialized or functional aspects. So accountability is but a partial thing; boards do not set policing policies so much as rely on the chief to ensure that these are in place and effectively implemented; they restrict themselves to the efficiencies of management and do not intrude into the policing area itself. (p. 164)

In practice, there is some difficulty experienced by conscientious, local governing authorities when they attempt to distinguish between broad guidelines for the efficient management of a police service and those that might have an impact on the *operational* policies of the department. Because management and operations are linked in a consistent continuum of policy formulation, implementation, and evaluation, the governing authority and senior police personnel often clash over the appropriate division of responsibilities (Martin, 1995). This area of uncertainty with regard to where the governing authority's responsibilities stop, and where the chief's professional expertise begins, is highlighted in the current wording of Section 31 of the Ontario *Police Services Act*, where the responsibilities of municipal police services boards are set out:

> A board is responsible for the provision of police services and for law enforcement and crime prevention in the municipality and shall,
>
> (a) appoint the members of the municipal police force;
> (b) generally determine, after consultation with the chief of police, objectives and priorities with respect to police services in the municipality;
> (c) establish policies for the effective management of the police force;
> (d) recruit and appoint the chief of police and any deputy chief of police, and annually determine their remuneration and working conditions, taking their submissions into account;
> (e) direct the chief of police and monitor his or her performance; ....

This partial listing of board responsibilities clearly shows that there is room for confusion and debate about the precise nature of the board's activities in guiding the police service and directing the chief of police. There is certainly an implication in this legislation that the board may extend itself deeply into the policy areas of "law enforcement" and "crime prevention" which can be distinguished from the realm of "police services" that appears to be the express preserve of the chief of police.

The need for higher levels of civilian governance of policing has grown over the last 30 years, with a movement away from the profound fears of undue political interference that were put forward in many discussions around this topic. The experience in the United States, where police departments were attempting to free themselves from what was seen as the corrupting influences of local partisan politics, has given way to a better understanding of the need for police services to be fully accountable and responsible to the public they serve and from whom they receive their authority and their considerable funding.

The issue of an appropriate model for civilian governance of policing in Canada is one that has generated some considerable attention (Oppal, 1994). The whole question of governance has provoked thought and research both in the private realm and in our many and varied public institutions. The need for responsible civilian governance of the police is fairly clear. The precise form which it should take may vary from jurisdiction to jurisdiction, bearing in mind Reiner's (1995) observation:

> To secure democratic accountability policing should be organized and controlled fundamentally on a local basis. This both facilitates responsiveness to local communities (and their varying priorities) and provides countervailing pressures against the dangers of a monolithic concentration of coercive state power. (p. 78)

Ken Kerr/Toronto Sun

Official meeting of a local police services board

OVERSIGHT OF POLICE ACTIVITY

The second category of police accountability may be seen in those mechanisms established to ensure that *individual* members of a police department follow the law and observe departmental policies and procedures in the execution of their duties. This may also be viewed as a form of accountability through the establishment of codes of conduct, disciplinary procedures, and a system for handling public complaints. The value of a general principle of police accountability through civilian oversight was articulated in Ontario's recent review of police services (Ontario. Ministry of the Solicitor General and Correctional Services, 1996):

> Today, the need for an established and transparent system of oversight of police has been universally accepted by government, the police, and the communities they serve. It is recognized that the ability of the police to protect the community and to apprehend those who break the law relies, in large measure, on the trust and co-operation of the public. The police would be profoundly hindered in the performance of their duties without the willing support of the public. (p. 56)

Because of the extensive discretion accorded to police officers in the application of their common law and statutory powers, there is strong justification for the development of standards of accountability that will deal directly and adequately with concerns about police misconduct. In order to satisfy the public interest in this area, policies and procedures for the oversight of individual police behaviour have been a central issue in the arena of police reform. Any system of police oversight should include the following elements:

- independence;
- fairness; and
- objectivity.

It is essential that while the police themselves have a profound role in the oversight of their operational mandate and the management of their own human resources, there must also be a pivotal civilian presence in the police oversight process to warrant public trust in the system. This presence, however, must not be at the expense of effectiveness, efficiency, and economy. Therefore, many jurisdictions are carefully examining their systems to ensure that disciplinary, public complaints, monitoring, investigative, adjudicative, and appellate processes have adequate levels of accountability and transparency, but do not become overly burdensome on individual officers or the public purse. In Ontario, the Attorney General began a review of the province's system of civilian oversight of police. The purpose of this review, in late 1996, was to develop recommendations based on research to:

- streamline oversight processes;
- eliminate unnecessary duplication within the system; and
- improve accountability to civilian authority.

INDEPENDENCE

In the Canadian context the idea of police independence has had a long history. The understanding currently applied in most organizations has its roots in the British experience and the decisions of various courts which have largely viewed the police as deserving high levels of independence from direct political control, particularly in their day-to-day operations. This perspective has come under increasing scrutiny from a number of sources (Hann et al., 1985; Stenning, 1995; Stenning, Briggs, and Crouch, 1996). Within police organizations, however, the strongly held view remains that police professionals should operate independently of political control that may be exercised over other departments which do not have such a high level of responsibility for the maintenance of order, public safety, and the enforcement of the law.

Because the police perform duties which derive from the common law and specific statutes, it is often maintained that they are not answerable to their civic authorities, but to the law and the courts (Stenning, 1981). Since the provinces hold constitutional responsibility for the administration of justice, derived from section 92 of the *Constitution Act, 1867*, it is further held that police are accountable to this level of authority.

In its thorough examination of the larger topic of police governance, Mr. Justice Oppal's Commission of Inquiry on Policing in British Columbia (1995) made the following observation about police independence that is broadly applicable throughout Canada:

> The Inquiry recognizes that the police have the professional expertise to know when and how to investigate alleged criminal behavior and,...what evidence is required to support a criminal charge...Citizens must be protected from abuses that may result from political interference in police investigations. On the other hand, the police cannot be a law unto themselves. Any system of governance that grants independence to police in the exercise of their special powers must also ensure that the police are accountable for their conduct. (p. B-6)

HIERARCHY

In modern organizations, hierarchy refers to a structured pattern of authority, where one level, or person, has power over another. The word, taken from the Greek, literally means, "the rule of the temple," and has its in origins in a time when the religious order guided all aspects of life. Today, it merely refers to some form of structure within which people operate. The number of levels within an organization will determine the extent to which it is hierarchical. For example, in Figure 6–3, the first of the two organizations is more hierarchical than the second one presented:

The first diagram in Figure 6–3 has a high level of hierarchy: the chief of police at the top of the structure and constables at the bottom, with four levels of hierarchy in between. The second diagram, with the same total number of personnel, has a much less hierarchical structure. Again, the chief of police is placed at the top, the constables at the bottom; however, there is only one level of hierarchy in between. While neither of these presentations is absolutely realistic, it does highlight significantly different results from two approaches to hierarchy in a police organization.

One author who has written extensively on the impact of hierarchy on organizations is Elliott Jacques. He notes that modern management theorists have a tendency to disparage both hierarchy and bureaucracy; however, Jacques takes a different view. He makes an argument in favour of hierarchy and notes that it is the *only* way to structure modern work in a unified, systematic, and coherent way (Jacques, 1990). The focus of his understanding of hierarchy is the fact that organizations employ and pay *individuals* to do work, in spite of the great benefits that have been seen in the creation and empowerment of *teams*. Jacques points out that the real nature of the present systems of employment rests firmly on this individual basis. As a result, innovations which do not sufficiently take stock of the importance of actually getting work done through individuals will improve neither overall organizational, nor individual, effectiveness. For Jacques (1990), managerial hierarchy:

> ...is and will remain the only way to structure unified working systems with hundreds, thousands, or tens of thousands of employees, for the very good reason that managerial hierarchy is the expression of two fundamental characteristics of real work. First, the tasks we carry out are not only more or less complex but they also become more complex as they separate out into discrete categories or types of complexity. Second, the same is true of the mental work that people do on the job.... (p. 129)

Because of the complexity and broad-ranging scope of modern police work in Canada, and, combined with the extreme emphasis on systems of accountability and oversight, it would appear that policing in this country requires a degree of hierarchy that will permit effective function and appropriate structure.

CHAIN OF COMMAND

The concept of a chain of command comes directly from the military model of organization. It is a formal arrangement that establishes the lines of communication that exist

FIGURE 6-3

TWO POLICE ORGANIZATIONS WITH DIFFERENT LEVELS OF HIERARCHY

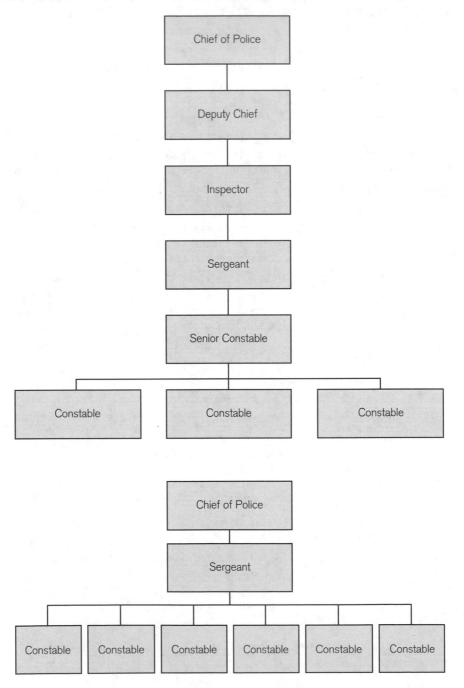

within a police department (Sheehan and Cordner, 1995). The thinking behind this model is that authority flows from the top of the organization down through increasingly subordinate ranks. Also known as the *scalar principle*, it creates a direct path of order and responsibility which can be seen in any organizational chart (Sheehan and Cordner, 1995). This chart is a diagram of the chain of command and tells the observer where a particular position on the chart reports to, and where that position, in turn, reports. Our examples of hierarchy in Figure 6–3 show two different chains of command; however, both include a strict reporting structure with a clear path of communication. A chain of command is expected to work in two directions: top-to-bottom and bottom-to-top. Therefore, it is as much a breach of the chain of command rule for the chief of police to give a direct communication to a constable, as it would be for that constable to provide a formal communication directly to the chief of police without passing through the intervening levels, or ranks, in the chain of command. While it is possible to reduce the levels of management and supervision that are contained in the chain of command, there should be fairly strict rules in place about the flow of information, instructions, and intelligence throughout the organizational structure. If the formal chain of command can be ignored for these purposes it is not an effective and efficient structure for conducting the business of the organization and should be revised.

If the organizational structure is suited to the needs and requirements of the department, then it should be closely adhered to in order to reinforce the chain of command and ensure that everyone in the process is included. We will learn more about adjustments to the chain of command and hierarchy in police organizations in Chapter 10; however, it should be understood that the command and control structure of police organizations was originally developed, and continues to be respected, for some extremely important reasons which relate both to officer safety and the protection of the public's well-being.

UNITY OF COMMAND

Organizational theory has traditionally stated that every individual employee should report to only one supervisor or "boss." This was usually known as the principle of unity of command. In policing, this would mean that a constable would receive orders and instructions from a sergeant/supervisor and would, in turn, report their activities only to that sergeant/supervisor. This one-to-one relationship became a convention of police administrative practice. The principle of unity of command has been defended by Souryal (1985) because it:

- strengthens the organization's authority and control;
- assists in determining responsibility for action, especially in crisis situations;
- facilitates communication and reduces confusion and contradictory orders; and
- enhances effective supervision of staff.

However, with modifications to the current theories of organizational development, the principle of unity of command has come under scrutiny and is often criticized because it:

- prevents employees from gaining advice and insight from other staff who are not immediate supervisors;
- extends the time it takes for communications to move through the hierarchy of the organization;
- offers potential for demoralizing staff when they must deal with uncooperative supervisors;
- diminishes the value of front-line staff; and
- promotes inflexibility.

Current organizational thinking tends to support a less rigid approach to command structures. However, in crisis situations, there remains a fairly high expectation from police managers and the public that unity of command will be adhered to for purposes of accountability. Where circumstances do not require rigorous command and control processes, the principle of unity of command may be appropriately relaxed. Because there are occasions when a more flexible approach may be highly effective, particularly in terms of proactive, problem-solving, or community policing, the principle of unity of command is not the only mode of operation for a progressive, modern police organization. However, it is not difficult to understand the need for a strict adherence to this principle in emergency response situations where opportunities for consultation, reflection, and experimentation are minimal.

SPAN OF RESPONSIBILITY

Also referred to as span of control in police organizations, this relates to the number of persons, or positions, which can reasonably be assigned to another person, or position, for the purposes of supervision and management. For example, if a chief of police has three deputy chiefs reporting to her position, then she is said to have a span of responsibility of three. A sergeant, however, with nine constables reporting to his position has a span of responsibility of nine. The literature on management has invested some time and thought into setting certain limits on the span of responsibility without arriving at any fixed formula for determining the ideal or optimal number. Span of responsibility should largely be determined by a number of conditions and circumstances. It is now generally accepted that spans of control should reduce in relation to the complexity and variability of the tasks and responsibilities which adhere to the positions in question. On the other hand, it is possible to suggest that spans of responsibility could expand in relation to the capabilities and capacities of the supervisors to effectively manage subordinates.

Some elements to be taken into account when considering appropriate spans of responsibility or control have been suggested by Souryal (1985):

- physical layout of the organization;
- complexity of the tasks involved;
- working conditions;
- knowledge, skills, and abilities of the employees;
- competencies of the supervisors;

- effectiveness of the communication system within the organization;
- financial capacity of the organization to assign supervisors; and
- organization's historical approach to supervision and management.

DELEGATION OF AUTHORITY

In a hierarchical organization, the process of delegating authority implies that someone of higher rank or position within the organization has assigned a task, or series of tasks, to someone of lower rank or position. The delegation of authority is usually specified in terms of time, activity, circumstances, conditions, and other factors. It is expected that the person who delegated this authority remains accountable for the actions of the person to whom the authority has been delegated. The amount of delegated authority tends to increase with the size of an organization or the complexity of the range of activities for which the organization is responsible. In large police departments which have an extensive jurisdiction and a full array of operational assignments, it is easy to understand that substantial amounts of delegated authority are required in order to function effectively. In fact, in some departments, it is necessary to include a process for sub-delegation, where the person originally delegated a task, or series of tasks, has some opportunity to further delegate to someone below them in the organizational hierarchy to undertake assignments that relate to the original delegated authority.

Because delegated authority resides so closely with the person who did the delegating, and since that person has, normally, defined the parameters of the tasks in fairly specific terms, it is seen as an impediment to the potential for creative and innovative problem solving for the person who has been delegated these responsibilities. In order to begin to address some of the rigidity that is often inherent in delegated authority, the idea of empowerment has become attractive in the theory and practice of modern management. Its effects are being felt in the world of police administration as we see below.

EMPOWERMENT

A number of authors, practitioners, and academics have tried to come to grips with the topic of empowerment. The term is fairly common in discussions about modern management and it is used quite freely when talking about new approaches for dealing with employees. However, there is a growing concern that much of the talk about empowerment is simply that, talk, with no real substance to inform its application. Kernaghan (1992) offers a very good summary of the thinking about this topic and offers some useful insights that may be applied within a policing context in Canada. He points out that from an organizational perspective, empowerment has internal and external aspects. Internally, empowerment implies some activity that increases individual and collective action on the part of employees which inclines to the benefit of the organization and its members. Externally, empowerment implies a similar kind of activity that is directed at clients or customers bringing them more fully into the decision-making processes of the organization. Kernaghan notes that empowerment may involve some blending of theory and practice from fields such as organizational design, quality circles, training, and leadership.

The truly empowered organization will be characterized by employees who are actively engaged in the workings of the organization and have a high degree of trust and respect among employees and managers. It will also operate with high levels of team involvement that allows for creative and innovative approaches to work and problem solving. Empowerment must include the responsibility, authority, and power to accomplish the work that is assigned to the individual or team. Otherwise, it is merely a delegation of work without any autonomy to produce new solutions or imaginative approaches.

There is recognition that in order to make empowerment work, organizations need to properly prepare people to accept this new kind of responsibility. Kernaghan (1992) notes that many public sector agencies have invested a great deal of effort in the training of senior managers and staff. A shared understanding of the framework and practice of empowerment is required in order that everyone can operate effectively in this climate of change. Because empowerment creates a new dynamic between managers and individual employees, particularly those operating in empowered teams, this approach needs substantial thought before it is implemented within a police organization. The empowerment approach is very different from the command and control model which must still have an important place within the department.

Within a public service, including police organizations, there will have to be some limitations to the application of empowerment. There must be a willingness to genuinely delegate decision-making power to employees who will then be able to operate effectively as individuals or in teams to accomplish the assignments, tasks, and projects which have been placed in their control. Real empowerment brings with it some important risks that cannot be underestimated when thinking about its application in a police organization, which, like many other public services, is bound by laws, regulations, policies, procedures, and standards that are interconnected in complex ways. Real empowerment also has the potential to run against the grain of the concept of ministerial responsibility that is central to Canadian public administration.

While at the working level it may be feasible to support and encourage risk-taking, problem-solving, and team-oriented approaches to work, at the senior executive level it may prove too problematic when the elected official appointed to manage a public service portfolio is called to account for errors or incompetence in the delivery of programs or services (Kernaghan, 1992). The freedom that is implied in any reasonable approach to empowerment will include errors, mistakes, false starts, and other seemingly negative aspects. If police organizations ensure that their employees are properly prepared to assume greater levels of empowerment, if they provide the best methods, materials, and means for their employees to succeed in their performance, and if they cultivate the acceptance of responsibility for individual and team action through performance measurement standards, the limitations inherent in our existing model of ministerial responsibility may be minimized. Kernaghan (1992) points out that the value of public service organizations seriously investing some effort in the application of empowerment is clear:

In the competition for skilled workers that is anticipated for the late 1990s, the advantage may well go to empowered private and public sector organizations. Thus, public service managers who do not at least investigate seriously the desirability and feasibility of empowering their organizations will do a long-term disservice to their employees, the government, and the public interest. (p. 214)

SPECIALIZATION

Police organizations tend to be attracted to specialization as an appropriate response to the complexities of their varied responsibilities. This can frequently be seen when looking at the department's organizational chart. There is often a division of the entire organization into functional "silos" that contain discrete areas of specialization as in Figure 6–4:

FIGURE 6-4

TYPICAL "SILOS" OF POLICE SPECIALIZATION

Silo One	Silo Two	Silo Three	Silo Four
Investigations	Specialized Operations	Investigative Support	Corporate Support
• Homicide • Fraud • Drug • Undercover	• Tactics & Rescue • Canine • Bomb Disposal • Scuba • Helicopter • Crowd Management • Motorcycle	• Surveillance • Identification • Wiretaps • Polygraph • Photography	• Policy/Planning • HR • Training • Finance • Technology • Legal Services • Audit • Internal Affairs • Communication

There are advantages and disadvantages to the use of specialization in a modern police service. Souryal (1985) has outlined some of those aspects which are worthy of careful attention in understanding this issue:

ADVANTAGES OF SPECIALIZATION

- streamlines work with specified tasks automatically being assigned to appropriate staff who are subject matter experts;
- ensures quality performance by specially trained personnel;
- reduces elapsed time spent on tasks when undertaken by skilled staff;
- contributes to staff motivation and enhances job satisfaction; and
- allows for appropriate levels of ongoing training, skills enhancement, or research and development in the area of expertise (e.g., bomb disposal).

DISADVANTAGES OF SPECIALIZATION

- contributes to the creation and perpetuation of "silos" in police departments;
- encourages a kind of "class consciousness" in the department where police generalists are, by definition, not "special";
- tends to complicate communications between different groups of specialists, and between specialists and generalists within the department;
- may isolate officers from the overall mission and goals of the organization as a result of a concentrated focus on their specialty;
- could contribute to unhealthy competition and rivalry in various parts of the organization;
- could foster resentment within the organization based on a perception of special treatment; and
- costs of dividing work into discrete specialties may become prohibitive and lead to stagnation of members who cannot be laterally transferred across the department because of their specialization.

CONCLUSION

Throughout this chapter we have looked at some of the basics of police administration in Canada. What should be clear from this examination is that the mandate and structure of police organizations requires special consideration in terms of management, leadership, and accountability. Because society continues to expect the police to offer a broad range of services that include emergency response, crime prevention, assistance to victims of crime, public order maintenance and law enforcement, senior police executives have a difficult challenge in ensuring that all possible means are in place to guarantee sound policies and appropriate action throughout their organizations.

The importance of public trust and accountability have increased substantially for police organizations over the last few decades. In order to assist them in their evolution to best practices, police managers have begun to seriously research and examine their own activities and are looking to the wider world of organizational leadership and development for models and systems to inspire innovation and change.

In trying to effectively balance their contract with the public for the delivery of important and significant services with a degree of independence that appropriately buffers them from undue political interference, police organizations have undertaken major corporate change initiatives with far-reaching impacts.

QUESTIONS FOR CONSIDERATION

1. What are the ways in which policing in Canada can be seen as part of a "system"?
2. What are some of the difficulties of applying a "systems" model to the criminal justice system in Canada?

3. What are some of the means by which police departments in Canada are made accountable?
4. Discuss the issue of police independence in Canada. Can police independence be combined with accountability?
5. What are some of the ways in which a police department can determine an appropriate span of responsibility?
6. Discuss empowerment in the context of modern policing in Canada. Can empowerment be applied effectively in a law enforcement agency?
7. Discuss the advantages and disadvantages of police specialization. Which approach provides for more effective policing services: the generalist officer or the specialist?
8. What are the merits of a clear and established chain of command? Under what circumstances should, or could, this chain of command be relaxed?

REFERENCES

Argyris, Chris. (1964). *Integrating the individual and the organization.* New York: Wiley.

Canada. Royal Commission on Financial Management and Accountability. (1979). *Final report.* Ottawa: Minister of Supply and Services Canada.

Hann, Robert G. et al. (1985). "Municipal police governance and accountability in Canada: an empirical study." *Canadian Police College Journal*, 9(1).

Ingstrup, Ole. (1995). *Public service renewal: from means to ends.* Ottawa: Canadian Centre for Management Development.

Jacques, Elliott. (1990). "In praise of hierarchy." *Harvard Business Review*, 68(1).

Kernaghan, Kenneth. (1992). "Empowerment and public administration: revolutionary advance or passing fancy?" *Canadian Public Administration*, 35(2).

Koontz, H. and C. O'Connell. (1968). *Principles of management: an analysis of managerial functions.* 4th ed. New York: McGraw-Hill.

Leclerc, Guy et al. (1996). *Accountability, performance reporting, comprehensive audit: an integrated approach.* Ottawa: CCAF-FCVI, Inc.

Lewis, Clare E., Sidney B. Linden, and Judith Keene. (1986). "Public complaints against police in Metropolitan Toronto: the history and operation of the Office of the Public Complaints Commissioner." *Criminal Law Quarterly*, 29(1).

Martin, Maurice A. (1995). *Urban policing in Canada: anatomy of an aging craft.* Montreal and Kingston: McGill-Queen's University Press.

McMahon, Maeve W. and Richard V. Ericson. (1984). *Policing reform: a study of the reform process and police institution in Toronto.* Toronto: Centre of Criminology, University of Toronto.

Ontario. Ministry of the Solicitor General and Correctional Services. (1996). *Review of police services in Ontario: a framework for discussion.* Toronto: The Ministry.

Oppal, The Honourable Mr. Justice Wallace T. (1994). *Closing the gap: policing and the community: the report, volume 1.* [Victoria, B.C.]: Policing in British Columbia Commission of Inquiry.

Price Waterhouse Associates and The Canada Consulting Group Inc. (1985). *A study of management and accountability in the Government of Ontario.* [Toronto]: Price Waterhouse Associate and The Canada Consulting Group Inc.

Reiner, Robert. (1995). "Counting the coppers: antinomies of accountability in policing." In Stenning, Philip C. (ed.). *Accountability for criminal justice: selected essays.* Toronto: University of Toronto Press.

Senge, Peter M. et al. (1994). *The fifth discipline fieldbook: strategies and tools for building a learning organization.* Toronto: Doubleday.

Sheehan, Robert and Gary W. Cordner. (1995). *Police administration. 3rd ed.* Cincinnati, Ohio: Anderson Publishing.

Souryal, Sam S. (1985). *Police organization & administration.* Cincinnati, Ohio: Anderson Publishing.

Stenning, Philip C. (1981). *Police commissions and boards in Canada.* Toronto: Centre of Criminology, University of Toronto.

Stenning, Philip C. (1994). "Police and politics: there and back and there again?" In MacLeod, R. and D. Schneiderman (eds.). *Police powers in Canada: the evolution and practice of authority.* Toronto: University of Toronto Press, pp. 209–240.

Stenning, Philip C. (ed.). (1995). *Accountability for criminal justice: selected essays.* Toronto: University of Toronto Press.

Stenning, Philip C., John Briggs, and Marnie Crouch. (1996). *Police governance in First Nations in Ontario.* Toronto: Centre of Criminology, University of Toronto.

Teal, Thomas. (1996). "The human side of management." *Harvard Business Review*, 74(6).

Wheatley, Margaret J. (1994). *Leadership and the new science: learning about organization from an orderly universe.* San Francisco: Berrett-Koehler.

TOWARD MORE LEARNING

A SYSTEMS THEORY OF ORGANIZATIONS

Senge, Peter et al. (1994). *The fifth discipline fieldbook: strategies and tools for building a learning organization.* New York: Currency Doubleday.

This publication offers a practical, accessible follow-up to Senge's enormously influential book, *The fifth discipline*. In this "fieldbook," Senge and his colleagues offer a number of valuable insights into the effectiveness of "systems thinking" as a problem-solving tool and provide some exercises which can be undertaken within any organization to foster the exploration of this approach. The book also contains a wealth of material relating to the other four "disciplines" (i.e., personal mastery, mental models, shared vision, and team learning).

The Systems Thinker: Building Shared Understanding. Cambridge, Mass.: Pegasus Communications, Inc.

Beginning in 1990, this newsletter has provided access to some very clear and valuable material about a "systems" perspective on important organizational issues. It offers case studies of the application of "systems thinking" as pioneered by Peter Senge and his colleagues and includes tools for dealing with problems in ways that are both innovative and effective.

The publisher of this useful service, Pegasus Communications, Inc., also maintains a Web site that includes details about some of its other related materials, especially in the area of organizational learning. The Web site can be found at: http://www.pegasuscom.com.

ACCOUNTABILITY

Hann, Robert G. et al. (1985). "Municipal police governance and accountability in Canada: an empirical study." *Canadian Police College Journal*, 9(1).

This article provides an extremely useful background reading on police governing authorities in Canada and, while dated, is helpful in understanding the development of this accountability mechanism and its variations across the country. It offers the only extended, empirical study of municipal police governance in Canada.

Stenning, Philip C. (ed.) (1995). *Accountability for criminal justice: selected essays*. Toronto: University of Toronto Press.

This recent Canadian publication brings together an international assortment of commentators on the broad topic of accountability within the criminal justice system. While the papers presented by scholars directly relevant to policing are most pertinent in the context of this textbook, there are other contributions which should be of general interest to the reader who wishes to probe the topic of accountability in greater depth. Stenning's study of accountability in the federal Solicitor General's department is particularly instructive in terms of its national role. David Bayley's treatment of police brutality provides some sound principles for a system of civilian oversight of police. Other papers deal directly with the role of public complaints, public inquiries in Canada, and a range of related accountability topics dealing with the justice system.

Walker, Samuel. (1995). *Citizen review resource manual*. Washington, D.C.: Police Executive Research Forum.

This U.S. publication is valuable because it contains an extensive selection of statutes, ordinances, executive and departmental orders, and other materials relating to citizen review of police activities. Walker has gathered information from more than 30 U.S. police departments and have packaged these sources for the benefit of police practitioners and others who wish to understand police accountability at a practical level.

EMPOWERMENT

Kernaghan, Kenneth. (1992). "Empowerment and public administration: revolutionary advance or passing fancy?" *Canadian Public Administration*, 35(2).

This article offers a good summary of this topic from a public administration perspective. Kernaghan examined the submissions made to the 1991 competition for the Institute of Public Administration of Canada's Award for Innovative Management, which had as its theme, "Empowerment: Employees, Managers, Organizations." On the basis of the 68 submissions, he has drawn some interesting conclusions about the application, and misapplication, of empowerment in the public sector. Kernaghan encourages the introduction of empowerment within a framework that includes: structural change, staff training (at all levels), rewards and recognition, and union involvement.

Holpp, Lawrence. (1995). "If empowerment is so good, why does it hurt?" *Training: The Human Side of Business*, 32(3).

The author offers some useful insights that form the basis for simple principles to guide the process of empowerment in any organization. He defines empowerment as:

...a process for helping the right people at the right levels make the right decisions for the right reasons.

In assisting organizations move toward this kind of appropriate empowerment, the author turns his attention to the role of team building and offers a useful model dealing with team development that progresses through four separate stages.

CHAPTER SEVEN

ASSIGNMENT TO DUTY

LEARNING OBJECTIVES

1. Describe the operational, administrative, and ancillary service functions of policing in Canada
2. Identify the key characteristics of each of these functional areas of activity
3. Explain the importance of these areas for the delivery of police services in Canada
4. Identify the components of the intelligence process
5. Distinguish between community relations programs and public relations programs

INTRODUCTION

This chapter begins to look at the actual assignments which police departments are responsible for undertaking in the delivery of their service to the public. Because there is a great deal of consistency across the country with regard to what police organizations *do*, this presentation should have general applicability for all Canadian readers. Of course, there will be some local variation depending on the size of a particular police department or its operational mandate. However, in trying to provide a broad understanding of the types of assignments which can be given to police officers, it is expected that this chapter will prove beneficial to those seeking a complete insight into the widest range of police duties and functions.

For the sake of simplicity, this chapter is divided into three main categories or subsystems:

- operational assignments;
- administrative functions; and
- ancillary services functions.

Each of these areas has its own subdivisions with areas of specialty that allow for considerable scope in the kinds of work that can be done on behalf of the organization in serving the public good. All of these areas have their own particular value for the overall efficiency and effectiveness of the police department, and each area attracts a particular kind of person who finds satisfaction and fulfillment in that particular field of endeavour. There is no special pre-eminence to any one of these areas and all can contribute to the overall mandate of the police service; indeed, in some instances, there is overlap between one area of activity and another. A more detailed treatment of *specialized* operational areas of police activity will be provided in Chapter 8 ("Organizational Strategies: Making the Best Use of Police Resources").

OPERATIONAL ASSIGNMENTS

Operational assignments include those front-line services that are most directly aimed at assisting the public. They are, therefore, the areas of police activity which are most commonly seen and best understood by the ordinary citizen. As a result, they are often the functions which require the highest levels of personnel deployment.

TRAFFIC FUNCTIONS

The traffic assignment may include a number of areas of activity which relate to motor vehicles and their movement and operation within the police jurisdiction. Some of these areas include: directing traffic (or stationary control), highway traffic law enforcement, radar operation (including photo-radar), parking enforcement, transportation of dangerous goods enforcement, vehicle inspections, and traffic accident investigation (including detailed accident reconstruction). In many police departments, the traffic function is often combined with responsibility for any marine or waterways patrol functions, if there are navigable bodies of water within the department's jurisdiction.

There is an important social value to the traffic function and its several subfunctions, which can be seen by anyone who has had to confront a serious slow-down on a major highway during rush hour. When traffic is stalled because of a multi-vehicle accident, it is clear that the normal flow of vehicles is something which does not simply happen. It is, in fact, the result of good road system design and careful highway safety enforcement by police officers assigned to this duty. There is a great deal of effort being focused on the preventative side of traffic enforcement to ensure that vehicles and people move efficiently. This area may also include responsibility for traffic safety that incorporates inspection of carriers of dangerous goods and the very detailed analysis of traffic accidents, which has developed into a precise science requiring high levels of education and training on the part of the officer.

In developing an appropriate mandate to guide the traffic function, a number of police services in Canada have begun to look at reengineering their processes in ways that combine proactive and reactive elements. The Metropolitan Toronto Police Service has undertaken

BRIEFING NOTE

One person dies in a motor vehicle accident *every eight hours*. Someone is injured in motor vehicle collision *every six minutes*.

Source: Metropolitan Toronto Police Service. Traffic Restructuring Project Team (1996). *Recommendations*. Toronto: Metropolitan Toronto Police Service. pp. 10–11. Used with permission.

such a review and has put forward recommendations designed to improve this area (Metropolitan Toronto Police Service, 1996). The following extract provides a good insight into the substance of a traffic function largely applicable to any major police department:

Traffic Policing Mandate:

The purpose of Traffic Policing is to contribute to the safe and free flow of traffic within Metropolitan Toronto and to influence driver and pedestrian behaviour so as to reduce death, injury, damage and costs to society by:

- focusing on community policing through partnership with all stakeholders
- enforcement
- education
- input on roadway design and traffic signage

The purpose of Traffic Services is to: provide specialized traffic planning and investigative functions, technical support, enforcement and educational programs; identify and deliver solutions to Service-wide traffic concerns; and to support the Community Policing strategies of the Division Traffic officers. Traffic Services will have specific responsibility for:

- fatals [sic] involving all modes of transportation
- all other collisions where injuries are life-threatening
- Service and Government vehicle collisions involving fatality [sic] or life-threatening injuries
- Provincial Special Investigations Unit (S.I.U.) traffic-related investigations (e.g., pursuit involving injury or death)
- specialized traffic enforcement (e.g., hazardous and dangerous goods, commercial vehicle enforcement, etc.)
- reconstruction program—management and training
- reconstruction of collisions when necessary
- property damage and fail to remain collisions as reported at the Collision Reporting Centres
- follow-up investigations on fail to remain personal injury collisions that remain unsolved after 48 hours of the occurrence being reported
- expressway patrol
- breath program—management, training and delivery

- radar program—management and training
- supervision of contract vehicle pounds
- roadway construction liaison on cross-jurisdictional projects
- investigate traffic-related charges and warrants
- development of Traffic Safety programs for delivery by Traffic Services and Divisional Traffic personnel
- testing and evaluation of Traffic Policing technology
- planning and liaison for major parades and special events occurring on roadways
- film liaison

The overall aim of an effective traffic patrol program is to ensure that there is road safety throughout the jurisdiction. In order to accomplish this goal, the following components of a suitable road safety system require constant attention and police awareness and involvement:

FIGURE 7-1

COMPONENTS OF A ROAD SAFETY SYSTEM

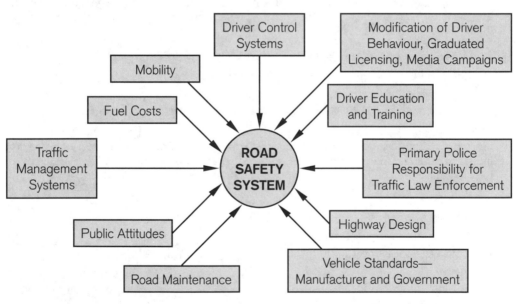

Adapted from: Ontario Provincial Police. Organizational Review Project. (1994). *Traffic/Waterways Management*. Orillia, Ont.: OPP, p. 43. Used with permission. Further reproduction without the consent of the OPP is prohibited.

PATROL FUNCTIONS

Patrol functions are at the core of most police operations. The first officer at the scene of a crime, or other emergency, is usually the patrol officer. The normal training of these officers provides them with a broad range of knowledge, skills, and abilities (KSAs) in preparation for dealing with a multitude of events which can occur. The presence of the patrol officer is one of the most widely recognized means by which citizens develop a sense of safety in the community. The sight of a patrol officer provides people with some sense that all is well and that the watch is being kept.

The patrol function is guided by considerations of time and geography. The shift schedule must be able to provide for adequate coverage of the police jurisdiction by officers working in the zones that have been defined for the jurisdiction. Originally, patrolling was done on foot, but eventually, with the greater availability of cars, there was a change to mobile patrols. This approach to the patrol function, as part of the "professional" model, was strongly supported in the United States under the reforms introduced by people like O.W. Wilson, a respected police administrator (Peak, 1993). The first major, scientific study of the effectiveness of police patrols was undertaken in Kansas City, Missouri, in 1972. Sponsored by the Police Foundation, this research was designed to examine the efficiency of this type of activity. A number of the city's police beats were selected to receive different kinds of patrol:

- *reactive*—no preventive patrol, with police only coming into the beat in response to a call for service;
- *proactive*—an increased number of patrol vehicles were assigned to this area; and
- *control*—a single marked patrol vehicle assigned to provide the normal level of service.

The Kansas City study produced some interesting findings. First, there were no statistically important differences in crime activity in any of the three patrol areas. Secondly, the citizen's fear of crime did not change in any material way when comparisons were made among the three different approaches to patrol. The attitude of people toward the police was not altered in any significant way as a result of the changes in patrol methods, and, finally, the response time of officers was not affected to any substantial degree by any of the three approaches to patrol (Kelling, et al., 1974). Subsequently, some of the elements of this experiment were challenged; however, it does stand as an important example of scientific research methods being applied to a practical police patrol issue. The Kansas City project was able to focus attention on some basic assumptions about the routine patrol function and made police administrators and the public aware that more police, more cars, and more funding would not necessarily solve crime and disorder problems. The inherent inefficiencies in the use of random police patrols has lead several police practitioners and academics to consider alternative approaches that are considered in detail in Chapter 8 ("Organizational Strategies: Making the Best Use of Police Resources").

The level of activity experienced by a patrol officer will be largely determined by the particular shift that is being worked. The importance of shift work in policing cannot be overlooked, and it has been the subject of much study and debate. There are basically three time divisions making up a typical eight-hour shift schedule:

- day shift (normally 7:00 a.m. to 3:00 p.m.);
- evening shift (normally 3:00 p.m. to 11:00 p.m.); and
- "graveyard" shift (normally 11:00 p.m. to 7:00 a.m.).

Because of the various activities that normally take place during these different time periods, it is not difficult to understand that the day shift has the highest potential for contact with people in the community. This is when the normal "business" of community life takes place, with children going to school, employees travelling to work, people shopping, sightseeing, or just gathering in the many and varied ways in which normal human interaction takes place. The day shift officer must be able to deal with the range of possible events that occur during these hours. This is the shift normally assigned to officers with more seniority.

The evening shift involves a high degree of involvement with the same groups of people returning from their daily chores of school, shopping, or work. It is also the time period when leisure activities are frequently engaged in, such as sporting events, entertainment, and pastimes. This often requires crowd management skills to ensure that people are safely and efficiently moved through the various venues where these events take place and that public order is maintained.

The "graveyard" shift is, as its unfortunate name implies, the least desirable shift and typically falls to those officers with the least job seniority. It is also the most difficult shift from a personal lifestyle perspective and is often considered a substantial source of stress in the police officer's life. This is the time of day when pubs and liquor establishments are closing, requiring a police presence to maintain the peace and ensure public safety. There is also a higher degree of illegal activity during this shift as businesses are closed and buildings are open to the threat of illegal entry.

The attraction of an established preventive patrol approach to policing was that it allowed for a high degree of standardization and centralization. As noted, this was part of O.W. Wilson's influence on the administration of police organizations. However, this rationalized approach to administrative control did not satisfy all of the changing demands on public safety. In Canada, this approach became widely accepted, and, as a result, the reactive model was little questioned, as Martin (1995) observes:

> The placid days of prewar, semirural Canada did not stimulate debate about the adequacy of justice-system programs, nor did the pinched days of the Depression. So with postwar growth, police had in preventive patrol a program that was readily standardized and therefore amenable to central supervision and expandable in uniform increments—in all, a manageable and suitable design for growth. When a standardized service is performing well, there is no pressing reason in the public mind why it should be done differently. (p. 126)

CRIMINAL INVESTIGATION FUNCTIONS

Once a criminal offence has occurred it is the task of officers assigned to the criminal investigation functions to move into action. Their responsibilities include the apprehension of persons responsible for committing these crimes. Their role includes crime scene investigation, the interviewing of witnesses, and the interrogation of suspects. Through the course of these activities it is intended that arrests will be made, crimes will be solved, and cases will be closed.

This area includes the detective function, which not only has a strong public appeal, but has been the subject of much literature and popular culture. It continues to hold a certain mystique that serves, rightly or wrongly, to attract people to the field of policing. The status of detectives, who normally work in plain clothes, is often highly elevated in the public eye and even within police departments themselves. The overall effectiveness of the detective function has been called into question in a number of studies, including an important survey done by the RAND Corporation, a highly respected U.S. think tank (Greenwood and Petersilia, 1975; Eck, 1996; Ericson, 1981). The issue of specialization within the criminal investigations department has also been examined where the efficiency of having highly specialized squads that deal only with one of the following types of crimes—homicides, sex assaults, hold-ups, auto thefts, fraud, pornography, etc.—is seriously questioned (Sheehan and Cordner, 1995, p. 69).

Weston and Wells (1986) have identified four basic components to the criminal investigation function:

- *preliminary investigation*—begins with the first officer at the scene, who is responsible for determining if a crime has been committed, securing and protecting the scene of the crime in order to preserve and locate any evidence that might be relevant to the crime, gathering any possible information from witnesses at the scene for follow-up, attempting to determine how the crime was committed and recording in detail any information on the crime for future reference, and making any necessary arrangements for photographing the crime scene and any victims;
- *continuing investigation*—conducting follow-up interviews with witnesses, developing theories about the crime, gathering any eyewitness information on the perpetrator, vehicles, weapons, in-depth interviews with the victims, furthering the search for any possible physical evidence (including fingerprints, footprints, blood stains), arranging for surveillance of suspects, preparing the case for the Crown prosecutor;
- *reconstructing the crime*—developing a detailed, scientific theory of the crime based on collected evidence, witness and victim information, and subject matter expertise; and
- *focusing the investigation*—narrowing the thrust of the investigation to build a case against a particular suspect or suspects based on the information, evidence, and investigation. This is the culmination of the criminal investigator's analysis of everything that has been brought together with regard to a particular crime.

Because there has been much study of the actual effectiveness of the detective function, considerable effort has gone into the development of "solvability" formulas. These are intended to provide a good approximation of how likely it would be for police detectives to solve a particular crime based on facts relating to that crime. This quantitative approach to crime allows detectives to make better decisions about cases they should be pursuing and those which have the characteristics associated with low solvability. Some of the informational components that can be used in such a formula include:

- estimated time from crime occurrence;
- availability of witness reports;
- availability of fingerprints;
- suspect information; and
- suspect vehicle information.

INTELLIGENCE FUNCTIONS

In defining intelligence as it relates to a law enforcement context, it pertains to the *output* of digested information resulting from a *process* that includes: planning, collection and evaluation, collation, analysis, concluding with the reporting and dissemination of the processed *input* of information. Intelligence operates to gather information in a structured manner in order to assist and guide the investigative functions discussed above. Criminal intelligence frequently targets the areas of organized crime that plague police departments and cross several jurisdictional lines, and requires, therefore, considerable cooperation among various police services. Figure 7–2 presents an outline of the intelligence process.

Intelligence can be further refined as being either *tactical* or *strategic* in nature. Tactical intelligence functions primarily as an investigative tool and relates to the support provided by an analytical unit for ongoing operational investigations. Its value lies in a capacity to focus investigations on the most effective areas of criminal activity and, therefore, best utilize the department's investigative resources. Strategic intelligence offers a management tool that gives overall perspective and direction to matters relating to criminal activity. It operates to provide a framework for a department's long-term plan of action with regard to emerging crime trends and activities (RCMP, 1991).

A police department's intelligence efforts may be directed at any one of the following groups and their activities:

- *outlaw motorcycle gangs*—these are highly organized, hierarchical groups that are engaged in a wide range of illegal activities, such as drug trafficking, extortion, contract killing, and prostitution;
- *traditional organized crime groups*—this category includes the Sicilian Mafia, N'Drangheta, the Camorra, and the U.S. Cosa Nostra;
- *ethnic crime groups*—while not restricted to the Canadian Asian community there has been an alarming growth in gangs whose origins are in the Triads and Vietnamese gangs, such as Kung Lok, 14K Triad, the Big Circle Boys Gang and others;
- *illegal immigration*—intelligence efforts are aimed at counteracting the flow of illegal aliens into the country and those illegal services that defraud those people through their activities;
- *smuggling and related activities*—across Canada there are various illegal activities related to the smuggling of tobacco products, liquor, currency, drugs, pornographic material, vehicles, and other items;

FIGURE 7-2

THE INTELLIGENCE PROCESS

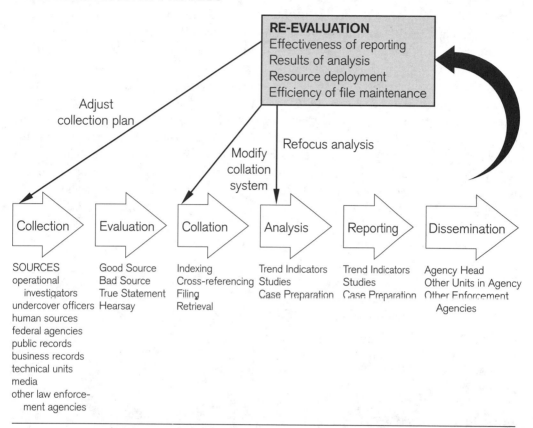

Adapted from: RCMP. (1991). *Criminal Intelligence Program: planning and direction: implementation guide.* Ottawa: RCMP, Criminal Intelligence Directorate. Reproduced with the permission of the Minister of Public Works and Government Services Canada, 1997.

- *illegal gambling*—with the growth of legal gambling there has been persistent difficulties surrounding the control of illegal gaming and gambling in Canada;
- *white collar crime*—intelligence efforts are made in order to address a wide range of illegal activities, such as bank inspector frauds, automated teller machine frauds, computer crimes, stock market manipulation, home improvement frauds, etc.;
- *youth gangs*—dealing with the illegal activities engaged in by these groups and the conflicts and violence carried out between rival gangs;
- *pornography*—the creation, distribution, and sale of illegal pornographic materials, especially those products which deal in child pornography; and
- *prostitution*—this includes the growing challenge of escort services; however, nearly 90% of illegal activity relates to street prostitution.

COMMUNITY POLICING AND CRIME PREVENTION FUNCTIONS

There will more detailed discussion of the topics of community policing and crime prevention in Chapter 10 ("Leading Innovation in Canadian Policing"); however, it is useful to offer some insight into the importance of these related areas as possible assignments for police personnel.

Traffic, patrol, and criminal investigation areas are largely, though not exclusively, reactive in nature. These functions are in place to ensure that there is an operational readiness to respond to particular occurrences through the availability of suitably trained and equipped officers. At the other end of the policing continuum, community policing and crime prevention areas of assignment are intended to be proactive in nature. Community policing as a concept has become very difficult to define in absolute terms and is the subject of considerable debate and variation across the spectrum of Canadian police organizations. However, at its most basic, community policing is an approach to the whole enterprise of policing that attempts to fully engage the public (in its various forms) in the overall challenge of community safety and security. Crime prevention, as an expression of

Community policing office

Ontario Provincial Police

the philosophy of community policing, relates to those areas of activity that operate to resist or suppress crime and frequently includes the use of properly trained and supervised volunteers within the community for that purpose.

Increasingly, police organizations are attempting to incorporate community policing and crime prevention functions into the overall thrust of their service delivery. Therefore, rather than being seen as a separate area of activity or as a single function or group of functions, community policing is expressed as the philosophy of service delivery and crime prevention as an approach to all categories of police operation.

BRIEFING NOTE

Debate about the true content of community policing has been taking place for a number of years with many departments moving away from the actual use of the term in their organizational literature. One astute observer of this debate, Chris Braiden, a retired Superintendent with the Edmonton Police now working as a consultant, has recently observed that talking about "community policing" is like saying that you are "...going fishing for fish...."

The simple fact that the old crime-fighting model of policing ignores a substantial amount of police activity makes it essential that attention be paid to some enlightened form of "community relations." Any effort that actively and directly engages the public in the identification, assessment, solution, and evaluation of community problems should be seen as valuable. There is an important distinction to be made between community relations (which can include community policing and crime prevention) and public relations, a discrete area of activity that is discussed later in this chapter, under the heading of Public Information and Media Relations.

ADMINISTRATIVE FUNCTIONS

The administrative functions which are discussed below are those which are largely unseen by the public; however, they serve to keep a police organization operating with some degree of efficiency, and they provide direct support to personnel working in the field. These functions are frequently aimed at the long-range viability of the organization and ensure that steps are being taken and procedures are in place to satisfy the resource needs of the department in order to meet the "business" needs of the service. Positions within this area are usually of the nine-to-five type of occupation and are often considered to be the corporate functions.

HUMAN RESOURCES

This is an area of responsibility within a police department that is critical; however, it is frequently given less attention and fewer resources than its importance warrants. Because the human resources of any organization should be looked upon as a significant investment that will ensure that organization's future, considerable support needs to be directed to this portion of the department. The staff, both uniform and civilian, who are engaged in this area of activity, may be concerned with any or all of the following:

- recruitment;
- employee selection criteria and processes;
- preparing and revising position descriptions and classifications;
- promotional processes;
- compensation and benefits programs;
- maintenance of personnel records;
- performance evaluation systems;
- human resources research and planning; and
- assistance with retirement planning and/or separation.

Because of its overwhelming importance to the viability and effectiveness of a police service, the area of staff training, development, and learning will be considered as a separate, specialized category. However, in many police departments, those responsible for this area of activity are attached to, or associated with, the human resource unit.

TRAINING, EDUCATION, DEVELOPMENT, AND LEARNING

This is a fundamental area within every police department and should be staffed with the most proficient individuals available. The impact that training, education, development, and learning has on a police service is profound; therefore, it calls for the most careful consideration by senior police managers. Individuals who are engaged in the various facets of this function will impart significant lessons to those who receive the programs. The leading edge practices which pertain to this field of endeavour will be considered in depth in Chapter 10 ("Leading Innovation in Canadian Policing"); however, the basic thrust of this area is worth considering for its immediate impact.

Whether policing is looked upon as a profession, a craft, a trade, or a vocation, it begins with people who have basically little or no exposure to the specialized knowledge, skills, and abilities (KSAs) that are required to function in the field as a police officer. New recruits brought in for initial training typically have not had any experience with high-speed vehicle pursuits, directing traffic, completing collision reports, administering a breathalyzer test, or any of the many other routine duties undertaken by a patrol officer. Therefore, the process of orientation training involves a steep learning curve that demands a high level of proficiency from the instructors. Police training has evolved with the job. Much greater emphasis is now being placed on sound adult learning principles, learner-centred instruction, and the continuous nature of learning. Furthermore, advances in technology have made it possible to introduce computers, videos, and CD-ROMs into the instructional mix for more effective, more flexible, more customized training. Given the complexities of the police function and the fact that it is affected on a continuous basis by changes in legislation, technology, and policies and procedures, we can see that retraining and new learning is especially important in this field. Those who design, develop, and evaluate training and education programs for police must be able to ensure that specific behavioural objectives are being met and measured. The U.S. Commission on Accreditation for Law Enforcement Agencies (1991) noted that:

> Training has often been cited as one of the most important responsibilities in any law enforcement agency. Training serves three broad purposes. First, well-trained officers are generally better prepared to act decisively and correctly in a broad spectrum of situations. Second, training results in greater productivity and effectiveness. Third, training fosters cooperation and unity of purpose. Moreover, agencies are now being held legally accountable for the actions of their personnel and for failing to provide initial or remedial training. (p. 33-1)

Police personnel who become involved in the training, education, and learning functions should have solid background in those KSAs that are appropriate for the interrelated tasks which make up this assignment. Many will have a particular subject matter expertise in specific operational or administrative functions (e.g., traffic accident investigation, criminal intelligence, policy development, etc.); however, above and beyond any specialized expertise, those attached to the training and learning function will need to understand some of the following areas which are directly pertinent to their educational roles and responsibilities:

- training needs assessment;
- lesson plan development;
- performance objective development;
- techniques of instruction;
- adult learning theory; and
- testing and evaluation methodologies.

POLICY DEVELOPMENT, PLANNING, AND ANALYSIS

The planning function within a police department is central to its long-term viability and effectiveness. It is worth making a clear distinction at the outset between two types of planning which can take place: strategic and operational. The strategic planning that should be undertaken on an ongoing basis within the department will be discussed in greater detail in Chapter 8, but it involves the development of a mission statement for the organization and, consistent with that mission, the articulation of key directions and priorities which the department will be pursuing over a set period of time, normally over a three- or five-year cycle. The focus of operational planning is on the day-to-day priorities that will guide the front-line functions of the organization.

Planning will provide input for the organization's decision makers to assist them in arriving at determinations about the overall management and administration of the police service. The individuals involved in this area of duty require special skills allowing them to contribute to the process of decision making within their organization. The planning function has grown significantly in police departments in Canada as these organizations have had to justify their resource needs more fully and openly. Municipal councils and those provincial and federal departments who approve police operating and management budgets have begun to require more substantial background for the budget submissions made by chiefs of police on behalf of their departments. Planning personnel are critical to providing input for these new levels of support and justification.

The planning area is typically tasked with the development of policies for the police department and will deal with both long-range (i.e., strategic) and short-term (i.e., tactical or operational) issues. A good definition of police planning is provided by Souryal (1985):

> Modern police planning is the process of facilitating management decision making by clarifying agency problems and recommending rational solutions through systematic, intellectual research. (p. 115)

Frequently, this function, because of its pivotal importance to the overall policies and directions of the organization, reports directly to the office of the chief of police. It will often include a number of subunits with responsibility for research, policy development, strategic planning (including environmental scanning), and statistics. Souryal (1985) refers to the work of the U.S. National Advisory Committee on Criminal Justice Standards and Goals (1973) with regard to some of the qualities necessary for individuals working in the planning area:

- *independent*—strongly self-motivated individual who can work with little direct supervision;
- *analytical*—capable of accessing and absorbing information in order to evaluate it carefully, perceive relationships and develop objective conclusions;
- *creative*—able to use imagination and creativity to consider innovative approaches and alternative solutions to organizational issues;
- *articulate*—able to effectively organize and express ideas and the results of research in both oral and written form; and
- *thorough*—capable of processing large amounts of information while meeting the organization's requirements for policy analysis and timelines for management decision-making submissions.

FINANCE AND BUDGET COORDINATION

This area of assignment requires obvious skills in accounting and financial management. As such, there is normally a strong civilian component in these units with individuals who have professional accounting qualifications. In some organizations, the budget is prepared by dealing with the finance department of the larger entity; for example, a small municipal police service may turn to the municipality's finance department for budget preparation expertise. However, many police departments have uniform staff assigned to these duties with high levels of appropriate skill and expertise. Because the police budget is central to the organization's ability to accomplish its mandate, it is important that this area of activity be undertaken with considerable care. The budget will include monies required for salaries, benefits, supplies, equipment, vehicles, maintenance, training and development, physical plant, and contracted services. In order to demonstrate the labour-intensive nature of a police service it should be remembered that normally about 80% to 90% of the department's budget will be devoted to salaries, wages, and benefits. The remaining percentage is applied to other direct operating expenses. Because of the nature of policing, certain highly unpredictable costs can have an impact on the most carefully planned budget projections. A particularly long and involved homicide investigation may require the assignment of resources that was not anticipated, as well as high levels of overtime payments.

Approaches to budgeting vary significantly from one jurisdiction to another. Two types of budgeting that have been used with varying degrees of satisfaction are outlined below:

- Program, Planning, and Budgeting System (PPBS); and
- Zero Base Budgeting (ZBB).

PROGRAM, PLANNING, AND BUDGETING SYSTEM (PPBS)

This approach to budgeting was developed in the U.S. Defense Department during the 1960s. It is relatively complicated; therefore, its use has been restricted to larger police departments. This approach has four major components that combine the areas of planning and budgeting:

- identification of a program structure that outlines results in terms of goals and objectives;
- development of a budget structure that will facilitate the accomplishment of the various program goals and objectives;
- identification of a reporting system to highlight problems in program implementation and any costs incurred in correcting those problems; and
- development of a planning system to research, assess, and identify solutions to problems identified.

ZERO BASE BUDGETING (ZBB)

This approach to budgeting was developed in order to move away from the practice of applying annual increases to traditional budgets. ZBB implies that every fiscal cycle begins at "zero" and all costs must be justified for each and every program. It operates on an assumption that nothing is guaranteed and that each year all program areas must account for their financial needs in detail. This approach to budgeting gained considerable respect in the 1970s and was applied in a number of jurisdictions. The advantages and disadvantages of this approach to budgeting are outlined below:

ADVANTAGES
- ensures decision makers have an opportunity to thoroughly review programs in order to eliminate those which are ineffective or outmoded;
- requires police services to carefully evaluate all programs on an annual basis for cost-effectiveness and to make comparisons with similar programs; and
- eliminates unnecessary duplication of services and reduces waste.

DISADVANTAGES
- very time-consuming approach which requires scrutiny of every budget decision;
- when dealing with police services there is normally no competitive incentive to make serious reductions in program delivery;
- ability to reduce or eliminate programs may not translate to an equal ability to reduce staffing levels; and
- may lead to a sense of instability when programs are scrutinized on an annual basis for their continued existence.

LEGAL SERVICES

Many larger police departments need skilled legal practitioners in order to undertake a number of specialized tasks on behalf of the department. One example involves civil litigation where suits are brought against the department for a variety of reasons, including officer negligence. Officers with legal training are frequently assigned to this function not only in order to avoid the costs of hiring outside legal counsel, but also because these officers can bring a deeper knowledge of specific police procedure and practice to bear on these issues. Increasingly, the complexities which confront police organizations call for fairly sophisticated levels of understanding of the legal impact of executive decisions, and many departments are creating units staffed by officers with law degrees closely aligned with the office of the chief in order to provide counsel and advice for legal matters. Frequently, legal advice is necessary in areas of policy development affecting the police service, liaison with the courts, or in administrative matters dealing with departmental hearings for disciplinary or other purposes. Some departments may contract for these services on an as-needed basis; however, many jurisdictions are finding it advantageous to have staff with appropriate law degrees assigned to the department for reasons of continuity and expertise.

PUBLIC INFORMATION AND MEDIA RELATIONS

Because police organizations are a public service, it is expected that they will provide significant amounts of information to their stakeholders. Police organizations in Canada are primarily funded by tax dollars at the municipal or provincial levels; therefore, it is essential that there be skilled individuals tasked with responsibility for providing current and accurate information to that public. The media in Canada is, by extension, a provider of information to the public and, therefore, they play a substantial role as intermediaries between the police and the public, which cannot be overlooked or minimized. Every police department requires a thoughtful approach to both public information and media relations if it is to function in a professional and effective manner.

Clear policies need to be established with regard to the release of information to the public, either directly or through the media. This relates not only to general information, but to serious criminal or operational matters that the public needs to know. Missing children reports, escaped convicts, criminals at large, threats to public safety, and requests for public assistance all need to be coordinated in a careful manner by the police service. This requires police personnel who have particular skills in the area of public relations and communications. Clearly, this is another area where civilian personnel may offer established levels of expertise and training.

Often police organizations will develop a position for a public information officer whose task is to engage with the media on a routine and regular basis, thus allowing other officers to continue with their operational duties and priorities. Some of the functions of a public information officer could include:

- assisting news personnel in covering routine news stories and at scenes of incidents;
- being available for on-call responses to the news media;
- preparing and distributing agency news releases;
- arranging for, and assisting at, news conferences;
- coordinating and authorizing the release of information about victims, witnesses, and suspects;
- assisting in crisis situations within the agency; and
- coordinating and authorizing the release of information concerning confidential agency investigations and operations. (Commission on Accreditation for Law Enforcement Agencies, March 1990, pp. 54-1 and 2)

In dealing with the public it may be worthwhile for some police organizations to formally survey their community in order to determine specific levels of "customer" satisfaction. This has been undertaken in a number of jurisdictions with extremely positive results. This approach requires skills in the area of survey design and analysis which may be available through a local university or college. It does require the department to make a genuine commitment to requesting honest feedback from the public and implies a willingness to take this feedback into account when setting organizational and operational priorities (Halton Regional Police Service, 1995; Horne, Forcese, and Thompson, 1989; Melchers and Roberts, 1994; Reno Police Department, 1993).

AUDITS, INSPECTIONS, AND PROGRAM REVIEW

Linked with the responsibility for developing adequate information for fiscal management is the need to offer substantial background on the effectiveness and efficiency of a police department's programs and operations. This is where the audit, inspection, and organizational review functions come into play. The personnel assigned to this area have an important and interesting duty that requires specialized skills and background. In Canada, the provision of internal audit systems within police departments is relatively new. For example, the Royal Canadian Mounted Police (RCMP) began to provide this function, by way of inspections, in 1973. Over time this area has grown to the point where detailed comprehensive audit programs have been introduced in a number of jurisdictions. These programs offer police executives and local governing authorities with the means to ensure that the administration and operation of the police department is properly monitored and reported upon in ways that satisfy the accountability standards established in that jurisdiction. Comprehensive audits are thorough reviews of key controls, processes, and systems in place within an organization to manage its financial, human, technological, informational, and physical assets. The Canadian Comprehensive Auditing Foundation (1983) offers the following definition:

> A comprehensive audit is an examination that provides an objective and constructive assessment of the extent to which:
>
> - financial, human and physical resources are managed with due regard to economy, efficiency and effectiveness; and
> - accountability relationships are reasonably served.
>
> The comprehensive audit examines both financial and management controls, including information systems and reporting practices, and recommends improvements where appropriate. (p. 8)

In order to assist police departments in developing personnel with this kind of skill base, the Canadian Police College in Ottawa offers a one-week course on comprehensive auditing that provides a solid basis for uniform or civilian members within a department.

INTERNAL AFFAIRS AND PROFESSIONAL STANDARDS

These areas of assignment are significant because they contribute to the maintenance of a responsible organization and the preservation of a department's reputation for integrity and honesty. In addressing this element of police service accountability the first point of contact should be a well-organized, reliable, and rigorous internal affairs unit. Normally, these functions are assigned to a specialized unit that is placed at an elevated level within the organization. It constitutes an important role within the department, although the assignment is particularly challenging because it requires that officers carrying this function be responsible for bringing their own colleagues to account when the need arises as a result of allegations of wrongdoing or improper conduct. Indeed the Knapp Commission in the United States, which investigated police corruption in New York in the 1970s, recommended that internal affairs officers remain in that department throughout their careers (Knapp Commission, 1972).

In a number of jurisdictions, a more proactive approach is being taken to the whole concept of ethical behaviour within a police service (Delattre, 1994). There has been considerable attention paid to the development of programs and practices that support high standards of police behaviour and provide training and learning to advance a deeper understanding of the need for proper ethical knowledge for police officers at all levels (Victoria Police (Australia), 1996). Police departments have a strong motivation to ensure the detection and prevention of corrupt or unethical behaviour on the part of their officers for many reasons, including morale, public perception, expense, viability, to name a few. By establishing a unit which is mandated to deal with complaints and investigations with respect to officer conduct, police organizations can ensure that the highest level of public confidence in the police is maintained.

A recent study by the Victoria Police, in Australia, classified all police complaints/investigations into eight key categories:

FIGURE 7-3

EIGHT CATEGORIES OF POLICE COMPLAINTS/INVESTIGATIONS

Category	Description
Minor Misconduct	Complaints that police have been neglectful, rude or otherwise have acted improperly, or internal matters of neglect or misconduct.
Serious Misconduct	Serious matters not involving criminality and corruption.
Criminality	Criminal offences committed while off duty and not Force related.
Corruption	The illegal use of police power for personal gain in some form, not necessarily financial.
Conciliation	Matters which can be concluded amicably by conciliation.
Correspondence	Call outs, complaint not specified or of a general nature.
Counter/Civil	Summons issued against [Force] member by member of public.
Serious Incident	Reported to I.I.D. [Internal Investigations Department] for oversight purposes only.

Source: Victoria Police (Australia). (1996). *Project Guardian: Ethical Standards Department: final report*, p. 29. Used with permission.

ANCILLARY SERVICES FUNCTIONS

As distinguished from the administrative functions outlined above, the following ancillary services functions include those areas of activity which are normally available at all times to the operational components of a police organization. Therefore, these are services which are accessible 24 hours a day during all shift cycles for providing important support to officer activity in the field. While they are vitally important to the ongoing effectiveness of a police organization, it will be readily apparent that this is an area where improvements in technology and opportunities for civilianization are having far-reaching impacts.

RECORDS

It is not difficult to understand that police organizations are the creators and custodians of huge files of records of many sorts and categories. There is almost no activity, procedure, or practice undertaken within a police service which does not have an accompanying form or record that must be completed by the officer. All of these records must be completed, collected, stored, disseminated, and retrieved in ways that are efficient and complete. As a result, all police departments require skilled individuals who are tasked with these interrelated functions. At the centre of these tasks is a records management *system*. This system will guide and direct the various types of forms that are used within the organization and will standardize and simplify the process of completing and accessing these forms for whatever institutional purposes may arise.

COMPUTERIZATION

The importance of computerization cannot be overstated in this context. The speed and consistency which is offered through large-scale automation of the records management function has been an enormous breakthrough for police services in Canada. One of the most obvious immediate benefits of the automation of the record management system is that it provides much better access for front-line officers. In order to ensure the security of these systems, however, most departments have assigned specially trained records officers who carry responsibility for control and accountability purposes.

COMMUNICATIONS

This function is significant to all areas of activity within a police department and will be treated in more detail in Chapter 9 ("Communication and Information Technology"). It is important to understand that personnel assigned to this area of duty may provide significant assistance to field officers by being able to handle incoming calls for service thereby relieving front-line officers of additional workload. Often a caller may be satisfied with information or assistance provided over the phone by the communications officer. This is an enormous efficiency for any police department and avoids the unnecessary dispatch of an officer to handle a call for service.

An ability to screen and prioritize calls for service is the essential skill required in this area of activity. These individuals will receive emergency calls, citizen complaints, requests for information and assistance, and they must be able to handle this wide range of inputs with a professional demeanour. As dispatchers, these individuals will need to be aware of the circumstances of each call and the requirement to ensure officer and public safety.

PROPERTY

Many police organizations have been criticized for lapses in the policies and procedures which guide their property and evidence-handling functions. Police have carriage of the following types of property which all require the highest levels of care and caution:

- prisoner's personal property;
- recovered stolen property;
- lost property;
- confiscated property;
- departmental property;
- abandoned or towed vehicles; and
- evidence (including drugs, firearms, dangerous goods, explosives, etc.)

The burden of responsibility in this regard is substantial, and police departments require special policies and procedures to ensure that they do not become open to criticism in this regard. Because a great deal of what is stored in these facilities will be returned to rightful owners or will be used as evidence in court, it is essential that these items be protected and maintained in good order. It is also important that personnel safety be ensured when items that could potentially be dangerous are stored. Proper records and receipts for items stored must also be provided in accordance with departmental policy or appropriate legislation.

FORENSIC IDENTIFICATION

This is a function that is becoming increasingly important to police organizations as developments are being made through scientific applications like DNA testing and the use of lasers and high-speed computers. There is a great deal of work being done through both private and public research centres to advance the art and science of forensic identification, and police services are continuously attempting to integrate new breakthroughs into their operational practices.

Because this area has a strong component of applied scientific method, it is not uncommon for this function to include large numbers of civilian staff trained in the specialized area of technology being applied. However, in Canada a number of police officers have developed incredible levels of expertise in the techniques of forensic identification through specialized learning through police colleges and public educational institutions. The growing significance of scientific evidence in all kinds of police investigations has lead to increased attention being paid to this area of activity.

In the Metropolitan Toronto Police Service, for example, a great deal of effort has gone into the process of identifying candidates for assignment to their Forensic

Identification Services area utilizing the General Aptitude Test Battery (G.A.T.B.), which is widely used for selecting entry-level police recruit candidates (see Chapter 4—"Becoming a Police Officer in Canada"). Collaborating with a qualified psychologist, this police service identified the following competencies that need to be demonstrated by applicants seeking positions in their Forensic Identification Services:

- *basic physical abilities and skills*—including physical strength, excellent eyesight (corrected or natural), no colour blindness, good hand/eye coordination, ability to climb and use ladders, free from latex or other allergies, demonstrated spatial relationship capabilities, free from dyslexia or other cognitive problems, free from any duty restrictions;
- *basic mechanical skills and abilities*—including proven driving ability to operate both light and medium duty vehicles, use of basic mechanical and power tools, cognizant of mechanical hazards, and able to work in both confined and open, outdoor areas;
- *basic technical knowledge and skills*—including keyboarding skills, knowledge of, and ability to use, service programs such as COPS, CPIC, MANIX, Microsoft Word, Windows, etc., and the ability to keep accurate legible handwritten notes;
- *scene management skills*—including evidence collection, continuity of evidence, biohazard protection procedures, evidence analysis, laws governing search and seizure, procedures for evidence control, and demonstrated understanding of costs associated with damage to property;
- *strong court-room abilities*—including appearance, bearing, self-confidence, professionalism, clearly demonstrated integrity, excellent case preparation skills, free of any criminal convictions or major disciplinary problems, and able to oath or affirm;
- *knowledge of basic investigative skills*—including ability to find and utilize all available resources, such as the RCMP, etc., be sensitive to victim concerns and issues, no sexual prohibitions, good time management, able to analyze and interpret evidence, good communication skills, able to function under pressure; and
- *display a high level of maturity*—including demonstrated high level of curiosity, ability to learn, open-mindedness, above-average intuitive capability, well-developed personal psychological coping mechanisms, ability to deal with distasteful or unpleasant investigative procedures and processes, self-discipline, and no aversion to the physical handling of dead bodies or other remains. (Metropolitan Toronto Police Service. Forensic Identification Services, 1997)

Because of the detailed and complex nature of the work being done in the forensic identification area, it is absolutely essential that members be highly competent individuals who do not make mistakes easily. The handling and preparation of items of physical evidence have to be completed with the utmost care if the evidence is to be accepted in court. The selection of personnel for these critical functions calls for the highest personal standards of excellence and professionalism. At the core of these functions two specific activities:

- fingerprinting; and
- photography.

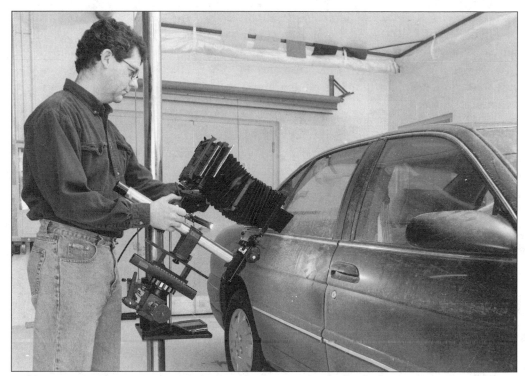

Ontario Provincial Police

Forensic technician photographing car for fingerprints

FINGERPRINTING

Fingerprinting is the fundamental skill required for work in the forensic identification area and constitutes a great deal of the evidence that is prepared for court cases. In line with other areas of police activity, fingerprinting has benefited from the application of technology with the creation of Automated Fingerprint Information Systems (AFIS). This allows for more rapid identification of fingerprint patterns and subsequent matching of latent fingerprints found at a crime scene and those held in the database. Officers continue to require a high level of sophistication with regard to fingerprinting techniques, and this can be acquired through the Canadian Police College, in Ottawa, which offers a highly regarded program on the theoretical knowledge and practical application of the Henry Fingerprint Classification System.

PHOTOGRAPHY

The application of photographic techniques to forensic identification are important because they allow for the exact recording of a crime scene, including the position and condition of the body, the arrangement of physical items within the crime scene, the presence of blood, or other substances, at the scene of the crime, as well as a number of other elements that may change or alter over time. Photographic skills in this area of assignment need to be quite extremely refined as the products of these efforts will be essential in any subsequent court proceedings and must, therefore, be of the highest quality. Forensic identification courses that prepare officers for work in this area place an enormous amount of emphasis on developing first-rate photographic skills with a view to the presentation of courtroom evidence.

In addition to the specialties discussed above, O'Brien and Sullivan (1980) point out that the front-line police officer may turn to the forensics area for the following assistance, which falls under the heading commonly known as criminalistics:

- Ammunition—including an analysis of bullets shot, wadding, cartridge casings, and shotgun shells;
- Blood—including blood samples found on objects floors, walls, rugs, and other surfaces;
- Clothing—including gunpowder residue, seminal stains, bloodstains, and paint;
- Documents—including letters and writings, altered documents, and cheques;
- Drugs—including dangerous substances and/or narcotics;
- Fibres—including wood, cotton, nylon, and hair;
- Firearms—including handguns, rifles, and shotguns;
- Glass—including fragments;
- Impressions—including shoes, tires;
- Liquor;
- Paint—on tools or chips found at the scene of a crime;
- Poisons;
- Soil; and
- Tools—including axes, bits, screwdrivers, tool marks, etc.

COURT SECURITY, DETENTION, AND PRISONER TRANSPORTATION

Police departments are frequently required to provide security for judges and those who are participating in or attending court proceedings. This will include prisoners, witnesses, and Crown and defence counsel. If this responsibility cannot be assigned to security personnel, sworn police officers will be required to undertake this function. There is also the need to have staff trained in the detention of prisoners prior to court appearance or while they are awaiting committal to a correctional facility. This places an obligation on police organizations to maintain lock-up facilities that satisfy local legislation and regulations with regard to the detention of young offenders, women, and prisoners with special health or medical needs.

There is a further responsibility for police departments to ensure that prisoners being transported to various locations are dealt with properly and in a secure manner.

ALCOHOL TESTING

With a strong emphasis on the prevention and control of impaired driving, police departments place considerable responsibility in the hands of officers who are skilled in the use of approved screening devices. Because the results of such screening are intended for possible use in court, it is essential that operators be qualified and certified in the application of any devices used for this purpose. Alcohol levels may be determined by examining breath, blood, and urine samples, with breath samples being the most easily acquired and analyzed. However, laboratory analysis of blood samples requires a slightly higher level of sophistication and skill.

FACILITIES MANAGEMENT

With police budgets being closely scrutinized and the likelihood of securing funding for new buildings being somewhat remote, it is important for police organizations to make the best use of their existing facilities and to plan carefully for growth. Due to the highly specialized nature of the interrelated police functions, the design of police headquarters and field offices should be informed with a full understanding of the functional flow of required activities. In recognizing this special need, the National Clearinghouse for Criminal Justice Planning and Architecture at the University of Illinois prepared appropriate guidelines for police facilities which have been widely accepted as a good basis for this area of planning (Sheehan and Cordner, 1995).

EQUIPMENT AND SUPPLY

There is a wide array of police equipment that needs to be researched, evaluated, tested, purchased and maintained in order to keep a police department functioning properly. Due to the constant changes in police technology, there is an ongoing requirement for a police service to have personnel who can take responsibility for these various functions and can provide suitable research, planning and development skills to ensure that officer safety is placed at an appropriately high level within the necessary financial constraints that will apply on new or replacement purchases.

Some of the types of equipment and supplies required of a normal police service include:

- *Police vehicles*—cruisers, motorcycles, motorboats, all-terrain vehicles, bicycles, helicopters, armoured vehicles, etc.;
- *Computer equipment*—personal computers, mainframe systems, printers, optical scanners, modems, etc.;
- *Firearms and ammunition*—revolvers, semi-automatic weapons, shotguns, long-guns, etc., and the appropriate ammunition for these weapons, including a sufficient supply for training and requalification purposes;

- *Photographic equipment*—high-speed cameras for surveillance work, videotape equipment for use in police lock-ups or for the production of training materials, developing equipment, enlargers, aerial photography, laser photography, etc.;
- *Uniforms*—belts, jackets, boots, soft body armour, hats, badges, seasonal wear, specially designed for various purposes (e.g., tactical uniform, ceremonial purposes, maternity wear for female officers, etc.); and
- *Specialized*—shields, bullhorns, batons, and other equipment for crowd management units, canine unit needs, including dogs and provision of food and training supplies, night-vision scopes for tactical units, ropes and related equipment for rappelling and other search and rescue purposes, underwater search and recovery equipment for scuba, explosives disposal equipment for training, remote mobile investigator, etc.

TRANSPORTATION, MAINTENANCE, AND PHYSICAL PLANT

Once the appropriate vehicles have been purchased for deployment and use throughout the police organization, there needs to be personnel assigned with the responsibility for ensuring that these investments are properly and routinely maintained and serviced for maximum efficiency and to satisfy any warranty requirements. Obviously, specialized mechanical skills will be essential in this area of assignment; however, a uniform police presence is considered important here to guarantee that this function is managed properly and according to the highest standards of safety and security.

Equally, the maintenance of equipment and the facilities where police functions are carried out is an important function that requires skill and supervision in order to adhere to proper standards. This area of assignment is typically contracted out by many police organizations; however, it is usually necessary for a police officer to be assigned overall coordination and management of these functions to protect the security and integrity of the materials, property, and information involved.

CONCLUSION

This chapter has outlined some of the wide range of duties that exist within most police departments. It should be apparent that the scope of possibilities for assignment are quite extensive and, invariably, challenging. In smaller police departments an incredible amount of flexibility is called for in order to accomplish many of these assignments which must necessarily be divided among fewer staff members and with fewer resources to support their efforts.

As police priorities change and evolve, the fundamental areas of activity outlined in this chapter will likely remain somewhat fixed. The public demand for crime prevention, law enforcement, order maintenance, assistance to victims of crime, and emergency response will require police organizations to structure themselves in ways that permit the effective and efficient delivery of flexible services focused on those demands. While the introduction of increasing levels of technology and continued civilianization in areas requiring highly specialized expertise may modify the details of the three main subsystems identified at the beginning of this chapter, there remains an ongoing need for highly motivated, fully sworn police officers with an incredibly flexible range of skills and abilities for assignment to duty.

QUESTIONS FOR CONSIDERATION

1. What are the ways in which the public comes into contact with front-line police officers?
2. What has contributed to the elevated status of police detectives?
3. Discuss various areas of police assignment in Canada. Where are there opportunities for civilianization in these areas?
4. Identify advantages and disadvantages associated with the various shifts found in a police department.
5. What are some of the major criminal investigations which have occurred in Canada over the last 10 years?
6. What are some ways in which the police can assist public safety by providing information?
7. Why are some crime prevention programs (e.g., Neighbourhood Watch) criticized as being unnecessary?

REFERENCES

Bigham, Steve. (1993). *Attitude and public opinion survey: Reno Police Department.* Reno, Nevada: Reno Police Department.

Canadian Comprehensive Auditing Foundation. (1983). *Comprehensive auditing: concepts, components and characteristics.* Ottawa: CCAF.

Commission on Accreditation for Law Enforcement Agencies, Inc. (1990–). [Loose-leaf]. *Standards for law enforcement agencies: the standards manual of the Law Enforcement Agency Accreditation Program.* Fairfax, Virginia: The Commission.

Cordner, Gary W. and Donna C. Hale (eds.) (1992). *What works in policing?: operations and administration examined.* Highland Heights, Kentucky and Cincinnati, Ohio: Academy of Criminal Justice Sciences, North Kentucky University and Anderson Publishing Co.

Eck, John E. (1983). *Solving crimes: the investigation of burglary and robbery.* Washington, D.C.: Police Executive Research Forum.

Eck, John E. (1996). "Rethinking detective management." In Hoover, Larry T. (ed.). *Quantifying quality in policing.* Washington, D.C.: Police Executive Research Forum.

Ericson, Richard V. (1981). *Making crime: a study of detective work.* Toronto: Butterworths Canada Ltd.

Greenwood, Peter W. and Joan Petersilia. (1975). *The criminal investigation process.* Santa Monica, Calif.: RAND Corporation.

Halton Regional Police Service. (1995). *Halton Regional Police Service public survey 1995*. Oakville, Ont.: Halton Regional Police Service.

Horne, David G., Dennis P. Forcese and Lester N. Thompson. (1989). *Gloucester Police Force: public needs survey preliminary findings: report number one*. Ottawa: Carleton University.

Kelling, George, et al. (1974). *The Kansas City Preventive Patrol Experiment: final report*. Washington, D.C.: Police Foundation.

Knapp Commission. (1972). *The Knapp Commission report on police corruption*. New York: George Braziller.

Martens, Frederick T. (1990). "The intelligence function." In Andrews, Jr., Paul P. and Marilyn Peterson (eds.). *Criminal intelligence analysis*. Loomis, Calif.: Palmer Enterprises.

Martin, Maurice A. (1995). *Urban policing: anatomy of an aging craft*. Montreal and Kingston: McGill-Queen's University Press.

Mayhall, Pamela D., Thomas Barker, and Ronald D. Hunter. (1995). *Police-community relations and the administration of justice. 4th ed.* Englewood Cliffs, N.J.: Prentice Hall, Inc.

Melchers, Ron and Julian Roberts. (1994). *Public opinion and policing in Canada: a review of recent findings and selected social trends and demands on policing*. Ottawa: Department of Criminology, University of Ottawa.

Metropolitan Toronto Police Service. Traffic Restructuring Project Team. (1996). *Recommendations*. Toronto: Metropolitan Toronto Police Service.

Metropolitan Toronto Police Service. Forensic Identification Services. (Draft, February 13, 1997).

O'Brien, Kevin P. and Robert C. Sullivan. (1980). *Criminalistics: theory and practice. 3rd ed.* Toronto: Allyn and Bacon, Inc.

Ontario. Ministry of the Solicitor General. Policing Services Division. (1992). [Loose-leaf]. *Policing standards manual for the Province of Ontario*. Toronto: The Ministry.

Ontario Provincial Police. Organizational Review Project. (1994). *Traffic/Waterways Management*. [Orillia, Ont.]: OPP.

Peak, Kenneth J. (1993). *Policing America: methods, issues, challenges*. Englewood Cliffs, N.J.: Regents/Prentice Hall.

Peak, Kenneth J. and Ronald W. Glensor. (1996). *Community policing and problem solving: strategies and practices*. Upper Saddle River, N.J.: Prentice Hall.

Royal Canadian Mounted Police. (1991). *Criminal intelligence program: planning and direction: implementation guide*. [Ottawa]: RCMP.

Shearing, Clifford D. (1984). *Dial-a-cop: a study of police mobilisation*. Toronto: Centre of Criminology, University of Toronto.

Sheehan, Robert and Gary W. Cordner. (1995). *Police administration. 3rd ed*. Cincinnati, Ohio: Anderson Publishing.

Victoria Police (Australia). (1996). *Project Guardian: Ethical Standards Department: final report*. [Melbourne]: Victoria Police.

Wells, Gary L. (1988). *Eyewitness identification: a system handbook*. Toronto: Carswell.

Weston, Paul B. and Kenneth M. Wells. (1986). *Criminal investigation: basic perspectives. 4th ed.* Englewood Cliffs, N.J.: Prentice Hall.

TOWARD MORE LEARNING

Ontario. Ministry of the Solicitor General. Policing Services Division. (1992). [Loose-leaf]. *Policing standards manual for the Province of Ontario*. Toronto: The Ministry.

This loose-leaf manual has been prepared as a reference tool and guide for use by police services across Ontario in developing policies and procedures to guide their activities in key areas. It is the result of ongoing consultation between the ministry and various groups that have an interest and/or expertise in the development of generic policing standards. The manual is designed around the following topical areas:

General

- Accommodation (Building Facilities; Cells in Police Stations)

Operations

- Care and Control of Prisoners
- Missing Persons
- Officer Note-taking
- Vehicle Pursuits
- Search of Premises
- Use of Force

Human Resources

- Personnel Selection
- Harassment in the Workplace
- Performance Appraisal
- Career Development

External Relations

- Media Relations
- Victim Assistance
- Cooperation with other Police Services

Crime Management

- Collection and Use of Crime Information
- Property

Financial Management
Health & Safety

Information Management & Communications

- Communications (Radio & Telephone)
- Information Services (Canadian Police Information Centre)
- Freedom of Information & Protection of Privacy
- Records Management
- Use of Force Reporting

Court Activities

- Court Security

Equipment

- Body Armour
- Condition of Uniforms and Equipment
- Secure Holster
- Use of Force (Aerosol Weapons, etc.)

While not exhaustive, this manual provides a good overview of standards that might pertain in virtually any police service and offers guidelines relevant to operational policies and procedures in these areas.

Commission on Accreditation for Law Enforcement Agencies, Inc. (1991). [Loose-leaf]. *Standards for law enforcement agencies: the standards manual of the Law Enforcement Agency Accreditation Program*. Fairfax, Virginia: The Commission.

This extensive resource provides substantial detail in more than 890 standards for application to law enforcement agencies. Aside from the fact that it is designed exclusively as an American product, it offers the Canadian reader some extensively researched insight into a number of assignment areas that would not differ substantially in our context. These standards were originally prepared through the collaboration of the following organizations:

- International Association of Chiefs of Police;
- National Organization of Black Law Enforcement Executives;
- National Sheriffs' Association; and the
- Police Executive Research Forum.

The standards, as originally prepared, were tested in field applications and revised. Since they first adopted by the Commission on Accreditation for Law Enforcement Agencies, Inc., in April 1983, the standards have been added to and amended as required. They have proven to be effective in making determinations about adherence to established standards. The detailed presentation provides a wealth of information for anyone seeking to gain a deeper insight into the functioning of a police organization; however, it is not a guarantee that the presence of policies and procedures will ensure flawless and complete front-line service delivery.

Webster, Jack, with Rosemary Aubert. (1991). *Copper Jack: my life on the force.* Toronto: Dundurn Press.

This is a fascinating account of one person's long and distinguished career with the Metropolitan Toronto Police. Beginning with his recruitment in 1945, Jack Webster provides the reader with a detailed account of his experiences in a large, urban police service that are both entertaining and educational. This officer provides us with an understanding of the fullest range of assignments from his personal experiences as a beat cop, motorcycle officer, accident investigator, member of the hold-up squad, homicide investigator, and senior police executive. When he retired in 1988, he had attained the rank of Staff Superintendent. His memoirs are a lasting tribute to the trials, tribulations, and triumphs of a working life devoted to the profession of policing.

CHAPTER EIGHT

ORGANIZATIONAL STRATEGIES: MAKING THE BEST USE OF RESOURCES

LEARNING OBJECTIVES

1. Identify the elements of a strategic management process
2. Identify the elements of a tactical planning process
3. Describe the differences between a generalist and a specialist model of policing in Canada
4. Describe the main differences between routine and directed patrol in Canadian policing
5. Explain the purpose of selective initial response
6. Describe key areas of special operational challenge for a police service in Canada

INTRODUCTION

This chapter will begin to look in some detail at the various ways in which police organizations in Canada have tried to make the best use of the human, financial, and technological resources which they have at their disposal. It will focus primarily on the specialized operational challenges that confront most police services and which create a need to deploy resources in ways that are calculated to have the maximum beneficial effect. The information in this chapter, while by no means exhaustive, attempts to give the reader a better understanding of the magnitude of the issues that confront police personnel on a continuous basis. It also tries to provide a deeper awareness of the functional duties which were introduced in Chapter 7 ("Assignment to Duty"). By reviewing an extensive range of specialized operational functions and the organizational strategies that are required to put resources into the field to deliver those functions, it is easier to understand the particular pressures and demands that are placed on police agencies when they develop their short-term (i.e., tactical) and long-range (i.e., strategic) plans.

STRATEGIC MANAGEMENT

Strategic management, which implies a continuous and sustained planning function, is a process that should be engaged in by any police organization that wants to be positioned properly for the delivery of its services. By doing a good job of strategic management, a police service will be able to visualize: what it should be doing in the future (for example, over the next five years); what it needs to move toward that vision of the future; and who will be needed within the organization to facilitate and lead that movement. As a specific skill, strategic management has some clear components that can be learned and practised; however, on an organizational level, there needs to be a serious commitment to the effort required to undertake this process in a meaningful and reliable manner. It is time-consuming and difficult but it can pay important dividends for everyone in the organization when it is done properly. It is also something that affects the entire organization and cannot be simply the product of deep thinking in the executive office of the police department. The more extensive the strategic management process is and the more broadly consultative the information gathering stages are, the more powerful the end results.

Strategic management attempts to answer the following key questions:

- Where are we now? (Organizational diagnosis)
- Where do we want to go? (Organizational prognosis)
- How are we going to get there? (Organizational prescriptions)

Each of these questions anticipates a whole series of additional questions that need to be answered if the organization is going to make some important decisions about how it intends to operate. This is where insight can be generated from everywhere within the organization. It is known that people who are new to a particular field of activity are often in an ideal position to offer constructive criticism of programs, processes, and practices for a number of reasons, including their lack of attachment to the *status quo*, their ability to clearly see any "anomalies" in the system, and their fresh perspective on the routines of the organization (Kuhn, 1986). By answering the questions outlined above, a police organization will be able to address a number of items that will support and sustain their strategic management process:

- mission statement;
- objectives; and
- action plans.

MISSION STATEMENT

This is a clear and usually brief expression of the police organization's vision, a statement or declaration of its overriding purpose. Such a document should be eloquent, direct, and meaningful for everyone within the organization and should also be accessible to the public as the recipients of the services being provided under the banner of this mission.

OBJECTIVES

These will serve to express the general results that the police organization wishes to accomplish in pursuing its mission. They will normally be fairly high-level statements of achievements the police department wishes to make over a certain period of time. These objectives should be stated in terms that can be *measured* in some manner in order to ensure that success or failure can be gauged.

ACTION PLANS

This part of the strategic management process begins to move into the tactical area of planning, insofar as they express in fairly close operational detail the specific steps that will be taken to achieve the objectives outlined above. Once an organization has clarified its vision and committed itself to moving toward certain clear objectives, it remains to plot a detailed course of concrete action in light of the mission and objectives. Action planning as an activity is really the bridge between tactical planning and strategic management. If action plans are not developed in ways that produce specific, measurable results that can be realistically accomplished at the front-line level of the organization, the whole strategic planning structure amounts to an exercise in futility.

The Peel Regional Police, for example, have demonstrated a strong understanding of the need for a systematic approach to the planning process and a continuous cycle of review of their organization's strategic plan. This understanding is exemplified in Figure 8–1.

TACTICAL PLANNING

This involves the process of planning a course of action for specific circumstances, under prescribed conditions, and relating to particular locations. Tactical plans are derived from the strategic plans which are guided by the overall mission and mandate of the organization, as well as being linked to any departmental objectives and action plans that have been produced out of a systematic strategic management process. Tactical planning amounts to the operationalization of the strategic plan of a police organization and will involve detailed behavioural objectives on the part of those assigned to this area of responsibility.

GENERALIST VS. SPECIALIST

Police organizations frequently engage in debate around the issue of whether they should be directed more toward a generalist or a specialist approach to the delivery of police services. On one hand, all police officers begin their careers with a basic level of education and training that places them in a generalist category. The entry-level officer is typically assigned to patrol duties that rest upon a broad range of generalist skills. On the other hand, there are particular areas of assignment within most police departments that require a highly focused level of aptitude and application that can normally only be acquired

FIGURE 8-1

STRATEGIC PLANNING FOR CONTINUOUS QUALITY IMPROVEMENT

Strategic Planning For Continuous Quality Improvement

The annual revision to the Strategic Plan ensures continuous enhancement of services in response to consumer and community needs, and identification of new opportunities for achievement.

Leadership

- Policing Priorities are reviewed and approved annually by the Peel Regional Police Services Board.
- Executive leadership provides direction and support throughout the strategic planning and management cycle and process.
- Cross-functional collaboration is facilitated by the Executive and Senior Management.

Customer Focus

- Community liaison and continuous consultation broadens our understanding of consumer needs and priorities.
- Decentralized problem-solving ensures that consumer and community needs are the primary focus of the pursuit of excellence at Peel Regional Police.

Planning for Improvement

- An annual update of the Strategic Plan clarifies the measurable results to be achieved in the long-term (3-5 years); builds on best practices and community assets; and keeps plans current.

People Focus

- Multi-level teams innovate, plan and monitor quality improvements; continuously learn from experience; and enhance individual skills for optimizing their full potential.

Process Optimization

- Strategic management practices are supported by a Feedback and Monitoring System which ensures that all organizational levels learn from experience.
- The Strategic Planning Cycle integrates annual service plans and the financial planning and budget management process.
- The planning process is evaluated annually and thrives on feedback from all Cost Centre Managers; members of Planning Teams; and consumer and community partnerships.

Supplier Focus

- Community partnerships are actively engaged in creative problem-solving processes.
- Collaboration within the Criminal Justice System and community service network ensures co-ordination of efforts; sharing of information; and improving working relationships.

PEEL REGIONAL
POLICE

 An Accredited Police Service

For further information contact: Manager, Strategic Planning Services, Peel Regional Police, 7750 Hurontario Street, Brampton, Ontario, L6V 3W6 Phone (905) 453-2121 Ext. 4050 or FAX (905) 453-4048

Source: Peel Regional Police. Used with permission.

through some degree of specialization. This presents a dilemma for many police organizations when they come to consider how to best deploy and utilize the resources which they have available. In some instances, police services have tried to balance both approaches through a concentration on the provision of generalist policing skills with the availability of a limited range of specialist officers.

Another approach that has been satisfactory in some jurisdictions is the use of agreements or protocols with other police jurisdictions, which provide for the sharing of certain specialist officers on an as-needed basis. This is seen, for example, where an emergency task force or tactical unit may be called upon by one jurisdiction only when there is a need for this kind of specialized capability. Otherwise, that jurisdiction does not have its own officers trained, equipped, or assigned for this purpose.

Generalist officers normally make up the highest percentage of a police service's front-line personnel allowing the department to have a fairly high degree of flexibility in the deployment of resources for a variety of police duties and operational assignments. In 1994, the Ontario Provincial Police (OPP) identified their philosophy as being community policing and their system of policing as being:

> ...based on a well-trained generalist policing service supported by traffic management, crime prevention and detection and administrative excellence. (OPP, 1994a)

This is an example of the kind of balance that is struck when a police organization must assume responsibility for a range of services that clearly fall into two distinct categories: generalist patrol functions and specialized operational activities.

ROUTINE PATROL

This is the term used to identify the kind of patrol work that is normally done by front-line officers. It may consist of driving around the patrol zone, parking in some location and observing general activity, or patrolling on foot within an assigned beat. There are some who perceive this kind of activity as being extremely wasteful; however, there are others who argue that this type of patrol has a strong preventative effect in most communities, and provides the positive reassurance of a visible police presence. Those who view this approach as being wasteful might call it random patrol. There have been occasions when an officer engaged in routine patrol has in fact come upon a crime in progress and has, as a result, been able to apprehend the criminal, prevent further violence, and protect the public. In such circumstances, there will be little argument that the officer's presence was valuable for overall public safety. However, for those who are concerned about the overall cost to the taxpayer of this kind of resource deployment, it is argued that there are better strategies for effective patrol. It has been noted that there is a degree of necessity implicit in the patrol function (Sheehan and Cordner, 1995). If officers are going to be available for service calls, they must be in a state of readiness that will allow them to be dispatched to any given location, at any given time. Part of the enormous cost of maintaining a police service results directly from this on-call availability of trained, equipped officers deployed throughout the jurisdiction to be patrolled.

DIRECTED PATROL

This form of patrol provides officers with specific instructions regarding activities to be followed when they are not actively engaged with a particular call for service. In some instances this may mean that patrol officers are directed to be on the alert for possible illegal activity in a particular area within the patrol zone. Frequently, this will be the result of some form of crime trend analysis that points to trouble or suspicious activity in a certain sector. It is intended that this approach will be more rational than the routine or random approach to patrolling which merely places an officer into the zone in a mobile state of readiness for whatever may occur, or for dispatch to a particular call. Directed patrol is an attempt to focus the operational assignment of officers and to present particular tactics which they may use when moving to specific target areas within their zone. To date, there has not been much sound research on the overall effectiveness of directed patrol (Sheehan and Cordner, 1995); however, its value lies in its tendency to balance police routine patrol with targeted responses which rely on the results of crime trend analysis.

FOOT PATROL

Before the introduction of the automobile, foot patrols were the means by which police officers provided coverage for their jurisdictions. The traditional image of the police officer walking the beat and keeping a watchful eye on the comings and goings of people is deeply ingrained.

When the car made its appearance, however, police departments began to organize themselves in ways that would take advantage of this new technology and allow for rapid, mobile coverage of the patrol zone. The police need for automobiles was particularly keen in small towns and rural areas where bank robbers and burglars could strike in an area without extensive policing and make a quick escape (Higley, 1984). The change from a visible police presence through foot patrols to the mobile patrol resulted in an entirely different approach to the whole concept of police presence and has created much of the current pressure for more proactive approaches to crime prevention and law enforcement. Because police officers were assigned to mobile patrols that kept them ready for dispatch, they were not available for regular, non-enforcement contact with members of the public. The sight of a passing patrol vehicle is a vastly different experience than passing an officer on foot patrol on the same streets that members of the public are using for their daily routines. There was an engagement of the community implicit in foot patrol that is absent in a mobile patrol approach. Many police commentators have lamented the change from foot patrols to mobile police strategies because it further distances officers from direct contact with the public in the normal course of their shifts. It meant that the

Ontario Provincial Police

Officers on street patrol

police only left the isolation of their vehicles to apprehend a suspect, make an arrest, or in some other way invoke their discretion or legal authority relating to specific occurrences requiring a police response.

Not only was it important for police departments to acquire automobiles for the purpose of giving chase to criminals, it was necessary if the limited number of police officers was going to begin to provide adequate coverage of the growing jurisdictions which they had to patrol. As towns, villages, and hamlets grew in both size and population, the police departments were faced with vast geographic areas which they had to oversee. Foot patrols became impractical in many instances because officers could not provide the kind of response time available to an officer in a mobile patrol unit.

Studies were done on foot patrols in order to determine their impact on the prevention of crime. Some of the evidence indicated that they were indeed helpful in this regard. On the other hand, a 1980 study of the foot patrol program in Newark, New Jersey, indicated that increases or decreases in this type of patrol had no significant effect on crime (Police Foundation, 1981). What this study did discover was that the public was more satisfied with the foot patrol approach than with mobile patrols and experienced less fear of crime. Such findings have prompted a number of police departments to reintroduce foot patrols as part of their overall policing strategy (Koller, 1990; Sheehan and Cordner, 1995). In taking more trouble to examine the nature of foot patrol assignments, Trojanowicz and Carter (1988) noted that these programs were evolving into something that could be effectively applied against crime and disorder problems in communities:

> As the concept evolved, the term foot patrol began to give way to community policing, reflecting a broad mandate. While many such efforts do employ foot patrol as the primary means of insuring the same officer has daily face-to-face interaction with the community, today's educated and trained officers do not approach the job in the same way the more passive beat officers of the political era did.
>
> Indeed, at least initially, the term foot patrol misled many into thinking this approach was simply a nostalgic desire to recapture the past. However, not only have today's foot officers been de-politicized, their functions extend far beyond what was expected of foot patrol officers in the political era, and, at the same time, their excesses have been curbed. (p. 5)

SELECTIVE INITIAL RESPONSE

Also referred to as differential response, tiered response, or a number of other terms, this approach really implies that the police service will prioritize every call for service that it receives and will assign resources to address these calls according to the call's individual characteristics. It has become widely accepted that police organizations cannot continue to simply dispatch officers, equipment, and resources equally to every single call that comes into the station. Some rank-ordering must be undertaken by the police in order to get the right resources into the rights hands at the right time.

A selective approach to the initial response to calls for police service can be introduced in order to increase the level of efficiency in an organization's handling of those calls. By applying certain principles for prioritizing calls for service it is possible to achieve the following:

- an increase in the number of non-emergency calls which can be dealt with by a trained telephone handler, by a delayed police response, or by some other form of alternative response;
- an increase in the amount of proactive, problem-solving, or community-oriented policing that can be undertaken by officers;
- a decrease in the total time spent by patrol officers in answering calls for service; and
- a decrease in the total number of calls requiring an immediate dispatch and response.

The OPP, as a result of a recent review of their processes, proposed an occurrence response program based on the following priorities:

- *Priority One: Immediate Mobile Response*—dealing with serious calls requiring rapid police response because of their potential for physical injury or damage to property;
- *Priority Two: Delayed Mobile Response/Officer Follow-up*—dealing with circumstances where an officer may reasonably delay response to the complaint without jeopardizing investigative procedures; and
- *Priority Three: Telephone Call Handling*—dealing with any type of call where a mobile police response would not be warranted and a telephone report could be taken.

By dividing all possible calls into one of these three priorities, it is expected that a more efficient handling of occurrences will result. The success of this prioritized approach relies heavily on a police department's efforts at educating the public about the rationale behind such a priority system and by ensuring that appropriate follow-ups are in fact undertaken on calls that have been placed on this level of priority.

SPECIAL OPERATIONAL CHALLENGES

In order to address the range of demands for police services, many organizations have developed strategies that ensure they have officers trained, equipped, and qualified for undertaking specialized assignments. In some cases, these officers function only in their area of specialty. In other cases, they may perform general duties and will be assigned to their specialist function only on an as-needed basis. The demands of many of the specialized operational assignments discussed below often require constant skill maintenance and practice; therefore, it is common for these officers to be dedicated exclusively to their specialty. What follows is an examination of some of these areas of specialization.

CROWD MANAGEMENT

In previous years this function would most likely be referred to as crowd control or riot control. However, in recent times this rather aggressive approach to crowds and the strategies that are most appropriate for dealing with them has undergone change. It is now more common to hear about techniques of crowd management, where the police participate in ways that are designed to more safely and peacefully deal with the challenge of large numbers of people gathered together for some common purpose. The spectacle of police officers pitted in an unequal battle with members of the public is something which any police organization should be attempting to avoid.

By taking a crowd management approach, police organizations are able to be considerably more proactive in their dealings with large gatherings of people. Under this approach, police officers make direct contact with members of the crowd before an event takes place and are often able to reduce tension and anxiety by the application of crisis intervention techniques. Officers who become members of a crowd management unit can be carefully trained in such techniques (Harman, 1995).

In the Metropolitan Toronto Police Service, there is a Public Safety Unit that applies this proactive approach to crowd management in a serious and consistent manner. Every officer who is assigned to this unit must complete a four-day training course which includes the following topics:

- introduction to the program;
- unit structure and duties;
- specialized equipment;

- theory of crowds—including orderly and disorderly crowds, crowd types, collective behaviour;
- crowd psychology;
- tactical formations—including theory and practice;
- use of force—gradual application of force; and
- dispersal tactics—including mounted units, dogs, moving formations, and pepper spray or tear gas.

In addition to this intensive training, Metropolitan Toronto Police officers in this unit are required to complete a one-week course in crisis resolution that further enhances the unit member's abilities and skills in applying a proactive approach to crowds (Metropolitan Toronto Police, 1997). This training includes the following components:

- critical thinking/exemplary reasoning;
- stages of crisis development;
- crisis assessment;
- officer response to crisis stages;
- communication—active listening/interviewing/decision making;
- kinesics and proxemics;
- verbal interventions;
- appropriate use of force;
- restorative interaction;
- applied human relations;
- team intervention;
- emotionally disturbed persons;
- role play; and
- assaultive subject restraint.

INCIDENT COMMAND

When serious occurrences take place within a police jurisdiction, there is a need for officers trained to a high level of proficiency who can take responsibility for the overall management and handling of such events. In most jurisdictions this person is referred to as the incident commander. The background knowledge, skills, and abilities (KSAs) required for this function are considerable and many police organizations do not have the resources to ensure that a sufficient number of their senior personnel are trained and continuously requalified in these KSAs. As a result, this is one area of police specialization where agreements or protocols are struck between two or more police organizations for the sharing of a fully qualified incident commander. There is a great deal of learning involved in assuming this important role; however, it is useless learning if incident commanders cannot practise their skills in realistic scenarios or mock exercises that truly test their knowledge and capacity to work under stressful circumstances. Some of the events which may require the specialized skills of an incident commander include:

- train derailments;
- hazardous material spills;
- air crashes;
- hostage situations;
- natural disasters;
- explosions or bomb threats;
- lost or missing persons; and
- nuclear or hydro incidents.

The following outlines some of the topical areas relevant to an incident commander:

- role of the incident commander;
- situational assessment;
- role of specialized units called to assist with the specific incident (e.g., tactics and rescue unit; explosives disposal unit; canine unit);
- establishing a command post (including the use of mobile command post);
- site management (including, location, decontamination, establishing a temporary morgue, evacuations, property recovery, staging areas, control points);
- media relations;
- briefings and debriefings; and
- critical incident stress.

TACTICAL AND EMERGENCY RESPONSE UNITS

These specialized units go by a variety of names, including tactics and rescue unit (TRU), emergency task force (ETF), hostage rescue team (HRT), and special weapons attack team (SWAT). In Canada, there has been an inclination toward the milder expression of this role; therefore, we have very few SWAT units deployed because the very name sounds overly aggressive. However, the critical importance of this specialized operational capacity is seen quite frequently when serious, violent crimes occur where highly trained, specially equipped, and properly supervised officers are mandatory. Such units require not only advanced equipment, but members of these units must be very carefully selected and constantly trained and retrained in order to maintain the highest levels of proficiency in the tactics and weapons required for safe operations.

Tactical units may be developed to provide a number of highly specialized services that may be divided into one of the following categories:

- containment;
- clearing;
- assault;
- security; and
- rescue.

Each of the categories noted above requires a precise set of skills and will likely utilize different tactical approaches. The police organization which proposes to establish some form of tactical unit will need to be very clear about the kind of mandate which their unit will have in order to fully prepare themselves for the selection, training, equipping, and qualification of unit members. Police officers who have an interest in this type of specialized assignment will need to be aware of the precise selection criteria being applied within their organization and also be prepared for the rigorous training and skills maintenance that goes along with this type of assignment. The following details on the basic models for tactics and rescue units are provided:

Armed officers responding to an emergency call

Brian Willer/Maclean's

- *Containment*—includes all approved tactical procedures that allow police personnel to gain dominance of a crisis area by means of tactical control, security, and observation in a safe and secure manner.
- *Clearing*—includes all approved tactical procedures that allows for police personnel to approach, enter, search, and secure a crisis area in a safe manner.
- *Assault*—includes all approved tactical procedures, especially relating to use of force provisions, to successfully resolve a hostage situation.
- *Security*—includes all approved tactical procedures relating to the provision of high risk security for persons, premises, or material in a safe manner.
- *Rescue*—includes the application of approved rescue techniques for the safe evacuation of individuals from isolated or remote areas.

In all tactical circumstances, it is important for unit members to have a full understanding of the briefing format which has been derived from the military for the logical gathering and recording of information. While not all questions will be relevant to each tactical event, nor will all answers be immediately available, it is essential that this framework be kept in mind for the collection of data. The acronym used to capture this format is SMEAC, which stands for:

S—Situation (the Who or Where?);
M—Mission (the What?);
E—Execution (the How and When?);
A—Administration (the Support System); and
C—Command, Control, and Communications (the Support System).

SITUATION

This component includes all available information on the occurrence. This data will assist in making any necessary tactical decisions and will include such things as:

- *General information*—including offence(s), type of occurrence, location, telephone number(s), deadlines;
- *Suspects*—including the number, type (e.g., suicidal, calm, mentally disabled), name(s), description, language(s), background (e.g., criminal record, medical history), physical condition, photographs, relationship to hostage(s);
- *Vehicles*—including year, make, model, licence plate number, colour, condition;
- *Weapons*—including type, quantity, ammunition, explosives, other equipment (e.g., body armour, gas masks);
- *Hostages*—including number, name(s), description, language(s), photographs, background, location (guarded or restraints); and
- *Scene*—including description, photographs, maps, floor plans, type of structure, access points, essential services (e.g., hydro, water, telephone, gas), obstacles, vantage points.

MISSION STATEMENT

This refers to the overall objective that is to be achieved. It should be a simple, clearly stated objective approved by the incident commander in charge of the tactical operation.

EXECUTION

This refers to the precise details or action plan as to how the mission will be accomplished. This tactical plan will include assignments or tasks given to individual elements within the team, the specific events that will take place, the sequence of team movements, routes to be followed, and coordinating instructions.

ADMINISTRATION

This area includes all elements of logistical support necessary to meet the tactical objectives. This may include the acquisition of special equipment (e.g., lights, ladders, explosives), transportation (e.g., helicopters, pontoon plane), clothing (e.g., camouflage gear, extreme weather clothing), emergency equipment (e.g., first aid, field dressings), and meals.

COMMAND, CONTROL, AND COMMUNICATIONS

A clear statement about the command structure relevant to this tactical assignment and the various lines and means of communication. This area will include detailed information about the Command Post, the Tactical Operations Centre, and communications (e.g., channels, frequencies, telephone numbers, pager numbers, code words, call signs, hand signals).

HOSTAGE NEGOTIATION AND BARRICADED PERSON(S)

This is essentially a tactical area of assignment that requires precise training to prepare an officer to function properly. The work of a hostage negotiator, or someone trying to communicate with barricaded persons (who may or may not be holding hostages), is *always* aimed at the peaceful resolution of a potentially lethal situation. The police officer operating as a negotiator must be a mature individual with considerable presence of mind and a calm, stable personality. This person needs to be able to inspire confidence when dealing with the captor and attempt to develop a strong interpersonal rapport. Negotiators apply their skills to bring the hostage-takers or barricaded persons to a point where they will release their hostages or surrender without any injury or lose of life. Negotiators are trained to apply patience, understanding, listening skills, and extraordinary verbal ability to relax the suspect and move toward the peaceful resolution of a situation. The information that these negotiators are able to gather from their careful interaction with hostage-takers or barricaded persons can be used by tactics and rescue unit members should the negotiations fail to bring about a peaceful resolution. However, it is always the priority for negotiators to invest as much time as it takes to resolve such situations without resorting to tactics that may result in injury or loss of life.

In order to function properly, the hostage negotiator needs to be aware of the different types of captors. Using this knowledge, the negotiator can ease tension and anxiety and, in certain circumstances, allow the captor to reassess their position through the consideration of different alternatives. By maintaining a continuous dialogue with the captor and by providing the captor with choices that require consideration and thought, the negotiator can keep that person preoccupied, thereby reducing the risk of injury to the hostages.

Negotiators can function best when they have detailed and accurate intelligence about the captor and the hostages. The following are some areas that should be immediately relevant for the negotiator's task:

- *medical history*—including information on possible alcohol or drug addiction, any medication being taken;
- *criminal record*—including any background details that may be available from correctional institutions associated with the captor;
- *military background*—including details about weapons or explosives training;
- *education and financial status*;
- *social and cultural background*; and
- *terrorist or political extremist background*.

From studies that have been done on hostage-takers, it has been determined that they typically fall into one of three main categories. By understanding the type of captor that one is dealing with, a negotiator can develop a strategy that is consistent with the captor's primary motivation. Each category has its own characteristics requiring different approaches. The categories are as follows:

- *psychological*—these individuals are moved by factors that can be extremely complex and unpredictable. Such a captors may be highly irrational and, as a result, it is difficult to logically anticipate their actions or their reaction to a negotiator's communication. These individuals' demands and behaviour may provide valuable clues to their mental states that can be applied in resolving the situation. In these circumstances, time is normally an ally of the police since the captor is typically expending a great deal of physical and mental energy and may be worn down through careful handling on the part of the negotiator;
- *criminal*—"professional" criminals are normally considered the least difficult type of captor to deal with because they are likely to be able to think rationally and calculate the precise nature of their situation. A skillful negotiator may be able to reason with this type of captor and bring about a peaceful resolution; and
- *political*—this is considered to be the most difficult type of captor for the police negotiator to deal with because of an extreme devotion to a larger cause. Highly organized and cohesive terrorist groups may be resigned to their own loss of life and, therefore, will be especially resistant to the negotiator's emphasis on peaceful resolution.

In terms of tactical police response to hostage-taking situations, there are really only five courses of action that can be considered:

- contain and negotiate;
- deploy chemical agents;
- use deception;
- authorize targeted sniper fire; and
- authorize assault tactics.

Ideally, the negotiator will begin at the first level and not need to move beyond this option. It is always possible to progress through these options, normally in a logical sequence; however, it is impossible to move back once the decision has been made to escalate the level of force used in the hostage situation. It is always preferable for the negotiator to remain at the first level of this continuum and use the utmost skill and patience in order to peacefully resolve the situation.

SEARCH AND RESCUE

Within Canada, police organizations are typically called upon to provide search and rescue functions. In the provinces other than Ontario and Quebec, this responsibility frequently falls to the Royal Canadian Mounted Police (RCMP). Following a review of the search and rescue (generally referred to as SAR) function, the RCMP identified the following key areas of focus:

- *Response*—development of detailed policy providing an outline of the various roles and responsibilities of police personnel to ensure coordination and investigation of lost or overdue persons using various SAR response methods (e.g., police search dogs, volunteer, helicopter, divers, etc.);

- *Training*—this includes the responsibility of developing police personnel in a wide range of KSAs that relate directly to the organization, management and execution of search and rescue functions. Many police organizations turn to the National Association for Search and Rescue in the United States for detailed curricula dealing with these areas. Also, there is a growing network of organizations in Canada that are developing considerable expertise based on the principles of basic, advanced, and management SAR courses already in existence;
- *Equipment*—highly specialized equipment is required for the conduct of SAR missions, including air, water, and land vehicles which can be used in all kinds of terrain and under a variety of geographic and weather conditions;
- *Interdepartmental Cooperation*—development of formal written agreements in each jurisdiction served by the police department to clarify the roles and responsibilities of various agencies (e.g., the Civilian Air Search & Rescue Association, the Canadian Marine Rescue Association, Canadian Parks Service, and the Departments of Forestry and Natural Resources) with regard to SAR;
- *Prevention*—including the design, delivery, and evaluation of public education programs. The RCMP is specifically directing their prevention efforts at three groups: children ages 5–12, special interest groups, and the general public; and
- *Volunteers*—emphasis is being placed on the preparation of an extensive network of trained civilian volunteers who may be more readily available than police personnel. It is expected that police will continue to retain authority for the organization and management of the search; however, there is considerable value to having a strong, trained volunteer SAR resource available. The extent of volunteer, civilian engagement in SAR is determined on a province-by-province basis according to various standards and guidelines in place in each jurisdiction.

As a specialized area of assignment, it requires particular knowledge and skills that are not acquired through normal police recruit training. Therefore, it will be undertaken by officers who have been developed in these particular skills.

Geographic considerations will be a significant factor in determining the need for such a function within any given police department. For example, in large urban settings, the nature of a search for a lost person will be substantially different from that in a remote, isolated community in a rugged, northern landscape. In many instances, there are both volunteer and other organizations available to undertake this search and rescue function or to augment the capabilities offered by a police service. Many of the skills required of the incident commander, outlined above, are relevant to the management of a search for a lost person. The skills needed for this legitimate function have been thoroughly documented by such organizations as the National Association for Search and Rescue (NASAR) based out of Fairfax, Virginia. They have also developed detailed checklists that are designed to guide the search process in a systematic manner (National Association for Search and Rescue, 1987).

The application of a precise planning process to this function can significantly increase the probability that lost persons will be rescued. In many instances, police agencies will enlist the support of canine units, auxiliaries or volunteers to increase the available rescues to undertake a search. The following factors can be used to determine the urgency of the search:

- subject profile—including age, medical condition, and number of subjects;
- subject experience profile;
- weather profile;
- equipment profile; and
- terrain/hazards profile.

On the basis of the above information, it is possible to make some determinations about the urgency of the search.

Canada has a National Search and Rescue Secretariat (NSS) that was created to provide a central focus and overall direction to the search and rescue (SAR) functions undertaken on a national basis.

UNDERWATER SEARCH AND RECOVERY

As a specialty within the overall category of search and rescue, the underwater search and recovery function is one that demands an extreme level of expert training, certification, and continuous requalification. Police divers, who are competent to provide this function, are required to develop a wide range of knowledge, skill, and ability (KSAs) relevant to the safe use of self-contained underwater breathing apparatus (scuba) and may be tasked with locating bodies, weapons, or other pieces of evidence, including explosives and other dangerous materials. This is a highly sophisticated skill leading some police services to consider the use of professional, civilian divers on an as-needed basis.

AIR SUPPORT

A number of police departments have seen the value of deploying various types of aircraft in order to augment their patrol function. This is particularly useful in jurisdictions which have large patrol areas, including portions of rough terrain that are difficult to provide coverage for using conventional land vehicles. The types of aircraft deployed may include helicopters, light aircraft, or seaplanes. For example, the OPP uses both helicopters and turbo-prop airplanes to service remote communities in its most northerly detachment areas (Higley, 1984). Innovations in technology have allowed helicopters to be extremely useful in providing support to the search and rescue function. The installation of forward-looking infrared (FLIR) equipment can substantially improve the chances of finding a lost person in isolated locations and allows for more rapid coverage of extensive search areas.

MARINE PATROL

In jurisdictions that include navigable bodies of water, the police are normally tasked with patrol functions which require that specially trained officers are assigned to ensure public safety and lawful operation of watercraft. When police departments carry this responsibility there are necessary expenditures for the acquisition of patrol boats and substantial training and certification requirements for officers assigned to this function.

In order to develop the KSAs necessary for this role, a police officer would require familiarity with some of these topic areas:

- *vessel transport*—including hook-up, safety checks, manoeuvring, launching, retrailering, handling of outboard motors;
- *vessel familiarization and equipment checks*—including checklists, cleaning, maintenance and activity logs, fuelling, and vessel startup;
- *operation*—including the docking, manoeuvring, and anchoring of police marine vessels;
- *navigation*—including day and night navigation exercises through various types of channels, using appropriate navigational aids; and
- *enforcement*—including an understanding of statutes dealing with common marine violations and their application. Various sections of the *Criminal Code*, the *Canada Shipping Act* and its regulations, and provincial statutes that pertain to vessel operation.

MOTORCYCLE PATROL

Many police departments have created special motorcycle squads as a means of providing economical, highly manoeuvrable patrol capabilities within their jurisdiction. As a result, there is a need for the selection, training, and development of officers who are competent in the use of this mode of transportation. The use of motorcycles for a highway patrol function is quite common in Canada; however, their effectiveness is somewhat hampered by weather conditions. They do provide an inexpensive and efficient means of patrol that is frequently used for special details, like VIP escorts, funeral processions, or wide-load convoys.

BRIEFING NOTE

The first formal training for OPP officers assigned to motorcycle patrol was delivered by the Canadian Provost Corps at Canadian Forces Base Borden in 1963. The military instructors provided skills training and made suggestions about proper equipment and protective clothing for these officers. From these beginnings developed the OPP's precision motorcycle riding team, known as the "Golden Helmets" which provide demonstrations at various events throughout Ontario. (Higley, 1984, pp. 419–420)

BICYCLE AND MOUNTED PATROLS

Several urban police departments have begun to place emphasis on the utility of officers assigned to a bicycle or mounted patrol functions. These have many of the advantages associated with a foot patrol by bringing officers into more direct and immediate contact with members of the public. However, it has the added advantage of making the officer more rapidly mobile in the event that they are called to an occurrence within their patrol zone. These types of patrols are less expensive than a police cruiser and require officers to be in excellent physical condition. As with the motorcycle patrol function, bicycle and mounted police patrols are subject to weather conditions. There is an additional value to mounted patrols in that they can be effectively used for crowd management purposes. The presence of a large horse with a uniformed rider can quickly bring peace to an unruly crowd and can be effective in peacefully resolving a potential crisis situation.

UNDERCOVER AND SURVEILLANCE ASSIGNMENTS

This is an area of specialized operation that is extremely difficult to undertake. When dealing with undercover work, officers must be selected with caution and trained with extensive understanding of the challenges faced during this type of assignment. Surveillance work is related to undercover operations; however, since it does not involve direct engagement with the target population it is less difficult from a personal, psychological perspective and does not normally hold the same degree of danger for the officer. It does, however, require a high level of technical competence that results from specialized training and continuous research and development.

Undercover officers may be assigned to any of the following areas operation:

- drugs;
- motorcycle gangs; and
- organized crime.

The undercover officer is expected to become completely engaged in the world of the criminal element which the police are attempting to control. These officers will be removing themselves from direct contact with their police station, their supervisors, their police colleagues, and, often, their families. They will be expected to assume a cover identity to allow them to infiltrate the criminal community and gather information and evidence that would not normally be available through conventional investigations.

Because of its nature, undercover work can be exceedingly dangerous. It can easily lead to situations where an officer's personal safety and security are at jeopardy. It can also lead to circumstances where an officer has difficulty maintaining appropriate detachment from the people being targeted through the undercover operation. When these assignments continue for some length of time, it is not uncommon for undercover officers to develop a degree of attachment to the individuals involved in criminal activity. This can provoke severe psychological problems for the officer and often requires a period of professional counselling before the officer can return to active duty. However, in spite of the considerable risks to the officers engaged in this type of assignment, it continues to be used by police organizations because it proves to be an effective means of gathering information and evidence in areas of organized criminal activity that are highly resistant to normal investigative procedures.

PORNOGRAPHY, HATE CRIMES, AND EXTREMIST GROUPS

Police organizations are authorized to enforce the laws dealing with all forms of pornographic material. What has complicated this area of specialized operation has been the incredible growth in the Internet and its ability to transmit information and pictorial representations at high speed across borders and international boundaries. The growth of pornographic material on the Internet and elsewhere has caused some police departments to assign investigators who focus their exclusive attention on this area of criminal activity. The appearance of Project "P" in Ontario is a good example of a cooperative approach to this crime challenge.

In addition to pornography, in its ordinary print or electronic forms, police services have had to deal with the issue of hate crime literature and the activities and publications of various kinds of extremist groups. The existence of such groups has created a special problem for police organizations that may be dealt with through a strategy of targeted enforcement. The existence of extremist groups in Canada has surfaced on a number of occasions and requires police response (Anti-Defamation League, 1996).

CANINE PATROL

The use of police dogs to augment regular patrols has had considerable success and wide public acceptance. Because particular breeds of dogs can be highly trained to undertake a number of specialized functions, they have become an essential part of many police departments' patrol strategy. By providing specialized training to both the police dog and the dog's handler, police organizations have created teams which are useful in a variety of areas, including:

- missing children searches;
- lost person searches;
- building searches;
- crowd management;
- explosives detection;
- narcotics detection; and
- high-risk arrests.

Officers selected for assignment to this specialized function will need to have a genuine interest in caring for their animal. The bond between the handler and the dog will be both strong and continuous. Police departments with canine programs typically have very clear selection criteria for officers who wish to become canine handlers, as well as for the dogs who are going to be trained for canine functions. The handler's responsibility extends to the nutrition, care, and grooming of the dog and the maintenance of kennel facilities for the animal. There are special uniform and equipment needs for this function, and the handler will have to be accomplished at maintaining control of their canine partner, following accepted tracking procedures, and deploying the animal appropriately for the apprehension and disarming of suspects. This area of assignment also requires officers to be of higher than average physical conditioning in order to keep pace with their animal, often over very rugged terrain. The additional exertion involved with handling a dog on a lead means that officers assigned to this specialized function will require additional firearms training.

EXPLOSIVES DISPOSAL

Another area of police specialization that is highly dangerous and requires substantial amounts of training and requalification is that of police explosives disposal. While not every police department has personnel who are trained in this specialty, there is normally some formal agreement with a neighbouring police organization for the provision of these skills when required. The events at the 1996 Summer Olympics in Altanta, Georgia, and the series of bombings in Montreal outside of the clubhouses of the local Hell's Angels and Rock Machine motorcycle gangs provide useful reminders as to the danger to public safety posed by explosives.

The police explosives technician must be someone who has received intensive training in a number of areas that will qualify them to undertake this dangerous assignment. A great deal of expertise has been developed in Canada through the military. Many police forces send their personnel to local military bases for their initial and refresher training, as well as for routine exercises which are designed to maintain high levels of competence in this discipline. As part of their training, police explosives technicians will require an understanding of the following:

- new tools and techniques;
- operation of portable x-ray equipment;
- operation of a remote mobile investigator (RMI);
- recognition of commercial explosives;
- conducting bomb searches;
- disposing of nitroglycerin (N.G.);
- disposing of explosives and the positive use of explosives;
- preparation of tools and equipment for explosives disposal operations; and
- engaging in "render safe" procedures.

SERIAL MURDER, SERIOUS SEXUAL ASSAULT, AND VIOLENT CRIME

Increasingly, the skills required to conduct investigations of serial murder and serious sexual assaults have become more demanding and complex. This area of specialization has been greatly enhanced by the advances made in the use of DNA analysis, which has been a powerful tool for police investigators. The study of serial killers and the analysis of information relating to serious sexual assaults can assist in the understanding of patterns of these crimes and has produced an area of specialty which many police organizations have begun to acknowledge.

Advances in the application of the behavioural sciences has done a great deal to assist in the investigation of serial killers and those predators who commit serious sexual assaults. These techniques were pioneered through the FBI; however, there are a number of Canadian police organizations that have begun to develop internal expertise in the application of these methods for dealing with such categories of offenders. The Violent Crime Linkage Analysis System (ViCLAS) has developed out of this growing skill and can be described as a means of collecting information about a number of crimes that can be stored, analyzed, and disseminating in ways that will assist investigators in closing these cases. The current criteria for ViCLAS crimes are as follows:

- homicide or attempted homicide (solved or unsolved);
- sexual assault (solved or unsolved);
- selected missing persons cases;
- unidentified body, homicide known to have occurred, or suspected; and
- non-parental abduction or attempted abduction.

ViCLAS has been used in Ontario since 1993 through the Behavioural Sciences Section of the OPP in Orillia. It is designed to capture, collate, and compare predatory/sexual crimes of violence through a careful analysis of victimology, suspect description, *modus operandi,* forensic and behavioural data (Campbell, 1996). Developed through a collaboration between the RCMP and OPP, ViCLAS has been recognized internationally as the most effective and practical automated system for the analysis of violent crime currently available. As a result, it is being considered for immediate introduction in several jurisdictions in Australia, the United States, and Europe.

ViCLAS requires that investigating officers complete details reports which include precisely structured questions that will facilitate analysis of known and established crime patterns on the part of offenders. This detailed information is submitted for entry into the ViCLAS database operated by the OPP's Behavioural Sciences Unit. A trained crime analyst will study this report in order to establish possible linkages with other similar crimes committed throughout Canada. If such linkages are identified, the police organization which submitted the original report will be notified for the purposes of follow-up.

BRIEFING NOTE

ViCLAS was successfully used in a 1994 case of sexual assault against a young girl in Surrey, B.C. The local RCMP received over 700 leads relating to this brutal attack; however, after three months, when all of those leads had been exhausted, they submitted a ViCLAS report on the crime. Almost immediately, a link was seen between this case and two other cases, one in Richmond and the other in Prince Rupert. When the victim was shown a photograph of the suspect in the Prince Rupert crime, she was able to identify him as her assailant. This suspect was arrested and later convicted.

As a result of the potential investigative power of ViCLAS and because of a perceived need to require its use in Ontario, Mr. Justice Archie Campbell, as part of his review of the Bernardo investigation, recommended that there be mandatory ViCLAS reporting for all police services in Ontario and that a regulation under the *Police Services Act* be developed for this purpose. Mr. Justice Campbell further recommended that this system be reinforced through appropriate training and auditing (Campbell, 1996).

Psychological profiling has been able to provide details leading to the classification and characteristics of rapists. The following categories have emerged from the research:

- *Power reassurance rapist*—assaults in order to provide reassurance about masculinity through domination of the victim(s). This type is the most common form of stranger-to-stranger rapist;
- *Power assertive rapist*—individual has no concerns about masculinity and is raping in order to assert his prerogative. This is the second most common type of rapist;
- *Anger retaliatory rapist*—individual who is angry with women generally and uses sexual contact as a weapon to punish them. This type of rapist will degrade the victim and frequently uses profanity;
- *Anger excitation rapist*—this category is also known as the sexual sadist. The individual derives sexual stimulation and/or gratification by way of the victim's response to degrees of physical and emotional anguish. This rapist seeks total submission on the part of the victim and is the least common type; and
- *Opportunistic rapist*—normally, his primary motive is to commit another crime (e.g., burglary). This type of rapist assaults for sexual gratification and does not usually injure the victim.

As a result of these detailed profiles, police investigators trained in this specialty can make some assessments about the *modus operandi* of these individuals, as well as being able to connect their behaviour to background history and social characteristics. Given patterns of reasonable predictability, police investigators can apply certain interview techniques for the interrogation of each category of rapist.

DOMESTIC VIOLENCE

A significant amount of attention has been devoted to the problem of domestic assault and violence. Much of this attention has been directed at the ways in which police organizations deal with this issue. In the past many departments adhered to a "hands-off" policy which viewed domestic issues as being outside the department's mandate. Efforts would be made by an officer to cool down a situation; however, it was assumed that the parties themselves would resolve the difficulties. Clearly this perspective has undergone considerable change over the last number of years with police services now pursuing clear policies that mandate their officers to lay criminal charges in cases where there are grounds to believe that an assault has taken place. Officers are no longer content to calm the immediate crisis down and leave matters to the disputing parties to resolve. There is a substantial public, moral, and ethical interest in taking domestic abuse seriously and bringing the force of law to bear in these circumstances.

Because domestic situations can be extremely dangerous for all parties concerned, especially for the responding officer, a number of police organizations have assigned special units to deal with these operational calls. As in certain other assignments, domestic violence calls require a range of skills on the part of the officer.

ELDER ABUSE

With changes in the demographics of Canadian society, we are beginning to be more aware of the special problems that result from an aging population. Police organizations are now more clearly conscious of the need to have officers skilled in recognizing and dealing with a range of forms of elder abuse, including:

- physical abuse;
- economic abuse (fraud and theft);
- sexual abuse; and
- psychological and emotional abuse.

This awareness has lead some police departments to use special squads that can resolve these issues with a range of interventions and techniques.

HOMELESS PERSONS AND/OR THE MENTALLY DISABLED

These two categories of people have generated a degree of attention on the part of the police in recent years. As a result, police organizations are beginning to consider the value of providing more training and education in the handling of homeless persons and the mentally disabled. Some police departments have established special units to address the problem of homeless persons. There is not always a direct connection between these two groups and, in fact, police are beginning to better understand the various types of individuals who find themselves labelled in this manner. There are complex psychological, emotional, and physical characteristics that distinguish the people who find themselves homeless in our cities and towns. Kelling and Coles (1996) provide some insight from the U.S.:

> For example, research conducted in New York City in 1989 on those who used the subway for shelter found them to be a particularly troubled and troublesome population, with many having lengthy histories of arrest for both minor and serious crimes. Metropolitan Transit Authority estimates indicated at least 40 percent of subway homeless were mentally ill, and substantial portions were chronic alcohol and drug abusers. More recent research indicates that 80 percent of the males in New York's armory shelters abuse drugs or alcohol. (p. 66)

Unfortunately, in the public arena there is a debate as to the proper role of municipal authorities with regard to the homeless. One view argues that homelessness is a social dilemma that cities should be addressing directly and not attempting to shift to other jurisdictions. This view supports local governments and police departments being involved in providing solutions to these issues and not prosecuting persons who are guilty of so-called economic offences (e.g., sleeping on park benches, squeegeeing, etc.). The other view recognizes that the problem of homelessness is real; however, it supports the application of strict enforcement and prosecution in an attempt to prevent or control disorder and fear within the jurisdiction. As Melekian (1990) indicates, this debate has left the police in a quandary which creates three distinct operational problems:

- conflicts over the proper use of public lands;
- pressure resulting from public demands for enforcement in dealing with activities that are not of a serious criminal nature; and
- ethical requirements for police to provide protection and service to a disadvantaged but deserving class of persons.

MISSING OR ABDUCTED CHILDREN

In recent years, police organizations have made significant advances in the training, establishment of standards, and overall investigation of instances of missing or abducted children. As a result of growing concern about family abductions, abductions by non-family members, and runaway children, police agencies have turned their attention to this problem. In the United States, the work of the National Center for Missing and Exploited Children (Steidel, 1994) has done a great deal of work in providing guidance to law enforcement organizations.

BRIEFING NOTE

Since its inception in 1984, the U.S. National Center for Missing and Exploited Children has achieved these important accomplishments:
- received over 760 000 calls on its toll-free hotline requesting assistance in cases of missing or exploited children;
- assisted law enforcement agencies and families in the recovery of more than 25 000 children;
- put into place a special unit with the capability to produce age-enhanced photographs of missing children;
- provided training for over 129 000 police, criminal/juvenile justice, and health-care professionals in the United States, Canada, and the United Kingdom in matters relating to child sexual exploitation, missing child detection, investigation, and prevention. (Steidel, 1994, p. viii)

YOUNG OFFENDERS

In light of the provisions of the federal *Young Offenders Act*, it is essential that police organizations handle young offenders in a manner that is consistent with that legislation. In order to accomplish this effectively, many police departments have assigned specially trained officers to these duties. In the area of youth gangs, police officers who are familiar with the requirements of the law are better able to deal with these operational challenges. An emphasis on crime prevention is important in this context, whereby young offenders are guided, through a variety of means, to avoid becoming adult offenders and further burdening the criminal justice system.

CONCLUSION

It may be seen from the areas dealt with in this chapter that police agencies have a difficult challenge before them when selecting the appropriate organizational strategies to most effectively deploy their resources. As the costs of public safety continue to increase, it is imperative that police decision makers have a degree of flexibility in the assignment of officers to specialized functions. It has become obvious that no police organization can be all things to all people; however, there continues to be an enormous amount of pressure on these organizations to offer an extremely broad spectrum of capabilities that relate to law enforcement, emergency response, public order maintenance, assistance to victims of crime, and crime prevention.

As long as the public continues to identify police officers as the appropriate deliverers of the kinds of specialist functions outlined above, there will be a pressing challenge for police leaders to select, train, equip, and qualify members from within their ranks for several specialist functions.

QUESTIONS FOR CONSIDERATION

1. What are the benefits of strategic management for a police service in Canada?
2. What are possible sources of environmental scanning information to assist a police service in developing a strategic plan?
3. Identify instances where tactical planning is important to a police department.
4. What are the advantages of maintaining a routine patrol function? What are the disadvantages?
5. Identify some instances where police organizations might choose to use directed patrols.
6. Identify events where a police service's crowd management unit would be required.
7. What are some advantages of a generalist approach to policing? What are the disadvantages of this approach?
8. What are some advantages of a specialist approach to policing? What are the disadvantages of this approach?

9. Identify circumstances where it would be appropriate to deal with a call for police service by simply taking a report over the telephone.
10. Identify circumstances where it is essential to dispatch a patrol officer to a call for service.
11. What are some occurrences where a police service would require the skills of an incident commander?
12. What are some circumstances where a police service would call upon a tactics and rescue unit?

REFERENCES

Anti-Defamation League. (1996). *Danger: extremism: the major vehicles and voices on America's far-right fringe.* New York: Anti-Defamation League.

Butterfield, Fox. (1995). *All God's children: the Bosket family and the American tradition of violence.* New York: Avon Books.

Campbell, Mr. Justice Archie. (1996). *Bernardo investigation review: report of Mr. Justice Archie Campbell.* [Toronto]: Ontario Ministry of the Solicitor General and Correctional Services.

Canadian Association of Chiefs of Police. Police Multicultural Liaison Committee. (1996). *Hate crimes in Canada: in your back yard: a resource guide.* Ottawa: CACP.

Chapman, Samuel G. (1979). *Police dogs in America.* Norman, Okla.: Bureau of Government Research, University of Oklahoma.

Chapman, Samuel G. (1983). "An update on United States and Canadian police dog programs." *Journal of Police Science and Administration,* 11(4).

Coordinating Council on Juvenile Justice and Delinquency Prevention. (1996). *Combating violence and delinquency: the national juvenile justice action plan: summary.* Washington, D.C.: U.S. Dept. Of Justice, Office of Juvenile Justice and Delinquency Prevention.

Cooper, H.H.A. (1977). *Hostage negotiations: options and alternatives.* Gaithersburg, Maryland: International Association of Chiefs of Police.

Harman, Alan. (1995). "Toronto's public order unit." *Law and Order,* September.

Hickey, Eric W. (1991). *Serial murderers and their victims.* Pacific Grove, Calif.: Brooks/Cole.

Higley, Dahn D. (1985). *O.P.P.: the history of the Ontario Provincial Police Force.* Toronto: Queen's Park.

House, John C. (1997, forthcoming). "Towards a practical application of offender profiling: the Royal Newfoundland Constabulary's criminal suspect prioritization system." In Jackson, J. and D. Berkerian (eds.). *Offender profiling: psychological support in criminal investigations.* Chichester: John C. Wiley.

Incident commander field handbook: search and rescue: managing the search function. (1987). Fairfax, Virginia: National Association for Search and Rescue.

Innovative training package for detecting and aiding victims of domestic elder abuse. (1993). Washington, D.C.: Police Executive Research Forum.

Kelling, George L. and Catherine M. Coles. (1996). *Fixing broken windows: restoring order & reducing crime in our communities.* New York: Free Press.

Keppel, Robert D. (1989). *Serial murder: future implications for police investigations*. Cincinnati, Ohio: Anderson Publishing.

Koller, Katherine. (1990). *Working the beat: the Edmonton neighborhood foot patrol*. Edmonton: Edmonton Police Service.

Kuhn, Thomas S. (1986). *The structure of scientific revolutions. 2nd ed*. Chicago: University of Chicago Press.

Layton, Elliott. (1986). *Hunting humans: the rise of the modern multiple murderer*. Toronto: McClelland and Stewart.

McCoy, Candace. (1986). "Enforcement workshop: policing the homeless." *Criminal Law Bulletin*, 22(3).

Meese III, Edwin, and Bob Carrico. (1990). "Taking back the streets: police methods that work." *Policy Review*, No. 54 (Fall).

Melekian, Barney. (1990). "Police and the homeless." *FBI Law Enforcement Bulletin*, 59(11).

Metropolitan Toronto Police. (1997). *Metropolitan Toronto Police crisis intervention training: module 1: course outline of material*. [Toronto]: Metropolitan Toronto Police, Charles O. Bick College.

Murphy, Gerard. (1986). *Special care: improving the police response to the mentally disabled*. Washington, D.C.: Police Executive Research Forum.

Murphy, Gerard. (1989). *Managing persons with mental disabilities: a curriculum guide for trainers*. Washington, D.C.: Police Executive Research Forum.

National Association for Search and Rescue. (1987). *Incident commander field handbook: search and rescue: managing the search function*. Fairfax, Virginia: NASAR.

Office of Juvenile Justice and Delinquency Prevention. (1996). *Reducing youth gun violence: an overview of programs and initiatives: program report*. Washington, D.C.: U.S. Dept. of Justice, Office of Juvenile Justice and Delinquency Prevention.

Ogle, Dan (ed.). (1991). *Strategic planning for police*. Ottawa: Canadian Police College.

Olesky, W. Ronald and David G. Born. (1983). "A behavioral approach to hostage situations." *FBI Law Enforcement Bulletin*, January.

Ontario. Ministry of the Solicitor General and Correctional Services. Policing Services Division. (1995). *Tactical response standard: consultation package*. [Toronto]: The Ministry.

Ontario. Ministry of the Solicitor General and Correctional Services. Policing Services Division. Policing Standards Section. (1996). *Police resource package on hate/bias motivated crimes: part A: open information*. [Toronto]: The Ministry.

Ontario Police Commission. (1989). *Review of tactical units 1989*. Toronto: The Commission. (2 vols.—Volume 1: Report; Volume 2: Appendices).

Ontario Provincial Police. (1994a). *Commissioner's directional statement 1994: "focus on the future."* [Toronto]: OPP.

Ontario Provincial Police. Organizational Review Project. (1994b). *Occurrence management*. [Orillia, Ont.]: OPP.

O'Reilly-Fleming, Thomas (ed.). (1996) *Serial and mass murder: theory, research, and policy*. Toronto: Canadian Scholars' Press.

Plotkin, Martha R. (1988). *A time for dignity: police and domestic abuse of the elderly*. Washington, D.C.: Police Executive Research Forum.

Plotkin, Martha R. and Ortwin A. Narr. (1993). *The police response to the homeless: a status report*. Washington, D.C.: Police Executive Research Forum.

Police Executive Research Forum. (1993). *Improving the police response to domestic elder abuse: prepared by the Police Executive Research Forum as a guide to law enforcement agencies*. Washington, D.C.: Police Executive Research Forum.

Police Foundation. (1981). *The Newark foot patrol experiment*. Washington, D.C.: Police Foundation.

Rapp, Jay. (1979). *How to organize a canine unit and train dogs for police work*. Fairfax, Virginia: Denlinger's Publishers.

Sharplin, Arthur. (1985). *Strategic management*. New York: McGraw-Hill.

Sheehan, Robert and Gary W. Cordner. (1995). *Police administration. 3rd ed*. Cincinnati, Ohio: Anderson Publishing Co.

Snyder, Howard N. and Melissa Sickmund. (1995). *Juvenile offenders and victims: a national report*. Washington, D.C.: U.S. Dept. of Justice, Office of Juvenile Justice and Delinquency Prevention.

Steidel, Stephen E. (ed.). (1994). *Missing and abducted children: a law enforcement guide to case investigation and program management*. Arlington, Virginia: National Center for Missing and Exploited Children.

Tafoya, William L. (1990). "Futures research: implications for criminal investigations." In Gilbert, James G. (ed.) *Criminal investigation: essays and cases*. Columbus, Ohio: Merrill Publishing Co.

Taroni, F. (1994). "Serial crime: a consideration of investigative problems." *Forensic Sciences International*, 65 (March).

Trojanowicz, Robert and David Carter. (1988). *The philosophy and role of community policing*. East Lansing, Mich.: National Neighborhood Foot Patrol Center, Michigan State University.

Watts, Sabina C. (1993). *Investigation into the psyches of serial killers: a Kleinean perspective*. Ottawa: National Library of Canada. Unpublished Masters thesis.

Weisel, Deborah Lamm and Ellen Painter. (1997). *The police response to gangs: case studies of five cities*. Washington, D.C.: Police Executive Research Forum.

TOWARD MORE LEARNING

STRATEGIC MANAGEMENT

Sharplin, Arthur. (1985). *Strategic management*. New York: McGraw-Hill.

This textbook deals with a the strategic management process in a very clear and accessible manner. It presents a model that places key considerations in the context of the organization and provides the reader with case studies from a broad range of corporations to illustrate each component. The author includes reference to the key elements of the environment which can have an impact on the organization's strategy (i.e., economic, political, social, and technological factors) and addresses overall strategic management from the following perspective:

Formulation
- mission determination;
- organizational/environmental assessment;

- objective or direction setting; and
- strategy determination.

Implementation
- strategic activation;
- strategic evaluation; and
- strategic control.

The book is clearly written and contains many references to additional sources of insight on related topics.

FOOT PATROL

Koller, Katherine. (1990). *Working the beat: the Edmonton neighborhood foot patrol*. Edmonton: Edmonton Police Service.

This publication is the result of a project within the City of Edmonton designed to apply an approach to policing with the following components: neighbourhood foot patrol constables, the use of storefront offices, and neighbourhood advisory committees.

Working the beat records a special application of community policing which brings officers into a more immediate and direct contact with the members of the community. The publication has an easily read format and is well illustrated with photographs reflecting the reality of this project. A more formal quantitative summary of this foot patrol experiment was prepared for the Edmonton Police Service by Dr. Joe Hornick, Executive Director of the Canadian Research Institute for Law and the Family, University of Calgary.

TACTICAL UNITS

Ontario Ministry of the Solicitor General and Correctional Services. Policing Services Division. (1996). *Tactical response standard: consultation package*. [Toronto]: The Ministry.

ELDER ABUSE

Innovative training package for detecting and aiding victims of domestic elder abuse. (1993). Washington, D.C.: Police Executive Research Forum.

This extensive material prepared by the Police Executive Research Forum (PERF) in the United States is the result of a substantial research and study. It is designed to be used as a guide for the training of police trainers, recruits, and veteran (i.e., in-service) officers. While the material is directed primarily at an American audience, the quality of the contents goes beyond the limits of American law and practice. The package is comprised of the following parts, each with detailed references and notes:

- Instructor Training Manual;
- Participant Training Manual;
- Model Role Call Training Bulletin;
- Model Procedures;
- Model Response and Investigative Protocol;
- Model Policy;
- Literature Review; and
- Assessment Report.

PERF provides a limited licence to reprint these materials for internal use, and the contents are in a camera-ready format for this purpose.

Plotkin, Martha R. (1988). *A time for dignity: police and domestic abuse of the elderly*. Washington, D.C.: Police Executive Research Forum.

HOMELESS PERSONS

Plotkin, Martha R. and Ortwin A. Narr. (1993). *The police response to the homeless: a status report*. Washington, D.C.: Police Executive Research Forum.

This report provides detailed background on the role of police as service providers to the homeless in the United States. It deals with the nature of the contact between police officers and homeless persons and outlines related issues, such a police policies and procedures, officer training, and interaction with non-police service providers. The report is the result of surveys and site visits in a number of American cities and offers practical information dealing with this topic, including extensive policy statements and references for further research.

MISSING AND EXPLOITED CHILDREN

Steidel, Stephen E. (ed.). (1994). *Missing and abducted children: a law enforcement guide to case investigation and program management*. Arlington, Virginia: National Center for Missing and Exploited Children.

YOUNG OFFENDERS

Bala, Nicholas et al. (1994). *A police reference manual on youth and violence*. Ottawa: Canadian Research Institute for Law and the Family and Solicitor General Canada.

An extensive resource for understanding, and dealing with youth violence in Canada. This publication has been specifically designed to assist police organizations, especially front-line officers. It provides insight into the *Young Offenders Act*, offers important legal definitions, and outlines the role of the police with regard to investigating incidents of youth violence. Several valuable checklists are included which provide assistance in guiding officers through investigations of school violence, dating violence, and cases involving children under 12 years of age.

Canadian Institute for Law and the Family. (1994). *A police reference manual on youth and violence*. Ottawa: Solicitor General Canada.

This manual includes information on crime and violence committed by youth and is designed to assist police officers who are working in their communities to develop effective and proactive approaches to the prevention of these kinds of occurrences. It is available through the federal Solicitor General, 340 Laurier Avenue West, 8th Floor, Ottawa, Ontario K1A 0P8 (telephone: (613) 991-3310).

Canadian Institute for Law and the Family. (1995). *Community resource committee: a community-based strategy for dealing with youth crime and violence in Calgary*. Calgary: Calgary Police Service.

This publication was undertaken for the Calgary Police Service by the Canadian Institute for Law and the Family and details the formation and function of the Community Resource Committee within the Calgary Police Service. This group was created to provide a process and framework for the delivery of police services and local resources to more effectively address the problems of youth crime and violence. The report is available through the Calgary Police Service, 133–6th Avenue South East, Calgary, Alberta T2G 4Z1 (telephone: (403) 266-1234).

Hornick, Joseph P. et al. (1996). *A police reference manual on crime prevention and diversion with youth*. Ottawa: Canadian Research Institute for Law and the Family and Solicitor General of Canada.

This manual was prepared for use by both front-line police officers and senior police managers. The text of this manual is available through the Internet at: http://www.sgc.gc.ca.

Mathews, Frederick. (1995). *The badge and the book: building effective police/school partnerships to combat youth violence*. Ottawa: Solicitor General of Canada.

This publication examines the problem of youth violence and provides the results of a study designed to identify the optimal role for the police in schools by gaining a deeper understanding of the attitudes and feelings which police, parents, educators, and students have regarding school violence and crime. It offers some suggestions for police policy and administrative practices relating to this area of program delivery.

Weiler, Richard et al. (1993). *A police reference manual for cases of child abduction and runaway youth*. Ottawa: Solicitor General Canada and Canadian Research Institute for Law and the Family.

This manual was designed as a guide for police officers in dealing with specific types of missing children and youth. It is intended to assist with the formulation of police strategies for managing the issue of missing children and youth. The publication includes references to helpful information and materials that are currently available to police and community organizations relating to these matters. There are several checklists dealing with the following:

- initial investigation of missing children cases;
- non-parental abductions;
- parental abductions; and
- runaways.

CHAPTER NINE

COMMUNICATION AND
INFORMATION TECHNOLOGY

LEARNING OBJECTIVES

1. Identify the components of a systems approach to communication
2. Understand distinctions between formal and informal communication
3. Understand distinctions between open and closed communication systems
4. Identify the barriers to effective communication
5. Explain the seven "C's" of effective communication
6. Describe the main developments in information technology that have effected policing in Canada
7. Describe the main developments in information technology that have affected policing in Canada

INTRODUCTION

This chapter will examine the role of communications in a police organization. The systems approach to communication allows for a clear understanding of the elements of communication and provides the basis for considering the attributes of effective communication. Because the transfer of information happens in many forms in a police service, this chapter looks at formal and informal styles, as well as open and closed systems of communication.

In making the multitude of police functions operate more smoothly, the application of information technology has been extremely beneficial. However, this aspect of policing in Canada is made complex by the speed at which the technology changes and the growing challenges that confront its implementation and coordination. This chapter begins to sort out some of these complexities by looking at distinct areas of policing that have been modified through the introduction of information technology.

COMMUNICATION IN POLICE ORGANIZATIONS

Communication is basically the process of taking information and conveying it to some receiver. Effective communication occurs when the information sent exactly matches the information received. Communication can be formal or informal; it may take oral, written, or electronic forms, and it can occur within open and closed systems. In all organizations, communication is an essential element of that organization's "business," and if the communication system is not operating effectively and efficiently, the organization will experience difficulties. This is particularly true in police organizations which must deal with enormous quantities of communication and must do so quickly, accurately, and in a form that can be stored and easily retrieved for a variety of uses. Figure 9–1 outlines a systems approach to communication that attempts to capture all of the key ingredients, including a mechanism for providing feedback which allows for continuous improvement within the system.

A SYSTEMS APPROACH TO COMMUNICATION

When *information* needs to be communicated by some *source*, it must first undergo a process of *encoding* through which the information is put into some understandable form (e.g., written, spoken, or electronic). Once this has been done, the information can then be transmitted. The process of *transmission* may include sounds, words, symbols, or other signs or representations that are intended by the source to convey meaning. However, since there is, by definition, some separation between the source of transmission and the receiver, it is possible that there will be varying degrees of *interference*. Any such interference has the potential to alter, distort, disrupt, or even block the message that is being transmitted. Once the message has been received by some medium (e.g., the ear or the eye) the encoded information is decoded by the *receiver*. The end-product of this process of *decoding* is the information which is absorbed at the *destination*. The extent to which there is a match between the information (source) and the information (destination) represents the degree of success of that communication. By understanding communication as a system, it is possible to better guard against poor communication. It is useful to always

FIGURE 9–1

A SYSTEMS APPROACH TO COMMUNICATION

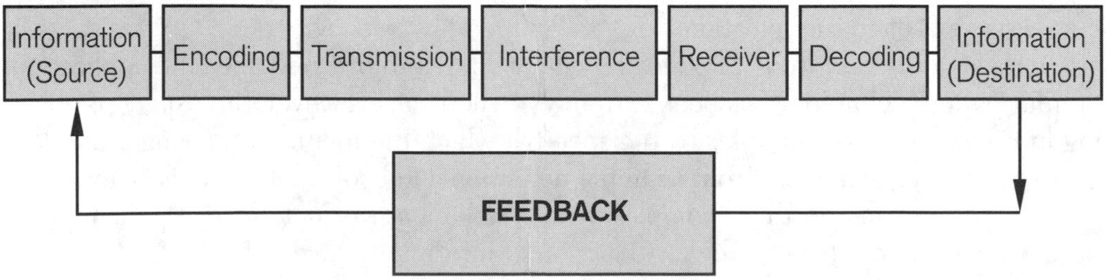

remember that it is the *receiver* of the communication that judges the quality of the communication. On the basis of the *feedback* (which the source is able to get from the destination of any communication), improvements, enhancements, modifications of future messages may be accomplished, thus completing the loop of the communication system.

According to Souryal (1985) communication in a police organization has the following significant functions:

- *Educate* police officers regarding departmental goals, formulation of policy, and execution of their duties, through a meaningful presentation of police procedures and standards for evaluation.
- *Resolve* controversial issues or misunderstandings with respect to police performance, and clarify the role of police in contemporary society.
- *Solicit* fresh ideas through personal communication and face-to-face encounters.
- *Motivate* police officers by keeping them informed of agency goals, agency progress, and the image of the agency in the community.
- *Unite* rank-and-file personnel in the department behind their leaders.
- *Stimulate* feedback from police officers and solicit their assessment of the successes and failures of the agency.
- *Facilitate* the expression of grievances by unhappy officers and expedite the redress of such grievances. (pp. 53–54)

FORMAL AND INFORMAL COMMUNICATION

Police organizations are typically characterized by high degrees of formal communication. However, a great deal of attention has been paid recently to the importance of informal communication. Formal communication refers to the normal or routine "channels" that allow for the transmission of information within the organization or among different organizations. It constitutes the official data of the organization and may relate to policies, procedures, directives, standing orders, and other such information. Because of its nature, formal communication tends to be in a written form. Informal communication, on the other hand, may be seen as the kind of communication that occurs outside of the official "channels," but which can clearly serve an important and useful organizational role. It is the type of communication that takes on a more personal tone and tends to be largely verbal. Both forms of communication have their own particular advantages and disadvantages (Souryal, 1985); however, they may be effectively combined to generate good lines of communication that emphasizes the advantages of either form.

OPEN AND CLOSED SYSTEMS OF COMMUNICATION

A police organization may chose to pursue either an open or a closed system of communication. Either approach will significantly affect the nature of communication both internally and externally (Southerland, 1992). Traditional police organizations favour a closed system of communication where corporate decisions are made at the executive level with little input from the rest of the organization, particularly at the front-line. This approach is consistent with the military model where formal communication tends to flow downward in the form of orders, directives, policies, commands, and other specific statements directed at operational and/or administrative matters. Increasingly, there is more acceptance of the need for, and value of, open channels of communication that can incorporate some of the benefits of formal, official downward communication along with the extensive, creative, supportive value of informal, upward communication throughout the organization. As Southerland (1992) observes:

> These open and closed models are polar extremes in decision-making style and in communication style. They require completely different management approaches. The open model of organizational communication cannot function in the traditional classical police organizational structure of top-down communication. It is problematic for open organizational communication to occur with the paramilitary symbols that are currently used in policing. The assumptions on which the classical structure and symbols are based have specific implications for organizational functioning and expectations of rewards and punishment. (p. 283)

BARRIERS TO EFFECTIVE POLICE COMMUNICATION

In any organization, there can be barriers to effective communication that can lead to confusion and error. In the systems model presented above, these barriers constitute a form of interference. In a police department, especially in an operational setting, failures in communication can lead to serious injury or death. Therefore, communication requires the most careful attention. Because communication typically occurs between human beings, there are several ways in which communication can be flawed beyond simple interference. For example, the person transmitting the message may introduce certain barriers through poor use of language or through the introduction of inappropriate connotations that colour the message, indistinct speech, or the imposition of personal bias or prejudice into the message. Likewise, the receiver of the message may introduce barriers to effective police communication through personal unwillingness to accept the message, a failure to properly listen and comprehend the communication, and a lack of understanding of the meaning of the message (particularly in the case of code words or specialized terminology).

The organization itself may introduce barriers to effective communication that are difficult for individual members to overcome. This includes the general, traditional police environment which provides an enormous amount of downward communication and may foster an unwillingness in its members to provide genuine, upward feedback. Also, the sheer size of many police organizations may make general and regular communication difficult. The effects of filtering in a hierarchical organization can degrade information as it passes from one level of the organization to another. Additionally, the overloading of the existing channels of communication, combined with a leadership that relies heavily on confidential or secret information can diminish the effectiveness of communication.

In the area of feedback, there are further barriers that may prevent or diminish effective communication, including an unwillingness to provide feedback, the failure of a message to reach the receiver, failure to understand the nature of the communication, disapproval of the communication, and fear of criticism.

THE SEVEN C'S OF EFFECTIVE COMMUNICATION

In order to ensure that effective oral, written, or electronic communication is created in any police organization, there are simple reminders that can be kept in mind. They all relate to the quality of the communication and can provide a firm basis on which to build both formal and informal messages within an organizational setting. Each one of the following "C's" of effective communication should be addressed *before* the message is delivered:

* *Complete*—ensuring that the message is as complete as the circumstances allow, thus making it possible for the receiver of the message to make decisions, act, or respond immediately on the basis of what has been provided without the need for follow-up information;
* *Correct*—ensuring that the information included in the message is accurate and factual. This may require the originator of the message to do some research in order to verify the contents of the message before it is transmitted;

FIGURE 9-2

THE SEVEN C'S OF EFFECTIVE COMMUNICATION

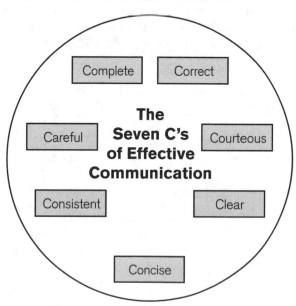

- *Courteous*—ensuring that the appropriate tone is taken in the message. Whether they are formal or informal, all messages should be polite and civilized in their expression. This does not mean that a message cannot be forceful; however, there should be discipline in the language used for conveying information;
- *Clear*—ensuring that the message does not contain any ambiguity that would lead to confusion or misunderstanding. The information should be stated with the least amount of wordiness and in language that is direct and easily understandable;
- *Concise*—ensuring that the information is provided in as short a form as possible to still satisfy the other "C's" of communication. Remember that members of the police department will receive many different messages and each individual message should get directly to the point—keep it short and simple;
- *Consistent*—ensuring that the information provided contains no contradictions. There should be a logical connection between the purpose of the message, its assumptions, observations, and any conclusions or recommendations contained in the message; and
- *Careful*—ensuring that care is taken to present a message or information that is free from errors (e.g., spelling, factual, or grammatical) and that the presentation is neat and acceptable to existing organizational standards.

INFORMATION TECHNOLOGY IN POLICE ORGANIZATIONS

Beyond the straightforward systems approach to communication outlined above, there is a requirement in police organizations for the formalized management of the various forms of information which must be handled. Information technology is the most common means available in a modern police organization for managing this important responsibility. Information technology (IT) can be seen as the grouping of the following elements which can be applied for the benefit of the organization:

- *data*—includes all forms of input that can be used as the basis for information;
- *application systems*—includes all varieties of procedures for handling data, both manual and programmed;
- *technology*—includes all hardware, operating systems, database management systems, networks, and multimedia programs;
- *facilities*—includes the resources required to accommodate and support all information systems; and
- *people*—includes the personnel assigned to undertake the planning, organizing, acquisition, delivery, support, and auditing of information systems and their related services.

These related resources provide the basis for the operation of any IT system that will assist the police organization in meeting its information needs and, thereby, satisfy its overall objectives. Figure 9–3 represents the connection of the various resources that combine to create the framework of information technology:

FIGURE 9-3

A FRAMEWORK OF INFORMATION TECHNOLOGY

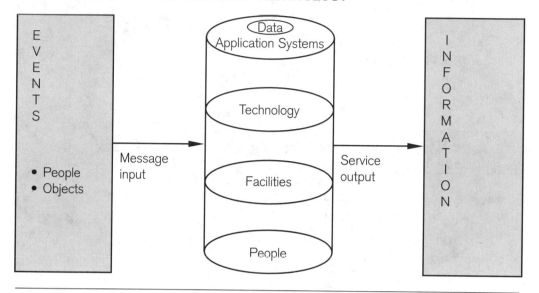

Excerpted from: *COBIT: control objectives for information and technology: executive summary.*
© 1996. Information Systems Audit and Control Foundation. Used with permission.

Police organizations need to develop and implement information technology processes and activities that will allow them to meet their operational needs in a timely, efficient, and effective manner. The management of these information technology processes and activities requires a great deal of expertise and represents an enormous investment for police services. However, because of the huge amounts of data and information that police departments are required to collect, collate, store, and disseminate, it is essential that such investments are made and constantly reviewed.

Manning (1992) notes that various studies have been done on the many forms of information technology applied within police departments.

> The information technology employed in these studies varies. Not only do computers used vary in speed, memory, capacity, and other engineering design features, they are products of different manufacturers. Departments sometimes find themselves with incompatible equipment, bought at different times, or with design features that never worked or were never developed because of budget constraints. (p. 256)

Information technology processes may be seen in the context of four groupings which allow for the most effective and efficient coordination of the available IT resources. Figure 9–4 illustrates the four "domains."

Within the context of the "domains" listed above there are specific elements that every police department should consider in order to best meet their business needs and ensure the proper use of their information technology resources:

FIGURE 9-4

INFORMATION TECHNOLOGY PROCESSES

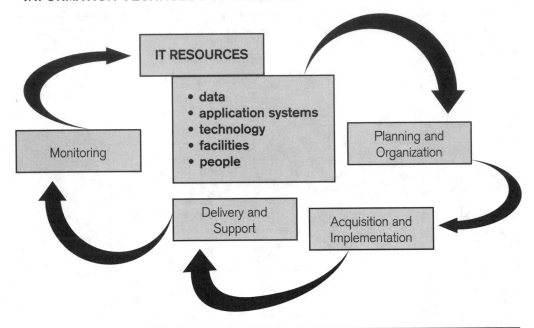

Excerpted from: *COBIT: control objectives for information and technology: executive summary.*
© 1996. Information Systems Audit and Control Foundation. Used with permission.

Planning & Organization

- define a strategic plan
- define the information architecture
- determine technological direction
- define the organization and relationships
- manage the investment
- communicate management aims and direction
- manage human resources
- ensure compliance with external requirements
- assess risks
- manage projects
- manage quality

Acquisition & Implementation

- identify automated solutions
- acquire and maintain application software

- acquire and maintain technology infrastructure
- develop and maintain procedures
- install and accredit systems
- manage changes

Delivery & Support

- define service levels
- manage third-party services
- manage performance and capacity
- ensure continuous service
- ensure systems security
- identify and attribute costs
- educate and train users
- assist and advise customers
- manage the configuration
- manage problems and incidents
- manage data
- manage facilities
- manage operations

Monitoring

- monitor the processes
- obtain independent assurance

Excerpted from: *COBIT: control objectives for information and technology: executive summary.* © 1996. Information Systems Audit and Control Foundation. Used with permission.

Within the structure of most police organizations, it is possible to define four separate categories where information technology resources can be effectively applied to advance organizational and operational needs:

- police communications systems;
- telephone and teleconferencing systems;
- automated computer systems; and
- management information systems.

POLICE COMMUNICATIONS SYSTEMS

As a separate category of information systems used within law enforcement agencies, the police communications systems in place are of special interest and importance. Especially important in this regard are the radio systems that allow for command and control to be in place within the organization. Through the radio system, front-line officers are able

Ontario Provincial Police

Officer communicating via radio with central dispatch

to be dispatched to particular calls for service, acknowledge their arrival at the scene, request further operational assistance, notify the dispatch centre when the call has been cleared, and provide any follow-up information on the nature of the call. The radio system allows police supervisors to direct officers to specific locations in order to undertake tasks consistent with a directed patrol function and maintain a dialogue with front-line officers while they are performing such duties.

The radio system allows for continuous contact to be maintained between patrol officers and the dispatch centre. In many instances, this contact provides higher levels of safety for the officer and the public. The application of technology in this area has been highly beneficial as Manning (1992) indicates:

> Information technology in policing include the hardware and software that permit (1) centralized call collection, usually based on a three-digit number such as 911 or 999; (2) computer-assisted dispatching (CAD), which uses computers and functionaries to screen, classify, prioritize, and distribute calls to units (most large urban departments now collect and queue calls using computers, and have adopted some form of CAD); (3) management information systems (MIS) employed for collection and analysis of data for strategic, short- and long-term planning, creation of positions or functions, and determining the depth of personnel assigned to given functions; (4) computer networking that facilitates data sharing via direct links between state and local police computers and FBI computers in the National Crime Information Center (NCIC). (pp. 257–258)

COMPUTER-ASSISTED DISPATCHING (CAD)

Computer-assisted dispatch (CAD) refers to systems that are designed to assist police communications staff with the dispatching of patrol personnel to particular sites in response to calls for service delivery. The application of computer technology to this function allows a structured approach that provides for consistent data collection and processing, as well as for the creation and storage of detailed records dealing with the dispatch function. The records created and stored provide the basis for statistical summaries that can be used to analyze this function for management and/or operational deployment purposes (Atchison et al., 1984).

TELEPHONE AND TELECONFERENCING SYSTEMS

This area relates to the management and development of all processes and facilities dealing with telephone and teleconferencing capabilities within the police organization. This has become more complex with the routine introduction of voice-mail and the establishment of satellite linkages that permit teleconferencing over significant distances. These capabilities allow for greater spans of control within a police organization whereby personnel can be remotely managed under the proper circumstances.

AUTOMATED COMPUTER SYSTEMS

While computers have penetrated many areas of police work, including operations and management, there is a continuous requirement for the overall coordination and guidance of the range of automated computer systems in place within any organization. This management can be broken down into four main categories:

- *systems implementation*—includes the planning, budgeting, and systematic introduction of computerized services within the organization;
- *systems maintenance*—includes the development of an organizational capacity to address overall maintenance issues in the area of computerized services. This involves having personnel who are trained and equipped to respond to service calls in order to minimize delay or "down time" and to maximize the efficiency of all computer systems;
- *systems operations*—includes the administration of all computerized operations in a consistent manner that coincides with organizational standards; and
- *systems research and integration*—includes the ongoing analysis of emerging technological solutions that may involve new hardware, software, or other equipment and the integration of existing and/or new systems.

MANAGEMENT INFORMATION SYSTEMS

This is a very broad category that includes the various systems that are designed to generate and disseminate information that supports or enhances management functions throughout the police organization. Atchison et al. (1984) present the following definition

Al Harvey

Automation has made an enormous contribution to policing in Canada

of management information systems (MIS):

> ... the process whereby data is collected, stored and retrieved to provide *specific information for decision-making*. A management information system begins with the way decisions are made in the entire organization and is designed to *target* information to the various levels and functions of decision-making. An MIS within a police department must be targeted to meet the information needs at all levels—operations as well as management. (p. 7, emphasis in original)

What follows is a listing of the some of the specific areas that can be considered as part of a police organization's overall management information system. While this listing may not be exhaustive, it should provide an extensive insight into the complex range of activities that require the support of increasingly sophisticated computer systems for their maintenance and management.

- *human resources information systems*—including the creation and maintenance of some of the following types of records:
  - personnel background information,
  - performance evaluation records,
  - disciplinary records,
  - skills inventory, and
  - training, education, and development records.

COMMUNICATION AND INFORMATION TECHNOLOGY 203

- *personnel deployment systems*—including the coordination and modification of the following areas of activity:
  - shift scheduling,
  - personnel deployment models and formulae,
  - special assignments,
  - court scheduling and attendance, and
  - duty rosters.
- *financial management information systems*—including the following specific elements:
  - overall budget,
  - specific cost centre allocations,
  - encumbered funds,
  - special expenditures, and
  - proper controls of all monies received or dispersed by the department.
- *fleet management information systems*—including the following components relating to this function:
  - mileage logs,
  - vehicle repair and maintenance,
  - vehicle deployment,
  - vehicle inventory,
  - vehicle replacement records, and
  - related equipment inventory.
- *operational support systems*—may include any of the following types of records and statistical summaries:
  - occurrence reporting,
  - field contact data,
  - dispatch records,
  - patrol summaries,
  - criminal occurrence data,
  - individual officer activity logs,
  - case follow-up data, and
  - ticket reporting.
- *property room and evidence control systems*—including detailed information that tracks the following areas:
  - intake tag information,
  - disposal of property information,
  - firearms and other weapons,
  - drugs and narcotics,
  - explosives and other dangerous materials,
  - cash and other negotiable instruments,
  - special items, and
  - detailed inventory records.

- *statistical information systems*—including the capability to provide a wide range of project-based services in all areas that must be reported upon by the police service, including:
  - simple statistical reports (i.e., raw data),
  - statistical analyses,
  - graphical presentation of statistics,
  - verification of data integrity and statistical quality assurance,
  - customized statistical projects, and
  - statistical reporting to Statistics Canada (legal requirement).
- *management reporting systems*—includes a wide variety of reports and summaries designed to meet the information needs of management for decision making, planning, and other purposes:
  - summary reports in all key categories of departmental activity,
  - clearance rates,
  - response times,
  - calls-for-service,
  - aggregate collision data,
  - cross-jurisdictional statistics,
  - personnel summaries, and
  - human resource strategic planning information.
- *inventory management systems*—includes general data on some of the following areas:
  - overall equipment inventory,
  - moveable assets inventory by zone or division, and
  - special item inventory.
- *registration and records management systems*—including data that is required by law or for special purposes within the police department, for example:
  - firearms registration,
  - private investigators and security guard registration, and
  - records maintenance schedules for the purposes of provincial Freedom of Information and Protection of Privacy legislation.
- *case management systems*—includes systems designed to generate case information and track the following:
  - case follow-up action,
  - case summary reports,
  - case status, and
  - case loads for investigating officers.

CONCLUSION

The information provided in this chapter is intended to reveal some of the complexities involved in making determinations about communication and information technology

(IT) in a modern police organization. Because technology is being constantly transformed, thus making earlier applications and systems obsolete, police decision makers must be extremely cautious in planning the systems that will be implemented. As with any communication, the effectiveness of an IT solution is determined largely by the users of that technology. This means that the officers or personnel who apply these solutions will be in the best position to assess the practical or operational value of technological innovations. Beyond this internal assessment, the public, who are, of course, the ultimate consumers of police services, will have an important and meaningful view on these applications.

The vast amounts of information that must be managed and maintained by police organizations requires that technology be harnessed in order to satisfactorily support a multitude of critical functions. Police managers need to be able to guide the allocation of human, material, financial, and intellectual resources in ways that are cost-efficient and consistent with the overall mandate and objectives of their organizations.

QUESTIONS FOR CONSIDERATION

1. What are some of the sources of interference that can distort the communication of information?
2. Discuss various types of communication that can occur within a police organization.
3. What are the possible advantages and disadvantages of formal communication within a police organization?
4. What are the possible advantages and disadvantages of informal communication within a police organization?
5. What are some of the sources of data that a police department would need to organize?
6. What are the advantages of having a computer-assisted dispatch (CAD) system in a police organization? Are there any possible disadvantages?
7. What are some ways in which information technology can assist with the police investigation function?

REFERENCES

Archambeault, William G. and Betty J. Archambeault. (1984). *Computers in criminal justice administration and management: introduction to emerging issues and applications.* Cincinnati, Ohio: Anderson Publishing Co.

Atchison, R.M. et al. (1984). *Study of police management information systems: volume iv: targeted information processing system: a developmental program for police management information systems.* Ottawa: Ministry of the Solicitor General of Canada.

Barley, S.R. (1986). "Technology as an occasion for structuring." *Administrative Science Quarterly,* 31, pp. 78–108.

Bezdikian, Veh and Clifford L. Karchmer. (1996). *Technology resources for police: a national assessment.* Washington, D.C.: Police Executive Research Forum.

Canadian Association of Chiefs of Police, Royal Canadian Mounted Police, and National Research Council of Canada. (1989). *Canadian program of science and technology in support of law enforcement*. Ottawa: RCMP.

Canadian Police Research Centre. (1996). *Annual report: 1995–1996*. Ottawa: Minister of Supply and Services Canada.

Information Systems Audit and Control Foundation. (1996). *COBIT: control objectives for information and technology: executive summary*. Rolling Meadows, Ill.: Information Systems Audit and Control Foundation.

Manning, Peter K. (1992). "Technological and material resource issues." In Hoover, Larry T. (ed.). *Police management: issues & perspectives*. Washington, D.C.: Police Executive Research Forum.

McPhee, R.D. (1985). "Formal structure and organizational communication." In McPhee, R.D. and P.K. Tompkins (eds.). *Organizational communication: traditional themes and new directions*. Beverly Hills, Calif.: Sage Publications.

Ontario Provincial Police. Systems Approach to Training Unit. (1990). *Recruit field training program: part II—coach officer's self-study package*. [Brampton, Ont.]: OPP, Provincial Police Academy.

Sheehan, Robert and Gary W. Cordner (1995). *Police administration. 3rd ed.* Cincinnati, Ohio: Anderson Publishing Co.

Souryal, Sam S. (1985). *Police organization & administration*. Cincinnati, Ohio: Anderson Publishing Co.

Southerland, Mittie D. (1992). "Organizational communication." In Hoover, Larry T. (ed.). *Police management: issues & perspectives*. Washington, D.C.: Police Executive Research Forum.

Stohl, Cynthia. (1995). *Organizational communication: connectedness in action*. Thousand Oaks, Calif.: Sage Publications.

TOWARD MORE LEARNING

COMMUNICATION

Barnard, Chester. (1938). *The functions of the executive*. Cambridge, Mass.: Harvard University Press.

This was a profoundly influential study of the modern executive which includes a careful analysis of the importance of organizational communication. Barnard was a senior executive in the telecommunications industry and brought a great deal of insight to bear on this topic.

INFORMATION TECHNOLOGY

Atchison, R.M. et al. (1984). *Study of police management information systems.* (5 volumes). Ottawa: Ministry of the Solicitor General of Canada.

In 1976, Decision Dynamics Corporation was engaged by the federal Solicitor General to undertake a study of police management information systems. The primary purpose of this study was to provide assistance in the development of management information systems specifications for the guidance of police services in Canada. The five volumes which resulted from this study provide strong background in an area of police activity that has been dramatically transformed over the last 20 years; however, this work remains instructive and provides good insight into some of the complexities relating to the automation of police functions and their resulting operational and administrative records. The following provides a brief summary of those five volumes:

Volume I

Technological alternatives and development initiatives for Canadian policing. This volume offers a projection of existing trends in Canadian municipal policing and considers the implications of these trends on management information systems (MIS).

Volume II

Police management information systems development in the United States: a comparative review. This volume includes a review of the development of MIS in U.S. jurisdictions and draws out some lessons relevant to applications in a Canadian setting;

Volume III

Police management information systems: the Canadian experience. This volume provides detail on what has already been accomplished in Canadian police organizations as it pertains to MIS.

Volume IV

Targeted information processing system: a developmental program for police management information systems. Contains a conceptual framework for the construction of MIS that is matched to the Canadian municipal police setting.

Volume V

Targeted information processing system (TIPS): general design specifications. This final volume contains some of the specific, technical design components relevant to the authors' proposed MIS model.

Canadian Program of Science and Technology in Support of Law Enforcement. (1979–). *Annual report*. Ottawa: RCMP.

Beginning in 1979, the federal Solicitor General assigned lead responsibility to the RCMP for the implementation of a program of science and technology supporting law enforcement in Canada. This program included the Operational Research Committee of the Canadian Association of Chiefs of Police (CACP) and the National

Research Council of Canada. The annual reports of this program are invaluable for learning about the progress made in terms of projects in some of the following areas:

- computerization of mug shots;
- software for bloodstain pattern analysis;
- evaluation of laptop computers for application in mobile patrol and intelligence units; and
- geographical resource allocation software system.

Canadian Police Research Centre (1990–). *Annual report*. Ottawa: Minister of Supply and Services Canada.

This body was created in 1990 to extend the work begun by the Canadian Program of Science and Technology in Support of Law Enforcement (outlined above). In 1995, the Canadian Police Research Centre (CPRC) expanded its reach through the establishment of a Technology Development Advisory Committee that included participation by the Department of National Defence, the Canadian Police Association, the Nova Scotia Policing Services, and the Policing Services Division of the Ontario Ministry of the Solicitor General and Correctional Services. Some of the projects which the CPRC has sponsored include the following:

- Canadian Bomb Data Centre automated database;
- Canadian law enforcement information management system (CLEIMS)—which allows for information dealing with large-scale commercial crime investigations to be scanned quickly for review and analysis, as well as for the creation of compact disks containing evidence for use in court;
- CACP Web site—this project was recommended by the Internet Subcommittee of the CACP's Informatics Committee.

CHAPTER TEN

LEADING INNOVATION IN CANADIAN POLICING

LEARNING OBJECTIVES

1. Identify sources of organizational reform in Canadian policing
2. Identify the characteristics of strategic alliances relevant to Canadian policing
3. Describe key elements of police performance measurement systems
4. Describe how business process reengineering relates to the reform of policing in Canada
5. Understand the value of organizational learning principles for policing in Canada
6. Describe the components of a problem-solving model of community policing
7. Identify the components of a problem-solving model of policing and its application in a Canadian context
8. Understand the components of a use of force continuum in Canada
9. Identify the importance of team building for innovation in policing
10. Describe the importance of stress management for policing in Canada

INTRODUCTION

Police organizations across Canada are subject to the same kinds of influences that affect all organizations, both public and private. Increasingly, as a result of those influences, police services are finding that they are being compelled to carefully study the nature of their work in order to find better ways of doing things. The pressure for change is coming from governments, at all levels, who are looking for more cost-efficient ways to deliver quality services to the public. Pressure is also coming from the public itself, which has a strong interest in issues relating to crime prevention, law enforcement, assistance to victims of crime, public order maintenance, and emergency response. Finally, pressure is coming from within police organizations themselves as different levels look for better ways to provide the services which constitute their "business" and to make the best use of the valuable resources which they have within their midst.

In response to these various pressures, there is evidence of considerable innovation within Canada's police organizations. By learning more about the nature of these innovations, the students of Canadian policing will be in a much better position to understand their own role in this dynamic area of activity. This chapter is designed to provide an insight into some of the leading innovations which are currently taking place in police organizations. However, this discussion is by no means complete since police services should be striving for continuous improvement, and it is expected that new initiatives will constantly appear on the horizon. A clear understanding that police organizations will pursue operational and administrative challenges with proactive solutions and creative approaches will gradually inform the individual officers' understanding of their own role: to constantly strive for enhanced performance and achievement.

This chapter will consider several areas of innovation which are being pursued in many modern police departments, such as:

- organizational reform;
- strategic alliances;
- performance indicators and measurement;
- organizational review and renewal;
- organizational learning;
- problem-solving and community-oriented policing;
- team building;
- use of force continuum; and
- stress management, psychological counselling, and peer counselling.

It is hoped that this detailed background will provide insight into the commitment made by police leaders, at all levels within their organizations, to bring about meaningful and worthwhile change in policing in Canada.

ORGANIZATIONAL REFORM

Organizational reform has been taking place in Canadian police organizations for decades. It is grossly unfair and inaccurate to assume that we are experiencing the first period when police agencies have engaged in institutional reform. A brief review of the history of policing in Canada indicates that there have been several important reform initiatives that have altered the face of policing (Higley, 1984; Marquis, 1993). It remains true, however, that we are now confronting a time where the pace and intensity of change are unprecedented. As Oettmeier (1992) emphasizes, police organizations are compelled to undertake some form of organizational reform in order to modify their structure when the department's objectives are transformed. He goes on to state, that:

. . . given today's economic and environmental demands and the perceived ineffectiveness of current strategies, police managers are now confronted with having to think differently about the nature of police work. Instead of focusing attention on procedural concerns brought about by the demand to react to incidents, police managers are beginning to think in terms of addressing substantive issues or problems. (p. 32)

What follows in this chapter is an examination of some specific approaches to organizational reform taking place in Canadian policing that are aimed at making significant improvements in the operation and administration of these institutions.

STRATEGIC ALLIANCES

A growing number of police organizations are working to develop alliances that can assist them to achieve their strategic objectives. The motivation to pursue these alliances has a number of causes rooted in the need for efficiency, effectiveness, and economy. However, it is also possible to view the major shifts made by many police organizations as being aimed at the most significant forms of strategic alliance available: full partnership with the community.

Strategic alliances may take any number of forms and meet a multitude of shared needs; however, any truly effective strategic alliance should have the following features:

- shared objectives or a joint mission;
- cooperation based on equality;
- openness, mutual trust and respect;
- building on individual strengths;
- mutual benefits;
- pooling of resources allowing for greater combined achievement;
- open channels of communication;
- shared commitment by leadership and middle managers; and
- shared opportunities for learning and development.

In order to properly maintain a viable strategic alliance, Devlin and Bleakley (1988) suggest that the following points be taken into account:

- set clearly defined goals and objectives;
- contribute sufficient resources to alliance;
- allocate accountability and responsibilities;
- implement an effective information retrieval process;
- transfer key people to partnership;
- enhance career prospects of alliance employees;
- monitor progress of alliance—including regular reporting, revision of the alliance agreement, and the duration of the alliance; and
- recognize limits of alliance.

PERFORMANCE INDICATORS AND MEASUREMENT

Throughout the public service, including police organizations, there has been an increasing amount of attention paid to performance indicators and the objective measurement of performance. This attention is, in part, a by-product of the desire to make our public services more accountable, responsive, and responsible. Police organizations are a prime example of an important public service that draws heavily on the resources of the taxpayer. Those who make the difficult decisions about the spending of public funds and, therefore, carry the weight of the public trust, are doing what they can to ensure that there is value for money in the services provided. In many jurisdictions, the need to establish performance indicators and measurements has led to some interesting debates and developments that will have a direct impact on the future of policing in Canada (Weatheritt, 1993).

In considering performance measurement, the Management Board Secretariat of Ontario (1996) offers three reasons for its importance:

- to provide a mechanism for public accountability;
- to drive change; and
- as a good management practice.

Performance measurement systems have been developed and advanced in Alberta, the United States, New Zealand, and Great Britain. The information gathered from these systems has many beneficial uses that relate both to organizational and individual achievement. What Weatheritt (1993) notes with respect to police organizations in Great Britain, is becoming increasingly valid in Canada:

> Since the 1970s, the police force has moved from being a largely closed institution to one that has become more open to outside scrutiny and more receptive to the need for critical evaluation. Part of this development has involved a greater emphasis than before on the importance of developing accessible and explicit definitions about what is to count as performance. (p. 24)

In providing a focus for the creation of performance measurements that are relevant to the public, many services in Great Britain have produced what are known as Citizen's Charters. These are published documents which contain indicators that apply the following principles of public service:

- *Standards*—the setting, monitoring and publication of explicit standards of public service that individuals can reasonably expect to receive. Actual performance against these standards will also be published;
- *Information and Openness*—the ready availability of complete and accurate information on how public services are operated, their cost, their performance, and who is responsible;
- *Choice and Consultation*—the provision of service choice, where practicable, along with regular and systematic consultation with those who use public services regarding such things as user satisfaction, priorities, and suggestions for service improvement;
- *Courtesy and Helpfulness*—the provision of services in a courteous and helpful manner, dispensed equally and conveniently;

- *Putting things right*—the acknowledgment that when things go wrong, or systems fail, the public is entitled to apologies, explanations, as well as rapid and effective remedial action. There will also be access to simple-to-use complaints procedures that are widely publicized and an opportunity for independent, impartial review, where possible; and
- *Value for money*—the assurance that public services will be delivered in ways that are efficient and economical and that the performance of these services will be validated against appropriate standards.

It is not difficult to set all of the above principles of public service into a context that would lead to the improvement of police services in Canada and could provide the basis for greater public understanding of those services. However, equally essential in this regard would be the process of establishing a sense among individual officers that improving police performance standards is both important and necessary (Weatheritt, 1993).

ORGANIZATIONAL REVIEW AND RENEWAL

Beyond the general idea of organizational reform that includes a vast array of approaches, there is a trend in police departments toward conducting comprehensive organizational reviews that are aimed at making fairly significant changes to a department's processes and structure. Such reviews have been undertaken in Vancouver, Edmonton, Metropolitan

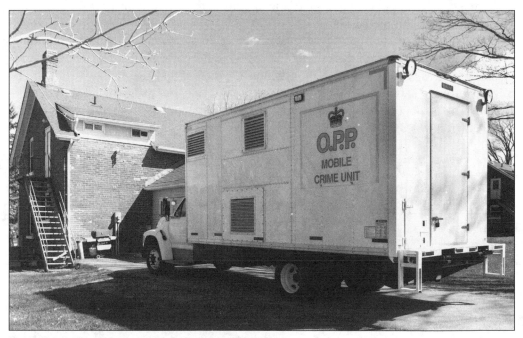

Ontario Provincial Police

Mobile Crime Unit takes the laboratory to the scene of the crime

Toronto, Halton Region, the Ontario Provincial Police, and Ottawa-Carleton Region, to name a few. In many instances, these reviews are aimed at creating a new vision of the police service and are attempts at addressing the kind of challenge put forward by Tully (1993):

> Like other organizations, police organizations suffer from the inability to adjust internally to change. In the simplest terms, what we are trying to build is an organizational structure able to listen to ideas generated by the people who are actually doing the work of the organization in the field, and react swiftly to address the problems identified. To the extent that extensive ranks or bureaucratic levels interrupt or interfere with the upward or downward communication process within an organization, they should be eliminated or modified. (p. 35)

This section will address the following specific approaches that can guide and inform major organizational review and renewal in Canadian policing:

- business process reengineering;
- benchmarking;
- attributes of effectiveness; and
- accreditation.

BUSINESS PROCESS REENGINEERING

As presented by Michael Hammer and James Champy (1993) reengineering is:

> The fundamental rethinking and *radical redesign* of business *processes* to bring about *dramatic* improvements in performance. (p. 3, emphasis in the original)

Some experts in this area of organizational reform have emphasized the radical transformation which this method inspires and offer the caution that business process reengineering requires a clear vision of the organization's future and will demand deep commitment on the part of the entire organization if it is to be successful. Reengineering is also a process that normally leads to the introduction of new technology that will tend to transform the nature of work within the organization and require changed attitudes, behaviour, and competencies. Coulson-Thomas (1994) distinguishes business process reengineering from process simplification:

FIGURE 10-1

PROCESS SIMPLIFICATION VS. BUSINESS PROCESS REENGINEERING

Process Simplification	Business Process Reengineering
• Incremental change	• Radical change
• Process led	• Vision led
• Within existing framework	• Review framework
• Improve application of technology	• Introduce new technology
• Assume existing attitudes and behaviour	• Establish new attitudes and behaviour
• Management led	• Director led
• Various simultaneous projects	• Limited number of corporate initiatives

Over the last few years, several organizations have applied the methods outlined by Hammer and Champy and others to reengineer their various processes. Some of these organizations have reported considerable success and satisfaction with this approach, which relies heavily on the enabling power of automation in all business processes. A number of police organizations have applied this method to their "business" and report degrees of success that are encouraging (OPP, 1995). In New York City, for example, the police have undergone an extensive restructuring that has resulted in substantial change within that organization. In simple terms, the Management Board Secretariat of Ontario (1993) cites the "three R's" of business reengineering:

- *Redesign*—fundamentally rethink how business processes should work;
- *Retool*—use information technology to enable change; and
- *Reorchestrate*—manage the human resource aspects, e.g., job design, organizational structure, rewards systems, etc. Lead the organization through the change process.

From their review of several organizations which applied the reengineering approach, Hammer and Stanton (1995) developed the following insights on what **not** to do if you are hoping to succeed in this kind of endeavour:

FIGURE 10-2

HAMMER AND STANTON ON REENGINEERING
The Ten Top Ways to Fail at Reengineering

1. Don't reengineer but say that you are.
2. Don't focus on processes.
3. Spend a lot of time analyzing the current situation.
4. Proceed without strong executive leadership.
5. Be timid in redesign.
6. Go directly from conceptual design to implementation.
7. Reengineer slowly.
8. Place some aspects of the business off-limits.
9. Adopt a conventional implementation style.
10. Ignore the concerns of your people.

Excerpted from: Hammer, Michael and Steven A. Stanton. *The reengineering revolution: a handbook.* New York: Harper Business. © 1995, Hammer and Company. p. 33. Used with permission

REENGINEERING IN THE ONTARIO PROVINCIAL POLICE

In November 1993, the Ontario Provincial Police began a process of corporate reform known as the Organizational Review Project, which was intended to apply the principles and techniques of business process reengineering as outlined by Michael Hammer and James Champy (McKenna, 1994). The OPP also had the example of previous Ontario government departments which had made efforts at applying this approach to organizational reform, notably the Ministry of Revenue and the Ministry of Natural Resources. The OPP looked at the potential for applying business process reengineering in the following 10 "businesses," which they defined as the key components of their service:

- Prevention of Victimization;
- Occurrence Management;
- Traffic/Waterways Management;
- External Investigative/Security Service Provision;
- Employee Selection and Competency Development;
- Resources Planning, Management, and Control;
- First Nations and Contract Policing Services;
- Firearms Acquisition and Control;
- Policing Services and Employee Standards; and
- Detachment Administration.

Throughout the life of this project, the OPP relied extensively on its internal resources to work within a network of sub-project teams in order to develop detailed process maps that would chart current practice within the organization, and then, using the techniques of business process reengineering, to redesign these processes to make them more effective, efficient, and economical. Finally, the teams would develop recommendations for review and consideration by OPP senior management. As a result of this enormous organizational effort, the OPP produced a significant number of process recommendations that led to the redesign of the entire organizational structure (OPP, 1995). The following chart represents the main categories into which the OPP's business process reengineering efforts were applied:

FIGURE 10-3

OPP BUSINESS PROCESS REENGINEERING RECOMMENDATIONS

Front-Line Service Delivery	Organizational Learning	Administrative and Support Service
enhanced differential response	operationalized principles	centralized
differential follow-up	continuous learning opportunities	better coordination
improved statistical analysis capabilities	systems to capture and share learning	reduced administration
"team" approach	connect the organization to the internal/external environment	better use of technology
enhanced community problem solving	creative application of technology to learning	
increased community participation		

Source: Ontario Provincial Police. (1995). *Organizational review: a process & model for change.* Toronto: Queen's Printer. © Queen's Printer for Ontario, 1995. p. 35. Reproduced with permission. Further reproduction requires the consent and approval of the OPP.

REENGINEERING IN THE NEW YORK CITY POLICE

Under the leadership of Commissioner Bill Bratton, the New York City Police undertook a major reengineering project aimed at producing significant organizational improvements. The department had nine key strategies which they were pursuing throughout this project:

1. Getting guns off the streets.
2. Curbing youth violence, especially in the schools.
3. Driving drug dealers off the streets.
4. Intervening in and breaking the cycle of domestic violence.
5. Reclaiming the public spaces in New York City.
6. Reducing auto-related crimes (including theft and vandalism).
7. Addressing police integrity and corruption.
8. Implementing zero-tolerance traffic control.
9. Encouraging police courtesy, professionalism and respect through training, supervisory guidance and reward system.

All of these strategies were focused at the precinct level of the New York City Police. In order to develop suitable responses to these strategies, 300 members from across the organization were selected to work on 12 reengineering teams. These teams addressed the following areas:

- integrity;
- administration;
- required equipment;
- technology;
- precinct organization (patrol zones);
- reward system and career path planning;
- productivity of members;
- building partnerships with communities;
- geographical responsibility versus specialized functions;
- discipline issues;
- innovation through empowerment; and
- in-service training.

As a result of the efforts of these reengineering teams and the recommendations which they put forward, the Commissioner of the New York City Police authorized the implementation of 418 revised strategies.

REENGINEERING IN THE HALTON REGIONAL POLICE SERVICE

In June 1995, the Halton Regional Police Service presented a proposal for a restructured and cost-efficient organization to their local governing authority. Over the previous nine months, there were more than 100 members of this police service engaged in an organizational review project which was intended to be a comprehensive review of that service, with the theme, *Eliminate, Combine, or Automate*. Various task force teams were equipped with guidelines to assist them in their efforts, as well as the police service's mission statement and the project's overall terms of reference. In order to generate comparative data, the Organizational Review Project studied other police services in Canada.

This project developed more than 170 recommendations for change, which were presented to the Halton Regional Police Services Board for approval. These recommendations fell under some of the following categories:

- community policing;
- criminal investigation branch operations;
- facilities;
- community support services;
- uniform operations;
- information services;
- records;
- courts;
- communications;
- headquarters and administration;
- training and development; and
- organization structure.

The organizational review conducted within the Halton Regional Police Service, along with other efforts, produced savings in the neighbourhood of $1.5 million, which matched the targeted financial savings set for the police department (Halton Regional Police Service, 1995).

BENCHMARKING

Benchmarking, as an activity, is aimed at continuously comparing your organization, its operations or management, with other organizations that are considered to be leaders in their field of endeavour. It implies a willingness on the part of the police organization to learn from others and make meaningful efforts to evolve. Benchmarking can operate by means of both quantitative and qualitative standards. It provides a means for arriving at "best practices" that can be adapted to the police organization for its improvement. It is important to emphasize that the process must be continuous and systematic if it is to be successful, and benchmarking can be applied to products, services, and practices within the police department. Benchmarking was pioneered in the United States within the private sector and has been very effectively used by large organizations, such as the Xerox Corporation, to produce remarkable results.

In order to ensure that a benchmarking project is successful, the following elements should be in place:

- *Involvement of stakeholders*—because of its potential to affect the work processes, resource allocation, and priorities of the organization, it is useful to engage managers, employees, unions, and "customers";

- *Understanding of your organization*—a clear understanding of the organization's current processes is essential for any improvement project and may include techniques like business process reengineering;
- *Selection of key processes*—there should be a careful identification of the areas of improvement that are critical to the internal and external "clients" of the organization. Ask the key question: What needs fixing? This element has a strong link to community policing because it makes the public and important component in the identification of key police processes that require improvement;
- *Development of appropriate indicators of performance*—attention needs to be given to the identification of the best means of determining success in meeting performance criteria. What is measured is what gets done, and the appropriate measures must be in place to focus on performance that produces meaningful results that meet public needs;
- *Benchmark appropriate partners*—selecting the best match for the benchmarking process is critical. It is important to look for partners who are engaged in similar functions or activities. In policing it not necessary to restrict the search to other police departments; there are many generic areas of activity that allow for broader partnerships (e.g., financial management processes, information technology functions, fleet management systems);
- *Balance between stability and change*—this element recognizes the important human need for a degree of stability, even in the midst of significant organizational change. Process changes resulting from benchmarking may require time and application to prove their value within any organizational setting;
- *Introduction of incentives*—there should be some effort made at reinvesting the savings that are realized through successful benchmarking;
- *Creation of a new culture*—recognize that staff will need to be made comfortable with the process of comparing oneself with superior performers, a culture that is willing to admit that it can learn from others and that there is no monopoly on good, creative ideas. Fostering a corporate culture that can overcome fear of, and resistance to, change; and
- *Linking benchmarking with evaluation*—as part of a cycle of continuous improvement, benchmarking can be tied to overall evaluation processes to ensure that innovation continues to thrive within the organization.

ATTRIBUTES OF EFFECTIVENESS

For several years the CCAF, formerly known as the Canadian Comprehensive Auditing Foundation, has been doing research to develop a framework for improving the effectiveness of organizations. The CCAF is made up of individuals and corporations that are seriously concerned with governance and accountability and has members from the public and private sector, auditors, and management consultants. They have refined a substantial amount of research into a number of packages which provide valuable background for anyone looking at organizational reform and improvement. One of the key outputs of the

CCAF's research are the "attributes of effectiveness." The following provides a listing of those attributes and the key questions that must be asked in order to make determinations about levels of effectiveness:

- *Management direction*—Does everyone understand what they are meant to be doing?
- *Relevance*—Do our activities continue to make sense in terms of the conditions, needs or problems to which they are intended to respond?
- *Appropriateness*—Are levels of effort and selected methods of pursuing objectives sensible and sufficient?
- *Achievement of intended results*—How challenging are our established goals, and have they been accomplished?
- *Acceptance*—Are clients and other key stakeholders satisfied with the organization and its products or services?
- *Secondary impacts*—What are the unintended effects of our activities, be they positive or negative?
- *Costs and productivity*—Are the relationships between costs, inputs and outputs favourable?
- *Responsiveness*—How well are we anticipating and responding to change?
- *Financial results*—How good are the financial results in terms of matching costs with revenues and appropriations, and financial assets with obligations?
- *Working environment*—Is it a happy, healthy and constructive working environment where staff are motivated to work together, adapt to change, and develop?
- *Protection of assets*—How well do we protect against surprise events or losses of key personnel, critical occupations, client information, facilities, equipment, inventories, processes or agreements?
- *Monitoring and reporting*—Do management have the information they need to support their decision-making and their own accountability, and do they use it appropriately?

Source: "Attributes of effectiveness." Excerpted from Leclerc, Guy et al. *Accountability, performance, reporting, comprehensive audit: an integrated perspective.* pp. 164–165. © 1996, CCAF-FCVI Inc. Used with permission.

ACCREDITATION

In August 1983, the Commission of Accreditation for Law Enforcement Agencies (CALEA) adopted a series of standards and approached American state and local police departments to gain their support by demonstrating adherence to those standards. CALEA's law enforcement standards were originally developed through collaboration with the following associations:

- International Association of Chiefs of Police (IACP);
- National Organization of Black Law Enforcement Officers (NOBLE);
- National Sheriffs' Association (NSA); and
- Police Executive Research Forum (PERF).

Increasingly, police departments began to adopt the CALEA standards and sought accreditation on the basis of their alignment with those standards. The overall goal of CALEA is "to improve the delivery of law enforcement services" and it has been widely accepted in the United States. In Canada, police services in Edmonton, Winnipeg, and Peel Region have sought CALEA accreditation. While there is some concern that the CALEA standards place an overemphasis on administrative and policy directives that may not be fulfilled at the operational level (Mastrofski, 1986), and that the current standards do not actively promote "community policing" (Cordner and Williams, 1996), they do provide a substantial amount of data that can be usefully adapted by individual police agencies.

ORGANIZATIONAL LEARNING

An increasing number of influential thinkers and practitioners have focused attention on the concept of organizational learning. This has happened, most notably, in the context of policing in Ontario (Ontario. Ministry of the Solicitor General. Strategic Planning Committee on Police Training and Education, 1992). However, major contributions to this innovative area of study and practice have been made over several years (Argyris, 1978; Argyris, 1992; Burgoyne, Pedlar, and Boydell, 1994; Dixon, 1994; Kline and Saunders, 1993; Senge, 1990; Senge et al., 1994; Watkins and Marsick, 1993).

What organizational learning requires is a dramatic magnification and intensification of the police organization's commitment to an all-encompassing enterprise of learning. Such learning will take place on three separate, but equally important, fronts:

- individual;
- team; and
- organization or system-wide.

By bringing together various aspects from a variety of disciplines including engineering, psychology, industrial relations, philosophy, organizational development, adult learning, physics, and political theory, a number of practitioners have emerged as strong proponents of organizational learning.

SOME CHARACTERISTICS OF ORGANIZATIONAL LEARNING

Without attempting to constrain the concept of organizational learning within a fixed definition, it is possible to offer the following characteristics that should be considered important:

- openness to new ideas;
- tolerance of error and risk taking;
- clear and shared vision;
- emphasis on teams;
- capacity for systems thinking;

- understanding of mental models;
- application of "action learning" or "action research";
- encouragement of personal growth and mastery;
- capacity to create, consolidate, and retrieve organizational memory;
- capacity to question fundamental assumptions and/or first principles; and
- capacity for "dialogue."

Many of the characteristics listed above are derived from the five "disciplines" pioneered by Senge (1990) and pursued by several progressive organizations seeking to achieve more effective ways of delivering their products, processes, or services.

In making conscious linkages across the three fronts of organizational learning (i.e., individual, team, and organization), it is possible for the organization to harness a higher level of flexible capability and capacity that continuously enriches the individuals who **are** the organization. Watkins and Marsick (1993) have developed the following useful diagram which captures the close relationship between work and the process of continuous learning that creates opportunities and insights that are beneficial for the individual learner as well as for the overall learning of the organization:

FIGURE 10–4

THE CONTINUOUS WORK AND LEARNING MODEL

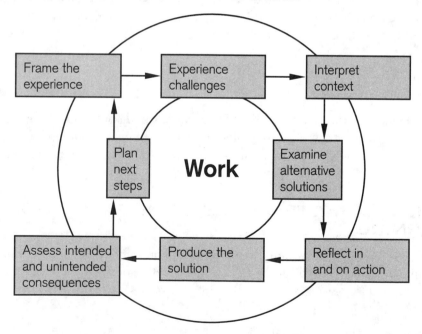

Excerpted from: Watkins, Karen E. and Virginia J. Marsick. *Sculpting the learning organization: lessons in the art and science of systemic change.* © 1993, Jossey-Bass Inc., Publishers. p. 27. Used with permission.

ORGANIZATIONAL LEARNING IN THE RCMP

Recently, the RCMP adopted a continuous learning approach for the delivery of their in-service training program. This new approach will include:

- training and provision of tools for supervisors and managers to develop individual learning plans;
- training for managers in the development of learning strategies to be incorporated in annual operational/business plans; and
- integration of the learning elements of business plans into an annual RCMP learning plan.

This approach confirms the RCMP's belief in continuous learning and the fundamental assumption that such learning is a responsibility shared between the individual member and the organization. Continuous learning is seen as an extension of the problem-solving approach to policing and is consistent with the commonly accepted principles of organizational learning. The RCMP is introducing an Employee Continuous Development Program (ECDP) that will advance the continuous

RCMP bicycle patrol (June 1995, Ottawa)

learning model and provide on-the-job and other opportunities for the growth and development of core organizational competencies based on identified individual learning needs.

PROBLEM-SOLVING POLICING, COMMUNITY-ORIENTED POLICING, AND COMMUNITY POLICING

Over several years, police leaders, practitioners, and academics have devoted a great deal of energy and effort in pursuing a functional understanding of "community policing" (Seagrave, 1997). As with many concepts which are called upon to satisfy radically different applications in substantially different circumstances, a simple, universal definition of "community policing" has proven to be elusive. However, of great practical value is the vision or philosophy of community policing that perceives a true partnership between the police and their various communities. This partnership involves the shared identification of crime and disorder problems, a joint formulation of responses to those problems, and mutually significant evaluation of the efficacy of those responses.

As the literature on community policing continues to grow, there have appeared some powerful insights which derive from the concepts of "problem-oriented policing" (Goldstein,

1990), "problem-solving," or "community-oriented policing"—all intellectual cousins. While there has been a substantial amount of research and writing on the theory and practice of community policing, nothing surpasses the practical simplicity of the applied approach known as problem-oriented policing. Problem-oriented policing (POP) can be understood as the application of the SARA model (Watson, Kenney, and Lusardi, 1995), which is outlined as follows:

- *Scanning*—the first stage of problem identification where community concerns are highlighted through a dialogue involving the police and the community;
- *Analysis*—the second stage involves the gathering of information and data relevant to the problems identified in the stage above. There is almost no limit to the sources which may be tapped into for this purpose; however, they could include of-ficial reports, interviews, surveys, focus groups, and presentations. The actual analy-sis will consider the forces operating on the problem, the events that are associated with the problem, an assessment of the impacts of the problem, and the resources that are available to deal with the problem;
- *Response*—the third stage entails the development of a coherent range of options for responding to the problem, the selection of a preferred and manageable re-sponse, and the implementation of that response option; and
- *Assessment*—the fourth stage involves evaluation of the effectiveness of the response based on data that is gathered. This data may be quantitative or qualitative in nature.

In studying the use of this problem-oriented approach to policing in several U.S. ju-risdictions, Watson, Kenney, and Lusardi (1995) have designed a curriculum to guide the training of police personnel. This curriculum has the following objectives:

FIGURE 10–5

OBJECTIVES FOR THE PROBLEM-SOLVING TRAINING

1. To understand and be able to complete each of the four broad stages of problem-solving.
2. To know and be able to practice the individual steps in each stage of problem-solving.
3. To use the problem-solving model as an effective tool for interacting with members of the community.
4. To be able to explain and mentor the problem-solving process to other officers and members in the community. This involves working collaboratively with members of the community instead of working alone as the expert.
5. To develop the communication skills required during the problem-solving process.
6. To develop the leadership skills necessary to elicit support from the community.
7. To encourage initiative and creativity from other problem-solving officers.

Excerpted from: Watson, T. Steuart, Dennis Jay Kenney, and John Lusardi. *Problem-solving: interme-diate curriculum guide.* © 1995, The Community Policing Consortium, Washington, D.C. p. 11. Used with permission.

As part of their commitment to providing a better understanding of community policing, the Ontario Association of Chiefs of Police (OACP) and the Ontario Ministry of the
Solicitor General and Correctional Services have collaborated on the development of a useful model for representing the interrelated components of community policing. The diagram below presents the five components of that model:

FIGURE 10-6

A FRAMEWORK FOR COMMUNITY POLICING

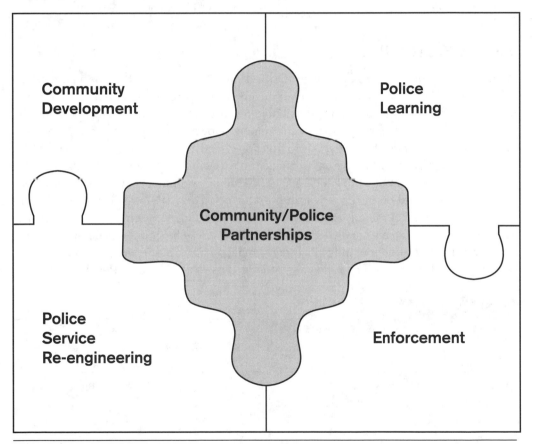

Adapted from: *Community Policing . . . Our Future Today.* © 1996 MSGCS – Policing Standards –
Policing Standards Division and OACP Community Policing Committee. Used with permission.

By combining each of the components outlined above, a police service can begin to develop effective approaches that will lead to service delivery and support mechanisms that
will enhance that organization's ability to provide genuine community policing. In more
detail, the components include:

- *Community development:* community led initiatives that contribute to solving crime and public order problems;
- *Community-police partnerships:* developing and maintaining partnerships in the community at both the front-line and corporate level, permitting meaningful community input into all aspects of policing
- *Police service reengineering:* affecting organizational change to support contemporary management styles and processes
- *Enforcement:* focusing on community safety concerns and serious violent crime
- *Police learning:* supporting continuous learning (Ontario Ministry of the Solicitor General and Correctional Services and Ontario Association of Chiefs of Police, 1996)

TEAM BUILDING

With police organizations undergoing rapid and substantial change, there is an increasing need for the high performance capacity of teams. When properly selected and prepared, teams can offer any organization a formidable resource for creativity, innovation, insight, and enormous capacity for productive achievement. However, team building requires a significant degree of understanding if it is to function effectively. Teams must be carefully constructed and given the wherewithal to tackle their specific assignments. Teams must also be allowed to cycle through the typical stages of team development. These stages have been extensively reported on in the research literature (Laiken, 1992). Not only is it important to ensure that your teams are assembled with care and attention, it is equally critical to establish effective team leadership and facilitation. These functions can be quite distinct and may call for two different individuals performing separate, but related, activities to guide the progress of the team. The following outlines those stages of team development:

FIGURE 10-7

STAGES OF TEAM DEVELOPMENT

Functional Focus	Stages of Team Development	Role of Facilitator
Developing an effective working environment; establishing "ground rules"	Forming	Guiding
Dealing with issues of power and control	Storming	Coaching
Managing conflict; re-negotiating "ground rules"	Norming	Supporting
Functioning as an effective team	Performing	Orchestrating
Concluding the team's work	Adjourning	Separating

Adapted from: Laiken, Marilyn. *The anatomy of high performing teams: a leader's handbook.* Toronto: OISE Press. © 1994, Laiken Associates. Used with permission. ("Stages of team development" based on Bruce Tuckman, 1977.)

In considering the basics of team activity, Katzenbach and Smith (1993) have designed an approach that captures team building across three main dimensions: skills, commitment, and accountability. Within those dimensions, they proceed to identify the need for specific performance results, collective work products, and personal growth.

In order to provide strong team leadership there are a number of factors that need to be taken into account. This is true in any team approach, including teams assembled for police operations or for organizational review projects. Isgar (1993) offers another good model for high performing teams that clarifies the internal and external factors that relate to effective team leadership:

FIGURE 10-8

MODEL FOR A HIGH PERFORMING TEAM

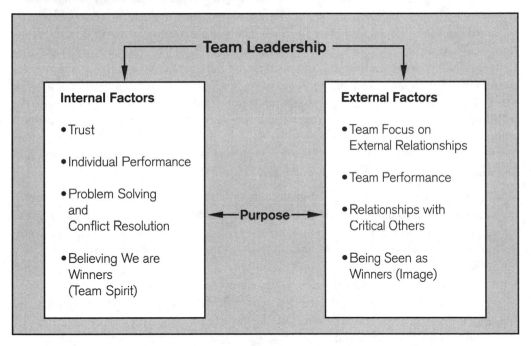

Excerpted from: Isgar, Thomas. *The ten minute team: 10 steps to building high performing teams.* *2nd ed.* Boulder, Colo.: Seluera Press. © 1993, Thomas Isgar. p. 10. Used with permission.

USE OF FORCE CONTINUUM

Much effort has been invested in understanding the issue of police use of force. Nothing serves to alienate the police from the public they serve more dramatically than the perception that officers are using excessive force in the exercise of their legal authority. Media coverage of police shootings or alleged police brutality focuses intense scrutiny on police organizations and can be the source of the deepest, most damaging criticism levelled against individual police officers, their supervisors, or their governing authorities. Accordingly, considerable thought has been given to the introduction of reasonable and responsible limits and parameters around police use of force and the application of alternatives to lethal force (Geller and Toch, 1995).

It is important to remember that police officers are required to use reasonable force in the protection of themselves and the public. This requirement derives from the *Criminal Code* which applies to all police officers in Canada. While the *Criminal Code* authorizes the use of necessary force for lawful purposes, officers are accountable to federal, and applicable provincial laws in their exercise of that authority. There are frequently detailed policies and procedures in place within each individual police service for the specific rules and regulations that pertain to the application of federal and provincial statutes regarding use of force.

As a result of comprehensive study, Geller and Toch (1995) have developed a table (Figure 10–9) that clearly indicates where the attention of a police department should be concentrated in matters relating to use of force. This presentation makes important distinctions between various levels of force and places the use of force into a range of reasonableness that can assist the organization, and the officers involved, in making appropriate responses.

In Ontario an enormous amount of attention has been given to the creation of a use of force continuum that is meant to be a guide to police officers, police executives, and the public with regard to the proportionate application of coercive force by police officers (Ontario. Ministry of the Solicitor General. Policing Services Division, 1992). In developing guidelines that will inform any local policy with respect to police use of force, some of the following topics must be taken into consideration:

- *Firearms*—including the type of weapon that will be authorized for use (revolver versus semi-automatic), the type of ammunition that will be authorized for use (hollow-point versus semi-wadcutter), holsters, reloaders, grip adapters or other adaptations of the issued weapon, and many other equipment issues that pertain to weapon selection;
- *Reporting systems*—including the requirements to report any discharge of the firearm or other weapons (including gas, chemical or aerosol weapons); training and requalification records and other related reports;
- *Training and requalification*—including the provision of an established cycle of instruction for all officers and the maintenance of full records on officers' performance during any training program. Topics may include legal requirements regarding the use of force, demonstration of judgment, review of safety considerations, theoretical framework for use of force legislation and policies, practical exercises designed to test and enhance proficiency, including handgun retention techniques; and
- *Use of Force Options*—including a configuration that permits officers to move along a continuum which emphasizes that the **least** amount of force should be employed

FIGURE 10-9

EXTENT OF DEPARTMENTAL ATTENTION TO DIFFERENT TYPES OF USE OF FORCE ISSUES

	Quality of Officer's Decision		
A *Amount of Force Used*	*B* *Unreasonable*	*C* *Reasonable*	*D* *Highly Skilled*
1 No force (or very minor force) used	Unreasonable Restraint	Justifiable Restraint	Commendable Restraint
2 Moderate force used (isolated incident)	Abuse of Force	Justifiable Use of Force	Commendable Use of Force
3 Serious force used (isolated incident)	Abuse of Force	Justifiable Use of Force	Commendable Use of Force
4 Moderate to Serious force used Frequently	Abuse of Force (Violence-prone officer and/or dept. problems)	Justifiable Use of Force (guidance, retraining, dept. changes)	Commendable Use of Force (Dept. strategic and/or tactical changes)

Key: Shaded cells represent police conduct that typically receives attention from most police departments. The behavior noted in unshaded cells receives far less consideration.

Excerpted from: Geller, William A. and Hans Toch. (eds.). *And justice for all: understanding and controlling police abuse of force.* © 1995, Police Executive Research Forum, Washington, D.C. p. 280. Used with permission.

in any given circumstance, while also recognizing that a situation may require the selection of the most extreme options in order to protect the officer or the public. This configuration includes the following elements:

- officer presence;
- tactical communications;
- empty-hand techniques—including soft (controlling techniques) and hard (empty hand strikes);
- impact weapons—including soft (weapon augmented restraint) and hard (defensive impact strikes);
- aerosol weapons; and
- firearms.

There has been a great deal of effort invested in the production of training scenarios that use simulators and other advanced educational technologies to provide realistic exercises for officers. These approaches have their advocates because they are able to build decision-making patterns that can be linked with operational and administrative policies within the police department. They can also be structured to generate reports on individual officer performance in these simulations in order to ensure that complete records are maintained and that any necessary remedial training can be scheduled quickly. However, Fyfe (1995) highlights the significant limitations of too heavy a reliance on even the most sophisticated electronic use of force training scenarios. Beyond the warning to resist the temptations of too much gadgetry, Fyfe recommends that broad use of force training policies cannot substitute for local proficiency enhancement that is tailored to immediate circumstances:

> The need to fit training to the needs of individual communities is yet another reason why police agencies should regard commercial or other out-of-house training as a complement to their own training effort. No commercial vendor who directs training at a wide market can possibly anticipate or address the characteristics of individual jurisdictions. And despite their greater proximity to the departments they serve, it is extremely difficult for state or regional academies to do so. Assuring that training is congruent with community demographics requires real *hands-on* effort by local police departments. (p. 171, emphasis in original)

STRESS MANAGEMENT, PSYCHOLOGICAL COUNSELLING, AND PEER COUNSELLING

Research has provided a great deal of assistance in drawing attention to the problems associated with stress in policing. While it is a given that stress will have an impact on every human being regardless of their occupation, the potential for dangerously high levels of stress among police personnel is considerable. Fortunately, what has resulted from the clinical and experimental studies of stress are a number of techniques and methods for dealing with the negative effects of stress. Also, we are constantly learning more about controlling the sources of stress in ways that will minimize their worst effects. Increasingly, progressive police organizations are making important investments in the resources that are necessary for these techniques and methods to be introduced in meaningful ways for the benefit of officers.

Anderson, Swenson, and Clay (1995) have identified some of the main sources of stress for police:

- discretionary power;
- death—including police shootings, mutilating accidents, suicides, murders, natural deaths;
- injury—to self and/or others;

- personal failure;
- dangerous situations;
- officer misconduct;
- supervision;
- handling disturbances;
- the judicial system;
- outside criticism and scrutiny;
- special assignments; and
- changes in working conditions.

Added to operational sources of stress, which have always been a characteristic of the occupation of policing, are the stressful influences of profound and extensive organizational change which is now so common in Canadian policing. The radical and fundamental transformation of the processes and structures of policing can have a powerfully stressful impact on officers who are resistant to such change and are not convinced of its value or necessity.

Beginning in the 1960s, police organizations worked with psychologists, largely to develop methods for screening applicants for recruitment. This collaboration resulted from recommendations made in the U.S. following serious urban riots in 1968 (Reese, 1987; Reiser, 1972). This initial purpose eventually grew to include some of the trained psychologists' other skills which were also adaptable to police work, including:

- critical incident response to police shootings;
- hostage-taking and/or barricaded person negotiation skills;
- criminal profiling;
- forensic hypnosis; and
- stress management and "wellness" training.

In addition to the professional expertise provided by psychologists, many police organizations in Canada have introduced peer counselling and support programs that have been highly effective. Also known as employee assistance programs (EAP), such initiatives are useful in reducing absenteeism, increasing productivity, decreasing the number of grievances and disciplinary actions, and generally raising morale within the department (Anderson, Swenson, and Clay, 1995). Frequently, training programs are designed to provide officers with the appropriate skills to undertake the functions of a peer counsellor. These individuals are then able to make themselves available to offer assistance following a traumatic incident, or to deal with a range of other stress-related matters that may be affecting officers. This approach allows the police service to provide qualified support to their members without provoking the officers' tendency to mistrust "outsiders" who are perceived as not understanding the circumstances of the police officer's experience.

CONCLUSION

When considering the many elements discussed above, it is possible to construct a strategic design for a police service that would include the key aspects that would assist any police service in building the capacity to develop innovations in these areas. While the effort here has been to provide only an introduction to some of the leading areas of innovation in contemporary policing, it is most certainly true that the new modes and orders that are appearing within Canadian police services are those which new officers should be learning about first and foremost. The strategic design which is presented below for a police service may also serve as a useful guide for police officers who hope to develop individual capacity to perform at the highest level of effectiveness within their organization and make meaningful contributions to the future of policing.

FIGURE 10-10

A STRATEGIC DESIGN FOR ORGANIZATIONAL REFORM, PROBLEM SOLVING AND RESEARCH, ORGANIZATIONAL LEARNING, AND CONTINUOUS IMPROVEMENT IN A POLICE SERVICE

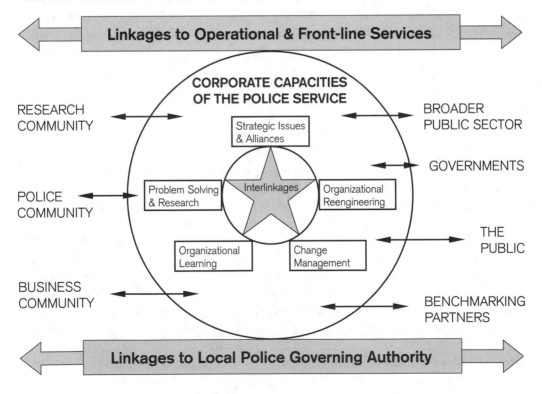

QUESTIONS FOR CONSIDERATION

1. What are some of the likely causes of organizational reform in Canadian policing?
2. What are the potential areas for strategic alliances that could benefit policing?
3. How could performance measurements improve policing in Canada?
4. Should performance measurements be applied to all levels within a police organization?
5. What are some of the processes in a police department that might be improved through business process reengineering?
6. Benchmarking seeks out partners that are leaders in an area of business practice. What are some possible benchmarking partners for police services in Canada?
7. What are the advantages of organizational learning in a police department? What are the disadvantages?
8. Problem solving offers an approach for dealing with crime and disorder issues. How can this approach be used to engage members of the community?
9. What are some of the difficulties that might be found in trying to implement a problem-solving approach?
10. What are some specific events in a police officer's work that could be the cause of negative stress?

REFERENCES

Abbey-Livingston, Diane and David Kelleher. (1989) *Managing for learning in organizations: the fundamentals*. Toronto: Ontario Ministry of Tourism and Recreation.

Anderson, Wayne, David Swenson, and Daniel Clay. (1995). *Stress management for law enforcement officers*. Englewood Cliffs, N.J.: Prentice Hall.

Argyris, Chris. (1993). *Knowledge for action: a guide to overcoming the barriers to organizational change*. San Francisco: Jossey-Bass Publishers.

Argyris, Chris and Donald Schon. (1978). *Organizational learning: a theory of action perspective*. Reading, Mass.: Addison-Wesley Publishing.

Belden, Ginny, Marcia Hyatt, and Deb Ackley. (1994). *Towards a learning organization: resource guide for the Ontario public service*. Toronto: Ontario Management Board Secretariat.

Burbeck, E. and A. Furnman. (1985). "Police officer selection: a critical review of the literature." *Journal of Police Science and Administration*, 13.

COPPS: community oriented policing & problem solving. [Sacramento, Calif.]: California Department of Justice, Crime Prevention Center, 1992.

Canadian Centre for Management Development. (1994). *Continuous learning: a CCMD report*. Ottawa: Canadian Centre for Management Development.

Commission on Accreditation for Law Enforcement Agencies, Inc. (1993). *Standards for law enforcement agencies: the standards manual of the law enforcement agency accreditation program*. Fairfax, Virginia: CALEA.

Community Policing Consortium. (1994). *Understanding community policing: a framework for action*. Washington, D.C.: U.S. Department of Justice. Bureau of Justice Assistance.

Cordner, Gary W. and Gerald L. Williams. (1996). "Community policing and accreditation: a content analysis of CALEA standards." In Hoover, Larry T. (ed.). *Quantifying quality in policing*. Washington, D.C.: Police Executive Research Forum.

Coulson-Thomas, Colin. (1992). *Transforming the company: bridging the gap between management myth and corporate reality*. London: Kogan Page.

Coulson-Thomas, Colin. (ed.). (1994). *Business process reengineering: myth or reality?* London: Kogan Page.

Devlin, G. and M. Bleakley. (1988). "Strategic alliances: guidelines for success." *Long Range Planning*, 21(5).

Dixon, Nancy M. (1993). *Organizational learning*. Ottawa: Conference Board of Canada.

Doob, Anthony N. (ed.) (1993). *Thinking about police resources*. Toronto: Centre of Criminology, University of Toronto.

Elledge, Robin L. and Steven L. Phillips. (1994). *Team building for the future: beyond the basics*. Toronto: Pfeiffer & Co.

Frederick, C.J. (1986). "Post-traumatic stress responses to victims of violent crime: information for law enforcement officials." In Reese, James T. and Harvey A. Goldstein (eds.). *Psychological services for law enforcement*. Washington, D.C.: Government Printing Office.

Fyfe, James. (1995). "Training to reduce police-civilian violence." In Geller, William A. and Hans Toch (eds.). *And justice for all: understanding and controlling police abuse of force*. Washington, D.C.: Police Executive Research Forum

Geller, William A. and Michael S. Scott. (1992). *Deadly force: what we know: a practitioner's desk reference on police-involved shootings*. Washington, D.C.: Police Executive Research Forum.

Geller, William A. and Hans Toch. (eds.). (1995a). *And justice for all: understanding and controlling police abuse of force*. Washington, D.C.: Police Executive Research Forum.

Geller, William A. and Guy Swanger. (1995b). *Managing innovation in policing: the untapped potential of the middle manager*. Washington, D.C.: Police Executive Research Forum.

Glensor, Ronald W. and Alissa J. Stern. (1995). *Dispute resolution and policing: a collaborative approach to effective problem solving*. Washington, D.C.: Police Executive Research Forum.

Goldstein, Herman. (1979). "Improving policing: a problem-oriented approach." *Crime & Delinquency*, April.

Goldstein, Herman. (1990). *Problem-oriented policing*. New York: McGraw-Hill, Inc.

Gow, James Iain. (1994). *Learning from others: administrative innovations among Canadian governments*. Toronto: Institute of Public Administration of Canada. (Monographs on Canadian Public Administration; no. 16).

Greene, Jack R. and Ralph B. Taylor. (1988). "Community-based policing and foot patrol: issues of theory and evaluation." In Greene, Jack R. and S.D. Mastroski (eds.). *Community policing: rhetoric or reality?* New York: Praeger.

Halton Regional Police Service. Organizational Review Project. (1995). *Media information package (June 22, 1995)*. Oakville: Halton Regional Police Service, Media Relations Bureau.

Hammer, Michael and James Champy. (1993). *Reengineering the corporation: a manifesto for business revolution*. New York: Harper Collins Publishers.

Hammer, Michael and Steven A. Stanton. (1995). *The reengineering revolution: a handbook*. New York: Harper Business.

Harbour, Jerry L. (1994). *The process reengineering workbook: practical steps to working faster and smarter through process improvement*. New York: Quality Resources.

Harbour, Jerry L. (1996). *Cycle time reduction: designing and streamlining work for high performance*. New York: Quality Resources.

Hastings, Ross. (1993). *Leadership for community policing in Canada*. Unpublished paper prepared for the Canadian Police College.

Heck, William P. (1990). *Creating a cadre of police leaders: a study of police executive development programs in the United States: a dissertation presented to the Faculty of the College of Criminal Justice, Sam Houston State University in partial fulfillment of the requirements of the degree of doctor of philosophy*. Huntsville, Texas: Sam Houston State University.

Higley, Dahn D. (1984). *O.P.P.: the history of the Ontario Provincial Police Force*. Toronto: Queen's Printer.

Hogan, R. (1971). "Personality characteristics of highly rated policemen." *Personnel Psychology*, 24.

Hoover, Larry T. (ed.). (1996). *Quantifying quality in policing*. Washington, D.C.: Police Executive Research Forum.

Ingstrup, Ole. (1995). *The strategic revolution in executive development: what does it mean for you and your organization?* Ottawa: Canadian Centre for Management Development.

Inkpen, A.C. and M.M. Crossan. (1995). "Believing is seeing: joint ventures and organization learning." *Journal of Management Studies*, 32(5).

Isgar, Thomas. (1993). *The ten minute team: 10 steps to building high performing teams. 2nd ed.* Boulder, Colo.: Seluera Press.

Janis, Irving L. (1989). *Crucial decisions: leadership in policymaking and crisis management*. New York: The Free Press.

Katzenbach, Jon R. and Douglas K. Smith. (1993). *The wisdom of teams: creating the high-performance organization*. Boston: Harvard Business School Press.

Kennedy, Leslie W. (1991). "The evaluation of community-based policing in Canada." *Canadian Police College Journal*, 15(4).

Kenney, Dennis Jay and T. Steuart Watson. (1996). "Reducing fear in the schools: managing conflict through student problem solving." *Education and Urban Society*, 28(4).

Kline, Peter and Bernard Saunders. (1993). *Ten steps to a learning organization*. Arlington, Virginia: Great Ocean Publishers.

Laiken, Marilyn E. (1994). *The anatomy of high performing teams: a leader's handbook*. Toronto: OISE Press.

Larson, Peter and Robert Mingie. (1993). *Leadership for a changing world: developing executive capability: detailed findings*. Ottawa: Conference Board of Canada.

Leclerc, Guy et al. (1996). *Accountability, performance reporting, comprehensive audit: an integrated perspective*. Ottawa: CCAF-FCVI Inc.

Leeuw, Frans L., Ray C. Rist, and Richard C. Sonnichsen. (1994). *Can governments learn?: comparative perspectives on evaluation and organizational learning*. New Brunswick, N.J.: Transaction Publishers.

Marquis, Greg. (1993). *Policing Canada's century: a history of the Canadian Association of Chiefs of Police*. Toronto: Published for the Osgoode Society by the University of Toronto Press.

Mastrofski, Stephen D. (1986). "Police agency accreditation: the prospects for reform." *American Journal of Police*, 5(2).

Mathie, Robert (1989). "Examining performance: some suggestions on measuring performances for evaluating police work." *Policing*, 5(4).

McKenna, Paul F. (1994). "Setting our sights for a focus on the future." *The O.P.P. Review*, 29 (4).

McKenna, Paul F. (1995). "Policing in 2020 & the application of organizational learning: grinding new lenses to view the development of human resources: a prolegomenon." Unpublished paper prepared for the Society of Police Futurists International (1995).

McKenna, Paul F. and Donald G. Evans (1995). "Leadership as learning: learning as leadership." *The Police Governor*, 5(2), pp. 13–18.

Meagher, M.S. and N.A. Yeates (1986). "Choosing a career in policing: a comparison of male and female perceptions." *Journal of Police Science and Administration*, 14.

Mintzberg, Henry (1981). "Organization design: fashion or fit?" *Harvard Business Review*, 59(1).

Murphy, Chris and Graham Muir. (1985). *Community-based policing: a review of the critical issues*. Ottawa: Solicitor General Canada.

O'Keefe, Garrett et al. (1993). *The social impact of the National Citizens' Crime Prevention Campaign: focus on what works*. Washington, D.C.: U.S. Department of Justice, Bureau of Justice Assistance.

Oettmeier, Timothy N. "Matching structure to objectives." In Hoover, Larry T. (ed.). *Police management: issues & perspectives*. Washington, D.C.: Police Executive Research Forum and Texas Law Enforcement Management Institute.

Ontario. Management Board Secretariat. (1993). *An introduction to business reengineering*. [Toronto]: Management Board Secretariat.

Ontario. Management Board Secretariat. (1996). *A framework for performance measurement in government programs and services*. [Toronto]: Management Board Secretariat.

Ontario. Ministry of Municipal Affairs. Subsidies Management Branch. (1993). *On becoming a learning organization: a practical guide for change*. Toronto: Queen's Printer.

Ontario. Ministry of the Solicitor General. Strategic Planning Committee on Police Education and Training. (1992). *A police learning system for Ontario: final report and recommendations*. Toronto: The Ministry.

Ontario. Ministry of the Solicitor General.. Policing Services Division. (1992). *Policing standards manual for the Province of Ontario*. Toronto: The Ministry.

Ontario Provincial Police. (1995). *Organizational review: a process & model for change*. Toronto: Queen's Printer.

Peak, Kenneth J. and Ronald W. Glensor. (1996). *Community policing & problem solving: strategies & practices*. Upper Saddle River, N.J.: Prentice Hall.

Piskurich, George M. (1993). *Self-directed learning: a practical guide to design, development, and implementation*. San Francisco: Jossey-Bass Publishers.

Pitney Bowes Management Services. (1994). *Reengineering among the Fortune 500: a Pitney Bowes Management Services study: summary of findings.* Stamford, Conn.: Pitney Bowes Management Services.

Police Executive Research Forum. (1996). *Themes and variations in community policing: case studies of community policing*. Washington, D.C.: Police Executive Research Forum.

Reese, J.T. (1987). *A history of police psychological services*. Washington, D.C.: U.S. Dept. of Justice.

Reiser, A.J. (1972). *The police department psychologist*. Springfield, Ill.: Charles C. Thomas.

Reno (Nevada) Police Department. (1990). *Problem oriented policing: training guide (supervisor)*. Reno: Reno Police Department.

Scrivner, Ellen M. (1994). *The role of police psychology in controlling excessive force*. Washington, D.C.: U.S. Dept. of Justice, National Institute of Justice.

Seagrave, Jayne. (1997). *Introduction to policing in Canada*. Scarborough, Ont.: Prentice Hall Canada.

Selye, H. (1974). *Stress without distress*. Philadelphia: J.B. Lippincott Co.

Selye, H. (1976). *The stress of life*. New York: McGraw-Hill.

Senge, Peter M. (1990). *The fifth discipline: the art and practice of the learning organization*. New York: Doubleday Currency.

Senge, Peter M. et al. (1994). *The fifth discipline fieldbook: strategies and tools for building a learning organization*. New York: Doubleday Currency.

Sewell, James D. (1981). "Police stress." *FBI Law Enforcement Bulletin*, April.

Sherman, Lawrence. (1987). "Effective community policing: research contributions and considerations." In Loree, D. and C. Murphy (eds.). *Community policing in the 1980s: recent advances in police programs*. Ottawa: Solicitor General Canada.

Snetsinger, Douglas. (1993). *Learning leaders: perspectives from Canadian CEOs*. Toronto: Institute of Market Driven Quality, Faculty of Management, University of Toronto, and Skill Dynamics Canada.

Stamper, Norman H. (1992). *Removing managerial barriers to effective police leadership: a study of executive leadership and executive management in big-city police departments*. Washington D.C.: Police Executive Research Forum.

Tilley, Nick. (1995). *Thinking about crime prevention performance indicators*. London: Home Office Police Research Group. (Crime Detection & Prevention series paper; no. 57).

Tully, Edward J. (1990). "The 1990s: new days, old problems." *Police Chief*, (January).

Wadman, Robert C. and Robert K. Olson. (1990). *Community wellness: a new theory of policing*. Washington, D.C.: Police Executive Research Forum.

Walker, Sandra Gail, Christopher R. Walker, and James C. McDavid. (1992). *The Victoria community police stations: a three-year evaluation*. Ottawa: The Canadian Police College.

Watkins, Karen E. and Victoria J. Marsick. (1993). *Sculpting the learning organization: lessons in the art and science of systemic change*. San Francisco: Jossey-Bass Publishers.

Watson, T. Steuart, Dennis Jay Kenney, and John Lusardi. (1995). *Problem-solving: intermediate curriculum guide*. Washington, D.C.: The Community Policing Consortium.

Weatheritt, Mollie. (1993). "Measuring police performance: accounting or accountability?" In Reiner, Robert and Sarah Spencer (eds.). *Accountable policing: effectiveness, empowerment and equity*. London: Institute for Public Policy Research.

Wheatley, Margaret J. (1992). *Leadership and the new science: learning about organization from an orderly universe*. San Francisco: Berrett-Koehler Publishers.

Williams, Gerald L. (1989). *Making the grade: the benefits of law enforcement accreditation*. Washington, D.C.: Police Executive Research Forum.

Wilson, James Q. and George L. Kelling. (1982). "Broken windows." *The Atlantic Monthly*, March.

Wilson, James Q. and George L. Kelling. (1989). "Making neighborhoods safe." *The Atlantic Monthly*, February.

Woolner, Paul. (1991). *Integrating work and learning: a developmental model of the learning organization: presented to the Commission of Professors of Adult Education, 1991 annual conference, Montreal, October 13–15*. Etobicoke, Ont.: Woolner, Lowy & Associates.

Zeffane, R. (1995). "The widening scope of inter-organizational networking: economic, sectoral and social dimensions." *Leadership & Organization Development Journal*, 16(4).

Zhao, Jihong. (1996). *Why police organizations change: a study of community-oriented policing*. Washington D.C.: Police Executive Research Forum.

Zhao, Jihong and Quint Thurman. (1996). *The nature of community policing innovations: do the ends justify the means?* Washington, D.C.: Police Executive Research Forum.

TOWARD MORE LEARNING

ORGANIZATIONAL REFORM

Marquis, Greg. (1993). *Policing Canada's century: a history of the Canadian Association of Chiefs of Police*. Toronto: Published for the Osgoode Society by the University of Toronto Press.

This recent study provides extensive, historical insight into the development of policing in Canada through an examination of the Canadian Association of Chiefs of Police (CACP). Marquis, through this analysis, clearly reveals that police organizations in Canada have had a tradition of change and adaptation, especially with regard to the introduction of new technology. This publication is worthwhile for placing the current situation of policing in Canada into a context that underlines the constant need for organizational reform.

PERFORMANCE INDICATORS AND MEASUREMENT

Ontario. Management Board Secretariat. (1996). *A framework for performance measurement in government programs and services*. [Toronto]: Management Board Secretariat.

This is a useful primer on the issues that relate to performance measurement and can be applied within the context of police organizations at any level. It contains a number of references for further reading in the areas of benchmarking, customer service surveys, critical success/output analysis, performance management, and process management.

ORGANIZATIONAL REVIEW AND RENEWAL

Metropolitan Toronto Police. Restructuring Task Force. (1994). *Beyond 2000: final report*. Toronto: Metropolitan Toronto Police.

This publication details the findings of the Beyond 2000 Restructuring Task Force established within the Metropolitan Toronto Police. This task force operated between April and November 1994 and undertook significant research and study on a wide range of topics relevant to their work. This final report also contains the recommendations of the task force designed to change the priorities, organizational structure, service delivery, and support systems within the police department. It is an effort to align the organization more with the strategic objectives set forth in the Beyond 2000 planning document which was originally published in 1991. The task force was comprised of 12 full-time members and 4 part-time personnel representing most areas and ranks within the police service, and together they produced 31 recommendations for change.

Ottawa-Carleton Regional Police Service. (1996). *Ottawa-Carleton Regional Police amalgamation report: submitted to the Ontario Civilian Commission on Police Services*. Ottawa: Ottawa-Carleton Regional Police Service.

With the creation of the Ottawa-Carleton Regional Police Service in January 1995, three former police services were brought together: the Gloucester, Nepean, and Ottawa Police Services. This report provides valuable detail on the process and strategy applied in facilitating and informing this amalgamation. It is divided into six sections, as follows:

- *Strategic analysis*—examines national and provincial trends with a concentration on the demographic profile of the Ottawa-Carleton area which provides a statistical basis for projections relating to police services;
- *Financial overview*—considers revenues and expenditures relating to the police service, with some discussion of alternative revenue-generating proposals;
- *Planning process*—includes aspects of the Organizational Change Project Team which was established in April 1995 to oversee all amalgamation activities and work toward to the development of a strategic plan that would facilitate transition to full amalgamation;
- *Police service delivery*—highlights the proposed organizational structure including the proposed service delivery model;
- *Adequacy of police services*—outlines the adherence of the proposed structure with available measures of police adequacy and effectiveness; and
- *Next steps*—outlines the implementation steps to be taken toward the realization of the amalgamated organizational structure and service delivery model.

The report also includes the internal and public opinion survey questionnaires that were employed to generate data for planning and design purposes.

Business Process Reengineering

Hammer, Michael and James Champy. (1993). *Reengineering the corporation: a manifesto for business revolution*. New York: Harper Collins Publishers.

This book gained a substantial reputation for guiding many corporations, public and private, in their reengineering initiatives. It is clearly written and provides a strong basis upon which to build a practical understanding of the need for, and benefits of, the radical redesign of processes and structures for greater efficiency and effectiveness.

Harbour, Jerry L. (1994). *The process reengineering workbook: practical steps to working faster and smarter through process improvement.* New York: Quality Resources.

A highly practical approach to process reengineering that makes a fundamental distinction between work and waste. Harbour has studied a number of organizations and offers suggestions for moving toward greater organizational efficiency.

Ontario Provincial Police. (1995). *Organizational review: a process and model for change.* Toronto: Queen's Printer.

This document provides a detailed overview of the entire Organizational Review Project undertaken by the OPP, beginning in November 1993. It offers thorough information on how the application of a business processing reengineering approach can contribute to meaningful and substantive organizational change within a police service.

Attributes of Effectiveness

Leclerc, Guy et al.(1996). *Accountability, performance reporting, comprehensive audit: an integrated perspective.* Ottawa: CCAF-FCVI Inc.

This publication provides a substantial reference tool covering 15 years of development, research, and learning dealing with the theory and practice of accountability. It covers a wide range of experience in providing valuable information on organizational effectiveness to governing bodies, and offers useful detail on the attributes of effectiveness which provides the basis for management reporting. As a Canadian organization committed to providing research and education leading to better accountability, governance, management, and audit in our private and public corporations, CCAF has much to offer in support of organizational change in policing.

Accreditation

Williams, Gerald L. (1989). *Making the grade: the benefits of law enforcement accreditation.* Washington, D.C.: Police Executive Research Forum.

This monograph is a condensed version of the author's doctoral dissertation in public administration. It examines the impact of the CALEA accreditation program on the 42 law enforcement agencies that had been formally granted accreditation by December 31, 1986. Williams used a questionnaire to gather data on the impact of accreditation in four key areas, namely, (1) the delineation of agency goals policies on (2) use of deadly force, (3) police pursuits, and (4) the collection and preservation of evidence. The author concludes by stating that the CALEA program can assist a police organization in making systematic improvements in its operation and management; however, it is recommended that further detailed study and research be conducted to further assess the effects of accreditation.

ORGANIZATIONAL LEARNING

Canadian Centre for Management Development. (1994). *Continuous learning: a CCMD report*. Ottawa: Canadian Centre for Management Development.

An extremely well-written Canadian resource on the topics of individual and organizational learning. It offers a distinction between formal and informal individual learning and provides valuable suggestions for pursuing self-development. It provides a linkage between organizational learning and strategic management and offers a summary of the "action learning" theories put forward by Chris Argyris and Donald Schon. This publication also includes extensive suggestions for further readings in the relevant topics.

Kline, Peter and Bernard Saunders. (1993). *Ten steps to a learning organization*. Arlington, Virginia: Great Ocean Publishers.

This is a practical introduction to the process of introducing and supporting organizational learning. It includes a "Learning Organization Assessment Matrix" that is designed to be completed in order to discover the current state of the organization in a number of important areas that relate to organizational learning, and which can be used as a blueprint for change and transformation.

Watkins, Karen E. and Victoria J. Marsick. (1993). *Sculpting the learning organization: lessons in the art and science of systemic change*. San Francisco: Jossey-Bass Publishers.

Written by two experienced adult educators, this textbook promotes the notion that individual learning can operate as a strong catalyst within any organization to advance team learning and organizational change. They draw on experiences in several corporations to present lessons that can be applied in many settings. By combining work and learning in an integrated fashion, it is possible to build effective individuals, teams, and organizations.

PROBLEM-SOLVING AND COMMUNITY-ORIENTED POLICING

Goldstein, Herman. (1990). *Problem-oriented policing*. New York: McGraw-Hill, Inc.

Herman Goldstein is considered by many to be one of the leading thinkers in the area of problem-oriented policing (POP). This book provides valuable insight for those seeking to better understand this approach to community policing and its practical application. Goldstein has written many other articles and essays on these and related topics, many of which are referred to in this publication.

Police Executive Research Forum. (1996). *Themes and variations in community policing: case studies of community policing*. Washington, D.C.: Police Executive Research Forum.

A recent study of the application of community policing in six jurisdictions: Edmonton, Alberta; Newport News, Virginia; Las Vegas, Nevada; Philadelphia, Pennsylvania; Santa Barbara, California; and San Diego, California. These sites were selected because of their commitment to some form of community policing and their varying approaches to its application. These case studies followed protocol that allowed for the consistent collection of information in the following areas: the environment, the department, community policing planning and implementation, the management of community policing, external collaboration (including the media, community, and other agencies), and results or outcomes.

Zhao, Jihong. (1996). *Why police organizations change: a study of community-oriented policing*. Washington D.C.: Police Executive Research Forum.

This is a comprehensive examination of organizational change in American policing as it relates to community-oriented policing (COP). The author looked at the inhibitors and facilitators of change in nearly 300 U.S. police departments. The book contains an overview of the literature on organizational change that is very useful. He concludes with the observation that change, in the form of COP, is largely forced in U.S. police agencies, and that organizational change overall is both marginal and incremental. This leads to the suggestion that more movement in the direction of organizational learning is required to make these changes more meaningful and sustainable.

TEAM BUILDING

Elledge, Robin L. and Steven L. Phillips. (1994). *Team building for the future: beyond the basics*. Toronto: Pfeiffer & Co.

Laiken, Marilyn E. (1994). *The anatomy of high performing teams: a leader's handbook*. Toronto: OISE Press.

USE OF FORCE CONTINUUM

Geller, William A. and Michael S. Scott. (1992). *Deadly force: what we know: a practitioner's desk reference on police-involved shootings*. Washington, D.C.: Police Executive Research Forum.

A very detailed and substantial treatment of the topic of police and deadly force in the United States. The work contains comprehensive statistics on shootings of and by police and provides analysis of these various statistics. The authors consider a number of shooting control strategies that include policy development, policy enforcement, training, weapons, and equipment. They also provide their thoughts on the establishment of agency standards relating to use of force and highlight areas of future operational research. The book contains an extensive bibliography of sources on the topic of deadly force and sample deadly force policy statements from several U.S. departments.

Geller, William A. and Hans Toch. (eds.). (1995). *And justice for all: understanding and controlling police abuse of force*. Washington, D.C.: Police Executive Research Forum.

This publication is an extension of the information provided in the item noted above. The book contains a series of essays that were commissioned by the Police Executive Research Forum in the wake of the Rodney King beating in Los Angeles in 1991. It is divided into five main categories that deal with the following general topics: What do we mean by "police abuse of force," why does it happen and how often?; violence, prejudice and public opinion; reducing the prevalence of abuse of force; international perspectives; and summary of recommendations for research and action.

STRESS MANAGEMENT, PSYCHOLOGICAL COUNSELLING, AND PEER COUNSELLING

Anderson, Wayne, David Swenson, and Daniel Clay. (1995). *Stress management for law enforcement officers*. Englewood Cliffs, N.J.: Prentice Hall.

A thorough study of the topic, written with the benefit of substantial and current research. It includes extensive references to the literature on the topics relating to stress in law enforcement, questions for discussion, and case studies.

CHAPTER ELEVEN

LOOKING FORWARD TO THE NEXT
MILLENNIUM OF CANADIAN
POLICE SERVICE

LEARNING OBJECTIVES

1. Identify selected elements of the future of policing in Canada
2. Identify the importance of change management in policing
3. Describe changes suggested for the improvement of police management
4. Review certain developments in policing in Canada that will affect its future
5. Understand the ongoing nature of personal and organizational change

INTRODUCTION

Persons pretending to forecast the future shall be considered disorderly under Subdivision 3, Section 901 of the Criminal Code and liable to a fine of $250 and/or six months in prison.

—Section 899, New York State Code of Criminal Procedure.

...to cherish traditions, old buildings, ancient cultures and graceful lifestyles is a worthy thing, but in the world of technology, to cling to outmoded methods of manufacture, old product lines, old markets or old attitudes among management and workers is a prescription for (organizational) suicide.

—Sir Ieuan Maddock. "Why industry must learn to forget." *New Scientist* (February 1982).

The consideration of the future is always difficult and controversial. Where someone sees signs of promise and prosperity, others have a premonition of disaster and disappointment. In policing, the transformation that has occurred over the last 10 years alone is sufficient to indicate that anyone interested in pursuing a career in law enforcement will need to be fully conscious of the continuous and dramatic nature of change and build that awareness into their planning for the future. Of course, the future can be seen as merely an extension of the present and the past and simply grows out of the seeds that have been planted in those time frames.

Therefore, preparing for the future can be done by having a good understanding of the past and how it has led to the present. That understanding will provide useful predictors of the future. In policing, the past has drawn heavily on a rigid military model of organization and structure. It is one that in Canada developed along with other institutions designed to contribute to our national goals of "peace, order, and good government." The present has witnessed huge changes in many areas of human endeavour, and police organizations have not been immune from the massive changes which are taking place in virtually every area of activity. By looking at the past and by comprehending the present, it is possible to project into the future in some measure. This chapter will attempt to shed some light on the possible future of policing in Canada and will emphasize the central significance of change as a watchword for that future. Nothing is certain but change; however, by learning what we can from experience, patience, and persistence, directions will emerge leading us to the creation of the kind of future we envision (Peak and Glensor, 1996).

By trying to make sense of the things that have brought us to where we are in Canadian policing, it is possible that what is useful and effective can be sustained by those who hold responsibility for the future of law enforcement. By learning more about the larger context in which policing operates, those who carry the future of policing will have an opportunity to contribute to its continuous improvement and evolution.

WHAT DOES THE FUTURE HOLD?

It is possible to point to certain aspects of the future of policing that can be seen quite clearly. Of course, as the view of the road ahead is constantly changing, this can be no more than a snapshot of the immediate horizon. Canada has witnessed some areas of advancement or enhancement that are beginning to affect law enforcement principles and practices. These selected areas reflect specific projects, undertakings, and trends that are worthy of note:

- Alternative Service Delivery;
- Internet, Intranet, and Information Technology;
- Civilianization;
- Globalization of Crime and Policing;
- Research and Development Initiatives:
  - Nathanson Centre for the Study of Organized Crime and Corruption;
  - Crime Prevention Through Environmental Design (CPTED);
  - Police Leadership Forum; and
  - *Policing: An International Journal of Police Strategies & Management*.

The next century will find Canada in the midst of significant social, political, economic, technological, and demographic transition. The stability of our very Confederation will be questioned and tested by several forces.

ALTERNATIVE SERVICE DELIVERY

Across Canada, governments are introducing projects and programs that attempt to restructure the way public services are being offered. Since policing and related public safety programs constitute such large investments of human, financial, and material resources, it is common for these public services to come under particular scrutiny. Lindquist and Sica (1995) have identified a number of factors which cause governments to undertake these reviews:

- reduction of deficits and accumulated debt;
- competition with other jurisdictions and sectors;
- delivery of services and provision of more hospitable environments for business and investment;
- provision and delivery of services that citizens want, in the manner they seek; and
- provision of a range of services consistent with the willingness of citizens and corporations to bear certain levels of taxation.

In order to satisfy these demands, police organizations are being challenged to redesign themselves in ways that will address the factors listed above. In order to prepare for an effective future in policing, individuals should be fully aware of the changes that are taking place and the kinds of skill sets that will be best tailored to these transforming institutions. Because the changes are happening rapidly and continuously, it is important that the demands of a new public service, which includes police services, be understood and addressed. New organizational structures will call for new kinds of managers; new information-based systems will require individuals who are increasingly sophisticated in their knowledge of information technologies and their applications. The demands for responsiveness to the public, sometimes presented as a customer-service orientation, will require individuals who are skilled at dealing with the public, making presentations, dealing effectively with conflict, problem solving, facilitation, and teamwork. Indeed, so much is happening across the country in various government departments that a proposal has been made for the establishment of a clearinghouse to collect and disseminate resources on this broad range of innovations and initiatives (Lindquist and Sica, 1995).

INTERNET, INTRANET, AND INFORMATION TECHNOLOGY

The Internet stands out clearly as the focus of future developments in the area of information technology. What began in the 1950s as a collection of research centres based in the United States has grown to a worldwide system that connects more than 60 million people and 15 million computers. The power of the Internet is remarkable and allows for the networking of incredible amounts of human intelligence. However, the Internet also opens new territory for the criminal. It has been estimated that computer crime is responsible for annual losses in excess of $10 billion in the United States (Rollock, 1996). With many institutions beginning to introduce programs that take advantage of the virtues of the

Internet, e.g., government agencies, financial institutions and banks, it is immediately feasible for policing organizations to implement changes that will harness some of the Internet's power. The following summarizes some of those applications (Rollock, 1996):

CRIME PREVENTION

- use of police bulletin boards;
- establishment of Neighbourhood Watch on the Internet;
- establishment of Web sites for individual police services;
- communities and police services connected through e-mail;
- posting of crime statistics relevant to the community; and
- establishment of information kiosks in communities.

PUBLIC ORDER MAINTENANCE

- posting of summonses and traffic citations on the Internet;
- notification of licence suspensions;
- Internet adaptations of "911";
- mobile access to the Internet;
- applications using an Intranet system to connect officers for computer-assisted dispatch (CAD), incident reporting, and downloading of departmental policies and procedures and other organizational information;
- dissemination of public information generated by the police service; and
- connection among police services for joint planning and response.

INVESTIGATIONS

- sharing of investigative information among police services;
- connection of federal/provincial/regional and municipal police agencies through Intranet systems;
- dissemination of high-resolution pictures of missing children, wanted suspects, or escapees;
- delivery of court documentation through Intranet systems; and
- sharing of sensitive criminal intelligence information through Intranet systems.

Of course, these applications of Internet and Intranet systems will require police personnel with a fairly high degree of computer literacy. The opportunities for working with such systems will increase the demand for skilled personnel who have strong information technology backgrounds.

CIVILIANIZATION

While this topic was dealt with briefly in Chapter 4 ("Becoming a Police Officer in Canada"), it is useful to pinpoint the potential for increasing civilianization as a feature of changing organizational priorities in policing. As the "business" of policing continues to grow in com-

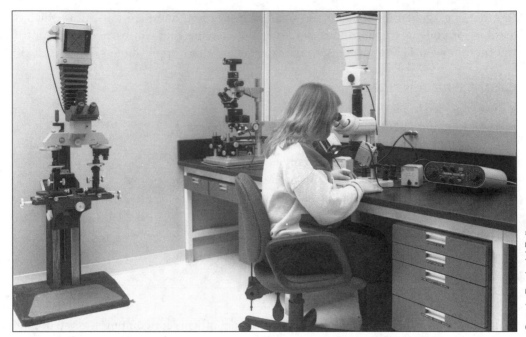

Ontario Provincial Police

Laboratory technicians and other civilian personnel provide valuable skills to police organizations

plexity and as levels of accountability and responsibility increase, it is not difficult to understand the pressures on police departments to introduce civilian personnel who have skills sets that are consistent with important organizational needs within those departments.

The evolution of civilianization has taken on some features that indicate a trend toward greater application of this approach for reasons of efficiency as well as economy (Berry, 1995). Distinct phases reveal the substance of the change in this area:

- *Manual*—cleaning, catering, and custodial functions;
- *Administrative and clerical*—typing, stenographic and other office-based functions;
- *Specialist*—mechanics, technical services, computer programmers and operators, photographers; and
- *Professional and managerial*—accounting, legal, human resources consultants, social science researchers, statisticians, information technology managers, systems analysts, architects, etc.

Linked to this evolution of civilianization within police services in Canada is the concept of volunteers. Increasingly, police organizations are beginning to make much more extensive use of this kind of resource in their delivery of service. This issue is one that has important implications for the success of community policing in many jurisdictions and is also a matter of utmost concern for police associations in Canada. The nature of the work done by the volunteer and the impact of that work on the nature and opportunity for paid duty using fully sworn, uniformed officers is a key point for the labour representatives of police officers. Many jurisdictions have extensive and impressive auxiliary police programs, as well as imaginative volunteer programs that harness community resources in a cost-efficient and collaborative manner.

BRIEFING NOTE

For the Police Service, the involvement of volunteer citizens is not at all seen as a form of cheap labour. On the contrary, volunteer involvement would lead to a demystification of police work in the eyes of citizens and favour closer ties between station staff and local communities.

In this perspective, volunteer citizens would be given specific mandates during particular activities of a communal nature and of interest to the community.

Source: Montréal Urban Community Police. (1995). *Neighbourhood policing,* p. 55.

GLOBALIZATION OF CRIME AND POLICING

At the edge of a new century it is not difficult to understand the growing concern being expressed by law enforcement organizations with regard to the increasing globalization of crime. As a result of the enormous advances made in the area of technology, the capacity for organized criminals to engage in illegal activities that cross international boundaries and borders is substantially increased. The movement to a global economy has made it attractive and lucrative for criminals to operate on a broader scale with more complex tools at their disposal. The breakdown of the Soviet Union and other geopolitical upheavals have made it obvious to law enforcement professionals that criminal activity is highly transportable and poses an important threat to social stability. The activities of international terrorism is but one feature of this globalization of crime; however, it is not the only element. Theft of computer information and proprietary data in the possession of large private and public corporations is a serious threat that requires considerable expertise and skill on the part of police investigators. Other forms of white collar crime that attack financial institutions and their clients is on the increase, again calling for international police cooperation, highly developed levels of computer literacy, and the technical wherewithal to detect and gather forensic evidence on such crimes.

RESEARCH AND DEVELOPMENT INITIATIVES

A number of research and development initiatives are being pursued within Canadian policing that demonstrate a solid commitment to excellence and innovation. While it is not possible to provide a comprehensive accounting of all the efforts being made in the area of research and development, the following examples have been selected to illustrate the vitality of Canadian policing and the ingenuity that is being invested in several projects that will contribute to its improvement.

NATHANSON CENTRE FOR THE STUDY OF ORGANIZED CRIME AND CORRUPTION

In March of 1997 an announcement was made regarding the creation of the Nathanson Centre for the Study of Organized Crime and Corruption at Osgoode Hall Law School of York University, Ontario. This is the first centre of its kind in Canada and is intended to meet important research, policy development, law reform, and educational needs in this area. The centre will examine relevant issues that fall under the general category of organized crime and corruption, including the impact of increased globalization of crime, the use and abuse of the Internet, the impacts of political changes in Eastern Europe, Russia, and Hong Kong.

The centre is the result of a $3 million endowment from Mark Nathanson, chairman and director of Marzen Holdings Company Ltd. and will facilitate a multi-disciplinary approach to the analysis of organized crime and corruption, including academic expertise in political science, sociology, business, criminology, criminal law, banking law, and international law. The centre will also provide scholarships in support of graduate research in relevant areas and will be the focus for linkages with international research institutes engaged in parallel studies. The Nathanson centre anticipates broad cooperation with experts in government agencies, police services, business and financial institutions, forensic accounting organizations, and other organizations concerned with the problems of organized crime and corruption. The centre will be guided by an Advisory Board that includes noted authorities from the relevant fields of professional activity and ex-officio members of York University. The first director of the centre is Dr. Margaret Beare, from the Department of Sociology (Criminology) at York University.

CRIME PREVENTION THROUGH ENVIRONMENTAL DESIGN (CPTED)

A significant approach to crime prevention that reflects the results of ongoing research and development is commonly referred to as crime prevention through environmental design (CPTED). Based on work begun in the 1960s and 1970s (Jacobs, 1962; Newman, 1972), this approach places considerable emphasis on the value of carefully designing the human environment to promote safety and security. It is possible to create public and private spaces in a manner that reduces or resists crime (sometimes referred to as "target hardening") by addressing the crime triangle, represented in Figure 11–1.

FIGURE 11-1

THE CRIME TRIANGLE

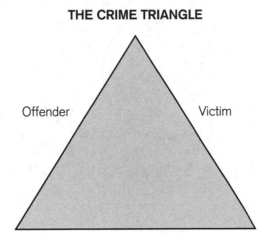

THE CRIME TRIANGLE

Offender

Victim

Location

By removing one, or more, of the elements of the crime triangle it becomes possible to affect the probability of a crime taking place. For example, if you create a location where the offender cannot confront the potential victim, through features such as lighting, high visibility, no escape route, etc., it is much less likely that the crime will take place. Many police organizations are developing an expertise in this field of research and are working with architects, city planners, and concerned citizens to introduce practical applications. This growing expertise is being shared with various community groups, and training programs dealing with the theory and practice of CPTED have been introduced as part of the regular curriculum at police colleges to ensure that such initiatives are widely available within the police community.

Additionally, there has been a great deal of attention paid to the study of crime and place at a "micro context" that has had promising results for crime prevention planners and policy makers (Eck and Weisburd, 1995). In part, this approach looks at the occurrence of crime events as the precise combination of a motivated offender and a desirable target in the same time and space. Figure 11–2 highlights this model and reveals where the overlap of each element provides the opportunity for a criminal occurrence.

POLICE LEADERSHIP FORUM

In October 1996, a two-day conference was held in Toronto that brought together approximately 200 people interested in the future of policing and, specifically, in the ongoing development of leadership. This conference took as its motto, *Leadership: an activity, not a position.* Several speakers made presentations on the changes and transformations

FIGURE 11-2

OCCURRENCE OF CRIME EVENTS

which have affected their organizations over the last few years, sharing their insights and observations for the benefit of all attendees. There were particular aspects of this event that are worth noting in the context of the future of policing in Canada. Some of the topics discussed at this conference are listed below, as well as the police service or organization represented by the speaker(s):

• Values, beliefs, and strategies for policing in the information age (Peel Regional Police);
• Fight Against Child Exploitation (FACES) program (Vancouver Police Department);
• Innovations in change leadership (Ottawa-Carleton Regional Police);
• Using teams in a problem-solving environment (Halton Regional Police);
• Community-based policing initiatives (Edmonton Police);
• Managing the future and environmental scanning (Canadian Police College);
• Quality principles in organizational leadership (Peel Regional Police);
• British Columbia supervisors' needs assessment (Justice Institute of B.C.);
• Community policing in Winnipeg: past, present, and future (Winnipeg Police);
• Forgotten issues of leadership (Hamilton-Wentworth Regional Police);
• Becoming a leadership organization (Abbotsford, B.C.);
• Business process reengineering of the occurrence process (Metro Toronto Police);
• Restructuring the Vancouver Police Department; and
• People issues during organizational change (Canadian Police College).

Evolving from the success of this conference and from a clear need within the law enforcement community in Canada for more opportunities for sharing information and insights with regard to leadership at every level of policing, the Police Leadership Forum was established to foster continuous improvement opportunities. The Police Leadership Forum is a federally incorporated, non-profit organization that has undertaken to pursue the following principles:

- To live by the highest ethical standards.
- To safeguard democratic rights and freedoms, while acknowledging the responsibilities of all members of society.
- To create and maintain learning environments in police organizations.
- To enhance career development and the performance of police leaders through superior management practices and continuous learning opportunities.
- To promote cross-training and benchmarking with other professionals and organizations who also demonstrate a strong focus on service.

In addition to the planning of further conferences dealing with topics relevant to the future development and enhancement of policing in Canada, the Police Leadership Forum has begun to publish a brief bulletin to keep members informed on issues and events. This periodical is called *The Mezzanine,* and is funded and published by the Canadian Police College, Ottawa.

POLICING: AN INTERNATIONAL JOURNAL OF POLICE STRATEGIES & MANAGEMENT

In order to keep abreast of international trends in modern law enforcement, the appearance of a new journal, *Policing: An International Journal of Police Strategies & Management*, will be useful for the serious study of policing. This new publication represents the merging of two previous published periodicals, *Police Studies: The International Review of Police Development* and the *American Journal of Police*. It is anticipated that this new journal will produce high quality articles on topics of relevance and importance to police services, policy makers, and academics in the field of law enforcement. It will offer summaries of recent research initiatives, book reviews, debates, and abstracts of topical articles from other journals. Some of the areas to be examined include:

- performance measurement and accountability;
- police pursuit policies and guidelines;
- crime trends and their analysis;
- organized crime;
- victimology;
- crime prevention;
- community policing;
- traffic enforcement;
- civil litigation; and
- investigations.

HOW DO I HOLD ON TO THE FUTURE?

The upheaval seen in private and public corporations across Canada, including the effects of downsizing, de-layering, outsourcing, restructuring, and reengineering have caused people to seriously question their future in these organizations and the stability of job prospects. It is not easy to offer convincing advice in the face of such massive change. However, there is some real wisdom available from those who have sustained these kinds of changes or who are knowledgeable and informed observers and have identified patterns and principles that can assist in this regard.

The surest way to weather the storms of the future is to become accomplished in the management of change. This is a lesson that has been taken to heart by many police organizations and is one of the most common insights that such services report on when they reflect on any major restructuring effort. Many departments that have undergone significant organizational transformation now know that they require an ongoing capacity to respond quickly and intelligently, almost instinctively, to the perpetual demands of change. They have also come to realize that change itself is inevitable, highly unpredictable, yet capable of being influenced to some degree. Of course, much of what is true of organizations is also true of individuals, since at a profound level, organizations are little more than the collective capacity of the people that comprise them.

MANAGING CHANGE

Give me somewhere to stand, and I will move the earth.

Archimedes, 287–212 B.C. (Source: Pappus. *Synagoge*. Edited by F. Hultsch, Berlin, 1876–1878, VIII, 10, xi.)

In taking a thoughtful approach to the management of change, there are some strategies that can be applied by individuals or organizations in order to make transitions more smoothly. While these strategies will express themselves differently, depending on precise circumstances, they will share certain common elements and should all be addressed with equal care and attention.

- establish open channels of communication;
- monitor perceptions;
- foster symbols;
- establish consistent values;
- identify custodians of change;
- establish shared responsibility;
- articulate your vision;
- foster team performance;
- support risk taking;
- address the Who, What, Why, Where, How questions;
- establish an overall game plan; and
- recognize the pioneers and experimenters.

There are some typical responses to change that have been derived from the research done by individuals, like Elisabeth Kübler-Ross, who have studied terminally ill patients. These responses move through time and may be more profound for some than others. The responses may be presented as follows:

- *Discovery*—the immediate awareness of change or a perception of the need for change;
- *Immobilization*—a reaction to the magnitude of the change and incapacitation at the prospect of change;
- *Denial*—a characteristic defence mechanism which attempts to negate the need for change or to "buy" time;
- *Anger*—an emotional reaction that is an expression of one's sense of resentment or fear at being compelled to change;
- *Bargaining*—attempts at negotiating the nature and/or the extent of anticipated change;
- *Upheaval*—an emotional response to the substance of the change process which may include depression, anxiety, confusion, excitement;
- *Exploration*—beginning to examine potential effects of change and analyze possible futures; and
- *Acceptance*—the movement toward positive attitudes regarding change and its opportunities for growth.

In addressing these stages individuals and leaders can do a number of things to better deal with the process.

FIGURE 11-3

THE CHANGE PROCESS

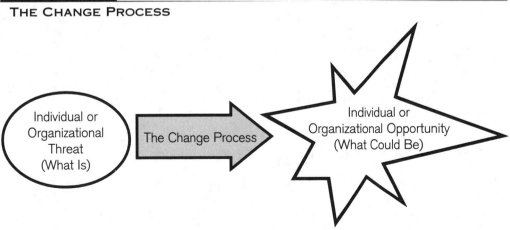

The OPP applied a model that was designed to guide their organizational renewal process and facilitate the management of change within their organization. As an approach to large-scale organizational change, this model is highly instructive. As a guide for the personnel mastery of change it provides a useful benchmark that can be adapted to individual circumstances with good effect.

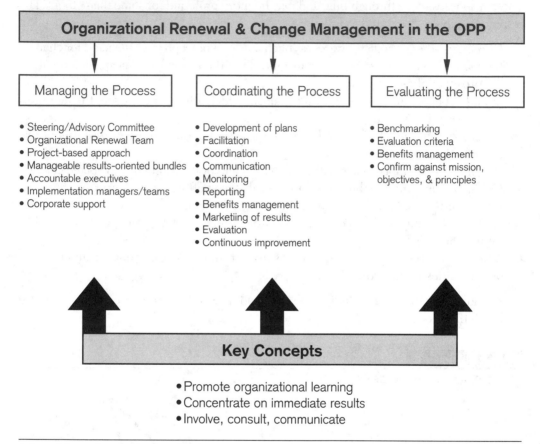

FIGURE 11-4

MODEL FOR CHANGE MANAGEMENT IN THE OPP

Organizational Renewal & Change Management in the OPP

Managing the Process	Coordinating the Process	Evaluating the Process
• Steering/Advisory Committee • Organizational Renewal Team • Project-based approach • Manageable results-oriented bundles • Accountable executives • Implementation managers/teams • Corporate support	• Development of plans • Facilitation • Coordination • Communication • Monitoring • Reporting • Benefits management • Marketiing of results • Evaluation • Continuous improvement	• Benchmarking • Evaluation criteria • Benefits management • Confirm against mission, objectives, & principles

Key Concepts

• Promote organizational learning
• Concentrate on immediate results
• Involve, consult, communicate

Adapted from: Ontario Provincial Police. Organizational Review Project. (1995). *Presentation material.* Orillia: OPP Organizational Review Project. Used with permission. Further reproduction requires the consent and approval of the OPP.

CHANGING MANAGEMENT

Nothing is more important to the future of policing in Canada than the now common observation that management approaches must be changed in order to promote and facilitate continuous improvement and growth (Geller and Swanger, 1995; Goldstein, 1990; Normandeau and Leighton, 1990; Stamper, 1992; Wadman and Olson, 1990). The past has embedded within it the model of a military paradigm that served a useful purpose for confronting the public order challenges of an earlier time. The present highlights the need for transforming that paradigm into one that has greater flexibility and empowerment

Ontario Provincial Police

Aerial photograph of new OPP headquarters in Orillia, Ontario

while still maintaining command and control in circumstances that do not permit broad consultation and rigorous problem solving. The immediate challenge for the future is to construct management layers that are more fully participative, team oriented, and populated with leaders who are equipped to function across a more complex range of knowledge, skills, and abilities than their predecessors. Changing policing in Canada, therefore, implies changing the management of police services. This is the responsibility of the police services themselves, their individual governing authorities, and the government bodies (at the federal and provincial levels) that oversee and legislate the administration of justice. The challenge of this change is enormous and calls for engagement throughout the entire system.

Drucker (1988) notes that the new organization, which is based on information, will be quite different from its predecessors:

> ...a good deal of work will be done differently in the information-based organization. Traditional departments will serve as guardians of standards, as centers of training and the assignments of specialists; they won't be where the work gets done. That will happen largely in task-focused teams. (p. 47)

Dalla Costa (1995) compares conventional management with an approach that promotes creativity and argues convincingly in favour of a "completeness" that results from their combination:

MANAGEMENT	CREATIVITY
Logical analysis	Discontinuity and reconnection
Accountability for results	Freedom to risk
Sequential process	Simultaneous combustion
Bias to reason	Bias to emotion
Organizational principles	Organizational values
Competition	Cooperation
Quest for reward	Quest for achievement
Appreciation of precedent	Appreciation of potential
Assurance of control	Stimulation of experimentation
Structures and systems	Short circuits and shortcuts
Lessons from mistakes	Lessons from life

It is important to emphasize that the nature of the change confronting organizations in society today highlights the need to seek ability and capacity from a much broader range of sources. It is no longer prudent or practical for organizations to draw only from within the existing management pool for talent. Many police organizations have begun to cast much wider nets in order to tap into operational levels and are beginning to look outside of traditional areas for new managers and senior executives. Indeed, some progressive police services have circumvented existing rank structures to promote talented officers to senior management positions without compelling them to progress through the intervening rank levels. This has brought praise because it reflects a new reality with regard to organizational need, as well as criticism because it amounts to a departure from the conventional wisdom which people have come to expect. This creates an unusual situation in the area of law enforcement and needs to be understood by those entering or contemplating a career in policing. As these organizations de-layer and downsize, as the role of public policing undergoes deliberate and inevitable transformation, there will always be opportunity for individuals with the potential for leadership, problem solving, facilitation, team building, and innovation. By enhancing and practicing these capabilities, including a mastery of change, there will be greater assurance that the future will unfold in ways that are more predictable.

CONCLUSION

While resisting the temptation to make predictions about the precise future of policing in Canada, it is valuable to study the signs and signals from everyday life in search of significant sources of insight. The attention given to issues of public safety in the socio-political realms and the constant watchfulness of the media in matters dealing with the police and the criminal justice system ensure that any future will be populated with persons who are officially tasked with the delivery of services that contribute to crime prevention, law enforcement, the maintenance of public order, the provision of assistance to victims of crime, and emergency response. The precise functions and responsibilities will vary and change over time and will be highly dependent on jurisdiction; however, the nature of human beings and society requires that such services be available and that appropriately skilled individuals bear responsibility for the provision of such services in accordance with the highest possible standards.

Like science, which has undergone several "paradigm shifts" over the last few centuries, modern policing in Canada is being challenged to change because of the inability of old rules and operating procedures to completely address new problems and realities. The search for a new paradigm for policing is the result of a crisis comparable to what Kuhn (1962) discovered in the scientific realm.

> Because it demands large-scale paradigm destruction and major shifts in the problems and techniques of normal science, the emergence of new theories is generally preceded by a period of pronounced professional insecurity. As one might expect, that insecurity is generated by the persistent failure of the puzzles of the normal science to come out as they should. Failure of existing rules is the prelude to a search for new ones. (pp. 67–68)

QUESTIONS FOR CONSIDERATION

1. What appear to be the most important trends likely to have an impact on the future of policing in Canada?
2. What are the positive influences of the Internet on policing in Canada? What are the negative influences of the Internet?
3. Discuss the importance of civilianization (including the use of paid staff and unpaid volunteers) in policing in Canada. Identify positions that could, or should, be civilianized. Identify positions that could not, or should not, be civilianized.
4. What are some of the operational challenges that may result from the increasing globalization of crime?
5. What effects will the transformation of organizational structures to more information-based models have on small police departments in Canada? On medium-sized police departments? On large police departments?
6. Identify ways in which an individual can learn about managing change.
7. Identify ways in which Crime Prevention Through Environmental Design (CPTED) could benefit a community.
8. What are some ways in which a police organization could communicate its approach to change management, both internally and externally?

REFERENCES

Adams, Michael. (1997). *Sex in the snow: Canadian social values at the end of the millennium.* Toronto: Viking.

Berry, Geoff D. (1995). "Civilianisation and the use of volunteers." In *Management challenges in 21st century policing: conference proceedings.* Conference held September 22–24, 1995 in Ottawa, Ontario, sponsored by the Centre for Police Management and Research (Staffordshire University, U.K.), the Canadian Institute for Law and the Family (University of Calgary), and the Solicitor General Canada.

Bolles, Richard Nelson. (1996). *What color is your parachute?: a practical manual for job-hunters & career changers.* Berkeley, Calif.: Ten Speed Press.

Brown, Jr., William F. (1992). "Thinking outside the dots: creative approaches to police funding." *The Police Chief*, April.

Campbell, John Henry. (1990). "Futures research: here and abroad." *The Police Chief*, January.

Carr, David K., H.J. Kelvin, and William J. Trahant. (1996). *Managing the change process: a fieldbook for change agents, team leaders, and reengineering managers.* New York: McGraw-Hill.

Carter, David L., Allen D. Sapp, and Darrel W. Stephens. (1989). *The state of police education: policy direction for the 21st century.* Washington, D.C.: Police Executive Research Forum.

Dalla Costa, John. (1995). *Working wisdom: the ultimate value in the new economy.* Toronto: Stoddart Publishing.

Drucker, Peter F. (1988). "The coming of the new organization." *Harvard Business Review*, 66(1).

Eck, John E. and David Weisburd (eds.). (1995). *Crime and place.* Monsey, N.Y.: Criminal Justice Press and the Police Executive Research Forum (Crime Prevention Studies; vol. 4).

Frame, J. Davidson. (1994). *The new project management: tools for an age of rapid change, corporate reengineering and other business realities.* San Francisco: Jossey-Bass Publishers.

Geller, William A. and Guy Swanger. (1995). *Managing innovation in policing: the untapped potential of the middle manager.* Washington, D.C.: Police Executive Research Forum, sponsored by the National Institute of Justice.

Goldstein, Herman. (1990). *Problem-oriented policing.* New York: McGraw-Hill, Inc.

Grant, Alan. (1980). *The police: a policy paper: a study prepared for the Law Reform Commission of Canada.* Ottawa: Law Reform Commission of Canada.

Handy, Charles. (1994). *The empty raincoat: making sense of the future.* [S.l.]: Arrow Business Books.

Helgesen, Sally. (1995). *The web of inclusion: a new architecture for building great organizations.* Toronto: Currency/Doubleday.

Ingstrup, Ole. (1995). *Public service renewal: from means to ends.* Ottawa: Canadian Centre for Management Development. (Explorations; no. 4).

Jacobs, Jane. (1962). *The death and life of great American cities.* New York: Vintage.

Jeffrey, C.R. (1977). *Crime prevention through environmental design.* Beverly Hills: Sage Publications.

Johnson, A.W. (1993). *What is public management?: an autobiographical view.* Ottawa: Canadian Centre for Management Development. (Research paper; no. 8).

Kübler-Ross, Elizabeth. (1986). *Death: the final stage of growth*. New York: Simon & Schuster.

Kuhn, Thomas S. (1962). *The structure of scientific revolutions*. Chicago: University of Chicago Press.

Lindquist, Evert and Tammy Sica. (1995). *Canadian governments and the search for alternative program delivery and financing: a preliminary survey*. Toronto: KPMG Centre for Government Foundation.

Management challenges in 21st century policing: conference proceedings. (1995). Conference held September 22–24, 1995, in Ottawa, Ontario, sponsored by the Centre for Police Management and Research (Staffordshire University, U.K.), the Canadian Institute for Law and the Family (University of Calgary), and the Solicitor General Canada.

Montréal Urban Community Police. (1995). *Neighbourhood policing*. Montréal: Montréal Urban Community Police.

Morgan, Gareth (1993). *Imaginization: the art of creative management*. Newbury Park, Calif.: Sage Publications.

Nadler, David A., Robert A. Shaw, A. Elise Walton and associates. (1995). *Discontinuous change: leading organizational transformation*. San Francisco: Jossey-Bass Publishers.

Newman, Oscar. (1972). *Defensible space: crime prevention through urban design*. New York: Macmillan.

Normandeau, André and Barry Leighton. (1990). *A vision of the future of policing in Canada: police-challenge 2000: background document*. Ottawa: Solicitor General Canada.

Peak, Kenneth J. and Ronald W. Glensor. (1996). *Community policing and problem solving: strategies and practices*. Upper Saddle River, N.J.: Prentice Hall.

Peters, B. Guy. (1993). *The public service, the changing state and governance*. Ottawa: Canadian Centre for Management Development. (Research paper; no. 13).

Police Association of Ontario. (1996). *Police employment in 1996: seeking the common sense solution: emerging issues, legal developments*. Toronto: Police Association of Ontario. Papers presented at conference held February 26 and 27, 1996, sponsored by the Police Association of Ontario

Portwood, John. (1997). "Force of change." *Chatelaine*, 70(5).

Pritchett, Price. (1996). *Resistance: moving beyond the barriers to change: a handbook for people who make things happen*. Dallas: Pritchett & Associates.

Pritchett, Price and Ron Pound. (1990). *The employee handbook for organizational change*. Dallas: Pritchett & Associates.

Pritchett, Price and Ron Pound. (1994). *Business as unusual: the handbook for managing and supervising organizational change. 2nd ed*. Dallas: Pritchett & Associates.

Pritchett, Price and Ron Pound. (1995). *A survival guide to the stress of organizational change*. Dallas: Pritchett & Associates.

Rollock, John A. (1996). "Internet and the future of policing." Unpublished paper presented by John A. Rollock, IBM Canada, Ltd.

Stamper, Norman H. (1992). *Removing managerial barriers to effective police leadership: a study of executive leadership and executive management in big-city police departments*. Washington, D.C.: Police Executive Research Forum.

Stansfield, Ronald T. (1996). *Issues in policing: a Canadian perspective*. Toronto: Thompson Educational Publishing.

Stevens, Nigel. (1993). "Future issues in policing." Unpublished paper prepared for the Edmonton Police Service.

Tafoya, William L. (1986). "A Delphi forecast of the future of law enforcement." Unpublished Ph.D. dissertation. College Park, Maryland: University of Maryland.

Tafoya, William L. (1990). "Futures research: implications for criminal investigations." In Gilbert, James N. (ed.). *Criminal investigations: essays and cases*. Columbus, Ohio: Merrill Publishing Co.

Toffler, Alvin and Heidi Toffler. (1995). *Creating a new civilization: the politics of the third wave*. Atlanta: Turner Publishing, Inc.

Wadman, Robert C. and Robert K. Olson. (1990). *Community wellness: a new theory of policing*. Washington, D.C.: Police Executive Research Forum.

Witham, Donald C. (1991). "Environmental scanning pays off." *The Police Chief*, March.

TOWARD MORE LEARNING

WHAT DOES THE FUTURE HOLD?

Cornish, Edward. (1977). *The study of the future*. Washington, D.C.: World Future Society.

This is a standard work which emphasizes the fundamental value of examining the future for the planning of the present. It has given rise to a considerable body of literature dealing with this area as a special discipline.

Flanagan, Timothy J. and Michael R. Buckman. (1976). *The Delphi technique: a tool for criminal justice planners*. Albany, N.Y.: State University of New York at Albany, School of Criminal Justice.

This book offers a good summary and assessment of the Delphi technique which has been applied in many organizational settings, including the study of the future of policing and the criminal justice system. The most extended application in the context of policing is that undertaken by William Tafoya (see below).

Tafoya, William L. (1986). "A Delphi forecast of the future of law enforcement." Unpublished Ph.D. dissertation. College Park, Maryland: University of Maryland.

This is a detailed and scholarly study of the application of the Delphi technique, which brings together subject matter experts from an area of human activity for a series of examinations of critical issues. The purpose of this application was to attempt to establish some authoritative forecasts relating to the future of law enforcement. It provides a solid insight into the technique as well as some interesting predictions based on the participants' extensive knowledge and exposure to key indicators. It has been widely circulated in police organizations and has been influential in causing police decision makers to think seriously about the future.

Periodicals

There are a number of journals which are published that take the future as their focus and provide interesting and valuable insights into new initiatives in technology and other areas that could potentially affect policing in Canada. The process of keeping up-to-date on such publications is a critical component of environmental scanning and is frequently included in police courses that promote learning about the future.

Futures Research Quarterly (U.S.)—a professional journal of strategic planning, policy analysis, and forecasting. Includes articles dealing with management in the future and other future-related issues.

Long Range Planning (U.K.)—this publication is designed to focus attention on the concepts and techniques involved in the process of developing and implementing long-range strategies and plans. Its intended audience includes senior managers, administrators, and academics.

Planning Review (U.S.)—a journal aimed at decision makers involved in strategic planning, as well as its financial and operational offshoots.

The Futurist (U.S.)—a journal devoted to the study of forecasts of the future, including the analysis of trends and future-oriented concepts.

HOW DO I HOLD ON TO THE FUTURE?

Bolles, Richard Nelson. (1996). *What color is your parachute?: a practical manual for job-hunters & career changers.* Berkeley, Calif.: Ten Speed Press.

This book has become the standard tool in preparing people for the difficult task of job hunting or career transition. It is updated on an annual basis and provides detailed insight into taking stock of your individual strengths, weaknesses, and interests and allows the reader to make some clear assessments about the job search, or career change, strategy. It is written in a encouraging tone and has substantial insight that makes it extremely useful.

MANAGING CHANGE

The series of booklets published by Pritchett & Associates (see items listed in "References") contain valuable material for managing change. There is a considerable body of literature which is available from several sources that offers insight and suggestions for developing this capacity.

CHANGING MANAGEMENT

Geller, William A. and Guy Swanger. (1995). *Managing innovation in policing: the untapped potential of the middle manager.* Washington, D.C.: Police Executive Research Forum, sponsored by the National Institute of Justice.

This recent publication from the Police Executive Research Forum (U.S.) provides insight into the means by which the middle managers in police organizations can be brought into the process of successful organizational change. Police organizations' commitment to some form of community policing requires new approaches to initiate and sustain innovative management that will affect existing managers, front-line staff, and the new recruits who will become managers of the future.

Ontario Provincial Police. (1995). *Organizational review: a process & model for change.* Toronto: Queen's Printer.

A thorough guide to the entire process of large-scale organizational change and the means by which it can be accomplished through business process reengineering. This publication also examines some of the lessons learned as a result of such an undertaking.

APPENDIX 1

SELECTED BIBLIOGRAPHY

Abbey-Livingston, Diane and David Kelleher. (1989). *Managing for learning in organizations: the fundamentals*. Toronto: Ontario Ministry of Tourism and Recreation.

Adams, Michael. (1997). *Sex in the snow: Canadian social values at the end of the millennium*. Toronto: Viking.

Anastaplo, George. (1975). *Human being and citizen: essays on virtue, freedom and the common good*. Chicago: The Swallow Press.

Anderson, Wayne, David Swenson, and Daniel Clay. (1995). *Stress management for law enforcement officers*. Englewood Cliffs, N.J.: Prentice Hall.

Anti-Defamation League. (1996). *Danger: extremism: the major vehicles and voices on America's far-right fringe*. New York: Anti-Defamation League.

Archambeault, W.G. and Betty J. Archambeault. (1984). *Computers in criminal justice administration and management: introduction to emerging issues and applications*. Cincinnati: Anderson Publishing.

Argyris, Chris. (1964). *Integrating the individual and the organization*. New York: Wiley.

Argyris, Chris. (1993). *Knowledge for action: a guide to overcoming the barriers to organizational change*. San Francisco: Jossey-Bass Publishers.

Argyris, Chris and Donald Schon. (1978). *Organizational learning: a theory of action perspective*. Reading, Mass.: Addison-Wesley Publishing.

Atchison, R.M. et al. (1984). *Study of police management information systems: volume iv targeted information processing system: a developmental program for police management information systems*. Ottawa: Ministry of the Solicitor General of Canada.

Barley, S.R. (1986). "Technology as an occasion for structuring." *Administrative Science Quarterly*, 31, pp. 78–108.

Belden, Ginny, Marcia Hyatt, and Deb Ackley. (1994). *Towards a learning organization: resource guide for the Ontario public service*. Toronto: Ontario Management Board Secretariat.

Bell, David and Lorne Tepperman. (1979). *The roots of disunity: a look at Canadian political culture*. Toronto: McClelland and Stewart.

Bellamy. David J., Jon H. Pammett and Donald C. Rowat. (1976). *The provincial political systems: comparative essays*. Toronto: Methuen.

Berry, Geoff D. (1995). "Civilianisation and the use of volunteers." In *Management challenges in 21st century policing: conference proceedings*. Conference held September 22–24, 1995 in Ottawa, Ontario, sponsored by the Centre for Police Management and Research (Staffordshire University, U.K.), the Canadian Institute for Law and the Family (University of Calgary), and the Solicitor General Canada

Bezdikian, Veh and Clifford L. Karchmer. (1996). *Technology resources for police: a national assessment*. Washington, D.C.: Police Executive Research Forum.

Bigham, Steve. (1993). *Attitude and public opinion survey: Reno Police Department*. Reno, Nevada: Reno Police Department.

Bloch, P. and D. Anderson. (1974). *Policewomen on patrol: final report: methodology, tables and measurement instruments*. Washington, D.C.: Urban Institute.

Bolles, Richard Nelson. (1996). *What color is your parachute?: a practical manual for job-hunters & career changers*. Berkeley, Calif.: Ten Speed Press.

Bothwell, L. (1983). *The art of leadership: skill building techniques that produce results*. Englewood Cliffs, N.J.: Prentice Hall.

Brodeur, Jean-Paul. (1992). "Professionalism and community policing." In *Managing diversity and change: a training strategy*. Regina: Police Educators Conference Board of Canada.

Brooks, S. (1993). *Public policy in Canada: an introduction. 2nd ed*. Toronto: McClelland and Stewart.

Brown, Jr., William F. (1992). "Thinking outside the dots: creative approaches to police funding." *The Police Chief*, April.

Buckley, Leslie B. and Michael G. Petrunik. (1995). "Socio-demographic factors, reference groups, and the career orientations, career aspirations and career satisfaction of Canadian police officers." *American Journal of Police*, 14(2).

Burbeck, E. and A. Furnman. (1985). "Police officer selection: a critical review of the literature." *Journal of Police Science and Administration*, 13.

Burns, James McGregor. (1975). *Leadership*. New York: Harper and Row.

Butterfield, Fox. (1995). *All God's children: the Bosket family and the American tradition of violence*. New York: Avon Books.

Campbell, John Henry. (1990). "Futures research: here and abroad." *The Police Chief*, January.

Campbell, Mr. Justice Archie. (1996). *Bernardo investigation review: report of Mr. Justice Archie Campbell*. [Toronto]: Ontario Ministry of the Solicitor General and Correctional Services.

Canada. Canadian Security Intelligence Service. (1990). *The Canadian Security Intelligence Service: helping to protect Canada and its people*. Ottawa: CSIS.

Canada. Criminal Intelligence Service Canada. (1996). *CISC annual report on organized crime in Canada*. Ottawa: CISC.

Canada. Royal Commission on Financial Management and Accountability. (1979). *Final report*. Ottawa: Minister of Supply and Services Canada.

Canada. Solicitor General Canada. (1996). *Outlook*. Ottawa: Solicitor General of Canada.

Canada. Solicitor General Canada. (1996a). *Establishing a national DNA data bank: consultation document*. Ottawa: Minister of Supply and Services Canada.

Canada. Solicitor General. Police and Security Branch. (1990). *Federal/Provincial/Territorial meeting on police policy issues*. Ottawa: Solicitor General Canada.

Canadian Association of Chiefs of Police. Organized Crime Committee. (1991). *Organized Crime Committee report*. [Ottawa]: Canadian Association of Chiefs of Police.

Canadian Association of Chiefs of Police. Police Multicultural Liaison Committee. (1996). *Hate crimes in Canada: in your back yard: a resource guide*. Ottawa: CACP.

Canadian Association of Chiefs of Police, Royal Canadian Mounted Police, and National Research Council of Canada. (1989). *Canadian program of science and technology in support of law enforcement*. Ottawa: RCMP.

Canadian Centre for Management Development. (1994). *Continuous learning: a CCMD report*. Ottawa: Canadian Centre for Management Development.

Canadian Comprehensive Auditing Foundation. (1983). *Comprehensive auditing: concepts, components and characteristics*. Ottawa: CCAF.

Canadian Police Research Centre. (1996). *Annual report: 1995–1996*. Ottawa: Minister of Supply and Services Canada.

Carr, David K., H.J. Kelvin, and William J. Trahant. (1996). *Managing the change process: a fieldbook for change agents, team leaders, and reengineering managers*. New York: McGraw-Hill.

Carter, David L., Allen D. Sapp, and Darrel W. Stephens. (1989). *The state of police education: policy direction for the 21st century*. Washington, D.C.: Police Executive Research Forum.

Cassels, D. (1995). "The role of technology on crime and policing." In *Management challenges in 21st century policing: conference proceedings*. Ottawa: Centre for Police Management and Research (Straffordshire University, U.K.) and Canadian Research Institute for Law and the Family (University of Calgary), and the Solicitor General Canada.

Castel, Jacqueline R. and Omeela K. Latchman. (1996). *The practical guide to Canadian legal research. 2nd ed.* Toronto: Carswell.

Ceyssens, P. (1994). [Loose-leaf]. *Legal aspects of policing*. Toronto: Carswell.

Chaiken, Marcia and Jan Chaiken. (1987). *Public policing: privately provided*. Washington, D.C.: National Institute of Justice.

Chapman, Samuel G. (1979). *Police dogs in America*. Norman, Okla.: Bureau of Government Research, University of Oklahoma.

Chapman, Samuel G. (1983). "An update on United States and Canadian police dog programs." *Journal of Police Science and Administration*, 11(4).

Commission on Accreditation for Law Enforcement Agencies, Inc. (1990). [Loose-leaf]. *Standards for law enforcement agencies: the standards manual of the law enforcement agency accreditation program*. Fairfax, Virginia: CALEA.

Community Policing Consortium. (1994). *Understanding community policing: a framework for action*. Washington, D.C.: U.S. Department of Justice. Bureau of Justice Assistance.

Cooper, H.H.A. (1977). *Hostage negotiations: options and alternatives*. Gaithersburg, Maryland: International Association of Chiefs of Police.

Cooper, H.S. (1981). "The evolution of Canadian police." McGrath, William T. and Michael Mitchell (eds.). *The police function in Canada*. Toronto: Methuen.

Coordinating Council on Juvenile Justice and Delinquency Prevention. (1996). *Combating violence and delinquency: the national juvenile justice action plan: summary*. Washington, D.C.: U.S. Dept. Of Justice, Office of Juvenile Justice and Delinquency Prevention.

COPPS: community oriented policing & problem solving. (1992). [Sacramento, Calif.]: California Department of Justice, Crime Prevention Center.

Cordner, Gary W. and Donna C. Hale (eds.). (1992). *What works in policing?: operations and administration examined*. Highland Heights, Kentucky and Cincinnati, Ohio: Academy of Criminal Justice Sciences, North Kentucky University and Anderson Publishing Co.

Cordner, Gary W. and Gerald L. Williams. (1996). "Community policing and accreditation: a content analysis of CALEA standards." In Hoover, Larry T. (ed.). *Quantifying quality in policing*. Washington, D.C.: Police Executive Research Forum.

Coulson-Thomas, Colin. (1992). *Transforming the company: bridging the gap between management myth and corporate reality*. London: Kogan Page.

Coulson-Thomas, Colin (ed.). (1994). *Business process reengineering: myth or reality?* London: Kogan Page.

Coutts, Larry M. "Police hiring and promotion: methods and outcomes." *Canadian Police College Journal*, 14(2).

Critchley, T.A. (1967). *A history of police in England and Wales 900–1966*. London: Constable & Co.

Cuadrado, Mary. (1995). "Female police officers: gender bias and professionalism." *American Journal of Police*, 14(2).

Cunningham, William C. and Todd H. Taylor. (1985). *Private security and police in America: the Hallcrest report I*. Boston: Butterworth-Heinemann.

Dalla Costa, John. (1995). *Working wisdom: the ultimate value in the new economy*. Toronto: Stoddart Publishing.

Delattre, Edwin J. (1994). *Character and cops: ethics in policing. 2nd ed.* Washington, D.C.: The AEI Press, Publisher for the American Enterprise Institute.

Devlin, G. and M. Bleakley. (1988). "Strategic alliances: guidelines for success." *Long Range Planning*, 21(5).

Dixon, Nancy M. (1993). *Organizational learning*. Ottawa: Conference Board of Canada.

Doern, G. Bruce and Peter Aucoin (eds.). (1979). *Public policy in Canada: organization, process, and management*. Toronto: Macmillan of Canada.

Doerner, William G. (1995). "Officer retention patterns: an affirmative action concern for police agencies?" *American Journal of Police*, 14(3/4).

Doob, Anthony N. (ed.) (1993). *Thinking about police resources*. Toronto: Centre of Criminology, University of Toronto.

Drucker, Peter F. (1988). "The coming of the new organization." *Harvard Business Review*, 66(1).

Drucker, Peter F. (1994). "The age of social transformation." *The Atlantic Monthly*, November, pp. 53–80.

Dyck, R. (1993). *Canadian politics: critical approaches*. Toronto: Nelson Canada.

Eck, John E. (1983). *Solving crimes: the investigation of burglary and robbery*. Washington, D.C.: Police Executive Research Forum.

Eck, John E. (1996). "Rethinking detective management." In Hoover, Larry T. (ed.) *Quantifying quality in policing*. Washington, D.C.: Police Executive Research Forum.

Eck, John E. and David Weisburd (eds.). (1995). *Crime and place*. Monsey, N.Y.: Criminal Justice Press and the Police Executive Research Forum (Crime Prevention Studies, vol. 4).

Elledge, Robin L. and Steven L. Phillips. (1994). *Team building for the future: beyond the basics*. Toronto: Pfeiffer & Co.

Ellis, Reginald T. (1991). "Perceptions, attitudes and beliefs of police recruits." *Canadian Police College Journal*, 15(2).

Ellul, J. (1964). *The technological society*. (Translated by John Wilkinson). New York: Vintage Books.

Ellul, J. (1990). *The technological bluff*. (Translated by Geoffrey W. Bromiley). Grand Rapids, Michigan: William B. Eerdmans Publishing.

Ericson, Richard V. (1981). *Making crime: a study of detective work*. Toronto: Butterworths Canada Ltd.

Fairweather, S.C. (1978). *A review of regionalized policing in Ontario*. Toronto: Ontario Police Commission.

Forcese, D.P. (1992). *Policing Canadian society*. Scarborough: Prentice Hall Canada.

Forsey, Eugene A. (1974). *Freedom and order: collected essays*. Toronto: McClelland and Stewart.

Frame, J. Davidson. (1994). *The new project management: tools for an age of rapid change, corporate reengineering and other business realities*. San Francisco: Jossey-Bass Publishers.

Frederick, C.J. (1986). "Post-traumatic stress responses to victims of violent crime: information for law enforcement officials." In Reese, James T. and Harvey A. Goldstein (eds.). *Psychological services for law enforcement*. Washington, D.C.: Government Printing Office.

Friedland, Martin L. (1984). *A century of criminal justice: perspectives on the development of Canadian law*. Toronto: Carswell Legal Publications.

Fyfe, James. (1995). "Training to reduce police-civilian violence." In Geller, William A. and Hans Toch (eds.). *And justice for all: understanding and controlling police abuse of force*. Washington, D.C.: Police Executive Research Forum

Gaffigan, Stephen J. and Phyllis P. McDonald. (1997). *Police integrity: public service with honor: a partnership between the National Institute of Justice and the Office of Community Oriented Policing Services*. Washington, D.C.: U.S. Dept. of Justice.

Geller, William A. and Michael S. Scott. (1992). *Deadly force: what we know: a practitioner's desk reference on police-involved shootings*. Washington, D.C.: Police Executive Research Forum.

Geller, William A. and Hans Toch (eds.). (1995a). *And justice for all: understanding and controlling police abuse of force*. Washington, D.C.: Police Executive Research Forum.

Geller, William A. and Guy Swanger. (1995b). *Managing innovation in policing: the untapped potential of the middle manager*. Washington, D.C.: Police Executive Research Forum.

Glensor, Ronald W. and Alissa J. Stern.. (1995). *Dispute resolution and policing: a collaborative approach to effective problem solving*. Washington, D.C.: Police Executive Research Forum.

Goldstein, Herman. (1979). "Improving policing: a problem-oriented approach." *Crime & Delinquency*, April.

Goldstein, Herman. (1990). *Problem-oriented policing*. New York: McGraw-Hill, Inc.

Gow, James Iain. (1994). *Learning from others: administrative innovations among Canadian governments*. Toronto: Institute of Public Administration of Canada. (Monographs on Canadian Public Administration, no. 16).

Grant, Alan. (1980). *The police: a policy paper: a study prepared for the Law Reform Commission of Canada*. Ottawa: Law Reform Commission of Canada.

Grant, Alan. (1992). *Policing arrangements in New Brunswick: 2000 and beyond*. [Fredericton, N.B.]: Published under the authority of the Department of the Solicitor General, Province of New Brunswick.

Grant, G.P. (1965). *Lament for a nation: the defeat of Canadian nationalism*. Toronto: McClelland and Stewart.

Grant, G.P. (1969). *Technology and empire: perspectives on North America*. Toronto: House of Anansi.

Grant, G.P. (1986). *Technology & justice*. Toronto: House of Anansi.

Greene, Jack R. and Ralph B. Taylor. (1988). "Community-based policing and foot patrol: issues of theory and evaluation." In Greene, Jack R. and S.D. Mastroski (eds.). *Community policing: rhetoric or reality?* New York: Praeger.

Greene, Jack R., Thomas M. Seamon, and Paul R. Levy. (1995). "Merging public and private security for collective benefit: Philadelphia's center city district." *American Journal of Police*, 14(2), 3–20.

Greenwood, Peter W. and Joan Petersilia. (1975). *The criminal investigation process*. Santa Monica, Calif.: RAND Corporation.

Guth, DeLloyd J. (1994). "The traditional common law constable, 1235–1829: from Bracton to the Fieldings to Canada." In MacLeod, R.C. and David Schneiderman (eds.). *Police powers in Canada: the evolution and practice of authority*. Toronto: Published in association with the Centre for Constitutional Studies, University of Alberta by the University of Toronto Press, pp. 3–23.

Guy, J.J. (1995). *How we are governed: the basics of Canadian politics and government*. Toronto: Harcourt Brace & Co. Canada.

Hale, D. (1992). "Women in policing." In Cordner, G. and D. Hale. (eds.). *What works in policing?: operations and administration examined*. Highland Heights, Kentucky and Cincinnati, Ohio: Academy of Criminal Justice Sciences, North Kentucky University and Anderson Publishing Co.

Halton Regional Police Service. (1995). *Halton Regional Police Service public survey 1995*. Oakville, Ont.: Halton Regional Police Service.

Halton Regional Police Service. Organizational Review Project. (1995). *Media information package (June 22, 1995)*. Oakville: Halton Regional Police Service, Media Relations Bureau.

Hamilton, Mr. Justice John F. et al. (1995). *The 1996 annotated Ontario Police Services Act*. Toronto: Carswell.

Hammer, Michael and James Champy. (1993). *Reengineering the corporation: a manifesto for business revolution*. New York: Harper Collins Publishers.

Hammer, Michael and Steven A. Stanton. (1995). *The reengineering revolution: a handbook*. New York: Harper Business.

Handy, Charles. (1994). *The empty raincoat: making sense of the future.* [S.l.]: Arrow Business Books.

Hann, Robert G. et al. (1985). "Municipal police governance and accountability in Canada: an empirical study." *Canadian Police College Journal,* 9(1).

Hann, Robert G. and Kathryn Asbury. (1992). *Change is the environment: Ontario region environmental scan: submitted to Ontario region, Ministry of the Solicitor General Canada.* Ottawa: Solicitor General Canada, Intergovernmental Affairs Regional Office.

Harbour, Jerry L. (1994). *The process reengineering workbook: practical steps to working faster and smarter through process improvement.* New York: Quality Resources.

Harbour, Jerry L. (1996). *Cycle time reduction: designing and streamlining work for high performance.* New York: Quality Resources.

Hargrave, G.E. and J.G. Berner. (1984). *POST psychological screening manual.* Sacramento, Calif.: California Commission on Police Officer Standards and Training.

Harman, Alan. (1995). "Toronto's public order unit." *Law and Order,* September.

Hastings, Ross. (1993). *Leadership for community policing in Canada.* Unpublished paper prepared for the Canadian Police College.

Hay Management Consultants and Dennis Strong & Associates. (1993). *Police constable selection: community recruiting—selecting constables for the future: phase II final report recommended design of the new selection system.* [Toronto: Ontario Ministry of the Solicitor General and Correctional Services].

Heck, William P. (1990). *Creating a cadre of police leaders: a study of police executive development programs in the United States: a dissertation presented to the Faculty of the College of Criminal Justice, Sam Houston State University in partial fulfillment of the requirements of the degree of doctor of philosophy.* Huntsville, Texas: Sam Houston State University.

Helgesen, Sally. (1995). *The web of inclusion: a new architecture for building great organizations.* Toronto: Currency/Doubleday.

Hickey, Eric W. (1991). *Serial murderers and their victims.* Pacific Grove, Calif.: Brooks/Cole.

Higgins, Donald J.H. (1977). *Urban Canada: its government and politics.* Toronto: Macmillan of Canada.

Higley, Dahn D. (1984). *O.P.P.: the history of the Ontario Provincial Police Force.* Toronto: Queen's Printer.

Hill, Dilys M. (1974). *Democratic theory and local government.* London: George Allen & Unwin Ltd.

Hockin, T.A. (1976). *Government in Canada.* Toronto: McGraw-Hill Ryerson Ltd.

Hockin, T.A. (ed.). (1977). *Apex of power: the Prime Minister and political leadership in Canada. 2nd ed.* Scarborough: Prentice Hall Canada.

Hogan, R. (1971). "Personality characteristics of highly rated policemen." *Personnel Psychology,* 24.

Holmes, John W. (1981). *Life with uncle: the Canadian-American relationship.* Toronto: University of Toronto Press.

Hoover, Larry T. (ed.). (1996). *Quantifying quality in policing.* Washington, D.C.: Police Executive Research Forum.

Horn, William G. (1975). *A study of police recruit training programs and the development of their curricula.* Unpublished doctoral dissertation, Michigan State University.

Horne, David G., Dennis P. Forcese and Lester N. Thompson. (1989). *Gloucester Police Force: public needs survey preliminary findings: report number one.* Ottawa: Carleton University.

House, John C. (1997, forthcoming). "Towards a practical application of offender profiling: the Royal Newfoundland Constabulary's criminal suspect prioritization system." In Jackson, J. and D. Berkerian (eds.). *Offender profiling: psychological support in criminal investigations.* Chichester: John C. Wiley.

Hutchison, Cathleen et al. (1988). *The Leadership Development Task Force: preliminary report.* Washington, D.C.: National Society for Performance and Instruction.

Incident commander field handbook: search and rescue: managing the search function. (1987). Fairfax, Virginia: National Association for Search and Rescue.

Information Systems Audit and Control Foundation. (1996). *COBIT: control objectives for information and technology: executive summary.* Rolling Meadows, Ill.: Information Systems Audit and Control Foundation.

Ingstrup, Ole. (1995a). *Public service renewal: from means to ends.* Ottawa: Canadian Centre for Management Development. (Explorations; no. 4)

Ingstrup, Ole. (1995b). *The strategic revolution in executive development: what does it mean for you and your organization?* Ottawa: Canadian Centre for Management Development.

Inkpen, A.C. and M.M. Crossan. (1995). "Believing is seeing: joint ventures and organization learning." *Journal of Management Studies*, 32(5).

Innovative training package for detecting and aiding victims of domestic elder abuse. (1993).

Washington, D.C.: Police Executive Research Forum.

Isgar, Thomas. (1993). *The ten minute team: 10 steps to building high performing teams. 2nd ed.* Boulder, Colo.: Seluera Press.

Jacobs, Jane. (1962). *The death and life of great American cities.* New York: Vintage.

Jacques, Elliott. (1990). "In praise of hierarchy." *Harvard Business Review*, 68(1).

Janis, Irving L. (1989). *Crucial decisions: leadership in policymaking and crisis management.* New York: The Free Press.

Jeffrey, C.R. (1977). *Crime prevention through environmental design.* Beverly Hills: Sage Publications.

Johnson, A.W. (1993). *What is public management?: an autobiographical view.* Ottawa: Canadian Centre for Management Development. (Research paper; no. 8).

KPMG Investigation and Security Inc. (1995a). *1995 Fraud survey report.* Toronto: KPMG ISI.

KPMG Investigation and Security Inc. (1995b). *1995 Chiefs of police survey.* Toronto: KPMG ISI.

KPMG Investigation and Security Inc. (1996). *1996 Fraud survey report.* Toronto: KPMG ISI.

Kaplan, William. (1996). *Bad judgment: the case of Mr. Justice Leo A. Landreville.* Toronto: University of Toronto Press for the Osgoode Society for Canadian Legal History.

Katzenbach, Jon R. and Douglas K. Smith. (1993). *The wisdom of teams: creating the high-performance organization.* Boston: Harvard Business School Press.

Kelling, George et al. (1974). *The Kansas City Preventive Patrol Experiment: final report.* Washington, D.C.: Police Foundation.

Kelling, George L. and Catherine M. Coles. (1996). *Fixing broken windows: restoring order & reducing crime in our communities*. New York: Free Press.

Kelly, W. and Nora Kelly. (1976). *Policing in Canada*. Toronto: Macmillan of Canada.

Kennedy, Leslie W. (1991). "The evaluation of community-based policing in Canada." *Canadian Police College Journal*, 15(4).

Kenney, Dennis Jay and T. Steuart Watson. (1996). "Reducing fear in the schools: managing conflict through student problem solving." *Education and Urban Society*, 28(4).

Kent, J.R. (1986). *The English village constable 1580–1642*. Oxford: Clarendon Press.

Keppel, Robert D. (1989). *Serial murder: future implications for police investigations*. Cincinnati, Ohio: Anderson Publishing.

Kernaghan, Kenneth. (1992). "Empowerment and public administration: revolutionary advance or passing fancy?" *Canadian Public Administration*, 35(2).

Kernaghan, Kenneth. (1994a). "The emerging public service culture: values, ethics, and reforms." *Canadian Public Administration*, 37(4).

Kernaghan, Kenneth. (1994b). "Ethics: do they provide a core of stability in a changing world?" In *Perspectives on public management: values in the public service*. Ottawa: Canadian Centre for Management Development.

Kline, Peter and Bernard Saunders. (1993). *Ten steps to a learning organization*. Arlington, Virginia: Great Ocean Publishers.

Knapp Commission. (1972). *The Knapp Commission report on police corruption*. New York: George Braziller.

Koller, Katherine. (1990). *Working the beat: the Edmonton neighborhood foot patrol*. Edmonton: Edmonton Police Service.

Koontz, H. and C. O'Connell. (1968). *Principles of management: an analysis of managerial functions. 4th ed*. New York: McGraw-Hill.

Kouzes, James. (1988). "Learning to lead." In Dixon, George. *What works at work: lessons from the masters*. Minneapolis: Lakewood Books.

Krimmel, John T. (1996). "The performance of college-educated police: a study of self-rated police performance measures." *American Journal of Police*, 25(1).

Kübler-Ross, Elizabeth. (1986). *Death: the final stage of growth*. New York: Simon & Schuster.

Kuhn, Thomas S. (1962). *The structure of scientific revolutions*. Chicago: University of Chicago Press.

Kuhn, Thomas S. (1986). *The structure of scientific revolutions. 2nd ed*. Chicago: University of Chicago Press.

Laiken, Marilyn E. (1994). *The anatomy of high performing teams: a leader's handbook*. Toronto: OISE Press.

Larson, Peter and Robert Mingie. (1992). *Leadership for a changing world: developing executive capability*. Ottawa: Conference Board of Canada and Canadian Centre for Management Development.

Layton, Elliott. (1986). *Hunting humans: the rise of the modern multiple murderer*. Toronto: McClelland and Stewart.

Leclerc, Guy et al.(1996). *Accountability, performance reporting, comprehensive audit: an integrated perspective*. Ottawa: CCAF-FCVI Inc.

Leeuw, Frans L., Ray C. Rist, and Richard C. Sonnichsen. (1994). *Can governments learn?: comparative perspectives on evaluation and organizational learning*. New Brunswick, N.J.: Transaction Publishers.

Lewis, Clare E., Sidney B. Linden, and Judith Keene. (1986). "Public complaints against police in Metropolitan Toronto: the history and operation of the Office of the Public Complaints Commissioner." *Criminal Law Quarterly*, 29(1).

Lindquist, E. and Tammy Sica. (1995). *Canadian governments and the search for alternative program delivery and financing: a preliminary survey*. Toronto: KPMG Centre for Government Foundation.

Lowman, R.L. (1989). *Pre-employment screening for psychopathology: a guide to professional practice*. Florida: Professional Resource Exchange.

Lunn, Janet and Christopher Moore. (1992). *The story of Canada*. Toronto: Lester Publishing and Key Porter Books.

Lunney, Robert. (1989). "The role of the police leader in the 21st century." In Loree, Donald J. (ed.). *Future issues in policing: symposium proceedings*. Ottawa: The Canadian Police College.

MacDonald, Victor N. (1986). *A study of leadership and supervision in policing*. Ottawa: The Canadian Police College.

MacIntosh, Donald A. (1989). *Fundamentals of the criminal justice system*. Toronto: Carswell.

Macpherson, C.B. (1965). *The real world of democracy*. Toronto: CBC Enterprises.

Mair, A.J. (1992). *E.P.S. the first 100 years: a history of the Edmonton Police Service*. Edmonton: Edmonton Police Service.

Management challenges in 21st century policing: conference proceedings. (1995). Conference held September 22–24, 1995 in Ottawa, Ontario, sponsored by the Centre for Police Management and Research (Staffordshire University, U.K.), the Canadian Institute for Law and the Family (University of Calgary), and the Solicitor General Canada.

Manning, M. (1983). *Rights, freedoms and the courts: a practical analysis of the Constitution Act, 1982*. Toronto: Emond-Montgomery.

Manning, Peter K. (1992). "Technological and material resource issues." In Hoover, Larry T. (ed.). *Police management: issues & perspectives*. Washington, D.C.: Police Executive Research Forum.

Manion, John L. (1989). *A management model*. Ottawa: Canadian Centre for Management Development.

Marchak, M.P. (1975). *Ideological perspectives on Canada*. Toronto: McGraw-Hill Ryerson Ltd.

Marquis, Greg. (1993). *Policing Canada's century: a history of the Canadian Association of Chiefs of Police*. Toronto: Published for the Osgoode Society by the University of Toronto Press.

Marsden, L.R. and E.B. Harvey. (1979). *Fragile federation: social change in Canada*. Toronto: McGraw-Hill Ryerson Ltd.

Martens, Frederick T. (1990). "The intelligence function." In Andrews, Jr., Paul P. and Marilyn Peterson (eds.). *Criminal intelligence analysis*. Loomis, Calif.: Palmer Enterprises.

Martin, Maurice A. (1995). *Urban policing: anatomy of an aging craft*. Montreal and Kingston: McGill-Queen's University Press.

Mastrofski, Stephen D. (1986). "Police agency accreditation: the prospects for reform." *American Journal of Police*, 5(2).

Mathie, Robert. (1989). "Examining performance: some suggestions on measuring performances for evaluating police work." *Policing*, 5(4).

Mayhall, Pamela D., Thomas Barker, and Ronald D. Hunter. (1995). *Police-community relations and the administration of justice. 4th ed.* Englewood Cliffs, N.J.: Prentice Hall, Inc.

McCoy, Candace. (1986). "Enforcement workshop: policing the homeless." *Criminal Law Bulletin*, 22(3).

McDonald, David C. (1980). *Commission of Inquiry Concerning Certain Activities of the Royal Canadian Mounted Police*. Ottawa: Supply and Services Canada.

McDonald, David C. (1982). *Legal rights in the Canadian Charter of Rights and Freedoms: a manual of issues and sources*. Toronto: Carswell Legal Publications (Western).

McKenna, Paul F. (1990a). "New demands mean police need improved training and education." *Carswell Police News*, 117.

McKenna, Paul F. (1990b). "To understand and cope: issues of multiculturalism and race in policing." *Carswell Police News*, 119.

McKenna, Paul F. (1990c). "Computers and word processors facilitate all phases of police training." *Carswell Police News*, 120.

McKenna, Paul F. (1990d). "Training police in a Charter-driven world." *Carswell Police News*, 121.

McKenna, Paul F. (1990e). "Firearms training is an ongoing need in modern policing." *Carswell Police News*, 122.

McKenna, Paul F. (1994). "Setting our sights for a focus on the future." *The O.P.P. Review*, 29(4).

McKenna, Paul F. and D.G. Evans. (1994). "Balancing police budgets and decision making: an experiment in disentanglement." *Canadian Public Administration*, 37(4).

McKenna, Paul F. (1995). "Policing in 2020 & the application of organizational learning: grinding new lenses to view the development of human resources: a prolegomenon." Unpublished paper prepared for the Society of Police Futurists International (1995).

McKenna, Paul F. and Donald G. Evans. (1995). "Leadership as learning: learning as leadership." *The Police Governor*, 5(2).

McMahon, Maeve W. and Richard V. Ericson. (1984). *Policing reform: a study of the reform process and police institution in Toronto*. Toronto: Centre of Criminology, University of Toronto.

McPhee, R.D. (1985). "Formal structure and organizational communication." In McPhee, R.D. and P.K. Tompkins (eds.). *Organizational communication: traditional themes and new directions*. Beverly Hills, Calif.: Sage Publications.

McRoberts, Kenneth and Dale Posgate. (1980). *Québec: social change and political crisis*. Toronto: McClelland and Stewart.

McWhinney, E. (1979). *Québec and the Constitution 1960–1978*. Toronto: University of Toronto Press.

Meagher, M.S. and N.A. Yeates. (1986). "Choosing a career in policing: a comparison of male and female perceptions." *Journal of Police Science and Administration*, 14.

Meekison, J.P. (ed.). (1977). *Canadian federalism: myth or reality. 3rd ed.* Toronto: Methuen.

Meese III, Edwin, and Bob Carrico. (1990). "Taking back the streets: police methods that work." *Policy Review*, No. 54 (Fall).

Melchers, Ron and Julian Roberts. (1994). *Public opinion and policing in Canada: a review of recent findings and selected social trends and demands on policing*. Ottawa: Department of Criminology, University of Ottawa.

Melekian, Barney. (1990). "Police and the homeless." *FBI Law Enforcement Bulletin*, 59(11).

Metropolitan Toronto Police. (1997). *Metropolitan Toronto Police crisis intervention training: module 1: course outline of material*. [Toronto]: Metropolitan Toronto Police, Charles O. Bick College.

Metropolitan Toronto Police Service. Traffic Restructuring Project Team. (1996). *Recommendations*. Toronto: Metropolitan Toronto Police Service.

Mewett, A.W. and M. Manning. (1985). *Criminal law. 2nd ed.* Toronto: Butterworths.

Milne, D. (1982). *The new Canadian constitution*. Toronto: James Lorimer & Company.

Mintzberg, Henry. (1981). "Organization design: fashion or fit?" *Harvard Business Review*, 59(1).

Montréal Urban Community Police. (1995). *Neighbourhood policing*. Montréal: Montréal Urban Community Police.

Morash, Merry and Jack R. Greene. (1986). "Evaluating women on patrol." *Evaluation Review*, 10(3).

Morgan, Gareth. (1993). *Imaginization: the art of creative management*. Newbury Park, Calif.: Sage Publications.

Murphy, Christopher. (1991). "The future of non-urban policing in Canada: modernization, regionalization, provincialization." *Canadian Journal of Criminology (Police and Society in Canada)*, 33(3/4).

Murphy, Christopher and Graham Muir. (1985). *Community-based policing: a review of the critical issues*. Ottawa: Solicitor General Canada.

Murphy, Gerard. (1986). *Special care: improving the police response to the mentally disabled*. Washington, D.C.: Police Executive Research Forum.

Murphy, Gerard. (1989). *Managing persons with mental disabilities: a curriculum guide for trainers*. Washington, D.C.: Police Executive Research Forum.

Nadler, David A., Robert A. Shaw, A. Elise Walton and associates. (1995). *Discontinuous change: leading organizational transformation*. San Francisco: Jossey-Bass Publishers.

Naismith, Clive et al. (1987). *A report on the constable training program: submitted by the Training Study Group*. Toronto: Ontario Police Commission.

National Association for Search and Rescue. (1987). *Incident commander field handbook: search and rescue: managing the search function*. Fairfax, Virginia: NASAR.

Nelson, E.D. (1992). "Employment equity and the Red Queen's hypothesis: recruitment and hiring in western Canadian municipal police departments." *Canadian Police College Journal*, 16(3).

Newman, Oscar. (1972). *Defensible space: crime prevention through urban design*. New York: Macmillan.

Normandeau, André and Barry Leighton. (1990). *A vision of the future of policing in Canada: police-challenge 2000: background document*. Ottawa: Solicitor General Canada.

O'Brien, Kevin P. and Robert C. Sullivan. (1980). *Criminalistics: theory and practice. 3rd ed.* Toronto: Allyn and Bacon, Inc.

Oettmeier, Timothy N. (1992). "Matching structure to objectives." In Hoover, Larry T. (ed.). *Police management: issues & perspectives*. Washington, D.C.: Police Executive Research Forum and Texas Law Enforcement Management Institute.

Office of Juvenile Justice and Delinquency Prevention. (1996). *Reducing youth gun violence: an overview of programs and initiatives: program report*. Washington, D.C.: U.S. Dept. of Justice, Office of Juvenile Justice and Delinquency Prevention.

Ogden, Frank. (1993). *The last book you'll ever read: and other lessons from the future*. Toronto: Macfarlane Walter & Ross.

Ogle, Dan (ed.). (1991). *Strategic planning for police*. Ottawa: Canadian Police College.

O'Keefe, Garrett et al. (1993). *The social impact of the National Citizens' Crime Prevention Campaign: focus on what works*. Washington, D.C.: U.S. Department of Justice, Bureau of Justice Assistance.

Olesky, W. Ronald and David G. Born. (1983). "A behavioral approach to hostage situations." *FBI Law Enforcement Bulletin*, January.

Ontario. Greater Toronto Area Task Force. (1996). *Greater Toronto: report of the GTA Task Force*. Toronto: Queen's Printer.

Ontario. Management Board Secretariat. (1993). *An introduction to business reengineering*. [Toronto]: Management Board Secretariat.

Ontario. Management Board Secretariat. (1996). *A framework for performance measurement in government programs and services*. [Toronto]: Management Board Secretariat.

Ontario. Ministry of Municipal Affairs. Subsidies Management Branch. (1993). *On becoming a learning organization: a practical guide for change*. Toronto: Queen's Printer.

Ontario. Ministry of the Solicitor General. (1991). *Future trends in society: an Ontario perspective*. Toronto: The Ministry.

Ontario. Ministry of the Solicitor General and Correctional Services. (1996). *Review of police services in Ontario: a framework for discussion*. Toronto: The Ministry.

Ontario. Ministry of the Solicitor General and Correctional Services. Police-Race Relations Monitoring Board. (1996). *Good beginnings: a catalogue of police-race relations initiatives in Ontario*. Toronto: The Ministry.

Ontario. Ministry of the Solicitor General. Policing Services Division. (1992). [Loose-leaf]. *Policing standards manual for the Province of Ontario*. Toronto: The Ministry.

Ontario. Ministry of the Solicitor General and Correctional Services. Policing Services Division. (1995). *Tactical response standard: consultation package*. [Toronto]: The Ministry.

Ontario. Ministry of the Solicitor General and Correctional Services. Policing Services Division. Policing Standards Section. (1996). *Police resource package on hate/bias motivated crimes: part A: open information*. [Toronto]: The Ministry.

Ontario. Ministry of the Solicitor General. Strategic Planning Committee on Police Training and Education. (1992a). *A police learning system for Ontario: final report and recommendations*. Toronto: The Ministry.

Ontario. Ministry of the Solicitor General. Strategic Planning Committee on Police Training and Education. (1992b). *Report on high impact learning methodologies*. Toronto: The Ministry.

Ontario. Ministry of the Solicitor General. Strategic Planning Committee on Police Training and Education. (1992c). *Report on police training and education in other jurisdictions*. Toronto: The Ministry.

Ontario. Ministry of the Solicitor General. Strategic Planning Committee on Police Training and Education. (1992d). *Report on consultations with the community on future policing and police training issues*. Toronto: The Ministry.

Ontario. Ministry of the Solicitor General. Strategic Planning Committee on Police Training and Education. (1992e). *Report on Ontario police community initial consultation*. Toronto: The Ministry.

Ontario. Ministry of the Solicitor General. Strategic Planning Committee on Police Training and Education. (1992f). *Report on private sector learning initiatives*. Toronto: The Ministry.

Ontario. Ministry of the Solicitor General. Strategic Planning Committee on Police Training and Education. (1992g). *Report on strategic learning requirements for police personnel*. Toronto: The Ministry.

Ontario. Ministry of the Solicitor General. Strategic Planning Committee on Police Training and Education. (1992h). *Report on the evaluation adult learning in the workplace*. Toronto: The Ministry.

Ontario. Ministry of the Solicitor General. Strategic Planning Committee on Police Training and Education. (1992i). *Report on evaluating learning systems*. Toronto: The Ministry.

Ontario. Ministry of the Solicitor General. Strategic Planning Committee on Police Training and Education. (1992j). *Report on consultation with the police community on police specialties in the future*. Toronto: The Ministry.

Ontario. Ministry of the Solicitor General. Strategic Planning Committee on Police Training and Education. (1992k). *Report on future policing issues in Ontario*. Toronto: The Ministry.

Ontario. Ministry of the Solicitor General. Strategic Planning Committee on Police Training and Education. (1992l). *Report on relationship between higher education and police learning requirements*. Toronto: The Ministry.

Ontario. Task Force on Policing in Ontario. (1974). *The Task Force on Policing in Ontario: report to the Solicitor General*. Toronto: Solicitor General of Ontario.

Ontario. Task Force on Race Relations and Policing. (1992). *The report of the Race Relations and Policing Task Force*. Toronto: Solicitor General of Ontario.

Ontario. Task Force on the Racial and Ethnic Implications of Police Hiring, Training, Promotion and Career Development. (1980).

Policing in Ontario for the eighties: perceptions and reflections: report of the Task Force on the Racial and Ethnic Implications of Police Hiring, Training, Promotion and Career Development. Toronto: Solicitor General of Ontario.

Ontario Police Commission. (1989). *Review of tactical units 1989*. Toronto: The Commission. (2 vols.—Volume 1: Report; Volume 2: Appendices).

Ontario Provincial Police. (1994). *Commissioner's directional statement 1994: "focus on the future."* [Toronto]: OPP.

Ontario Provincial Police. (1995). *Organizational review: a process & model for change*. Toronto: Queen's Printer.

Ontario Provincial Police. (1996). *Annual report, 1994*. Orillia: Ontario Provincial Police.

Ontario Provincial Police. Organizational Review Project. (1994a). *Occurrence management*. [Orillia, Ont.]: OPP.

Ontario Provincial Police. Organizational Review Project. (1994b). *Traffic/Waterways Management*. [Orillia, Ont.]: OPP.

Ontario Provincial Police. Systems Approach to Training Unit. (1990). *Recruit field training program: part II—coach officer's self-study package*. [Brampton, Ont.]: OPP, Provincial Police Academy.

Oppal, The Honourable Mr. Justice Wallace T. (1994). *Closing the gap: policing and the community: the report, volume 1*. [Victoria, B.C.]: Policing in British Columbia Commission of Inquiry.

O'Reilly-Fleming, Thomas (ed.). (1996) *Serial and mass murder: theory, research, and policy*. Toronto: Canadian Scholars' Press.

Pangle, Thomas L. (1992). *The ennobling of democracy: the challenge of the postmodern age*. Baltimore: The Johns Hopkins University Press.

Parker, Graham. (1981). "The origins of the Canadian Criminal Code." In Flaherty, David H. (ed.) *Essays in the history of Canadian law*. Toronto: Published for the Osgoode Society by University of Toronto Press.

Peak, Kenneth J. (1993). *Policing America: methods, issues, challenges*. Englewood Cliffs, N.J.: Regents/Prentice Hall.

Peak, Kenneth J. and Ronald W. Glensor. (1996). *Community policing and problem solving: strategies and practices*. Upper Saddle River, N.J.: Prentice Hall.

Peters, B. Guy. (1993). *The public service, the changing state and governance*. Ottawa: Canadian Centre for Management Development. (Research paper; no. 13).

Piskurich, George M. (1993). *Self-directed learning: a practical guide to design, development, and implementation*. San Francisco: Jossey-Bass Publishers.

Pitney Bowes Management Services. (1994). *Reengineering among the Fortune 500: a Pitney Bowes Management Services study: summary of findings.* Stamford, Conn.: Pitney Bowes Management Services.

Plotkin, Martha R. (1988). *A time for dignity: police and domestic abuse of the elderly*. Washington, D.C.: Police Executive Research Forum.

Plotkin, Martha R. (1996). "Improving the police response to domestic elder abuse victims." *Aging, 367*.

Plotkin, Martha R. and Ortwin A. Narr. (1993). *The police response to the homeless: a status report*. Washington, D.C.: Police Executive Research Forum.

Police Association of Ontario. (1996). *Police employment in 1996: seeking the common sense solution: emerging issues, legal developments*. Toronto: Police Association of Ontario. Papers presented at conference held February 26 and 27, 1996, sponsored by the Police Association of Ontario.

Police Executive Research Forum. (1993). *Improving the police response to domestic elder abuse: prepared by the Police Executive Research Forum as a guide to law enforcement agencies*. Washington, D.C.: Police Executive Research Forum.

Police Executive Research Forum. (1996). *Themes and variations in community policing: case studies of community policing*. Washington, D.C.: Police Executive Research Forum.

Police Foundation. (1981). *The Newark foot patrol experiment*. Washington, D.C.: Police Foundation.

Portwood, John. (1997). "Force of change." *Chatelaine*, 70(5).

Price Waterhouse Associates and The Canada Consulting Group Inc. (1985). *A study of management and accountability in the Government of Ontario*. [Toronto]: Price Waterhouse Associates and The Canada Consulting Group Inc.

Pritchett, Price. (1996). *Resistance: moving beyond the barriers to change: a handbook for people who make things happen*. Dallas: Pritchett & Associates.

Pritchett, Price and Ron Pound. (1990). *The employee handbook for organizational change*. Dallas: Pritchett & Associates.

Pritchett, Price and Ron Pound. (1994). *Business as unusual: the handbook for managing and supervising organizational change. 2nd ed.* Dallas: Pritchett & Associates.

Pritchett, Price and Ron Pound. (1995). *A survival guide to the stress of organizational change*. Dallas: Pritchett & Associates.

Rapp, Jay. (1979). *How to organize a canine unit and train dogs for police work*. Fairfax, Virginia: Denlinger's Publishers.

Reese, J.T. (1987). *A history of police psychological services*. Washington, D.C.: U.S. Dept. of Justice.

Reiner, Robert. (1995). "Counting the coppers: antinomies of accountability in policing." In Stenning, Philip C. (ed.). *Accountability for criminal justice: selected essays*. Toronto: University of Toronto Press.

Reiser, A.J. (1972). *The police department psychologist*. Springfield, Ill.: Charles C. Thomas.

Reith, C. (1948). *A short history of the British police*. London: Oxford University Press.

Reno (Nevada) Police Department. (1990). *Problem oriented policing: training guide (supervisor)*. Reno: Reno Police Department.

Roach, Kent. (1995). "Canadian public inquiries and accountability." In Stenning, Philip C. (ed.). *Accountability for criminal justice*. Toronto: University of Toronto Press.

Rollock, John A. (1996). "Internet and the future of policing." Unpublished paper presented by John A. Rollock, IBM Canada, Ltd.

Royal Canadian Mounted Police. (1990). *The International Criminal Police Organization: INTERPOL Ottawa: Canada's law enforcement link with the world*. Ottawa: Published by the Royal Canadian Mounted Police Public Affairs Directorate for INTERPOL Ottawa.

Royal Canadian Mounted Police. (1991). *Criminal intelligence program: planning and direction: implementation guide*. [Ottawa]: RCMP.

Royal Canadian Mounted Police. (1996). *Partners in policing: the Royal Canadian Mounted Police contract policing program*. Ottawa: RCMP.

Russell, Peter H. (1982). *Leading constitutional decisions. 3rd ed*. Toronto: Carleton University Press.

Sancton, Andrew. (1996). "Reducing costs by consolidating municipalities: New Brunswick, Nova Scotia and Ontario." *Canadian Public Administration*, 39(3).

Schein, Edgar. (1985). *Organizational culture and leadership*. San Francisco: Jossey-Bass

Scissons, Ed. (1988). *Police leadership part I: interpersonal decision making*. Ottawa: The Canadian Police College.

Scissons, Ed. (1990). *Police leadership part II: organizational decision making*. Ottawa: Canadian Police College.

Scrivner, Ellen M. (1994). *The role of police psychology in controlling excessive force*. Washington, D.C.: U.S. Dept. of Justice, National Institute of Justice.

Seagrave, Jayne. (1997). *Introduction to policing in Canada*. Scarborough: Prentice Hall Canada.

Selye, H. (1974). *Stress without distress*. Philadelphia: J.B. Lippincott Co.

Selye, H. (1976). *The stress of life*. New York: McGraw-Hill.

Senge, Peter M. (1990). *The fifth discipline: the art and practice of the learning organization*. New York: Doubleday Currency.

Senge, Peter M. et al. (1994). *The fifth discipline fieldbook: strategies and tools for building a learning organization*. New York: Doubleday Currency.

Sewell, James D. (1981). "Police stress." *FBI Law Enforcement Bulletin*, April.

Sewell, John. (1985). *Police: urban policing in Canada*. Toronto: James Lorimer & Company.

Sharplin, Arthur. (1985). *Strategic management*. New York: McGraw-Hill.

Shearing, Clifford D. (1984). *Dial-a-cop: a study of police mobilisation*. Toronto: Centre of Criminology, University of Toronto.

Sheehan, Robert and Gary W. Cordner. (1995). *Police administration. 3rd ed.* Cincinnati, Ohio: Anderson Publishing.

Sherman, Lawrence. (1987). "Effective community policing: research contributions and considerations." In Loree, D. and C. Murphy (eds.). *Community policing in the 1980s: recent advances in police programs*. Ottawa: Solicitor General Canada.

Shusta, Robert M. et al. (1995). *Multicultural law enforcement: strategies for peacekeeping in a diverse society*. Englewood Cliffs, N.J.: Prentice Hall.

Skiff, Dana Allen. (1976). *An approach to designing a police recruit training program reflecting the readiness to learn and the developmental tasks of the police recruit*. Unpublished thesis, Boston University, School of Education.

Snell, James G. and Frederick Vaughan. (1985). *The Supreme Court of Canada: history of the institution*. Toronto: Published for the Osgoode Society by the University of Toronto Press.

Snetsinger, Douglas. (1993). *Learning leaders: perspectives from Canadian CEOs*. Toronto: Institute of Market Driven Quality, Faculty of Management, University of Toronto, and Skill Dynamics Canada.

Snyder, Howard N. and Melissa Sickmund. (1995). *Juvenile offenders and victims: a national report*. Washington, D.C.: U.S. Dept. of Justice, Office of Juvenile Justice and Delinquency Prevention.

Souryal, Sam S. (1985). *Police organization & administration*. Cincinnati, Ohio: Anderson Publishing Co.

Southerland, Mittie D. (1992). "Organizational communication." In Hoover, Larry T. (ed.). *Police management: issues & perspectives*. Washington, D.C.: Police Executive Research Forum.

Stamper, Norman H. (1992). *Removing managerial barriers to effective police leadership: a study of executive leadership and executive management in big-city police departments*. Washington, D.C.: Police Executive Research Forum.

Stansfield, Ronald T. (1996). *Issues in policing: a Canadian perspective*. Toronto: Thompson Educational Publishing.

Statistics Canada. Canadian Centre for Justice Statistics. (1996a). "Police personnel and expenditures in Canada, 1994." In *Juristat*, 16(1).

Statistics Canada. Canadian Centre for Justice Statistics. (1996b). *Selected police administration characteristics of municipal police departments, 1994*. Ottawa: Statistics Canada.

Stayer, Ralph. (1990). "How I learned to let my workers lead." *Harvard Business Review*, 68(6).

Steidel, Stephen E. (ed.). (1994). *Missing and abducted children: a law enforcement guide to case investigation and program management*. Arlington, Virginia: National Center for Missing and Exploited Children.

Stenning, Philip C. (1981). *Police commissions and boards in Canada*. Toronto: Centre of Criminology, University of Toronto.

Stenning, Philip C. (1982). *Legal status of the police: a study paper prepared for the Law Reform Commission of Canada*. Ottawa: Law Reform Commission of Canada.

Stenning, Philip C. (1989). "Private police and public police: toward a redefinition of the police role." In Loree, Donald J. (ed.). *Future issues in policing: symposium proceedings*. Ottawa: Canadian Police College.

Stenning, Philip C. (1994). "Police and politics: there and back and there again?" In MacLeod,

R.C. and David Schneiderman (eds.). *Police powers in Canada: the evolution and practice of authority*. Toronto: Published in association with the Centre for Constitutional Studies, University of Alberta by University of Toronto Press, pp. 209–240.

Stenning, Philip C. (ed.). (1995). *Accountability for criminal justice: selected essays*. Toronto: University of Toronto Press.

Stenning, Philip C., John Briggs, and Marnie Crouch. (1996). *Police governance in First Nations in Ontario*. Toronto: Centre of Criminology, University of Toronto.

Stevens, Nigel. (1993). "Future issues in policing." Unpublished paper prepared for the Edmonton Police Service.

Stohl, Cynthia. (1995). *Organizational communication: connectedness in action*. Thousand Oaks, Calif.: Sage Publications.

Stowell, Steven J. (1988). "Coaching: a commitment to leadership." *Training and Development Journal*, 42(6).

Strayer, B.L. (1983). *The Canadian constitution and the courts: the function and scope of judicial review. 2nd ed.* Toronto: Butterworths.

Stuart D. (1994). "Policing under the Charter." In MacLeod, R.C. and David Schneiderman. (eds.). *Police powers in Canada: the evolution and practice of authority*. Toronto: Published in association with the Centre for Constitutional Studies, University of Alberta by University of Toronto Press, pp. 74–99.

Sunahara, David F. (1992). "Public inquiries into policing." *Canadian Police College Journal*, 16(2).

Tafoya, William L. (1986). "A Delphi forecast of the future of law enforcement." Unpublished Ph.D. dissertation. College Park, Maryland: University of Maryland.

Tafoya, William L. (1990). "Futures research: implications for criminal investigations." In Gilbert, James N. (ed.). *Criminal investigations: essays and cases*. Columbus, Ohio: Merrill Publishing Co.

Talbot, C.K., C.H.S. Jayewardene, and T.J. Juliani. (1985). *Canada's constables: the historical development of policing in Canada*. Ottawa: Crimcare Inc.

Taroni, F. (1994). "Serial crime: a consideration of investigative problems." *Forensic Sciences International,* 65 (March).

Teal, Thomas. (1996). "The human side of management." *Harvard Business Review*, 74(6).

Tilley, Nick. (1995). *Thinking about crime prevention performance indicators*. London: Home Office Police Research Group. (Crime Detection & Prevention series paper; no. 57).

Toffler, Alvin and Heidi Toffler. (1995). *Creating a new civilization: the politics of the third wave*. Atlanta: Turner Publishing, Inc.

Trojanowicz, Robert and David Carter. (1988). *The philosophy and role of community policing*. East Lansing, Mich.: National Neighborhood Foot Patrol Center, Michigan State University.

Trompetter, P.S. (1993). "Pre-employment psychological screening of violence-prone peace officer applicants." *The Journal of Criminal Law Enforcement*, 27(1).

Tully, Edward J. (1990). "The 1990s: new days, old problems." *Police Chief*, (January).

Vancouver Police Department. (1997). *"Make a difference every day": a policing career in the City of Vancouver*. Vancouver: Vancouver Police Department.

Vastel, M. (1990). *The outsider: the life of Pierre Elliott Trudeau*. (Translated by H. Bauch). Toronto: Macmillan of Canada.

Victoria Police (Australia). (1996). *Project Guardian: Ethical Standards Department: final report*. [Melbourne]: Victoria Police.

Volti, R. (1995). *Society and technological change. 3rd ed.* New York: St. Martin's Press.

Wadman, Robert C. and Robert K. Olson. (1990). *Community wellness: a new theory of policing*. Washington, D.C.: Police Executive Research Forum.

Walinsky, A. (1995). "The crisis of public order." *The Atlantic Monthly*, July 1995.

Walker, Sandra Gail. (1993). *The status of women in Canadian policing: 1993*. Ottawa: Solicitor General Canada.

Walker, Sandra Gail, Christopher R. Walker, and James C. McDavid. (1992). *The Victoria community police stations: a three-year evaluation*. Ottawa: The Canadian Police College.

Watkins, Karen E. and Victoria J. Marsick. (1993). *Sculpting the learning organization: lessons in the art and science of systemic change*. San Francisco: Jossey-Bass Publishers.

Watson, T. Steuart, Dennis Jay Kenney, and John Lusardi. (1995). *Problem-solving: intermediate curriculum guide*. Washington, D.C.: The Community Policing Consortium.

Watt, The Honourable Mr. Justice David and Michelle K. Fuerst. (1996). *The annotated 1997 Tremeear's Criminal Code*. Toronto: Carswell.

Watts, Sabina C. (1993). *Investigation into the psyches of serial killers: a Kleinean perspective*. Ottawa: National Library of Canada. Unpublished Masters thesis.

Weatheritt, Mollie. (1993). "Measuring police performance: accounting or accountability?" In Reiner, Robert and Sarah Spencer (eds.). *Accountable policing: effectiveness, empowerment and equity*. London: Institute for Public Policy Research.

Webster, Jack with Rosemary Aubert. (1991). *Copper Jack: my life on the force*. Toronto: Dundurn Press.

Weisel, Deborah Lamm and Ellen Painter. (1997). *The police response to gangs: case studies of five cities*. Washington, D.C.: Police Executive Research Forum.

Wells, Gary L. (1988). *Eyewitness identification: a system handbook*. Toronto: Carswell.

Weston, Paul B. and Kenneth M. Wells. (1986). *Criminal investigation: basic perspectives. 4th ed.* Englewood Cliffs, N.J.: Prentice Hall.

Wheatley, Margaret J. (1994). *Leadership and the new science: learning about organization from an orderly universe*. San Francisco: Berrett-Koehler Publishers.

White, Walter L., Ronald H. Wagenberg, and Ralph C. Nelson. (1994). *Introduction to Canadian politics and government. 6th ed.* Toronto: Harcourt Brace Canada.

Williams, Gerald L. (1989). *Making the grade: the benefits of law enforcement accreditation*. Washington, D.C.: Police Executive Research Forum.

Wilson, James Q. and George L. Kelling. (1982). "Broken windows." *The Atlantic Monthly*, March.

Wilson, James Q. and George L. Kelling. (1989). "Making neighborhoods safe." *The Atlantic Monthly*, February.

Witham, Donald C. (1991). "Environmental scanning pays off." *The Police Chief*, March.

Woolner, Paul. (1991). *Integrating work and learning: a developmental model of the learning organization: presented to the Commission of Professors of Adult Education, 1991 annual conference, Montreal, October 13–15*. Etobicoke, Ont.: Woolner, Lowy & Associates.

Worden, Robert E. (1990). "A badge and a bac-calaureate: policies, hypotheses, and further evidence." *Justice Quarterly*, 7(3).

Zeffane, R. (1995). "The widening scope of inter-organizational networking: economic, sectoral and social dimensions." *Leadership & Organization Development Journal*, 16(4).

Zhao, Jihong. (1996). *Why police organizations change: a study of community-oriented policing*. Washington D.C.: Police Executive Research Forum.

Zhao, Jihong and Quint Thurman. (1996). *The nature of community policing innovations: do the ends justify the means?* Washington, D.C.: Police Executive Research Forum.

CANADIAN POLICE CASE STUDIES

INTRODUCTION

While the case study method, popularized at Harvard University earlier this century, has its detractors and deficiencies, it continues to provide a useful and practical approach for learning about organizational issues and offers students an opportunity to apply various principles and theories to practical problems.

Essentially, a case provides a formal description of a particular organization and, typically, focuses on a specific management or operational issue. Cases usually include some background information on the history of the organization, its operation, and the environment in which the organization operates. A useful case study allows students to enter a realistic situation where they can apply decision-making or problem-solving skills in a risk-free setting. Case studies should provide the student with an opportunity to discuss organizational challenges in detail and to debate alternative solutions for addressing specific issues, based on their reading and research.

Part of the inherent value of the case study method is that it compels participants to move toward possible solutions without the benefit of complete information. Since organizations in the real world rarely have all the facts and figures on hand for making perfect decisions, the case method simulates this less than ideal environment. Something has to be done, even in the absence of every piece of desirable information. Also, the case method serves to illustrate that there is never one precise and perfect answer to organizational problems. Students are encouraged to make valid decisions based on available information and to take into account the constraints that exist in the realm of organizational problem solving.

The case study method, then, should address the following objectives:

1. To develop skill in the practical application of textbook knowledge.
2. To move the student from a passive mode of receiving data, details, theories and concepts to an active mode where issues are analyzed and solutions are formulated.

3. To develop a capacity for independent thinking based on relevant theories and practices.
4. To enhance understanding of a wide range of realistic organizational situations and circumstances.

In approaching any case study, the student should follow the following simple steps:

1. *Description*—read the case carefully (at least twice) and highlight the relevant points which the case contains.
2. *Diagnosis*—utilize the concepts and theories learned to pinpoint the key problem(s) presented in the case.
3. *Prescription*—apply relevant concepts and theories in the formulation of possible solutions to the problem(s) presented in the case.
4. *Implementation*—identify specific actions to address the problem(s) presented in the case with a rationale for those actions.

The following six case studies have been prepared based on real experiences within Canadian police services, with some modifications to provide a suitable context for the application of theory from the textbook. Each case study contains a degree of detail on the issue(s) being addressed and should be discussed using the sample questions provided at the end of each study. However, in reviewing these samples, it may be useful to broaden your examination to include other questions and points of consideration.

Case Study #1
THE BEST AND THE BRIGHTEST: A RECRUITMENT CHALLENGE

Background

You are a policy officer with the Great Lakes Regional Police Service in Ontario, and have been given the assignment of reviewing your department's recruitment practices and procedures. Basic criteria for the hiring of police officers have been established by the province through the *Police Services Act*, as follows:

- Canadian citizen or permanent resident of Canada;
- at least eighteen years of age;
- is physically and mentally able to perform the duties of the position, having regard to his or her own safety and the safety of members of the public;
- is of good moral character and habits; and
- has successfully completed at least four years of secondary school education or its equivalent.

Your project involves making recommendations for changes to departmental policies and practices that will reflect good police recruitment practices consistent with that legislation. The legislation sets out what may be considered the *minimum* criteria for recruitment. Given the assumption that the personnel selection process is one of the most important investments of the police department, you are keenly aware of the significance of this project. Decisions about the hiring of candidates have long-term implications for the service. Mistakes are very difficult to correct, often involving considerable expense and embarrassment for the department. Because of the strength of civil service agreements in place, once an officer has passed the probationary period, they can only be dismissed on the basis of serious disciplinary action.

You recognize that there is an important interrelationship between the recruitment and selection processes. Different phases in these processes include:

- specifying appropriate labour markets;
- seeking out and attracting qualified applicants;
- presenting the police service in a positive manner as an enlightened and progressive employer;
- establishing specific selection criteria for the acceptance, or rejection, of applicants;
- gathering job information relevant to the selection criteria; and
- making final selection decisions.

Of course, it's also important to bear in mind all the related legislation that will affect the department's personnel selection procedures. For example, the Ontario *Human Rights Code*, the *Employment Standards Act*, and other provincial and federal statutes will provide a legal framework for the recommendations you are to make. You will also need to distinguish between standards and tests. Standards are criteria that are necessary for applicant to hold a position. They are usually quite rigid and require applicants to meet specified qualifications before being eligible for employment in the agency. Typical standards include:

- vision standards;
- educational standards;
- drug use standards;
- physical ability standards;
- background and work history standards; and
- psychological standards.

In the area of testing, your department may elect to administer a series of written or oral tests that will measure certain qualities or characteristics of the applicant. Tests are used to establish if a candidate meets, or exceeds, a given standard. Oral interviews, pen-and-paper exercises, and assessment centres are often used to test applicants in specific areas of qualification.

In the instructions relating to this project, you are being asked to take into account the following elements:

- *merit-based employment practices* —includes competency-based selection process (the essential knowledge, skills, and abilities required to perform the specific job functions), as well as assessment tools that are valid indicators of performance capabilities;

- *barrier-free employment practices*—includes an analysis of complaints regarding barriers to employment which may be found through exit interviews and other means;
- *elimination of discrimination and harassment*; and
- *provision of employment accommodation*—includes taking reasonable steps to make it possible for categories of applicants to secure employment within your organization, e.g., providing access and equipment for persons with disabilities.

You are also aware that your constable selection process should be:

- consistent with other police services, and should include:
  - standardized assessment tools,
  - support for the merit principle,
  - job relevant tests, and
  - application of modern assessment methods;
- legally defensible;
- without unnecessary duplication;
- affordable;
- helpful to community policing efforts;
- fair to all applicants; and
- congruent with goals of equal opportunity.

You realize that it is important to give consideration to the needs of First Nations, visible minorities, persons with disabilities, women, gays and lesbians and other segments of society who may have been overlooked in earlier recruitment processes. It is clear that such persons are under-represented in your police service. There are compelling operational reasons for attention to this issue as well as simple fairness considerations.

You have been instructed to look at recent demographic trends within your jurisdiction and use that information to assist in the formulation of your recommendations for improving the recruitment policies and practices. The project has been mandated to ensure that employment practices within the department do not perpetuate the under-representation of certain groups of people. It is expected that recommendations will be made on removing systemic barriers and undertaking meaningful outreach programs for better recruitment. Previous study in area of systemic barriers has indicated that some of the following difficulties should be addressed by progressive police departments:

- resistance to civilianization of certain positions that would open up employment for persons with disabilities;
- absence of day care or flexible shift scheduling;
- culturally biased entrance requirements and testing;
- sense of isolation felt by members of under-represented groups, particularly women; and
- perceived need to suppress gender or culture-based traits in order to conform to the dominant group.

It is quite apparent that quota systems are not highly regarded. For example, the affirmative action approach in the United States has apparently tended to marginalize legitimate applicants; however, a distinction can be made between equal treatment and special treatment.

Your project has been asked to give special consideration to the recruitment of women officers. It is fairly widely known that the primary barrier to their recruitment has typically been physical testing, in particular as it pertains to upper body strength. The elimination of age limits and minimum height requirements might help in this regard. You are being asked to determine ways in which the police service can attract more women applicants.

You have on hand the following statistics which provide an insight into the gradual growth of women in policing in Canada. It is anticipated that your project will be able to produce some useful recommendations for improving recruitment policies and practices in the Great Lakes Regional Police Service.

TRENDS IN POLICE PERSONNEL—CANADA, 1965–1992			
Year	Male	Female	Percentage Female
1965	29 965	181	0.6%
1970	37 759	190	0.5%
1975	47 188	525	1.1%
1980	48 794	1047	2.1%
1985	48 538	1813	3.6%
1988	50 604	2708	5.1%
1989	51 809	3144	5.8%
1990	52 461	3537	6.4%
1991	52 810	3964	6.9%
1992	52 705	4286	7.5%

Source: Statistics Canada, 1993. Walker, S. Gail. *The Status of Women in Canadian Policing: 1993.* No.: 1993-22. Solicitor General Canada .

Discussion Questions

1. What are some of the standards that should be used in the recruitment process?
2. How should approved tests be administered? Who should administer those tests?
3. Provide some detail on different outreach approaches that you would recommend to attract the broadest range of potential candidates to your police department.
4. What are the qualifications/characteristics of your recruitment personnel? Should they receive any special training or development? If yes, what would be the content of their training or development?
5. What pieces of legislation might have an impact on a Canadian police department's selection policies and procedures?

6. What initiatives could be taken to encourage and increase the number of women applicants to a police department?
7. What are some areas of police work that could be assigned to persons with disabilities?

Case Study #2
IS BIGGER BETTER?: AMALGAMATING POLICE SERVICES

Background

Watertown and Southport are two communities of approximately equal size on the east coast of Canada. Due to financial constraints, increased public demands for higher levels of police service, pressure from the provincial government for greater cost-efficiency in the area of policing, and a spirit of partnership between the two municipal governments, there is a desire to examine the possibility of amalgamating the two police services of these communities into one agency. Other choices include contracting with the provincial police service or sharing police services with another community.

These two communities (i.e., Watertown and Southport) have enjoyed a good level of cooperation between the two existing police services boards. This is also true of the relationship between the uniform and civilian members of the two police services. It appears feasible to look at offering joint police services through some form of amalgamation. As a result, working committees, made up of local politicians, municipal staff, and police administrators, were established to look at some of the following topics:

- administration and cost-sharing;
- budget;
- staffing;
- shift scheduling;
- contracts;
- structure of the new police services board; and
- location and name of the new police service.

These working committees deliberated for some time on their assignments and have considered a number of issues relevant to a combined police department. Some vital statistics about the assets of the two police services are provided below:

ASSETS Police Service	Replacement Cost	Disposal Cost
Watertown	$140 000	$ 60 000
Southport	$110 000	$ 40 000
TOTAL	$250 000	$100 000

It has been determined that the liabilities of the two police services will be disposed of prior to the development of any shared services agreement. In order to arrive at a reasonable method of cost sharing for the two communities, it was proposed that an average be taken of the population, the number of dwellings, and the assessment for the two communities. This results in the following figures:

Police Service	(A) Population	(B) Dwellings	(C) Assessment	Average of (A), (B), & (C)
Watertown	6857	2482	$106 787 496	65%
Southport	3118	1223	$ 71 862 771	35%

In developing this method of cost-sharing it became clear that the two communities could establish a joint police service that would provide them with adequate and effective law enforcement services. By combining their existing strengths, a new police service could operate with a budget of approximately $1.4 million.

The combination of the two police services was thought to allow for some efficiencies. Obviously an amalgamated police service would only need one Chief of police, one dispatch centre, one crew of vehicle mechanics. Also, there could be several areas where savings might be found through streamlining or redeployment of resources. However, it is also recognized that the two police associations want to do everything possible to protect their members to the greatest extent possible and would like to ensure that their salaries, wages, and benefits are given a high priority throughout this process. Some statistics for the two police services are presented below:

STATISTICS	Watertown	Southport
Population	6857	3118
Uniform Staff	11	6
Civilian Staff	1.5	1
1996 Budget	$898 299	$479 166
1996 Cost Per Capita	$131	$153

There are certain advantages to be found in the amalgamation of the Watertown and Southport police departments. It appears likely that this proposal will be put forward for approval within the two communities. However, even when this decision has been made locally, it requires the approval of the provincial government according to the local *Police Services Act*.

Discussion Questions

1. Identify some of the considerations which the various working committees (e.g., administration, shift scheduling, and budget) will need to take into account when developing recommendations.
2. What the advantages and disadvantages of such an amalgamated police service?
3. What are some of the alternatives that could be reviewed?
4. What direction should be taken in this case study? Explain your answer.

Case Study #3
ACTIVE LISTENING: GAUGING PUBLIC OPINION

Background

The Braemar Regional Police Service provides law enforcement within Braemar Region, a strong, well-established community in central Canada. The region has a rich history as well as a fairly stable and diversified economy with active commercial, agricultural, and residential communities. The area is experiencing substantial growth in retail and light industrial outlets. It also has a large number of health care facilities, several well-known post-secondary educational institutions, and many cultural, ethnic, and social associations and activities.

Following recent changes in the leadership of this department and, in order to get quantifiable information about the public's opinion about the police, the new chief has committed his department to undertake a public survey. Experience has shown that many other jurisdictions (especially Reno, Nevada) are able to make substantial and meaningful improvements in their service delivery through the use of such surveys where direct questions are asked of the community.

STATISTICS RELEVANT TO THE BRAEMAR REGIONAL POLICE SERVICE						
Total Population	Police Personnel			Budget (in thousands)	Per Capita Costs	Population Per Officer
	Officers	*Civilians*	*Other*			
328 300	367	128	15	$41 607	$127	895

You've been assigned as part of the team that will be developing this survey and delivering it within your jurisdiction. You will also be asked to ensure that the results of this survey are interpreted properly in order to provide the department with some good indicators about service delivery improvements. The team is made up of representatives from the key areas in the department: administration, operations, support services, special units, and policy and planning. The survey group reports directly to the chief of police for the purposes of this project. Your team has been asked to look at some of the following areas relating to the Braemar Regional Police Service:

- performance;
- dealing with lawbreakers;
- image;
- public safety; and
- key enforcement problems.

You understand that survey design, delivery, and interpretation are essential ingredients for acceptable results. Your project team has assurances that it will receive a budget to undertake this assignment in a professional manner with required expertise.

Discussion Questions

1. Where would your team go for the appropriate expertise in developing a survey?
2. What questions would you ask to generate useful information for the police service?
3. Who should be asked to answer the questions contained in the survey?
4. How often should the department undertake such surveys?
5. How should the results be published?
6. Who should be responsible for administering the survey questions?

Case Study #4
LOOKING INTO THE FUTURE: STRATEGIC PLANNING

Background

Silverville is a large city in the Prairies that has been growing steadily for the last decade. As a vital community with a strong base in natural resources, industry, manufacturing and other economic supports, this city has experienced a sustained period of development. The police department plays an important role in the stability of the community and is regarded as quite effective in providing for the public safety concerns of the residents. Over time, a number of challenges have arisen making it essential that the police service carefully understand what it is going to do over the next five years with regard to identifying and addressing policing priorities.

Indications are strong that youth gangs are growing in this jurisdiction, along with the violence often associated with these groups. There has been an apparent increase in drug-related crime in parts of the community, and some abandoned buildings in the inner city have been commandeered by street-level pushers and addicts. White collar crime, especially fraud artists who victimize the elderly, has been on the increase, and levels of domestic violence and reported child abuse cases seem to be increasing. There also is considerable pressure from the provincial government to ensure that all public services are cost-effective in their delivery of programs, and senior managers are going to have their salaries tied to specific performance agreements that will require their departments to meet specific program objectives and outcomes on an annual basis.

STATISTICS RELEVANT TO THE SILVERVILLE POLICE SERVICE				Budget (in thousands)	Per Capita Costs	Population Per Officer
Total Population	Police Personnel					
	Officers	Civilians	Other			
740 000	1150	483	24	$116 344	$156	648

In order to plan for the future of the police department, the chief of police has initiated a new strategic planning process that is expected to provide the city council with a clear blueprint dealing with the future of the organization. Because there is a strong commitment on the part of the management of the city to this kind of planning process, the chief has considerable support for this undertaking; however, the budget is tight and it is expected that costs for the planning process will not be too excessive. There are some members of the Policing Committee of Council who are not sure that such an effort will be valuable and would be quick to criticize if the results of this process did not prove to be effective at setting some important goals and objectives for the police service.

The approach to be taken involves four phases:

- assessment;
- strategic planning;
- operational planning; and
- annual planning and action.

Each of the phases identified above has its own focus and function. The personnel involved in this project have a number of examples of strategic planning documents from other police services across the country, including access to strategic planning consultants within the city to assist in the methodology. There is an expectation that the police service will deliver a strategic plan to the city managers by the end of the calendar year. It is now the beginning of April and the chief expects great things from this process to which everyone is committed.

Discussion Questions

1. Identify sources of internal data that would help the project team with the assessment phase of this project.
2. Identify sources of external data that would help the project team with this assignment.
3. How would the police department determine the expectations that exist regarding their services?

4. Who should be involved in the strategic planning project? How should project team members be selected?

5. What kinds of preparation should the project team members have before beginning their work, if any?

Case Study #5
BENDING GRANITE: RESISTANCE TO CHANGE

Background

Fort Douglas is a large city on the west coast of Canada. Recently, the chief of police has become a strong proponent of community policing and has attended a few seminars and workshops sponsored by several police organizations in order to develop a deeper understanding of this approach and has returned to the police service with many ideas about things that can be done to implement a new philosophy of policing in their jurisdiction. Accordingly, the chief has set in place a new mission statement for the department that clearly announces that the organization will be pursuing the philosophy of community policing in all of its various units and that every officer in the department is committed to delivering services in a way that enhances the principles of community policing. The chief has been very active and visible in "selling" this new philosophy. He has received a great deal of exposure through the local media on account of his crusade. Indeed, the chief has become known as the "Champion of Change" for his efforts. Almost overnight, it seems that community policing has become the answer to all the ills of Fort Douglas.

In order to make the principles of community policing known throughout the organization, the chief held an intensive series of half-day information sessions in all of the districts of the police department, including a full-day session for all staff members (uniform and civilian) in headquarters. These sessions were introduced by the chief himself, with great enthusiasm and eloquence. The sessions were lead by a consultant who was specifically engaged for her expertise in the theory of community policing. She is a faculty member of the social sciences department of a large university and has published a great deal in the academic literature on community policing. She is highly regarded in the scholarly community for her expertise in this area.

The sessions were well-run and included some very sophisticated presentation materials that were prepared at no small cost to the police department. Everyone in attendance enjoyed the presentations and it seemed that there was positive reception to the overall message. The chief was pleased with his initiative and considered the sessions quite a success.

However, as time went on the chief began to get feedback from his field commanders and operational senior managers that there was not really any change in the way the department's services were being delivered. Many constables on the front-line had been quite enthusiastic about the change to a community-based, problem-solving approach to policing. It was generally hoped that such an approach would empower them to work more closely with their communities in a partnership which placed a priority on proactive solutions to public safety and disorder problems. The chief was surprised, disappointed, and a little bit annoyed that he was not getting the kind of support and action he had expected with this important initiative. He was hoping that his organization might qualify for a national award for innovative policing that was presented every year by an esteemed association of government officials and public service associations. The chief wanted to find the source of the problem and set to work correcting it as quickly as possible. He suspected that his middle managers (i.e., the sergeants, staff sergeants, and inspectors) were sabotaging his efforts at meaningful change. The chief knew that people often fear change, but he thought that the way had been cleared for progress in his organization. The *status quo* was not acceptable, and he was determined to make community policing work in Fort Douglas.

Discussion Questions

1. What information does the chief need in order to find out what the problem is with this initiative?
2. What are some possible sources of this problem that can be identified immediately?
3. What things could the chief of police have done to smooth the transition to the new model of community policing?

Case Study #6
FINDING THE TOP COP: SELECTING A NEW CHIEF OF POLICE

Background

Acropolis, one the largest municipal centres in Canada, is in the process of selecting a new chief of police for their police service. This is an important event in the life of the organization, and the police services board has the responsibility for undertaking this task. You are a new member of the Acropolis Police Services Board. You were appointed by the province to this board and have a strong interest in public safety issues within your community. You have been active as a volunteer in many of the programs established by the police department, own a small local business in the downtown core of the city, and feel that you have a fairly good appreciation for the problems which affect the delivery of services within the police organization. Your police services board is made up of local municipal politicians, including some very vocal councillors who are interested in finding cost-savings in all municipal departments, including the police service, and have made it clear that they are looking for a chief who will be able to cut expenditures in the department. Your own interest is in finding a chief who will meet the public safety needs of the community at large, but especially the downtown business community that drives a great deal of the local economy.

There were hundreds of applications for the position of chief of police from many highly qualified and capable police executives. The Police Services Board had placed a position notice in local and national newspapers in order to generate interest from a wide pool of police executives. The board had also contracted with a well-known executive search firm to assist them with the screening and evaluation of the candidates for this important position. Based on the initial efforts of the board, which included in-depth interviews, as well as the submission and presentation of an essay discussing the future issues of policing in Acropolis, a short list of four candidates has been established for the second round of interviews. The board is searching for an extremely strong leader who will take this police service through significant organizational change in the face of some severe financial restraints. They are also looking for a chief of police who will work hard to introduce innovation within the police service while maintaining a tradition of operational excellence. These shortlisted candidates are profiled as follows:

CANDIDATE "A"—DEPUTY CHIEF DAVIDSON:

This internal candidate is an experienced senior officer with more than 25 years experience with the Acropolis Police Service. He has most recently been involved as head of detectives and has spent the last 18 years in the area of criminal investigations. His skills are extensive in this area and he has been responsible for some high-profile investigations that resulted in the arrest and conviction of a dangerous serial killer and other violent criminals. He is highly regarded by the rank and file of the organization and was deeply involved in the police association before he became a senior officer within the department about 15 years ago. His career has been one of steady progression through the ranks and he has had a great deal of additional training and development at the Canadian Police College, as well as at the FBI Academy in Quantico, Virginia, where he attended a Senior Police Management program designed for officers with significant career promise. He is married with two teenage children and is a long-term resident in one of the suburbs of the city.

CANDIDATE "B"—DETECTIVE INSPECTOR TEMPLE:

This officer is extremely bright with a solid background in the police service. He has been on the job for 10 years. He earned a law degree from Osgoode Hall Law School before joining the police force and also has a master's degree in public administration. This second degree was acquired through dedicated part-time study through the local university and where he stood at the top of his class. His thesis dealt with the introduction of performance evaluation systems in police organizations and the application of computer technology in the maintenance of these systems. His work experience has included a number of years in patrol areas throughout the city, time spent as an instructor at the Acropolis Police Academy with special concentration on the training of new recruits in effective communications, report writing, and legal research. He has also gained considerable experience in financial management through his work with the department's budget coordinator in the preparation of several budget submissions to the chief. He has only recently been assigned to the investigation division, along with a promotion to the rank of Detective Inspector, where he has already distinguished himself through a number of very practical suggestions for the automation of certain routine functions within the fraud investigations unit. He has a strong work ethic that makes him a dedicated officer; however, his drive and ambition have alienated not only some of his fellow officers who are not willing to work as hard as he does, but also some of his superior officers who have felt a little threatened by his talent and determination. D/Insp. Temple has never been insubordinate in any way, but he is equipped with the strength of his convictions and will not back down when confronting an obstacle to the achievement of personal or organizational goals, which are usually quite consistent. He is recently married to a woman who works in the personnel department of the police service, and, while they do not have any children, they are planning to begin their family very soon. Many were surprised when they learned that he had applied for the chief's position; however, his performance during the first round of board interviews was superlative.

Candidate "C"—Deputy Chief McClung:

This candidate was shortlisted with the highest qualifying marks from the earlier screening process. She is the deputy chief of a smaller, but substantial, regional police service with over 600 uniformed officers and was in charge of the administration of the department, which has many similar challenges to the Acropolis Police Service. Deputy Chief McClung has had about 20 years' experience in the field of law enforcement, beginning as constable in an organization that did not easily accept the presence of women. She made rapid progress through the ranks in spite of a great deal of opposition and resistance. She has been able to acquire advanced degrees in criminology and administration over her career through part-time study. She has also had important secondments to government departments where policy and standards are developed for law enforcement throughout the province, and she has become familiar with the corporate context within which policing occurs on a provincial and federal basis.

Her determination to excel is apparent in everything she does, both on and off the job. She has enormous levels of energy and a superb memory for facts, figures, and faces. As a result of her negative experiences in the early days of her career, Deputy Chief McClung has developed an aggressive personality that is focused on results and she places little stock in the social elements of the job. She can be friendly and accommodating with a broad range of people; however, she is less than patient with those who are apt to slack off or not take the responsibilities of policing as seriously as she does. In her current position she has had a number of battles with the president of the local police association over a number of issues, including disciplinary action, promotional processes, and restructuring. In every instance, the association executive has fuelled a campaign to malign the deputy chief and undermine support for her both within the department and the community. There have been rumors that the morale in the police service is at rock bottom because of the deputy chief and that her leadership skills are non-existent. Members of the association have launched a whispering campaign against the deputy chief that has made her controversial. She has been able to balance these controversies with some very effective innovations within the department and has the steadfast support of her chief, who is singularly impressed with her commitment, competence, and professionalism. Deputy Chief McClung is single and is an avid athlete with interests in skiing, sailing, and motorcycle touring. Her main focus is her job and she devotes the bulk of her time to the responsibilities of her position.

CANDIDATE "D"—CHIEF MACDONALD:

This short-listed candidate is the chief of police for a local municipal police service that is about half the size of Acropolis. He has been the chief of police for over eight years and has not had any major crises to severely test or tarnish his reputation as a moderately skilled and competent senior executive. His application for this job as the chief of police in Acropolis has caused quite a stir in his local community with everyone assuming that he would stay in this position until his retirement, which would likely occur in the next six years. The local media has begun to lament the possible loss of Chief MacDonald, who has been able to secure himself a good reputation in the public's mind through workmanlike application to the job and the avoidance of any hint of scandal or corruption within the department. Chief MacDonald is popular with his front-line officers and has good relations with police association. He is relatively easygoing in his style; however, he expects his officers to closely follow the chain of command. His department has not had to face too many crises. The population is largely homogeneous and quite stable, with solid economic conditions tied to a world-class manufacturing base.

STATISTICS RELEVANT TO THE ACROPOLIS POLICE SERVICE:					
Total Population	Police Personnel			Budget (in thousands)	Per Capita Costs	Population Per Officer
	Officers	Civilians	Other			
1 565 000	2650	769	238	$256 924	$164	591

Discussion Questions

1. How should the police services board evaluate the short-listed candidates for chief of police?
2. What are the management skills and knowledge that would be most important to this position?
3. What are some of the key challenges which the new chief of police should be expected to address, regardless of the choice made by your board?

4. What are the advantages and disadvantages to hiring the new chief of police from within the department?
5. What are the advantages and disadvantages to hiring the new chief of police from outside of the department?
6. Based on the information provided in this case study, who would you select as the new chief of police for Acropolis? Provide reasons to support your answer.

APPENDIX III

SELECTED LISTING OF
ASSOCIATIONS, ORGANIZATIONS,
AND WEB SITES FOR
CANADIAN POLICING

INTRODUCTION

This appendix provides a listing of some important associations, organizations and Web sites that pertain to policing in Canada. There are references to some of the larger Canadian police services which have substantial home pages established on the Internet, along with addresses and other contact information. Several police services are in the process of establishing their own Web sites and these will begin to appear in the "links" section of other home pages. In this appendix an effort has been made to provide current, accurate data regarding the organizations and resources listed below; however, it is by no means comprehensive and the reader is encouraged to supplement this information with other contacts that might be useful. A brief description of individual listings is provided on a selected basis.

CANADA
Associations

Atlantic Association of Chiefs of Police
c/o Fredericton Police Department
311 Queen Street
Fredericton, NB E3B 1B1
Tel.: (506) 452-9701

British Columbia Federation of Police Officers
190 Alexander Street, #603
Vancouver, BC V6A 1B5
Tel.: (604) 685-6441
Fax.: (604) 685-5228

Brotherhood of Constables of Highway Traffic Controllers of the Québec Provincial Police/ Fraternité des constables du contrôle routier de la Sûreté du Québec
4165, rue Chauveau
Sherbrooke, QC J1L 1R9
Tel.: (819) 567-9784

Canadian Association of Chiefs of Police
130 Albert Street, Suite 1710
Ottawa, ON K1P 5G4
Tel.: (613) 233-1106
Fax.: (613) 23-6960
Web site: http://www.sass.ca/cacppage.html

Canadian Association for Civilian Oversight of Law Enforcement
c/o Secretariat
595 Bay Street, 9th Floor
P.O. Box 23
Toronto, ON M5G 2C2
Tel.: (416) 325-4700
Fax.: (416) 325-4704

Canadian Association of Police Boards
10 Peel Centre Drive
Brampton, ON L6T 4B9
Tel.: (905) 458-1342
Fax.: (905) 458-7278

Canadian Police Association
141 Catherine Street
Ottawa, ON K2P 1C3
Tel.: (613) 231-4168
Fax.: (613) 231-3254

Ontario Association of Chiefs of Police
P.O. Box 193
Sault Ste. Marie, ON P6A 5L6
Tel.: (705) 946-6389
Fax.: (705) 942-2093

Ontario Association of Police Services Boards
637 Second Avenue East, 2nd Floor
Owen Sound, ON N4K 2G7
Tel.: (519) 372-9291
Fax.: (519) 372-9339

Ontario Provincial Police Association
119 Ferris Lane, #7
Barrie, ON L4M 2Y1
Tel.: (705) 728-6161
Fax.: (705) 721-4867
Web site: http://www.oppa.on.ca

Police Association of Nova Scotia/Association des policiers de la Nouvelle-Écosse
P.O. Box 1557
Station Central RPO
Halifax, NS B3J 2Y3
Tel.: (902) 423-7477

Police Association of Ontario
6370 Davand Drive, Unit #1
Mississauga, ON L5T 2K8
Tel.: (905) 670-9770
Fax.: (905) 670-9755

Police Brotherhood of the Royal Newfoundland Constabulary Association
P.O. Box 7247, Station C
St. John's, NF A1E 3Y4
Tel.: (709) 739-5946
Fax.: (709) 739-6276

Training, Education, and Research

Atlantic Police Academy
Holland College of Applied Arts & Technology
P.O. Box 156
Slemon Park
Charlottetown, PE C0A 2A0
Tel.: (902) 888-6700
Fax.: (902) 888-6725

Canadian Police College
P.O. Box 8900
Ottawa, ON K1G 3J2
Tel.: (613)
Fax.: (613) 990-9738
Web site: http://www.cpc.gc.ca

Criminology Information Service
Centre of Criminology
University of Toronto
130 St. George Street, Room 8001
Toronto, ON M5S 3H1
Tel.: (416) 978-7068
Fax.: (416) 978-4195
Web site: http://library.utoronto.ca/www/
   libraries_crim/crimhome.html

Description: The Centre's information service provides information relevant to policing, corrections, young offenders, and criminal justice, including publications by faculty, bibliographies, listings of serial holdings, and recent acquisitions.

Dalhousie University
Henson College of Public Affairs & Continuing Education
Centre for Public Management
6100 University Avenue
Halifax, NS B3H 3J5
Tel.: (902) 494-2526
Fax.: (902) 494-2598

Description: The Centre offers a number of distance education programs leading to a certificate in police studies. Topics include: police leadership, police budgeting, and communication skills for police personnel.

Institut de police du Québec

350 rue Margarite d'Youville
C.P. 1120
Nicolet, QC J3T 1X4
Tel.: (819) 293-8631
Fax.: (819) 293-4018

Description: Academy responsible for the training, education, and development of police personnel in the province of Québec.

McMaster University

Centre for Continuing Education
Commons 116
1280 Main Street West
Hamilton, ON L8S 4K1
Tel.: (905) 525-9140 Ext. 24321
Tel.: 1-800-INFO CCE
Fax.: (905) 546-1690
Web site: http://www.mcmaster.ca/conted

Description: The Centre offers a Police Studies certificate program designed to provide learners with current, practical knowledge and skills in this area of study.

Nathanson Centre for the Study of Organized Crime and Corruption

c/o Dr. Margaret Beare, Director
Osgoode Hall Law School, Room 321A
York University
4700 Keele Street
North York, ON M3J 1P3
Tel.: (416) 736-5907
E-mail: mbeare@yorku.ca

Ontario Association of Police Educators

c/o Catherine Nanton, President
Ontario Police College
P.O. Box 1190
Aylmer, ON N5H 2T2
Tel.: (519) 773-4230
Fax.: (519) 773-5762
Web site: http://www.oape.org

Description: Association formed to promote standardized training procedures for personnel involved in police training and education, including research and application of new technology and equipment to policing.

Simon Fraser University

School of Criminology
Burnaby, BC V5A 1S6
Tel.: (604) 291-4641
Fax.: (604) 291-4860

Justice Institute of British Columbia

4180 West 4th Avenue
Vancouver, BC V6R 4J5
Tel.: (604) 228-9771

Police Leadership Forum

c/o Canadian Police College
P.O. Box 8900
Ottawa, ON K1G 3J2

Government Agencies and Departments

FEDERAL

Canadian Centre for Justice Statistics

Information and Client Services
19th Floor, R.H. Coats Building
Ottawa, ON K1A 0T6
Tel.: (613) 951-9023
Fax.: (613) 951-6615

Canadian Police Research Centre

P.O. Box 8885
Ottawa, ON K1G 3M8
Tel.: (613) 998-6343
Fax.: (613) 952-0156

Justice Canada

Ottawa, ON K1A 0H8
Tel.: (613) 991-3283
Fax.: (613) 952-2240
Web site: http://canada.justice.gc.ca/

National Search and Rescue Secretariat

Standard Life Building, 4th Floor
275 Slater Street
Ottawa, ON K1A 0K2
Tel.: (613) 992-0063
Tel.: 1-800-727-9414
Fax.: (613) 996-3746
Web site: http://www.nss.gc.ca

Solicitor General Canada
340 Laurier Avenue West, 8th Floor
Ottawa, ON K1A 0P8
Tel.:(613) 990-2703
Fax.: (613) 993-5252
Web site: http://www.sgc.gc.ca

Statistics Canada
Statistical Research Centre
Ottawa, ON K1A 0T6
Tel.: (613) 951-8116
Fax.: (613) 951-0581
Web site: http://www.statcan.ca/

PROVINCIAL

Alberta Justice
Law Enforcement Division
10365 - 97 Street, 10th Floor
Edmonton, AB T5J 3W7
Tel.: (403) 427-3457
Fax.: (403) 427-5916

British Columbia Attorney General
Police Services Division
#5, 910 Government Street
Victoria, BC V8V 1X4
Tel.: (604) 387-1751
Fax.: (604) 356-7747

Manitoba Justice
Law Enforcement Services
405 Broadway, 5th Floor
Winnipeg, MB R3B 3L6
Tel.: (204) 945-2825
Fax.: (204) 945-2217

**New Brunswick Dept. of the Solicitor
General Policing Services**
P.O. Box 6000
Fredericton, NB E3B 5H1
Tel.: (506) 453-3603
Fax.: (506) 457-4957

Newfoundland Dept. of Justice
Confederation Bldg.
P.O. Box 8700
St. John's, NF A1B 4J6
Tel.: (709) 729-2872
Fax.: (709) 729-2129

Nova Scotia Police Commission
P.O. Box 1573
Halifax, NS B3J 2Y3
Tel.: (902) 424-3246
Fax.: (902) 424-3919

Nova Scotia Dept. of Justice
Policing Services Division
P.O. Box 217
Station M
Halifax, NS B3J 2M4
Tel.: (902) 424-7795
Fax.: (902) 424-0700

**Ontario Ministry of the Solicitor General
and Correctional Services**
Policing Services Division
12th Floor
25 Grosvenor Street
Toronto, ON M7A 2H3
Tel.: (416) 314-3377
Fax.: (416) 314-4037

**Prince Edward Island Dept. of Provincial
Affairs & Attorney General**
P.O. Box 2000
Charlottetown, PE C1A 7N8
Tel.: (902) 368-5250
Fax.: (902) 368-4121

Québec Ministère de la Sécurité publique
Direction générale de la sécurité et de la
prévention
2525 boul. Laurier, 8e étage
Ste-Foy, QC G1V 2L2
Tel.: (418) 643-5691
Fax.: (418) 646-3564

Saskatchewan Justice
Law Enforcement Services Division
1874 Scarth Street
7th Floor
Regina, SK S4P 3V7
Tel.: (306) 787-5560
Fax.: (306) 787-8084

Selected Canadian Police Services

FEDERAL

Royal Canadian Mounted Police
Public Affairs Directorate
1200 Vanier Parkway
Ottawa, ON K1A 0R2
Tel.: (613) 993-1085
Fax.: (613) 993-5894
Web site: http://www.rcmp-grc.gc.ca/

PROVINCIAL

Ontario Provincial Police
777 Memorial Avenue
Orillia, ON L3V 7V3
Tel.: (705) 329-6111
Fax.: (705) 329-6077
Web site: http://www.gov.on.ca/OPP/

Royal Newfoundland Constabulary
P.O. Box 7247
St. John's, NF A1E 3Y4
Tel.: (709) 729-8000
Fax.: (709) 729-8214
Web site:
http://www.gov.nf.ca/just/publicpr/rnc.html

Sûreté du Québec
1701, rue Parthenais
C.P. 1400, succ. C
Montréal, QC H2L 4K7
Tel.: (514) 598-4488
Fax.: (514) 598-4957
Web site:
http://www.suretequebec.gouv.qc.ca/index.html

MUNICIPAL AND REGIONAL

Calgary Police Service
133 - 6th Avenue S.E.
Calgary, AB T2G 4Z1
Tel.: (403) 266-1234
Fax.: (403) 268-4552
Web site:
http://www.gov.calgary.ab.ca/75/75B00000.html

Edmonton Police Service
9620 - 103 Avenue
Edmonton, AB T5H 0H7
Tel.: (413) 421-3333
Web site: http://www.gov.edmonton.ab.ca/
   police/service.html

Fredericton Police Force
311 Queen Street
Fredericton, NB E3B 1B1
Tel.: (506) 452-9701
Fax.: (506) 450-2102
Web site: http://www.city.fredericton.nb.ca/
   cityhall/departments/police.html

Kingston Police
11 Queen Street
P.O. Box 1001
Kingston, ON K7L 4X8
Tel.: (613) 549-4660
Fax.: (613) 549-7111 (Operations)
Fax.: (613) 549-3111 (Administration)
Web site: http://www.police.kingston.on.ca/

Lethbridge Police Service
135 –1 Avenue South
Lethbridge, AB T1J 0A1
Tel.: (403) 327-2210
Fax.: (403) 328-6999
Web site: http://www.city.lethbridge.ab.ca/
   police/

Metropolitan Toronto Police Service
40 College Street
Toronto, ON M5G 2J3
Tel.: (416) 8089-2222
Fax.: (416) 808-8002
Web site: http://www.mtps.on.ca/

Montréal Urban Community Police
750, rue Bonsecours
Montréal, QC H2Y 3C7
Tel.: (514) 280-8550
Web site: http://www.spcum.qc.ca/

Niagara Regional Police Service
68 Church Street
St. Catherines, ON L2R 3C6
Tel.: (905) 688-4111
Fax.: (905) 685-5081
Web site: http://www.nrps.com/main.eht

Ottawa-Carleton Regional Police Service
474 Elgin Street
Ottawa, ON K2P 2J6
Tel.: (613) 236-1222
Fax.: (613) 236-9360
Web site: http://mail.compmore.net/~police

Peel Regional Police
P.O. Box 7750
7750 Hurontario Street
Brampton, ON L6V 3W6
Tel.: (905) 453-3311
Web site: http://www.peelpolice.gov/#index

Vancouver Police Department
312 Main Street
Vancouver, BC V6A 2T2
Tel.: (604) 665-3535
Fax: (604) 257-3716
Web site: http://www.city.vancouver.bc.ca/police

Winnipeg Police Service
P.O. Box 1680
Winnipeg, MB R3C 2Z7
Tel.: (204) 986-6037
Fax.: (204) 944-8468
Web site: http://www.winnipeg.freenet.mb.ca/
  iphome/w/wps/index.html

Miscellaneous

CPINet
Web site: http://www.cpinet.org/index.html

KPMG Investigation and Security Inc.
Suite 3300 Commerce Court West
P.O. Box 31, Stn. Commerce Court
Toronto, ON M5L 1B2
Tel.: (416) 777-8500
Fax.: (416) 777-3519
Web site: http://www.kpmg.ca/isi

UNITED STATES
Associations

American Federation of Police
3801 Biscayne Boulevard
Miami, FL 33137
Tel.: (303) 573-0070
Fax.: (303) 573-9819

**Association of Police Planners and
Research Officers International**
910 Sleater Kinney South East, Suite 187
Lacy, WA 98503
Tel.: (206) 754-4160

Blacks in Law Enforcement
256 East McLemore Avenue
Memphis, TN 38106
Tel.: (901) 774-1118
Fax.: (901) 774-1139

**International Association of Campus Law
Enforcement Administrators**
638 Prospect Avenue
Hartford, CT 06105
Tel.: (203) 233-4531

International Association of Chiefs of Police
515 North Washington Street
Alexandria, VA 22314
Tel.: (703) 836-6767
Web site: http://www.amdahl.com/ext/iacp

**International Society of Crime Prevention
Practitioners**
1696 Connor Drive
Pittsburgh, PA 15129-9035
Tel.: (412) 655-1600

National Association of Police Organizations
750 1st Street Northwest, Suite 935
Washington, DC 20002-4241
Tel.: (202) 842-4420
Fax.: (202) 842-4396

National Black Police Association
3251 Mount Pleasant Street Northwest
Washington, DC 20010-2103
Tel.: (202) 986-2070
Fax.: (202) 986-0410

National Criminal Justice Association
444 North Capital Street Northwest
Suite 618
Washington, DC 20001
Tel.: (202) 347-4900
Fax.: (202) 508-3859

National Institute for Victimology
2333 North Vernon Street
Arlington, VA 22207
Tel.: (703) 528-3387

Description: Offers consulting services and publications to assist individuals and organizations within the criminal justice system.

National Organization of Black Law Enforcement Executives (NOBLE)
4609 Pinecrest Office Park Drive, 2nd Floor
Alexandria, VA 22312
Tel.: (703) 658-1529
Fax.: (703) 658-9479

National Police Officers Association of America
P.O. Box 2219
Louisville, KY 40252-0129
Tel.: 1-800-467-6762
Fax.: (502) 452-9512

National Sheriffs' Association
1450 Duke Street
Alexandria, VA 22314-3490
Tel.: (703) 836-7827
Web site: http://www.sheriffs.org

Training, Education, and Research

American Police Academy
1000 Connecticut Avenue Northwest
Suite 9
Washington, DC 20036
Tel.: (202) 293-9088
Fax.: (202) 573-9819

American Society of Criminology
1314 Kinnear Road, Suite 212
Columbus, OH 43212
Tel.: (614) 292-9207

American Society of Law Enforcement Trainers
102 Dock Road, P.O. Box 361
Lewes, DE 19958
Tel.: (302) 645-4080
Fax.: (302) 645-4084

Description: Formed to organize law enforcement training personnel and develop innovative approaches to training. Offers training and publications.

Center for Research in Law and Justice
University of Illinois at Chicago
400 South Peoria Street, #2100
Chicago, IL 60680
Tel.: (312) 996-4632
Fax.: (312) 996-5755

FBI Academy
Web site: http://www.fbi.gov/academy/academy.html

Institute of Police Technology & Management
University of North Florida
4567 St. Johns Bluff Road South
Jacksonville, FL 32224-2645
Tel.: (904) 646-2722
Fax.: (904) 646-2453

International Association for the Study of Organized Crime
1033 W. Van Buren Street
Suite 500
Chicago, IL 60607-2919
Tel.: (312) 996-9636
Fax.: (312) 996-0458

International Association of Directors of Law Enforcement Standards and Training
John Jay College of Criminal Justice
444 West 56th Street
New York, NY 10019
Tel.: (212) 237-8695
Web site: http://ns1.dpscs.state.md.us/iadlest/

Justice Research and Studies Association
444 North Capitol Street Northwest, Suite 445
Washington, DC 20001
Tel.: (202) 624-8560
Fax.: (202) 624-5269

Law Enforcement Training Network
1303 Marsh Lane
Carrollton, TX 75006
Tel.: 1-800-535-LETN (5386)
Fax.: (214) 716-5302

Description: Organization that provides video and satellite training to police departments and other criminal justice organizations.

Law Enforcement Video Association
5942 Edinger, #113
Huntington Beach, CA 92649
Tel.: (714) 892-7251

National Archive of Criminal Justice Data
Web site:
http://www.icpsr.umich.edu/NACJD/home.html

Description: Established in 1978 by the Inter-university Consortium for Political and Social Research and the Bureau of Justice Statistics (U.S. Dept. of Justice) to facilitate research in the field of criminal justice.

National Center for Community Policing
School of Criminal Justice
Michigan State University
560 Baker Hall
East Lansing, MI 48824-1118
Tel.: (517) 355-2322

National Crime Prevention Institute
University of Louisville
Brigman Hall
Louisville, KY 40292-0001
Tel.: (502) 588-6987

Description: Institute established to provide training to police officers, criminal justice planners, private security personnel, and community representatives in the area of crime prevention.

National Institute of Justice
633 Indiana Avenue, N.W.
Washington, DC 20531
Tel.: (202) 514-4787
Fax.: (202) 307-6394
Web site: http://www.ncjrs.org/nijhome.html

Description: NIJ is the research and development agency of the U.S. Dept. of Justice. It has a mandate to sponsor special projects in the area of criminal justice aimed at the prevention and/or reduction of crime, develop new technologies, evaluate criminal justice program effectiveness, undertake research, and develop new research methods.

Northwestern University Traffic Institute
405 Church Street
Evanston, IL 60204
Tel.: (708) 491-5230
Fax.: (708) 491-5270

Office of International Criminal Justice
The University of Chicago at Illinois
Web site: http://www.acsp.uic.edu/index.html

Description: Founded in 1984 as a centre of excellence in education, research, development, and training within the University of Illinois at Chicago. It contributes to improved understanding of criminal justice systems through professional development, consulting, and publications. This organization's Web site includes access to Crime & Justice International, *which is a periodical that tracks worldwide news and trends relevant to policing and criminal justice.*

Police Executive Research Forum
1120 Connecticut Avenue N.W., Suite 930
Washington, DC 20036
Tel.: (202) 466-7820
Fax.: (202) 466-2670
Web site: http://www.policeforum.org

Police Foundation
1001 22nd Street Northwest, Suite 200
Washington, DC 20037
Tel.: (202) 833-1460
Fax.: (202) 659-9149

Description: Established to improve police effectiveness through the operation of the Center for the Study of Police and Civil Disorder. Also sponsors workshops, provides assistance, and disseminates publications.

Police Law Institute
University of Iowa Technology Innovation Center
Room 225
P.O. Box 161
Oakdale, IA 52319
Tel.: (319) 335-4665

Rutgers University
School of Criminal Justice
15 Washington Street
Newark, NJ 07102
Tel.: (201) 648-5870

Sam Houston State University
College of Criminal Justice
Huntsville, TX 77341
Tel.: (409) 294-1631

Sellin Center for Studies in Criminology and Criminal Justice
3733 Spruce Street, Room 437
Philadelphia, PA 19104
Tel.: (215) 898-7411

University of Albany
State University of New York
School of Criminal Justice
135 Western Avenue
Albany, NY 12222
Tel.: (518) 442-5210

University of Maryland
Institute of Criminal Justice and Criminology
2200 LeFrak Hall
College Park, MD 20742-8235
Tel.: (301) 405-4703

Government Agencies and Departments

Bureau of Justice Statistics
Office of Justice Programs
U.S. Dept. of Justice
633 Indiana Avenue, N.W.
Washington, DC 20531
Tel.: 1-800-732-3277
Web site: http://www.ojp.usdoj.gov

Office of Juvenile Justice and Delinquency Prevention
Office of Justice Programs
U.S. Dept. of Justice
633 Indiana Avenue, N.W.
Washington, DC 20531
Tel.: 1-800-638-8736
Web site: http://www.ncjrs.org/ojjhome.html

Description: This is the federal government's central agency for matters relating to juvenile justice and delinquency prevention.

National Institute of Justice
P.O. Box 6000
Rockville, MD 20849-6000
Tel.: (301) 251-5500
Web site: http://www.ncjrs.org/nijhome.html

Community Policing Consortium
1726 M Street, N.W., Suite 801
Washington, DC 20036
Tel.: 1-800-833-3085
Fax.: (202) 833-9295
Web site: http://www.communitypolicing.org

Selected United States Police Services

Federal Bureau of Investigation
Web site: http://www.fbi.gov/homepage.html
New York City Police Department
One Police Plaza, 7th Floor
New York, NY 10038
Web site:
http://www.ci.nyc.ny.us/html/nypd/home.html

San Diego Police Department
1401 Broadway
San Diego, CA 92101-5729
Tel.: (619) 531-2777
Web site: http://www.sannet.gov/police/
   sdpdhome.html

Miscellaneous

Commission on Accreditation for Law Enforcement Agencies, Inc.
10306 Eaton Place, Suite 320
Fairfax, VA 22030-2201
Tel.: 1-800-368-3757
Tel.: (703) 352-4225
Fax.: (703) 591-2206

National Archive of Criminal Justice Data
Web site: http://www.icpsr.umich.edu/nacjd

RAND Organization
Peter Greenwood, Director
Criminal Justice Program
P.O. Box 2138
Santa Monica, CA 90407-2138
Tel.: (310) 393-0411, Ext. 6321
Web site: http://www.rand.org

Police Officer's Internet Directory
Web site: http://www.officer.com
Law Enforcement Sites on the Web
Web site: http://www.ih2000.net/ira/ira.html

Police Guide
Web site: http://www.policeguide.com

A law enforcement guide to the Internet's World Wide Web
Web site: http://www.leolinks.com

Police Net
Web site: http://www.policenet.org

Copnet
Web site: http://www.copnet.org/

GREAT BRITAIN
Associations

Police Federation of England & Wales
Web site: http://www.pfed.demon.co.uk/

Description: This is the home page for the organization that represents police officers below the rank of Superintendent with regard to their labour interests and the efficiency of their respective police services. This organization has a membership of approximately 126 000 and was established by legislation in 1919.

Training, Education and Research

Home Office
Police Research Group
50 Queen Anne's Gate
London SW1H 9AT
U.K.
Tel.: 0171-273-4000
Fax.: 0171-273-2190
Web site:
http://www.open.gov.uk/home_off/prghome.html

Description: This body provides the U.K. police service with a source of centralized social science and management information to assist in research and development.

Government Agencies and Departments

Home Office
50 Queen Anne's Gate
London, SW1H 9AT
U.K.
Web site: http://www.open.gov.uk/home_off/

Great Britain Police Services

The Police Services of the U.K.
Web site: http://www.police.uk

Description: This is an official listing of police forces and police-related organizations in the U.K, including:

- The National Training Centre for Scientific Support to Crime Investigation;
- Durham Police;
- Dyfed Powys Police;
- Greater Manchester Police;
- Lancashire Police;
- Merseyside Police;
- Metropolitan Police (Scotland Yard);
- North Wales Police;
- Royal Ulster Constabulary;
- South Yorkshire Police;
- Tayside Police;
- West Mercia Constabulary; and
- West Yorkshire Police.

INDEX